The Limits to Rational Expectations

To Marion
Bijan, Jamal, and Eva-Leila

The Limits to Rational Expectations

M. Hashem Pesaran

Basil Blackwell

First published 1987
First published in USA 1988

Basil Blackwell Ltd
108 Cowley Road, Oxford

Basil Blackwell Inc.
432 Park Avenue South, Suite 1503
New York, NY 10016, USA

British Library Cataloguing in Publication Data

Pesaran, Hashem
The limits to rational expectations.
1. Rational expectations (Economic theory)
— Mathematical models 2. Macroeconomics 3. Econometrics
I. Title
339.3′01 HB199

ISBN 0-631-14036-0

Library of Congress Cataloging in Publication Data

Pesaran, M. Hashem, 1946–
The limits to rational expectations.
Bibliography: p.
Includes index.
1. Rational expectations (Economic theory). I. Title.
HB172.5.P445 1988 339 87-20877

ISBN 0-631-14036-0

Typeset in Scantext 9½ on 11pt Times by Unicus Graphics Ltd, Horsham, Sussex
Printed in Great Britain by T. J. Press Ltd, Padstow

Contents

Preface

The general acceptance of the rational expectations hypothesis, especially in the USA, has already had far-reaching implications both for the development of economic theory and for the analysis and the interpretation of economic time series data. This book provides a critical assessment of this influential hypothesis, and examines the methodological and empirical considerations upon which it is based. It covers a broad range of topics in the literature of the rational expectations hypothesis, including the nature and sources of uncertainty, the problems of information heterogeneity, learning and information acquisition, and the non-uniqueness of the solution of rational expectations models with future expectations. In addition, for the first time, it brings together in one place the diverse contributions recently made to the econometric analysis of rational expectations models, and it deals in detail with the problems of identification, estimation and hypothesis testing in a variety of rational expectations models.

The book argues that the rational expectations hypothesis, and the adaptive expectations hypothesis that preceded it, represent two different extremes, both of which are based on untenable assumptions and are empirically unsatisfactory. What is needed is a greater reliance on survey data on expectations, and the formulation of expectations formation models that explicitly take account of the learning process. In this vein I shall propose a new method for quantification of categorical survey data, and put forward an augmented adaptive-learning expectations formation hypothesis which does not suffer from the shortcomings of the purely extrapolative schemes, and which at the same time is not based on the extreme information assumptions that underlie the rational expectations hypothesis.

In writing this book I have benefited from the comments and suggestions of a large number of individuals. In particular I am grateful to Roy Batchelor, Peter Burridge, Sheila Dow, Christian Gourieroux, Geoff Harcourt, Mike McAleer, Adrian Pagan, Rick van der Ploeg, Fabio Schiantarelli, Ron Smith, Pravin Trivedi and, above all, to Ignazio Visco, for reading various parts of the manuscript and for their constructive criticisms. I have also benefited from comments by participants in the seminars/workshops at the Australian

National University; the London School of Economics; Queen Mary College, London and at the Universities of Birmingham, Liverpool, Rome and Groningen. I should like to thank Ann Widdop, Christine Molton, Christine Hudson, and Nguyet Thu Luu for their skilful typing of the manuscript, and Alison Rowlatt for helping me with the index. Finally, I should like to thank Sue Corbett of Basil Blackwell for encouraging me to write a book on rational expectations.

M. Hashem Pesaran
Cambridge

1 Introduction: Aims and Scopes

The past decade has witnessed important developments in the study of the expectations formation process and the problem of decision-making under uncertainty. How expectations are formed, the way they influence economic behaviour, and whether they lend themselves to formal analysis have become issues of central importance both in the development of dynamic economic theory and in econometric analysis of time-series data. Out of the theories of expectations formation so far advanced the 'rational expectations hypothesis' has attracted by far the greatest attention. A weak version of the hypothesis postulates that 'rational' agents form expectations by acquiring and processing information up to the point where the expected marginal cost and expected marginal benefit of gathering and processing the information are equated. This weak version, although plausible, lacks operational significance and does not imply that expectations formed in this way will necessarily be free from *systematic* errors. The stronger version of the rational expectations hypothesis (REH), due to Muth, is much bolder, and states that subjective expectations held by economic agents will be the same as the conditional mathematical expectations based on the 'true' probability model of the economy, or more generally, that the agents' subjective probability distribution coincides with the 'objective' probability distribution of events. It is this strong version that concerns us here in this volume.

Although, the REH was advanced by Muth in 1961 it was the work of Lucas (1972a, 1973, 1975), Sargent (1973), Barro (1977) and others on the new classical explanations of output and inflation in the early 1970s that brought it into prominence. The adoption of the REH has in turn led to important developments in macroeconomic theory and time-series econometric research. By arguing that economic agents form their expectations *endogenously* on the basis of the *true* model of the economy and a *correct* understanding of the government policy, the REH has raised serious doubts about the invariance of the structural parameters of the mainstream Keynesian macroeconometric models in the face of changes in government policy. This has been highlighted in Lucas's (1976) critique of macroeconometric policy evaluation. The application of the REH has not been confined to the analysis of macroeconomic problems. It has found its way into numerous fields of research in economics, including econometric analysis of consumption, investment, commodity and security prices, labour markets, etc. It would indeed be fair to say that over the past 15 years the REH has been the single most important factor in the development of dynamic economic models and the econometric analysis of time-series data.

The prominence given to the REH in the literature clearly calls for a critical assessment of this influential hypothesis, and the present book is intended as a contribution towards this end. The primary aim of this book is, therefore, to provide the reader with a critical examination of the methodological and empirical basis of the REH. This critical approach is followed in the belief that only by identifying and plotting the limits of ideas or concepts is it possible to achieve a full understanding of their true significance.

The analysis is not, however, confined to the REH; other models of expectations formation will also be considered. I shall argue that the REH, like the adaptive expectations hypothesis that preceded it, is based on extreme assumptions and cannot be maintained outside the tranquillity of a long-period steady state, and that in conditions of dynamic disequilibrium greater reliance needs to be placed on direct measurement of expectations. This is important both for the analysis of the effect of expectations on economic behaviour, and for the study of the expectations formation process itself. I also emphasize the importance of formulating expectations formation models that explicitly take account of the learning process. With this in mind the book develops an augmented adaptive-learning expectations formation hypothesis which does not suffer from the shortcomings of the purely extrapolative schemes, and which at the same time is not based on extreme information assumptions that underlie the REH. The book concludes with an application of these ideas to the problem of the formation of inflation expectations in the UK manufacturing industries.

The book is in three parts. The first part (chapters 2–4) is concerned with the methodological basis of the REH, and examines the circumstances under which it is valid to apply this hypothesis to economic problems. Chapter 2 deals with the basic concepts and ideas that underlie the problem of expectations formation in economics. It makes a distinction between 'behavioural' and 'exogenous' uncertainty, and discusses the importance of this distinction for the evaluation and assessment of the limits to the REH. It then introduces the adaptive and rational expectations hypotheses, and gives a formal account of their optimal properties. It will be pointed out that, in advancing his theory of expectations formation, Muth (1961) was primarily concerned with the criterion of statistical optimality, and viewed the REH as a purely *descriptive* hypothesis in the positivist sense emphasized by Friedman (1953). Further, it will be argued that for rational expectations to have the desired (statistical) properties of unbiasedness and orthogonality it is not enough, as is often stated by some authors, that individuals form expectations 'as if' they knew the 'true' model of the economy. They should actually know the 'true' model, or else they should be capable of learning what the 'true' model is, given their *a priori* beliefs and the past history of the economy.

The problem of learning is addressed in chapter 3, which considers both the 'rational learning models', and the 'boundedly rational learning models' discussed in the literature. In the case of the former we reiterate the conclusion reached by Bray and Kreps (1984), and point out that the idea of rational learning, although intellectually appealing, is of limited relevance to actual problems. In the case of the boundedly rational learning models we review the recent literature on the convergence of the learning process in the context of a simple cobweb model. The convergence results so far obtained for the cobweb model are encouraging, but are still based on very demanding 'common knowledge' assumptions, and assume that the acquisition and processing of information is costless. When information is costly the problem of learning becomes much more complicated. First, the decision to collect information, and hence the possibility of learning, can be stifled by agents' *a priori* held subjective beliefs. Second, when information is costly it may not be worthwhile to learn the 'true' model even if it were in fact possible to do so. Thus, in the face of costly information, contrary to what is predicted by the Muth version of the REH, there is no ground for believing that 'rational' optimizing agents will necessarily form expectations that are free of systematic errors. The difficulties involved in the learning process when information acquisition is costly are demonstrated by a simple search example due to Stigler (1961). We also briefly discuss the literature on the existence of informationally efficient markets recently spearheaded by the work of Grossman and Stiglitz (1976, 1980) and comment on the relevance of this literature for the problem of learning in the face of costly information.

Chapter 4 discusses the often overlooked problem of information heterogeneity across agents, and considers the implications that it has for the REH. This problem is of particular importance for the optimization approach advocated by Lucas, Sargent, Hansen and others. (See, for example, the various contributions in Lucas and Sargent (1981).) Under this approach the REH is viewed as an integral part of the development of a theoretically consistent dynamic model of decision-making under uncertainty, and therefore an important extension of the neoclassical research programme. There it is argued that although the optimization approach can provide a plausible micro-foundation for the REH in situations where information is homogeneous across agents, the same need not be true under heterogeneous information. In particular, by means of simple examples involving economic optimization. I show that under information heterogeneity decision-making will, in general, be subject to behavioural uncertainty, and a rigorous derivation of the REH from principles of economic optimization invariably involves the infinite regress in expectations discussed by Keynes (1936). A general solution to the problem of infinite regress in the case of a simple linear rational expectations model with heterogeneous information is given in appendix B, where a formalization of Keynes's beauty contest example may also be found. By implication, chapter 4 also provides a critique of the Marshallian concept of the 'representative' firm (or household) as the basis for the formulation of the REH from the principles of economic optimization.

This in turn casts serious doubt on the validity of the optimization approach advocated by Sargent and others, who base their analysis on the behaviour of the 'representative' firm or household.

The second part (chapters 5–7) is concerned with the econometric issues that arise in the analysis of a variety of linear rational expectations models, containing current and/or future expectations of the endogenous variables. The econometric problems are demonstrated by means of examples from the new classical macroeconomic model, the efficient market hypothesis, the dynamic partial adjustment model, the inventory speculation model, and the forward exchange rate model. The analysis of some of the econometric problems covered in this part is rather technical, and assumes knowledge of theoretical econometrics at an advanced undergraduate level.

The first chapter in the second part reviews the various techniques proposed in the literature for the solution of linear rational expectations models. The solution of models containing only *current* expectations of the endogenous variables, formed on the basis of information available at different points in time in the past, is covered in detail in section 5.2. Following Aoki and Canzoneri (1979), Visco (1981, 1984a), and Broze and Szafarz (1984) we show that, save for a number of degenerate cases, the rational expectations models with current expectations admit a unique solution, and that the hypothesis of rationality in the case of these models does not pose any new technical problems. The same is not, however, true of rational expectations models with future expectations of the endogenous variables. In the case of these models information on the past history of the endogenous variables is not sufficient for the determination of a unique solution, and solution of such models in general depends on *arbitrary* martingale processes. (A description of what is meant by a martingale process, together with a brief account of its properties, is given in appendix A.) To highlight the nature of this non-uniqueness problem we consider five different solution techniques proposed in the literature, namely *the method of undetermined coefficients* first introduced by Muth (1961), *the operator, or the z-transform method*, used by Shiller (1978), and Sargent (1979a), *the forward recursive substitution method*, first employed by Sargent and Wallace (1973), *the martingale method*, proposed by Pesaran (1981), and Gourieroux et al. (1982), and finally *the martingale difference method*, recently put forward by Broze et al. (1985). It will be shown that the degree to which the solution of the rational expectations models with future expectations is subject to the non-uniqueness problem can be fully recognized only when the martingale solution methods are employed. The other three solution techniques proposed in the literature generally fail to identify all the possible solutions. This chapter also reviews the various criteria, such as economic optimality, stationarity, minimum variance, and the minimal use of state variables that are proposed in the literature for narrowing down the range of feasible solutions in the case of models with future expectations. It will be argued that none of these selection criteria is really satisfactory. They either fail to lead to a unique solution or they are *ad hoc* and lack a proper economic rationale. The various technical problems associated with the solution of rational expectations models are demonstrated with the help of three important examples of linear rational expectations models, of the type frequently encountered in the literature, namely the new classical macroeconomic model, Taylor's (1977) macroeconomic model, and a generalization of Muth's (1961) inventory speculation model.

Chapter 6 is concerned with the problem of identification. In the case of the REH the problem presents itself at two levels. First, at the level of a single equation, where the substitution of unobserved expectations by functions of observables poses the problem of whether the unknown parameters can be consistently estimated from the observed history of the variables. Second, at a simultaneous equation level where, in addition to the difficulty of unobserved expectations, there is also the further problem of consistently estimating the structural parameters from the (pseudo)-reduced form parameters. The necessary and sufficient conditions for identification of rational expectations models will be investigated at both levels. The first part of chapter 6 deals with single-equation models containing current and future expectations of the endogenous variables. In the case of models with future expectations the chapter discusses the identification problem both when the model under consideration has a unique stationary solution (the 'regular case'), and when it has an infinite number of stationary solutions (the 'irregular case'). It is shown that the identification problem in the regular case can be viewed as a special case of the identification problem in the irregular case. The second part of chapter 6 considers the simultaneous equation case and reviews the results already derived in the literature by Wallis (1980), Pesaran (1981), and Wegge and Feldman (1983a). Here we derive the relevant rank and order conditions for identification explicitly in terms of the structural parameters and the coefficients of the identifying restrictions. The main results are summarized in theorems 6.1 and 6.2. The problem of identification is particularly troublesome in the case of models with future expectations. Identification of these models requires *a priori* information regarding both the type of solution these models have (whether they have a unique stationary solution or a multiplicity of stationary solutions), and the lag lengths of the exogenous variables that they contain. Two general conclusions emerge from the analysis of the identification problem. The better informed economic agents are about the future course of the exogenous variables the less likely it is that an outside observer (econometrician) will be able to discover the structural relations that underlie the agents' decision rules. And in the absence of *a priori* information concerning the order of lags in economic relations, or *a priori* knowledge of restrictions on the processes generating the exogenous variables and the disturbances, it will not be possible to empirically distinguish between linear rational expectations models and general distributed lag models. This problem of 'observational equivalence' of RE and non-RE linear dynamic models presents important difficulties for empirical analysis of Keynesian and the new classical explanations of output and employment.

The problems of estimation and hypothesis testing are covered in chapter 7, which divides the various procedures proposed in the literature for the estimation of rational expectations models into two broad categories depending on the extent to which information concerning the processes generating the exogenous variables of the model is utilized in the estimation process. The 'full-information' methods require a complete specification of all the stochastic processes involved, while the 'limited-information' methods do not need such a complete characterization. Both types of estimators are considered in this chapter. The chapter also discusses the problems associated with the use of cross-equation tests as tests of the REH, and examines the relationship that exists between Granger non-causality tests and the joint tests of the neutrality and rationality propositions of the new classical macroeconomics. The chapter is set out in two parts: part A deals with models containing current and past expectations, and part B focuses attention on models with future expectations. In the case of the latter we first study the estimation problem in the context of rational expectations models of exchange rate determination, and then turn to more general rational expectations models with lagged dependent variables and future expectations of the endogenous variables. We review the estimators proposed by Hansen (1982), Cumby et al. (1983), and Hayashi and Sims (1983), and show the importance of distinguishing between the 'regular' and the 'irregular' cases referred to above for the consistent and efficient estimation of rational expectations models with future expectations of the endogenous variables. It will be shown that fully efficient estimation of the rational expectations models with future expectations requires *a priori* knowledge of the number of unstable roots of the model. The pitfalls inherent in the indiscriminate use of the instrumental variable method for a consistent estimation of rational expectations models with future expectations, an issue which is often overlooked in the literature, are also demonstrated.

The third part (chapters 8–9) is concerned with the use of direct observations on expectations for testing the REH, and for the empirical analysis of the expectations formation process in general. While it is possible to test the REH via tests of cross-equation restrictions, the outcome of such tests will generally be ambiguous, and it is important that such indirect tests be supplemented with direct tests based on observed expectations whenever possible. When there are no direct observations on expectations, empirical analysis of the expectations formation process can be carried out only indirectly, and on the assumption that the behavioural model that embodies the expectational variables is in fact valid. In these circumstances, although tests of cross-equation restrictions are useful as tests of the consistency of the expectations formation process and the underlying behavioural model, they are of little help as tests of theories of expectations formation. What is needed, we argue, is direct reliable observations on expectations.

Chapter 8 deals with the problem of quantification of qualitative expectations data and discusses the alternative approaches that are employed in the literature for this purpose. In particular it reviews the probability method proposed by Theil (1952), and Carlson and Parkin (1975), and contrasts it with the regression method discussed in Pesaran (1984b). In the analysis particular attention is paid to the problem of measurement errors in expectations, and we emphasize the importance of allowing for these errors in the econometric analysis of the expectations formation process. Methods are suggested that can be used to shed light on the nature of the measurement errors involved and to show how to allow for such errors when testing the REH. (The econometric implications of the measurement errors for the modelling of expectations is discussed in chapter 9.) This chapter also considers the aggregation problem involved in the use of expectations data obtained by conversion of qualitative responses into quantitative measures. This problem is particularly important in testing the REH, where individual agents, and not some fictitious 'representative' agent, are the subject of the analysis. Finally, we derive a test of the REH which is based on assumptions that are less restrictive than the ones that underlie the familiar orthogonality tests, and apply it to test the 'rationality' of inflation expectations series in the UK manufacturing industries. (The empirical results reported in this chapter update those already published in Pesaran (1985).)

Chapter 9 considers the problem of modelling of expectations using direct observations on expectations. The chapter focuses on models of expectations formation that are informationally less demanding than the REH. We first briefly review the various adaptive/extrapolative models that have been proposed in the literature. These purely extrapolative models are, however, subject to one important objection. They ignore relevant information that may be available to economic agents at the time expectations are formed. While the REH attributes to agents information which they may not possess, the purely extrapolative hypothesis assumes agents form their expectations on the basis of an information set far more restricted than the one they may actually have. Seen from this perspective the purely extrapolative schemes stand at the other extreme to the REH. This chapter develops expectations formation models assuming that agents form their expectations on the basis of a reduced-form model of the economy, and emphasizes the importance of learning in the process of expectations formation. This reduced-form approach to modelling expectations has the advantage of explicitly allowing variables other than the past history of the variable under consideration to influence expectations without invoking the extreme information assumptions that underlie the REH. We derive an augmented adaptive-learning model and, on the basis of inflation expectations data obtained in chapter 8, examine its empirical validity in relation to other models of expectations formation.

The final chapter of the book provides some conclusions and indicates areas of further research.

Part I

Methodological Issues

2 Uncertainty and the Process of Expectations Formation

2.1 The Source and Nature of Uncertainty

The need to form expectations arises primarily because individuals in deciding which course of action to follow are constantly faced with an uncertain environment. How expectations are formed, and whether they can be characterized by means of formal mathematical models, are central issues in the development of dynamic economic theory and time-series econometrics; and like most issues of central importance are also highly controversial. The types of answers that can be given to these questions very much depend on the nature and the source of the uncertainty that surrounds a particular decision. Given the complexity and the variety of economic environments encountered in practice this is hardly surprising. Even as far as the concept of uncertainty itself is concerned there are different meanings attached to it in the literature. In ordinary usage the word 'uncertainty' is often used synonymously with 'not knowing' or 'lack of certainty', but on occasions it is also used in a non-cognitive sense to convey 'feelings' or 'perception' of uncertainty. Here we employ the concept of uncertainty in the formal sense developed in the literature of the statistical decision theory, and define uncertainty in the context of the decision-making process. Accordingly we say that *a decision-making process is subject to 'uncertainty' if the individual decision-maker is not perfectly aware (or knowledgeable) of the consequences of his/her own action.* In this broad sense uncertainty may involve imperfect information or unpredictable events, it may be due to 'ignorance' or 'chance' or a combination of both.[1]

The outcome of a toss of a 'fair' coin is uncertain because of the element of pure chance involved; but the uncertainty associated with the moves of one's rival in a game of chess is basically due to ignorance. In reality both

[1] Whether there is such a thing as chance in the world is a controversial matter which has attracted the attention of many philosophers. Hume, for example, maintained that when we attribute an event to chance (like turning head in the toss of a coin), we are confessing our ignorance (Hume, 1975, p. 56). Even if true this does not mean that the concept of chance is redundant. It is often useful to identify one's ignorance that cannot be reduced any further as chance. In other words chance can be viewed as 'irreducible ignorance'.

types of uncertainty are usually present. A simple example due to Dubey and Shubik (1977) can be used to illustrate this point further. Consider two individuals, one with normal eyesight and the other blind, both of whom wish to cross a road where there is a probability p that a truck is approaching *silently* and a probability $1 - p$ that the truck is not approaching. Assume now that the person who is blind is told (but not accompanied) by the one who can see whether it is safe to cross the road. In this example the blind man faces two distinct types of uncertainty: the uncertainty associated with the state of nature (i.e. whether the truck approaches or not) and the blind person's uncertainty concerning the motivation and the strategy of the person who can see. The blind person may not be sure of the sincerity of the advice he is offered. We call the former type of uncertainty 'exogenous' uncertainty, and refer to the latter as 'behavioural' uncertainty. Put more formally, when the probability of the occurrence of a given event is invariant to an individual's action, we say (for that individual) the uncertainty which surrounds the occurrence of the event is exogenous; otherwise we say it is 'behavioural' or 'endogenous'.

In the above example, behavioural uncertainty can only exist if there is uncertainty about the state of nature. But in general this need not be the case. The uncertainty involved in the outcome of a game of chess can be regarded as purely behavioural. In monopolistic or oligopolistic market conditions where actions by one market participant have a potentially non-negligible impact upon the actions of other participants, behavioural uncertainty will be present even if demand for the industry's output and the individual firm's cost functions happen to be known with certainty. It is the capacity of individuals to adapt and react to one another (in a non-negligible manner) which is the root cause of the existence and prevalence of behavioural uncertainty in economic and social systems.

The famous example of a 'beauty contest' given by Keynes (1936, p. 156) whereby it is required to anticipate 'what average opinion expects the average opinion to be', provides a vivid illustration of the nature and the source of what we have called behavioural uncertainty.[2] (A formalization of Keynes's beauty contest can be found in appendix B.) When the source of uncertainty is

---

[2] However, Keynes under the influence of Marshallian analysis was preoccupied with a distinction between the state of 'short-run' and 'long-run' expectations. He did not make any attempt to distinguish explicitly between exogenous and behavioural sources of uncertainty. For recent appraisals of Keynes's view on uncertainty and expectations see Lawson (1981), Coddington (1982), Begg (1982b), Patinkin (1984), Hodgson (1985) and Dow and Dow (1985). Coddington argues that Keynes's position on uncertainty is 'odd and unhelpful', and suggests that 'Keynes's forays into this area [uncertainty] was an opportunistic but mild flirtation with subjectivism'. Coddington's sweeping dismissal of Keynes's views on uncertainty is not convincing, and misses the main points of Keynes's objections to frequency interpretation of probability and uncertainty. A more balanced account of Keynes's views concerning the state of long-term expectations is given in Lawson (1981), Hodgson (1985), and Dow and Dow (1985). Begg and Patinkin are mainly concerned with the issue of how Keynes would have responded to the REH. Patinkin argues that Keynes would have been willing to accept the REH in a short-run context. A similar viewpoint is also put forward by Begg.

solely 'behavioural', the probability distributions involved will not generally be invariant to individual actions, and unless one makes the extreme assumption that, apart from exogenous shocks, agents are perfectly aware of the reactions of others, the assignment of an objective probability distribution to the behaviourally uncertain events in general will not be possible. This problem clearly does not arise if the source of uncertainty is exogenous to the behaviour of economic agents. On the other hand, it is often possible, through trading or exchanging of information, or by adhering to institutional arrangements, customs, or rules of conduct, to reduce the degree of behavioural uncertainty involved in a given situation. The same cannot, however, be said about exogenous uncertainty. We can learn about the degree of exogenous uncertainty that may be present in a given situation, or it may be feasible to prepare for, counteract, or insure against the unfavourable consequences of natural disasters, but it is hard to envisage how the probability of the occurrence of exogenous events can be reduced.

Our concepts of exogenous and behavioural uncertainties are also closely related to Knight's notions of 'true uncertainty' and 'risk', but they are not the same. For Knight 'true uncertainty' exists whenever it is not possible to reduce the uncertainty surrounding a decision to 'an objective quantitatively determined probability' (Knight, 1921, p. 321). A similar distinction between 'uncertain' and 'probable' events has also been made by Keynes (1921, 1937). The basis of Knight's distinction between 'true uncertainty' and 'risk' in effect lies in the position one may take concerning the question of whether the probability of various pairs of possible outcomes of a decision can be compared. The problem of measurability of probability can arise irrespective of whether the source of uncertainty is behavioural or exogenous; although it may be reasonably argued that 'true uncertainty' in the sense of Knight or Keynes is likely to be more prevalent in the case of behavioural rather than exogenous uncertainty. Our concern here is not so much with the controversial problem of whether 'probability' is measurable, but whether *the subjective probability distributions attached to uncertain events faced by individuals remain invariant with respect to their own actions or the perception they have of others' actions.*

The extent of behavioural uncertainty in a market environment is closely related to the degree to which individual market participants are potentially capable of influencing the action of others by their own actions, or are themselves influenced by what they perceive others participating in the market are likely to do. In reality all decentralized systems of economic decision-making are subject to behavioural uncertainty. For there to be no behavioural uncertainty in a market environment, there should exist a full set of Arrow–Debreu contingent markets where trade in commodities contingent on any conceivable state of nature can take place.[3] In this set-up all market partici-

[3] In the Arrow–Debreu world, commodities are distinguished not only by their physical characteristics and location, but also by their date of delivery and the state of nature. As a result the standard application of the theory of competitive equilibrium to this expanded commodity world necessitates that there should exist a full set of markets (and prices) for every conceivable contingency. For further details and analysis see, for example, Arrow and Hahn (1971), and Radner (1982).

pants are price-taking profit or utility maximizers and are completely informed about the potential outcome of their actions and make their demand and supply decisions in the light of market clearing prices for every possible contingency. When perfect competition prevails and a complete set of Arrow–Debreu markets exists, agents need only consider uncertainties associated with the state of nature which are exogenous to the functioning of the market mechanism. This is, however, an extremely idealized characterization of the workings of a decentralized market economy which has very little to do with reality. The Arrow–Debreu model is an ingenious mathematical abstraction which should only be taken seriously as a characterization of reality if its emergence from an initial economic situation (given endowments, tastes and technology) can be shown rather than assumed. In reality, markets are far from being complete or perfectly competitive, and there is no reason to believe that, starting from a given market condition, there should be any tendency towards the Arrow–Debreu world. If anything, the reverse seems more likely to be the case. In the words of Joan Robinson (1971, p. 102) 'where competition is vigorous, there must be a tendency toward monopoly, which is often held up at the stage of oligopoly when a few powerful firms prefer armed neutrality to the final battle of supremacy'. In conditions of incomplete and imperfectly competitive markets behavioural uncertainty is an integral part of the market environment, and any study of uncertainty and expectations in economics has to recognize the importance of behavioural uncertainty and find appropriate ways of dealing with it.

2.2 Process of Expectations Formation

We now turn our attention to the problems connected with the formation and modelling of expectations both when the uncertainty surrounding future events is exogenous to the decision process and when it is behavioural in the sense discussed above.

By expectations is usually meant 'attitudes, dispositions or psychological states of mind' that relate to events the outcomes of which are uncertain.[4] Expectations are usually formed about future events which have not been experienced in the past, although expectations may also be formed about present or past events which are unknown to the individual forming expectations. In this general sense expectations are psychologically held subjective beliefs that may or may not be related to the individual's past experience or his present perception. Whether such subjective beliefs can be represented by probability measures is itself the subject of an old controversy which was considerably revived (in economics) by the appearance of Keynes's (1921) *Treatise on Probability* and Shackle's (1949, 1955) subsequent work on expectations and uncertainty. Shackle's view of expectations is based on a historical conceptualization of time, and rejects the logical-time analysis that

[4] For a discussion of the meaning of expectations from a psychological viewpoint see, for example, Katona (1951, pp. 52–3).

underlies the treatment of uncertainty in the statistical decision theory. Shackle's scheme does not allow comparison or addition of probabilities. According to Shackle expectations are creative acts of imagination and fantasy, and do not lend themselves to formal representations by means of probabilistic models. A contrast between Shackle's view of expectations and the hypothesis of rational expectations is given by Bausor (1983). In this connection the view expressed by Davidson (1982/3) is also of some interest. Davidson interprets Shackle's position in terms of the 'ergodicity' property of stochastic processes.

The logical impossibility of the probabilistic formalization of 'knowledge' was first emphasized by Hume, who maintained that it is not logically justifiable to infer from *repeated* instances of which we have experience to the probability of instances of which we have no experience. According to this epistemological position the characterization of subjective expectations by probability distributions cannot be logically justified, irrespective of whether the source of uncertainty is exogenous or behavioural. This position is, however, unduly pessimistic, especially as far as the exogenous uncertainty is concerned. It may be possible to defend the representation of exogenous uncertainty by means of stable probability distributions on the grounds that the 'Law of Uniformity of Nature', needed for the validity of induction, is likely to be satisfied in the case of exogenous uncertainty where individuals, through their own actions, cannot influence the data generation process. Unfortunately, the same cannot be said when the source of uncertainty is behavioural and agents face the additional difficulty that the data generation process itself may change as a result of their actions. In these circumstances it is doubtful that the uncertainty surrounding economic decisions could be represented by stable stochastic processes, and Keynes's and Shackle's objections to the use of probability models as the basis for formation of expectations is likely to be valid. In the case of exogenous uncertainty, a probabilistic representation of uncertainty will be invariant to the action of economic agents. Decision by an individual not to carry an umbrella does not alter (so we believe!) the probability of rain, but a decision by an oligopolist to reduce his price is unlikely to have no effect on the probability of a price change by other oligopolists. Under behavioural uncertainty, even if we ignore Hume's objection to induction, the knowledge of past evolution of a system may be of little guide to its likely future development. The decision-making process will generally be in the form of a non-cooperative non-zero-sum game where mixed strategies and unstable outcomes cannot be ruled out, and may even become quite prevalent over certain periods. The breakdown of business confidence, the occurrence of social unrest and revolutionary upheavals are examples that immediately come to mind. The highly interactive nature of decision-making under behavioural uncertainty also initiates and involves changes in economic and social institutions.[5] There is no stable and exogenously given data generation process that agents can hope to learn about. The

[5] See Schotter and Schwödiauer (1980) for a comprehensive survey of game theory in which the importance of endogenization of a theory of institution creation is emphasized.

basis for formation of expectations as mathematical expectations derived from economic theory simply does not exist; not necessarily because of Hume's or Keynes's objections to the frequency interpretation of probability and inference, but due to the interactive nature of decision-making under behavioural uncertainty.

The fact that an objective basis for a probability representation of behavioural uncertainty may not exist does not, however, mean that individuals will not form expectations, or that their expectations would necessarily be unstable for all variables at all times. Possible reasons for this have been suggested by Hume, himself an arch-critic of the inductive method of inference. According to Hume 'custom and habit' condition individuals to form expectations in which they have great confidence. A similar point of view has also been advanced by Keynes (1936) in chapter 12 of his *General Theory.* Popper (1972) even goes a step further and points to 'the immensely powerful need for regularity' which makes individuals seek for regularities. The need for regularities arises because of the individual's desire to solve the recurrent problems that he is constantly facing, which in turn leads to the creation of institutions within which conventions, norms and habits can be exercised with ease. He habitually uses certain rules of thumb in the conduct of his business affairs even if it means not acting in an 'optimal' manner at all times.[6] The fact that erratic changes in business expectations are not usually observed is largely due to the relatively stable nature of our economic and social institutions.

It should, however, be noted that, apart from the individual's desire for order and regularity, the reasons for institutional stability are not very well understood (but see Schotter, 1981). Spurts of institutional instability and periods of collapse of business confidence clearly cannot be ruled out, as is often painfully demonstrated at times of social unrest and revolutionary upheavals. In conditions where *behavioural uncertainty is predominant*, the best that can be hoped for is to detect past patterns of regularity, to attempt to understand such regularities and to watch for possible changes in society's institutions, customs and habits. It may then be necessary to fall back on 'history' as an explanation of why certain customs and habits dominate others.

The preceding discussion strongly suggests that a search for a general and all-encompassing theory of expectations formation may be futile. For some events, such as variations in gold prices or changes in policy regimes, a formal modelling of expectations may not be possible. But, as pointed out above, this does not necessarily mean that expectations *cannot* be modelled at all. The possibility of modelling expectations depends on the nature of uncertainty that surrounds the decision-making process, the pervasiveness of customs and habits in the society, and the degree to which regularities exist and are exploited by individuals. However, without direct measurement of expectations it will be difficult, if not impossible, to say whether an indi-

---

[6] For an interesting discussion of the importance of 'habitual' as opposed to 'genuine' decisions or 'programmed' as opposed to 'unprogrammed' decisions, see Katona (1951), and Simon (1958).

vidual's expectations of a particular economic phenomenon can be modelled formally. Only when reliable direct observations on expectations are available would it be possible to compare and contrast alternative models of expectations formation. The problems associated with the quantitative measurement of expectations from survey data and the utilization of such data in empirical analysis of models of expectations formation will be dealt with in some detail later on in this volume (see chapters 8 and 9). First, we need to consider some of the models of expectations formations already advanced in the literature and critically examine the premises upon which they are based.

2.3 The Adaptive Expectations Hypothesis

In its most general form the adaptive hypothesis states that in any one period expectations are revised (linearly) in the light of past errors of expectations. In its simplest form the adaptive expectations hypothesis can be written as

$$\Pi_t^* - \Pi_{t-1}^* = \theta(\Pi_{t-1} - \Pi_{t-1}^*), \tag{2.1}$$

where Π_{t-i}^* stand for expectations of Π_{t-i} (say, the rate of inflation at $t-i$), formed at time $t-i-1$.[7] The magnitude of the revision in expectations is determined by the coefficient θ assumed to lie in the range $0<\theta<2$. A high value for θ means a rapid adjustment. The simple expectations formation mechanism (2.1) is usually referred to as a first-order adaptive scheme or a first-order error-correction mechanism, and was initially applied in economics by Koyck (1954) in a study of investment, by Cagan (1956) in a study of demand for money in conditions of hyper-inflation, and by Nerlove (1958) in a study of the cobweb phenomena. Up until the early 1970s, adaptive schemes were also used extensively in empirical studies of the relationship between inflation and unemployment.

The simple adaptive process (2.1) can also be generalized in a straightforward manner to higher-order schemes. (For other generalizations of (2.1) see chapter 9.) The rth-order adaptive expectations model may be written as

$$\Pi_t^* - \Pi_{t-1}^* = \sum_{i=1}^{r} \theta_i(\Pi_{t-i} - \Pi_{t-i}^*). \tag{2.2}$$

One important feature of the adaptive mechanism lies in the fact that it can be written as a fixed-coefficient infinite distributed lag function in Π_{t-i} $(i \geqslant 1)$, with suitable restrictions on the lag-coefficients. Using the one-period lag operator $L(L\Pi_t = \Pi_{t-1})$, equation (2.1), for example, may be rewritten as

$$\{1-(1-\theta)L\}\Pi_t^* = \theta\Pi_{t-1}$$

[7] The expression (2.1) may also contain a disturbance term, unobservable to the econometrician, which we have suppressed here for expositional convenience.

and since $|1-\theta|<1$, the inversion of the linear lag operator function on Π_t^* yields,

$$\Pi_t^* = \theta\{1-(1-\theta)L\}^{-1}\Pi_{t-1}$$

or

$$= \theta \sum_{i=1}^{\infty}(1-\theta)^{i-1}\Pi_{t-i}. \tag{2.3}$$

Therefore, the first-order adaptive expectations hypothesis can also be viewed as a special case of a more general hypothesis that postulates

$$\Pi_t^* = \sum_{i=1}^{\infty} \omega_i \Pi_{t-i} = W(L)\Pi_{t-1}, \tag{2.4}$$

with the weights $\{\omega_i\}$ restricted to follow a geometrically declining sequence. A comparison of (2.3) and (2.4) reveals that

$$\omega_i = \theta(1-\theta)^{i-1}, \quad i=1,2,\ldots$$

and that $\Sigma_{i=1}^{\infty}\omega_i=1$. Clearly, the use of higher-order adaptive schemes will result in less restrictive patterns for ω_i. Notice, however, that under the adaptive expectations hypothesis the restriction $\Sigma_{i=1}^{\infty}\omega_i=1$ cannot be relaxed. For the general adaptive scheme the infinite order polynomial $W(L)$ in the lag operator L is given by[8]

$$W(L) = \frac{\sum_{i=1}^{r}\theta_i L^i}{1-(1-\theta_1)L+\sum_{i=2}^{r}\theta_i L^i},$$

and $\Sigma_{i=1}^{\infty}\omega_i = W(1) = 1$, for all values of r.

The adaptive expectations hypothesis, whether in its simple form (2.1) or the general distributed lag form (2.4), is, however, subject to two important objections. Firstly, in periods when the rate of inflation (Π_t) is accelerating expectations of the inflation rate formed according to the adaptive hypothesis will systematically underestimate the actual rate of inflation. This undesirable property can be illustrated by means of the following simple example. Suppose the actual rate of inflation is accelerating at a constant rate g. That is

$$\Pi_t = \Pi_0(1+g)^t, \quad g>0.$$

Using this expression in (2.3) gives

[8] It is assumed that all the roots of the equation $1-(1-\theta_1)x+\Sigma_{i=2}^{r}\theta_i x^i=0$, lie outside the unit-circle.

$$\Pi_t^* = \Pi_0 \theta \sum_{i=1}^{\infty} (1-\theta)^{i-1}(1+g)^{t-i},$$

$$= \Pi_t \theta (1+g)^{-1} \sum_{i=1}^{\infty} \{(1-\theta)/(1+g)\}^{i-1}.$$

But since by assumption $\theta > 0$, $g > 0$, then $(1-\theta)/(1+g) < 1$, and we have $\Pi_t^*/\Pi_t = \theta/(g+\theta)$. Therefore, for positive values of θ and g, it follows that $\Pi_t^* < \Pi_t$ for all t. This in turn establishes that when the rate of inflation is accelerating, Π_t^* will be systematically below the actual rate of inflation.[9] This example also shows that when the rate of inflation is falling ($g < 0$), the inflation expectations obtained according to the adaptive scheme will be systematically above the actual rate of inflation (assuming θ is large enough to ensure that $\theta + g > 0$).

The second objection to the simple adaptive expectations hypothesis or the general extrapolative formulation (2.4) is more fundamental, and concerns the limited information set upon which the adaptive or purely extrapolative hypotheses are based. The adaptive hypothesis ignores relevant information that may be available to economic agents at the time of expectations formation other than past rates of inflation. Obvious examples of such relevant pieces of information are the size of current wage settlements and (credible) announced changes in government policy. But, as we shall see in chapter 9, it is possible to modify the adaptive hypothesis by augmenting it with information on changes in other variables.

2.4 Optimality of the Adaptive Expectations Hypothesis

The adaptive expectations hypothesis was put forward originally as a plausible 'rule of thumb' for updating or revising expectations in the light of past observed expectations errors. Only in certain especial circumstances, as shown by Muth (1960), is the simple adaptive expectations hypothesis optimal in the sense of yielding minimum mean squared forecast errors.[10] Suppose the change in the rate of inflation ($\Delta\Pi_t$) follows the invertible first-order moving-average process

$$\Delta\Pi_t = \varepsilon_t - (1-\theta)\varepsilon_{t-1}, \quad 0 < \theta < 2, \tag{2.5}$$

where ε_t are identically, independently distributed random variables with zero means and a constant variance. That is Π_t has an integrated autoregressive

---

[9] This shortcoming of the adaptive expectations hypothesis can, however, be rectified by specifying the adaptive scheme in terms of the rate of change of the inflation rate, or if need be in terms of the rate of acceleration of the inflation rate, and so on.

[10] The minimum mean squared error criterion employed by Muth is primarily a statistical criterion and should not be confused with the notion of economic optimality which is based on expected profit or expected utility maximization. These two optimality criteria (the statistical and the economic ones) in general will have different implications.

moving average representation ARIMA (0,1,1).[11] Then the optimal forecast of Π_t, formed at $t-1$, which we denote by $\tilde{\Pi}_t$ will be

$$\tilde{\Pi}_t = E(\Pi_t | \Pi_{t-1}, \Pi_{t-2} \dots),$$
$$= \Pi_{t-1} - (1-\theta)\varepsilon_{t-1},$$

where $E(\Pi_t | \Pi_{t-1}, \Pi_{t-2}, \dots)$ is the conditional mathematical expectations operator. (See appendix A for a definition of conditional mathematical expectations and their properties.) Now using (2.5) we have

$$\varepsilon_{t-1} = \{1-(1-\theta)L\}^{-1}\Delta\Pi_{t-1}.$$

Replacing this result in the expression for $\tilde{\Pi}_t$ gives

$$\tilde{\Pi}_t = \theta\{1-(1-\theta)L\}^{-1}\Pi_{t-1},$$

or

$$\tilde{\Pi}_t - (1-\theta)\tilde{\Pi}_{t-1} = \theta\,\Pi_{t-1},$$

which can also be written in the form of the first-order adaptive expectations hypothesis (2.1).

This statistical optimality property of the adaptive expectations hypothesis does not, however, hold in general. For example, when it is *known* that Π_t follows a first-order autoregressive process [i.e. AR(1)],

$$\Pi_t = \alpha + \beta\Pi_{t-1} + \varepsilon_t,$$

the 'optimal' expectations (again in the sense of yielding minimum mean squared forecast errors) will be given by

$$\tilde{\Pi}_t = E(\Pi_t | \Pi_{t-1}, \Pi_{t-2} \dots),$$
$$= \alpha + \beta\Pi_{t-1},$$

and the 'optimal' method of updating expectations in this case will be

$$\tilde{\Pi}_t - \tilde{\Pi}_{t-1} = \beta(\Pi_{t-1} - \Pi_{t-2}). \qquad (2.6)$$

This simply states that expectations should be revised only if the rate of inflation in the past has been accelerating or decelerating. We shall refer to (2.6) as

---

[11] Notice that the assumption (2.5) also implies that Π_t is non-stationary, which is essential if the weights w_i in (2.4) are to add up to unity. To see this consider the following infinite autoregressive representation of Π_t,

$$\Pi_t = \sum_{i=1}^{\infty} w_i \Pi_{t-i} + u_t = W(L)\Pi_{t-1} + u_t,$$

or

$$A(L)\Pi_t = u_t,$$

where u_t is a white-noise process and $A(L) = 1 - W(L)$. The optimal forecast of Π_t conditional on $\Pi_{t-1}, \Pi_{t-2}, \dots$ is given by $\tilde{\Pi}_t = W(L)\Pi_{t-1}$, and the condition for the weights w_i *to add up to unity is* $W(1) = 1$. Hence, $A(1) = 1 - W(1) = 0$, which means that the autoregressive process generating Π_t should have a root on the unit circle. This is possible only if Π_t is non-stationary. (On this result also see Rose, 1976.)

the first-order accelerator expectations hypothesis. Like the adaptive hypothesis the accelerator hypothesis can also be generalized in a straightforward manner. The *r*th-order accelerator hypothesis may be written as

$$\tilde{\Pi}_t - \tilde{\Pi}_{t-1} = \sum_{i=1}^{r} \beta_i(\Pi_{t-i} - \Pi_{t-i-1}). \tag{2.7}$$

The above examples clearly show that the 'optimality' of expectations formation models will crucially depend on the 'true' process that generates the data. If it were *known* that Π_t follows an AR(1) process, it is clearly sub-optimal if expectations were updated by the adaptive scheme. Similarly when it is known that Π_t is generated according to (2.5), it would not be optimal to adopt the accelerator hypothesis for the purpose of revising expectations. The issue of 'optimality' or 'rationality' of alternative expectations formation processes can only be addressed meaningfully if the 'true' underlying data generating process is known by economic agents.

2.5 The Rational Expectations Hypothesis

The emphasis of Muth's 1960 paper on 'optimal' forecast errors in the case of univariate time-series models such as (2.5) led him to propose the 'rational expectations hypothesis' (REH), thus extending the idea of 'optimality' of expectations formed on the basis of univariate models to expectations formed on the basis of structural economic models. Muth (1961) postulated that economic agents form their expectations on the basis of the 'true' structural model of the economy. Muth's own definition of what he means by rational expectations is given in the following familiar quotation, 'expectations, since they are informed predictions of future events, are essentially the same as the predictions of the relevant economic theory' (p. 316); or put more precisely, in the words of Begg (1982a): 'The hypothesis of Rational Expectations asserts that the unobservable subjective expectations of individuals are exactly the true mathematical conditional expectations implied by the model itself' (p. 30). However, the two crucial issues of what the relevant economic theory or model is, and how individuals are supposed to learn to form expectations that are 'rational' in the above sense, were left, perhaps intentionally, unexplained. Muth himself certainly did not regard the REH as a prescription of how individuals ought to form expectations. He viewed it rather as a purely descriptive hypothesis emphasizing the relationship between the way expectations are formed and 'the structure of the relevant system describing the economy'. Muth was more interested in the predictive power of the hypothesis he was advancing than in the realism of its premises. His aim in proposing the REH was to explain two phenomena observed by other researchers in their studies of expectations data obtained from sample surveys of firms:

1 Averages of expectations in an industry are more accurate than naive models and as accurate as elaborate equation systems, although there are considerable cross-sectional differences of opinion.

2 Reported expectations generally underestimate the extent of changes that actually take place (p. 316).

Muth saw the REH as a 'positive' hypothesis in the sense of Friedman (1953), and advocated it not because he believed that the REH hypothesis represented how individuals actually formed expectations, but because he thought it could yield useful predictions capable of explaining the two observed phenomena, cited above, which concerned him. In his own words, 'The only real test [of the REH], however, is whether theories involving rationality explain observed phenomena any better than alternative theories,' (p. 330). This clearly places Muth firmly in Friedman's 'instrumentalist' methodological camp, which emphasizes the predictive usefulness of a hypothesis with little or no attention to the realism of its assumptions. For Muth the value of the REH lies not in its realism but in its predictive power. Whether this is an acceptable methodological position to hold has been the subject of an on-going debate in economics,[12] which we cannot enter into here. We would like, however, to point out that the application of Friedman's methodology to models of expectations formation involves additional difficulties that chiefly emanate from the nature of expectations themselves. This is because expectations are either unobservable or can only be observed with errors, thus making direct tests of the predictive performance of models of expectations formation either impossible or at best subject to a high degree of uncertainty not usually present in other applications of the methodology in economics. An alternative approach would be to adopt indirect tests of the REH, which do not require direct observations on expectations. But such indirect tests can be carried out only conditional on the behavioural model which embodies the expectational variables. This means that conclusions concerning the expectations process will not be invariant to the choice of the underlying behavioural model. The results of the predictive tests of the REH, whether based on direct or indirect methods, can be challenged effectively by the proponents as well as the opponents of the hypothesis. In the case of direct tests of the REH, it can be argued that the data used on expectations are not reliable enough, while the result of indirect tests can be dismissed on the grounds that the behavioural model upon which the REH is based is misspecified. Consequently, the application of Friedman's methodology to the REH may not be fruitful even if one accepts the usefulness of the instrumentalist position in applied economic research. The inherently unobservable nature of expectations in effect immunizes the REH against possible falsification. Of course, what we have just described is not exclusive to the REH and is symptomatic of a more general problem that afflicts applied research in economics. Our aim here has been to emphasize the additional difficulties that the unobservability of 'true' expectations are likely to present for empirical analysis of the expectations formation processes and/or the economic models that contain expectational variables. (The issues surrounding the *direct* and

[12] See, for example, Nagel (1963), Papandreou (1963), Samuelson (1963), Wong (1973), Boland (1979) and Caldwell (1982, ch. 8).

the *indirect* methods of testing the REH will be discussed more fully later, in chapters 7 and 8.)

2.6 'As If' Principle and the Optimality of the REH

The above 'instrumentalist' view of the REH has led some to argue that the validity of the REH does not really depend on whether economic agents know the true model of the economy. All that is required is that individuals form expectations 'as if' they knew the 'true' model. (See for example Shaw (1984, p. 57), and Begg (1982a, p. 30).) This may very well be how expectations are formed in reality. Individuals only having an incomplete understanding of the way the economy functions may indeed form expectations rationally on the basis of a model which they believe to be an adequate representation of the reality. It is not, however, valid to conclude from this that the expectations so formed will necessarily possess any of the 'optimality' properties (to be discussed below) that are usually attributed to the rational expectations. The issue of whether the REH yield 'optimal' forecasts is similar to that of the optimality of the adaptive expectations hypothesis which we discussed above. Like the adaptive hypothesis, the optimality of the REH crucially depends on the validity of the economic model employed by agents to form their expectations. Clearly, when rational expectations are formed on the basis of the true model of the economy, the subjective probability distributions held by economic agents will be the same as the objective probability distributions of the relevant variables. But there is no reason to believe that the rational expectations formed on the basis of a mis-specified model will have the desired properties of an optimal forecast. The emotive label of 'rationality' should not be automatically taken to mean that the REH always yields expectations that are 'optimal' forecasts. The optimality properties of the rational expectations will follow if agents know, or are capable of learning, the true model of the economy. It is not enough that agents act 'as if' they know the true model.

There are examples of self-fulfilling expectations that seem to contradict what has been said above. The case of self-fulfilling expectations can arise when a possibly false model is taken by all market participants to be 'common knowledge', in the sense that everyone acts 'as if' the model is correct and knows that everyone else also believes and acts in the same way.[13] As a result rational expectations formed on the basis of such a model will be self-fulfilling despite the fact that the model may be false in the sense of misrepresenting certain aspects of the 'objective reality' bearing on individuals' decisions. Such 'common beliefs' in a false model can and do arise in practice, but often with unfortunate consequences. These models do not necessarily possess stable outcomes. This is because a chance discovery of the 'truth' by one or more individuals in the economy can *potentially* cause the overthrow of the falsely held common belief. In such a situation the belief in the model ceases to be

---

[13] For a formalization of the concept of 'common knowledge' see Aumann (1976).

'common knowledge'! In the literature of asset market pricing such outcomes are often referred to as 'speculative bubbles', to highlight the precarious nature of the equilibrium outcomes that result from falsely held common beliefs. This kind of instability usually arises in rational expectations or perfect foresight models with multiple equilibria. For example, if everyone expects that the price of a particular share is going to rise, say by 10 per cent, the share price does indeed rise by the expected amount. There is, however, a limit to such a self-fulfilling process. When the share price reaches a high enough level, a level well above the yield expected on the share, expectations of further rises in the share price may be frustrated by those traders who realize the wide gap that exists between the market price and the yield expected on the share.[14] The bubble bursts and unexpectedly (at least to some!) the price of the share starts to fall.

2.7 Optimal Properties of the REH

Turning now to the situation where individuals know the 'true' underlying model, the rational expectations hypothesis can be shown to possess a number of important optimality properties. Let Ω_{t-1} be the information set that is available to an individual economic agent at time $t-1$. This information set contains *all* the data on the past history of all the variables that enter the relevant economic model, and any other information that may be available to the agent at time $t-1$ including past expectations. Suppose now that conditional on the information set Ω_{t-1}, the joint probability distribution of the random variables entering the agent's economic model (say a finite dimensional vector $\mathbf{x}_t$) is given by $f(\mathbf{x}_t | \Omega_{t-1})$. The REH postulates that the subjective conditional distribution of $\mathbf{x}_t$ coincides, exactly, with the objective conditional distribution of $\mathbf{x}_t$. Thus, under the REH there exists a one-to-one relationship between the moments of the subject conditional probability distribution and the corresponding moments of the objective conditional probability distribution (assuming, of course, that these moments exist). Focusing on the first moments of these distributions, under the REH we have

$$\mathbf{x}_t^* = E(\mathbf{x}_t | \Omega_{t-1}) = \int_R \mathbf{x}_t f(\mathbf{x}_t | \Omega_{t-1}) \, d\mathbf{x}_t$$

where $\mathbf{x}_t^*$ stands for the subjective expectations of the mean of $\mathbf{x}_t$ (i.e. the first moments of the subjective conditional probability distribution of $\mathbf{x}_t$) formed at time $t-1$, E is the mathematical expectations operator, and R denotes the region over which $\mathbf{x}_t$ can vary. (For a definition of conditional mathematical expectations see appendix A.) Clearly similar expressions can also be written

---

[14] Under the efficient market hypothesis the yield of a share is calculated as the discounted value of the dividends expected on the share plus the expected capital gains or losses associated with the ownership of the share. For more details see example 6.3 in chapter 6, pp. 138–141.

down for the subjective expectations of the variance and higher order moments of $\mathbf{x}_t$ conditional on Ω_{t-1}. For example, the subjective expectations of the covariance matrix of $\mathbf{x}_t$ under the REH will be

$$\Sigma_t^* = E\{[\mathbf{x}_t - E(\mathbf{x}_t | \Omega_{t-1})]'[\mathbf{x}_t - E(\mathbf{x}_t | \Omega_{t-1})] | \Omega_{t-1}\}.$$

In general it is therefore necessary that rational expectations are formed about all moments of the subjective probability distribution of the random variables. In practice, especially in the macroeconomics literature, the emphasis has largely been placed on the formation of expectations of the mean of the random variables, generally ignoring expectations about other measures such as median, mode or higher order moments. (But see Pagan and Ullah, 1986). This is difficult to justify, unless it is believed that $\mathbf{x}_t$ are jointly normally distributed with a non-stochastic conditional covariance matrix (i.e. $\Sigma_t^* = \Sigma^*$, for all t), or that the relevant economic model and the expectations formation processes are all linear in components of Ω_t. By contrast the microeconomic literature – being primarily concerned with the more abstract issues such as learning, the existence of rational expectations equilibrium, and economics of information – is firmly based on the general postulate of the REH as is set out above (for a brief discussion of this latter literature and related references see chapter 3). In the rest of this section we examine the optimality properties of the REH only in relation to the first-order moments of $\mathbf{x}_t$. As we shall see later, two of these properties are crucial to the validity of the 'policy ineffectiveness' propositions of the new classical school. These are

1. the expectations errors conditioned on the available information set have zero means;
2. the expectations errors are uncorrelated with the values of all the variables in the information set and therefore with their own past values.

The proof of these propositions is quite straightforward. Denoting the error of expectations by ξ_t, we have $\xi_t = \mathbf{x}_t - \mathbf{x}_t^*$, or under the REH

$$\xi_t = \mathbf{x}_t - E(\mathbf{x}_t | \Omega_{t-1}),$$

and

$$E(\xi_t | \Omega_{t-1}) = E\{[\mathbf{x}_t - E(\mathbf{x}_t | \Omega_{t-1})] | \Omega_{t-1}].$$

Now using known properties of conditional mathematical expectations (see appendix A), it is easily seen that

$$\begin{aligned} E(\xi_t | \Omega_{t-1}) &= E(\mathbf{x}_t | \Omega_{t-1}) - E[E(\mathbf{x}_t | \Omega_{t-1}) | \Omega_{t-1}], \\ &= E(\mathbf{x}_t | \Omega_{t-1}) - E(\mathbf{x}_t | \Omega_{t-1}), \\ &= 0. \end{aligned}$$

In fact for any subset of Ω_t, say S_t (i.e. $S_t \subset \Omega_t$) we have

$$E(\xi_t | S_{t-1}) = 0. \qquad (2.9)$$

The proof of the second property also follows immediately from the fact that for $i \geqslant 1$,

$$E(\xi_t \xi_{t-i} | \Omega_{t-i}) = \xi_{t-i} E(\xi_t | \Omega_{t-i})$$

and since Ω_{t-i} $(i \geqslant 1)$ is a subset of Ω_{t-1}, then by (2.9) it follows that

$$E(\xi_t \xi_{t-i}) = 0, \quad \text{for } i \geqslant 1. \tag{2.10a}$$

Similarly,

$$E(\xi_t \xi_{t+i} | \Omega_{t+i-1}) = \xi_t E(\xi_{t+i} | \Omega_{t+i-1}), \quad \text{for } i \geqslant 1,$$

and since under the REH $E(\xi_{t+i} | \Omega_{t+i-1}) = 0$, then we also have

$$E(\xi_t \xi_{t+i}) = 0, \quad \text{for } i \geqslant 1, \tag{2.10b}$$

which together with (2.10a) establish that exectations errors ξ_t are serially independent.

The first result (2.9) is generally known as the *orthogonality* property, and the second result (2.10), is sometimes referred to as the *lack of serial correlation* property. The orthogonality property (2.9) also implies the two properties known as *unbiasedness* and *efficiency*. These are:

$$\text{'Unbiasedness property'} \quad E(\xi_t) = 0, \tag{2.11}$$

and

$$\text{'efficiency property'} \quad E(\xi_t | \mathbf{x}_t, \mathbf{x}_{t-1}, \ldots) = 0. \tag{2.12}$$

To prove the unbiasedness property first note that by property P5 in appendix A we have

$$E\{E(\xi_t | S_{t-1})\} = E(\xi_t).$$

But by (2.9), $E(\xi_t | S_{t-1}) = 0$ which establishes that $E(\xi_t) = 0$. The 'efficiency' property is a special case of the orthogonality property where S_{t-1} is now taken to include only past values of the variables which are the subject of expectations formation, namely $\mathbf{x}_{t-1}, \mathbf{x}_{t-2}, \ldots$

The above properties need not, however, hold if expectations are formed on the basis of a mis-specified model or a correct model structure but with incorrect parameter values. A few simple examples would be helpful in clarifying some of these points.

Example 2.1 A Simple Neoclassical Model (True Model Known)

Consider the following simple example of a Lucasian aggregate supply function,

$$y_t^s - \bar{y}_t = \alpha(\Pi_t - \Pi_t^*) + \varepsilon_t \tag{2.13}$$

where y_t^s is the logarithm of real output, $\bar{y}_t$ is the logarithm of the 'natural level' of output, and ε_t is assumed to be a zero mean serially uncorrelated disturbance term representing the effect of unobservable random factors on the aggregate supply. It is also usually assumed that $0<\alpha<1$. A detailed discussion of the theoretical underpinnings of this aggregate supply function and the relevant references to the literature can be found, for example, in Pesaran (1984a).

Suppose now, following Lucas (1972a), the aggregate demand function is given by

$$y_t^d + p_t = x_t \tag{2.14}$$

where p_t is the logarithm of the price level, y_t^d is the logarithm of real demand in the economy, and x_t is the logarithm of nominal income taken here to be a policy variable. We note also that $p_t - p_{t-1} = \log(1+\Pi_t) \approx \Pi_t$ and hence approximating $\Pi_t - \Pi_t^*$ by $p_t - p_t^*$ the aggregate supply function (2.13) may also be written as,[15]

$$y_t^s - \bar{y}_t = \alpha(p_t - p_t^*) + \varepsilon_t. \tag{2.15}$$

The relations (2.14) and (2.15) together with the market clearing condition $y_t^d = y_t^s = y_t$ represent a simple structural model, which if true, can be used to derive p_t^* as the 'optimal' forecast of p_t. Eliminating y_t^s and y_t^d from (2.14) and (2.15) gives,

$$p_t = \mu p_t^* + (1-\mu) z_t, \quad 0 \leqslant \mu < 1 \tag{2.16}$$

where $\mu = \alpha/(1+\alpha)$, and $z_t = x_t - \bar{y}_t - \varepsilon_t$. The optimal forecast of p_t conditional on the information available at time $t-1$ (i.e. Ω_{t-1}) is obtained by replacing z_t by its conditional mathematical expectations with respect to Ω_{t-1}. Denoting the 'optimal' forecast of p_t by $\tilde{p}_t$, we have

$$\tilde{p}_t = \mu p_t^* + (1-\mu) E(z_t \mid \Omega_{t-1}). \tag{2.17}$$

The REH (in terms of the first-order moments) postulates that p_t^*, the subjective expectations, will be equal to $\tilde{p}_t$, the optimal forecast of p_t derived from the 'true' structural model. Thus imposing the 'optimality' condition $p_t^* = \tilde{p}_t$ on (2.17) yields

$$p_t^* = \tilde{p}_t = E(z_t \mid \Omega_{t-1}). \tag{2.18}$$

Replacing this result in (2.16) now gives the following equilibrium equation for the price level

$$p_t = \mu E(z_t \mid \Omega_{t-1}) + (1-\mu) z_t. \tag{2.19}$$

The familiar result of the REH that $p_t^* = E(p_t \mid \Omega_{t-1})$ now readily follows from (2.19). Taking expectations of both sides of (2.19) conditional on the information set Ω_{t-1} gives

$$E(p_t \mid \Omega_{t-1}) = E(z_t \mid \Omega_{t-1}),$$

---

[15] Here we assume that higher-order terms in the expansion of $\log(1+\Pi_t)$ can be ignored, otherwise the model will be non-linear in Π_t (or p_t), and therefore analytically rather difficult to deal with.

which together with (2.18) establishes that $p_t^* = \tilde{p}_t = E(p_t | \Omega_{t-1})$. The 'optimality' of expectations formed under the REH in this particular example follows directly from the assumption that agents when forming their expectations know that relations (2.14) and (2.15) and the equilibrium condition $y_t^s = y_t^d$ provide a true characterization of the process generating output and prices.

An important feature of the REH, also present in the above example, is the way it transforms the problem of forming expectations of the endogenous variables to one of forming expectations of the exogenous and policy variables of the model. The REH provides a specific procedure for solving the expectations of endogenous variables of the model in terms of the parameters, the past history, and the expectations of the exogenous policy and the exogenous non-policy variables of the model. The hypothesis can only provide a complete specification of expectations when the processes generating the exogenous variables are also fully specified. Under the REH, the traditional dichotomy of the variables of a model into the endogenous and the exogenous categories is no longer relevant. Agents in forming rational expectations need to know how *all* the variables that enter the economic model are generated. This requires formal modelling not only of the endogeneous variables such as output and prices, but also of exogenous variables ranging from changes in economic policy to technological innovations, fashion, and wars. This is indeed a tall order and highlights the severe informational demand that the REH places on economic agents. In effect the REH assumes that the uncertainty surrounding *all* the variables entering the decision-making process including the exogenous variables can be represented by stable probability distributions.

In the case of the above example, a complete specification of $E(p_t | \Omega_{t-1})$, the rational expectations of p_t, entails knowledge of the way the three components of z_t (namely, $\bar{y}_t$, ε_t, and x_t) are generated. In the literature of the new classical macroeconomics it is usually assumed that $\bar{y}_t$ (the logarithm of the natural level of output) is exogenously given and is determined by market conditions in a rational expectations equilibrium. It is also invariably assumed that $\bar{y}_t$ is not affected by changes in the nominal magnitudes including money expenditure, x_t. The disturbances ε_t are assumed to be serially uncorrelated with zero means. For x_t the following simple autoregressive policy rule is often adopted

$$x_t = \rho x_{t-1} + v_t, \tag{2.20}$$

where $\{v_t\}$ represents a serially uncorrelated sequence with zero mean and a constant variance. Given these assumptions and choosing a linear specification for $\bar{y}_t (= a_0 + a_1 t)$ the following expressions for the components of z_t can be obtained

$$E(\varepsilon_t | \Omega_{t-1}) = 0,$$
$$E(\bar{y}_t | \Omega_{t-1}) = a_0 + a_1 t,$$
$$E(x_t | \Omega_{t-1}) = \rho x_{t-1}$$

Therefore using these results in (2.18), the rational expectations of p_t will be

$$p_t^* = \tilde{p}_t = E(p_t \mid \Omega_{t-1}) = \rho x_{t-1} - a_0 - a_1 t. \tag{2.21}$$

Substituting this result in (2.16) yields the following RE solution for p_t:

$$p_t = (1-\mu)x_t + \rho\mu x_{t-1} - a_0 - a_1 t - (1-\mu)\varepsilon_t. \tag{2.22}$$

The expectations errors of p_t, or the inflation rate, can now be obtained by subtracting (2.21) from (2.22). That is

$$\xi_t = p_t - p_t^* = (1-\mu)(x_t - \rho x_{t-1}) - (1-\mu)\varepsilon_t$$

or upon using (2.20)

$$\varepsilon_t = (1-\mu)(v_t - \varepsilon_t). \tag{2.23}$$

It is clear that ε_t satisfies all the four properties possessed by optimal forecasts, namely *unbiasedness* (i.e. $E(\varepsilon_t)=0$), *lack of serial correlation*, (i.e. $E(\varepsilon_t\varepsilon_{t-i})=0$, for $i \geqslant 1$), *efficiency* (i.e. $E(\varepsilon_t \mid p_{t-1}, p_{t-2}, \ldots)=0$), *and orthogonality* (i.e. $E(\varepsilon_t \mid S_{t-1})=0$, where S_{t-1} is a subset of Ω_{t-1}).

Example 2.2 Inflation-augmented Phillips Curve (True Model Not Known)

Suppose now expectations of p_t are formed rationally on the basis of (2.22), but the 'true' inflation model is different from the simple new classical model of example 2.1, and is composed of the mark-up equation

$$p_t - p_{t-1} = \alpha_1(w_t - w_{t-1}) + \varepsilon_{t1}, \tag{2.24}$$

and the inflation-augmented Phillips relation given by

$$w_t - w_{t-1} = \beta_1(p_t^* - p_{t-1}) + \beta_2(y_t^s - \bar{y}_t) + \varepsilon_{t2}, \tag{2.25}$$

where w_t is the logarithm of money wages, and ε_{t1} and ε_{t2} are white noise processes.[16]

For expositional convenience we are assuming that the labour productivity, the price of imported inputs, and the mark-up over costs are fixed. The aggregate demand function is still given by (2.14). Under the market clearing assumption $y_t^s = y_t^d = y_t$, the variables w_t and y_t can be eliminated from the relations (2.14), (2.24) and (2.25). This yields the following price equation

$$(1+\alpha_1\beta_2)p_t = \alpha_1\beta_1 p_t^* + (1-\alpha_1\beta_1)p_{t-1} + \alpha_1\beta_2\rho x_{t-1} - \alpha_1\beta_2\bar{y}_t + \eta_t, \tag{2.26}$$

where

$$\eta_t = \varepsilon_{t1} + \alpha_1\varepsilon_{t2} + \alpha_1\beta_2 v_t.$$

But since it is assumed that economic agents (wrongly) form their price expectations according to the simple new classical macroeconomic model of

[16] A stochastic process is said to be a white noise process if it is serially uncorrelated, has mean zero, and a constant variance.

example 2.1, p_t^* will be determined by relation (2.21) which then feeds back onto actual prices through the equation (2.26). Therefore, the errors in inflation expectations will be given by,

$$\xi_t = p_t - p_t^* = \left(\frac{1-\alpha_1\beta_1}{1+\alpha_1\beta_2}\right)(p_{t-1} - \rho x_{t-1} + \bar{y}_t) + \left(\frac{1}{1+\alpha_1\beta_2}\right)\eta_t,$$

and, unless $\alpha_1\beta_1 = 1$, the rational expectations of p_t^* formed on the basis of the model of example 2.1, do not satisfy any of the optimality properties enumerated above. The expectations errors ξ_t in general will be biased, inefficient and serially correlated.

When $\alpha_1\beta_1 = 1$ is satisfied, expectations errors ξ_t collapse to the white noise process $(1+\alpha_1\beta_2)^{-1}\eta_t$, and inflation expectations will become optimal again. This result, however, is hardly surprising and follows from the fact that the new classical model of example 2.1, is nested within the mark-up pricing model set out above. Under $\alpha_1\beta_1 = 1$, the mark-up model and the new classical model will become 'observationally equivalent'.[17] To see this substitute $w_t - w_{t-1}$ from (2.24) in (2.25). This gives

$$p_t - p_{t-1} = \alpha_1\beta_1(p_t^* - p_{t-1}) + \alpha_1\beta_2(y_t^s - \bar{y}_t) + \alpha_1\varepsilon_{t2} + \varepsilon_{t1},$$

which under $\alpha_1\beta_1 = 1$, simplifies to

$$y_t^s - \bar{y}_t = (\beta_1/\beta_2)(p_t - p_t^*) - (\beta_1\varepsilon_{t1} + \beta_2^{-1}\varepsilon_{t2}),$$

and is clearly observationally equivalent to the aggregate supply function (2.15). The parameter $\alpha_1\beta_1$ is usually referred to as the money-illusion parameter, and plays an important role in the debate over the possible trade-offs between output and inflation.

The REH also ceases to yield optimal forecasts whenever agents know the true model but are uncertain of the values of some of the parameters in the policy rules or other processes generating non-policy exogenous variables. Suppose the aggregate supply and demand functions are correctly specified, but the true value of ρ, the parameter of the policy rule (2.20), is not known. The rational expectations of p_t are formed instead using an incorrect value of ρ, say $\bar{\rho}$. In this case (2.22) is no longer valid and the error of price expectations will be given by

$$\xi_t = (1-\mu)(\rho - \bar{\rho})x_{t-1} + (1-\mu)(v_t - \varepsilon_t).$$

Hence

$$E(\xi_t | \Omega_{t-1}) = (1-\mu)(\rho - \bar{\rho})x_{t-1},$$

which shows that unless $\rho = \bar{\rho}$, the 'orthogonality' property no longer holds.[18]

---

[17] Broadly speaking two models are said to be 'observationally equivalent' if neither model can be distinguished from the other by means of empirical analysis. A formalization of the concept of observational equivalence will be given in chapter 6.

[18] But in this particular example, although the true value of ρ is not known, expectations are still unbiased and efficient. This is because by assumption $E(x_t) = 0$, and ξ_t are distributed independently of $p_{t-1}, p_{t-2}, \ldots$.

The above examples clearly demonstrate that the optimality of the REH fundamentally depends on whether agents know the correct model of the economy. In reality the 'true' model is rarely known, and in the presence of behavioural uncertainty it may not even be unique or stable.

2.8 Concluding Remarks

In this chapter we have argued that when the decision-making process is dominated by behavioural uncertainty, the necessary basis for a formal representation of the process of expectations formation along the lines suggested by Muth may not exist. Under such circumstances an institutional and conventional view of the expectations formation process advanced by Keynes (1936, ch. 12) and Simon (1958) may be much more fruitful. From this standpoint we have discussed the alternative models of the expectations formation process advanced in the literature, and have emphasized the extreme information assumptions that underlie the REH. For the rational expectations hypothesis to have the desired optimal properties it is not enough, we argue, that individuals form rational expectations 'as if' they know the 'true' model. They should actually know the 'true' model, or else they should have the ability to learn it from past observations including past forecast errors. The problem of learning will be discussed in the next chapter. In chapter 4 by means of simple examples of economic optimisation under uncertainty, we also examine how and under what circumstances the REH can be derived directly from the optimization principles.

3 The Process of Learning and the Rational Expectations Hypothesis

3.1 Introduction

There is no doubt that individuals do learn from their own experience as well as from the experience of others. Generally speaking, learning takes place through two separate but closely connected mechanisms, namely 'repetition', and 'understanding'.[1] Learning by repetition alone is possible, but is generally confined to events that are 'seriable', in the sense that they can be repeated many times under the *same* circumstances. A simple example would be learning the probability of a head turning up in the tossing of a possibly biased coin. This is an example of an almost perfectly replicable experiment, where the relevant probabilities can be learned with a high degree of accuracy. In practice, however, events that are seriable are rather rare and, as a result, learning by mere repetition is generally of limited relevance, especially in the case of economic phenomena which are subject to behavioural uncertainty. In situations where the underlying model structure is known and is also invariant to individuals' actions, it may be possible to learn the value of some of the unknown parameters of the model. But when the structure of the underlying model is unknown or is not invariant to individuals' actions, there is no

[1] Locke was perhaps the first philosopher to have emphasized these two aspects of the learning process. In Book II of his *Essay Concerning Human Understanding* he states

> Let us then suppose the Mind to be, as we say, white Paper, void of all Characters, without any Ideas; How comes it to be furnished? Whence comes it by that vast store, which the busy and boundless Fancy of Man has painted on it, with an almost endless variety? Whence has it all the materials of Reason and Knowledge? To this I answer, in one word, From *Experience*: In that, all our Knowledge is founded; and from that it ultimately derives it self. Our Observation employ'd either about *external, sensible Objects; or about the internal Operations of our Minds, perceived and reflected on by our selves, is that, which supplies our Understandings with all the materials of thinking.* These two are the Fountains of Knowledge, from whence all the Ideas we have, or can naturally have, do spring (chapter 1, section 2).

guarantee that mere repetition would lead individuals to the true model. In general, learning involves a trial-and-error elimination process. Trial (or formulation) of new theories, and elimination (or rejection) of false theories or models is the basic process according to which learning normally takes place. In practice, this on-going process of formulation, rejection, and revision of models can be carried out either by means of classical statistical inference or by resort to Bayesian techniques. Whether such a learning process is capable of narrowing down the discrepancy that may exist between subjective beliefs and the true state of the world very much depends on the nature of the data generation process, the available information, and the agents' degree of *a priori* 'understanding' of the way the economic system functions.

The problem of 'learning' that underlies the REH has been the subject of a number of studies over the past decade. These studies are carried out mainly, but not exclusively, in the context of microeconomic models that permit a rational expectations equilibrium (REE). The concept of the REE is formalized in a number of different ways and the interested reader should consult the survey papers by Radner (1982), and Jordan and Radner (1982) for details. But it is important to note that the idea of REE involves much more than the familiar and well-understood concept of the equilibrium of supply and demand. Broadly speaking, a REE refers to a state of affairs where all acts of 'learning' are complete, in the sense that there is no incentive on the part of agents to change the beliefs they hold about their economic environment.[2] A rational expectations equilibrium can be characterized by three main features: (1) all markets clear at equilibrium prices, (2) every agent knows the relationship between equilibrium prices and private information of all other agents, and (3) the information contained in equilibrium prices is fully exploited by all agents in making inferences about the private information of others. Thus in a REE prices perform a dual role – apart from clearing the markets they also reveal to every agent the *private* information of all the other agents.

The concept of the REE in effect requires that everybody knows (in a probabilistic sense) everything about the way the market economy functions. But as Hayek (1937) puts it:

> The statement that, if people know everything, they are in equilibrium is true simply because that is how we define equilibrium. The assumption of a perfect market in that sense is just another way of saying that equilibrium exists, but does not get us any nearer an explanation of when and how such a state will come about. It is clear that if we want to make the assertion that under certain conditions people will approach that state we must explain by what process they will acquire the necessary knowledge (p. 45).

---

[2] While interest in the REE is rather recent, the basic ideas behind it were first discussed about half a century ago in important contributions by Hayek (1937), and Hicks (1939, ch. X). In a similar vein see also Hahn (1952).

That is, for the REE to have any operational meaning it is necessary that the processes by means of which people learn from experience and acquire the common knowledge necessary for the achievement of the REE are specified fully and explicitly.

This chapter briefly reviews some of the learning models discussed in the literature. In the context of the microeconomic rational expectations literature the problem of learning has been studied using two types of frameworks. These we refer to as 'rational learning models' and 'boundedly rational learning models'. In this literature it is generally assumed that a REE does in fact exist and can somehow be implemented.[3] Here we follow this tradition and focus on the problems involved in the convergence of the learning process to the REE. Section 3.2 considers the rational learning models and echoes the conclusion reached by Bray and Kreps (1984). The idea of rational learning, although intellectually appealing, is of limited relevance to actual problems. Section 3.3 considers the boundedly rational learning models and gives a review of some of the results obtained in this field for the cobweb model. Although there are no general theories available on the convergence of the boundedly rational learning models, the results so far obtained in the case of cobweb models are quite encouraging. It should, however, be recognized that the boundedly rational learning models are still based on the assumption that the reduced-form relations of the true model are common knowledge, and that information acquisition is costless. In section 3.5 we consider the implications of costly information for the learning process. With costly information, the decision to acquire information itself becomes an integral part of the decision-making process. Systematic errors of expectations may now persist simply because agents (perhaps incorrectly) believe that these errors are not *worth* correcting for. The main conclusions of the chapter are set out in the final section.

3.2 Rational Learning Models

The rational learning framework assumes that agents know the correct specification of the equilibrium relationships between market prices and private signals, but are uncertain about some of the parameters of those relationships. The problem of 'rational learning' then centres on estimation of a finite number of unknown parameters in an interactive setting where there is a feedback from the incorrectly estimated parameters to the actual outcomes. This feedback from expectations to outcomes that takes place during the learning period, by introducing an additional source of variability into the model, further complicates the act of learning. Cyert and DeGroot (1974), Taylor (1975), Friedman (1979), Townsend (1978, 1983), Bray and Kreps (1984), and Brandenburger (1985) all study the problem of learning in

[3] The problems connected with the existence and the implementation of the REE are dealt with, for example, in Radner (1982).

situations where, except for a finite number of parameters, the true economic model is taken to be common knowledge. In the examples studied by Friedman and Taylor there are no feedbacks from expectations to outcomes, and the standard results on the consistency and the asymptotic efficiency of the estimators can be used directly to establish the convergence of the learning process to the rational expectations solution. In the more general case where expectations affect outcomes, the act of learning, by its very nature, alters the data generation process and causes it to become non-stationary, even if the underlying REE happens to be stationary. Simple examples of rational learning models with feedbacks have been studied, for example, by Frydman (1982). Townsend (1978, 1983), and Brandenburger (1985). These studies have all found convergence to the REE. More recently Bray and Kreps (1984) have also shown that in the context of rational learning subjective beliefs will (nearly) always converge, although not necessarily to a REE. These results at first appear to be very favourable to the REH. However, a closer examination of the concept of 'rational learning' reveals a different picture. This is primarily due to the fact that rational learning assumes that, apart from the values of a finite number of unknown parameters, agents know the true equilibrium relations of the economy. It is not, however, explained how agents in fact come to learn these 'true' structural relationships of the economy. As Bray and Kreps put it

> This [that agents know the structural relationships] is at least as demanding in terms of the analytic ability of agents as the original story in which agents calculate the rational expectations equilibrium. Indeed, we have done nothing more than generate a *grander* rational expectations equilibrium that allows for subjective uncertainty about variables which are treated as known parameters in standard models (p. 4).

The concept of rational learning is therefore of limited relevance to the problem of how learning actually takes place. A less demanding framework would be to adopt the learning models that are, in a broad sense, based on Simon's idea of 'bounded rationality'.

3.3 Boundedly Rational Learning Models

This alternative model does not require that agents should know the structural equilibrium relations, but assumes instead that agents use some 'plausible' or 'reasonable' rule of learning to which they remain committed over the whole period that learning is taking place. The informational requirements of this approach are not as severe as the rational learning models, but are subject to two important shortcomings. Firstly, the idea of 'bounded rationality' is not fully spelled out. Agents are supposed to follow a 'reasonable' learning rule, but it is not explained what constitutes a reasonable rule, nor is it explained how, before the commencement of the act of learning, agents collectively come to choose the same learning rule. Secondly, the approach does not allow for a revision of the learning rule, which is justifiable only if it can be shown that the rule chosen does in fact ensure convergence to the REE. Whether this is so in turn depends on the learning rule chosen in the first place. Clearly, it will not be possible to establish whether a learning rule is reasonable or not, unless some *a priori* knowledge of the way the economy functions is assumed. Indeed all the authors who have studied the problem of convergence in boundedly rational learning models have assumed that agents' choice of the learning rule is based on some common *a priori* knowledge of the REE. The learning rules adopted in these models necessitate that agents know the reduced form equations of the true model except for a finite number of unknown parameters. The main difference between the rational learning models and the boundedly rational learning models lies in the type of *a priori* information each model supposes that agents have. Under the former class of models it is assumed that agents know the true structural relations of the economy, while under the latter agents are only required to know the reduced-form equations of the economic model. It is in this sense of utilizing knowledge of the reduced-form relations instead of the structural-form relations that boundedly rational learning models make a less demanding assumption about the *a priori* knowledge and the analytical ability of agents. But it should be recognized that even with boundedly rational learning models, the reduced-form relations of the true model are taken to be common knowledge.

The convergence of boundedly rational learning models has been examined by DeCanio (1979), Radner (1982), Blume and Easley (1982), Frydman (1982), Bray (1983), Fourgeaud et al. (1986), Bray and Savin (1986), and Bowden (1984). These authors show that, in the case of the simple examples they study, convergence to the REE is possible, although the presence of cycles and divergence from the REE cannot be ruled out. For example Blume and Easley (1982) show that when agents are faced with a number of finite models, one of which is known to be the correct one, there is no guarantee that the learning process would not get stuck at an incorrect model. Although there are as yet no general theorems about the convergence of boundedly rational learning models, the results so far obtained in the context of a simple cobweb model are nevertheless encouraging. We now turn our attention to this simple model.

3.4 Learning in a Cobweb Model

The model is composed of a linear supply function relating total quantity supplied (q_t^s) to a vector $\mathbf{x}_{t1}$ of exogenous variables and producers' (average) price expectations in period t formed at $t-1$ (i.e. ${}_{t-1}p_t^*$, or simply p_t^*). The quantity demanded (q_t^d) is assumed to be a linear function of the current price (p_t), and a vector of exogenous variables $\mathbf{x}_{t2}$. Both demand and supply are assumed subject to random shocks ε_{t1}, and ε_{t2}. Here we assume that these random shocks are white-noise processes distributed independently of all the exogenous variables of the model.[4] The full model can be written as

Supply function:	$q_t^s = \mathbf{x}_{t1}'\boldsymbol{\alpha}_1 + \beta_1 p_t^* + \varepsilon_{t1}$,	(3.1)
Demand function:	$q_t^d = \mathbf{x}_{t2}'\boldsymbol{\alpha}_2 - \beta_2 p_t + \varepsilon_{t2}$,	(3.2)
Market clearing condition:	$q_t = q_t^s = q_t^d$,	(3.3)

where we assume that the scalars β_1 and β_2 are strictly positive. This ensures that the supply and demand are sensitive to actual and expected price changes in an *a priori* plausible manner; that is, the supply curve is upward-sloping, and the demand curve is downward sloping. The (pseudo)-reduced form equation of this model in terms of the prediction errors $\xi_t = p_t - p_t^*$, can be easily seen to be[5]

$$p_t = \mathbf{x}_t'\boldsymbol{\alpha} + \beta(p_t - p_t^*) + \varepsilon_t = \mathbf{x}_t'\boldsymbol{\alpha} + \beta\xi_t + \varepsilon_t, \tag{3.4}$$

where

$$\mathbf{x}_t'\boldsymbol{\alpha} = \frac{1}{\beta_1 + \beta_2}(\mathbf{x}_{t2}'\boldsymbol{\alpha}_2 - \mathbf{x}_{t1}'\boldsymbol{\alpha}_1), \quad \mathbf{x}_t' = (\mathbf{x}_{t1}', \mathbf{x}_{t2}'),$$

$$\varepsilon_t = (\varepsilon_{t2} - \varepsilon_{t1})/(\beta_1 + \beta_2), \qquad \boldsymbol{\alpha}' = \left(\frac{1}{\beta_1 + \beta_2}\right)(-\boldsymbol{\alpha}_1', \boldsymbol{\alpha}_2'),$$

and

$$\beta = \beta_1/(\beta_1 + \beta_2) > 0.$$

In the highly idealized conditions where the structural model given by (3.1)–(3.3) is common knowledge, and all producers know the value of $\mathbf{x}_t$ at the time they are forming price expectations,[6] the REH can then be invoked to yield the following expression for price expectations.[7]

$$p_{t0}^* = \mathbf{x}_t'\boldsymbol{\alpha}. \tag{3.5}$$

Substituting this result in (3.4) gives (assuming that $\beta \neq 1$), the REE solution for p_t, which we denote by p_{t0} to distinguish it from the realizations, p_t. The actual values of prices coincide with the REE value, p_{t0}, only when producers

[4] Bowden also considers the case where the ε_{t1} and ε_{t2} are serially correlated.

[5] Note that usually the reduced-form equation of systems such as (3.1) to (3.3) is written in terms of the price expectations p_t^*. But in studying the convergence of the learning process it is often helpful to write the reduced-form equation as (3.4), in terms of the prediction or expectations errors.

[6] The assumption that agents know $\mathbf{x}_t$ at time $t-1$ is rather restrictive but, as is discussed in Bowden (1984), it can be relaxed. For the present model one can take $\mathbf{x}_t$ to contain only the lagged values of the variables observed by the producers at the time they are making their output decisions.

[7] Notice that in the REE the price expectations p_t^* will be the same across all producers.

know the structural model (including its parameters), and the expectations formation processes of the other producers. In the REE we have

$$p_{t0} = \mathbf{x}_t'\boldsymbol{\alpha} + (1-\beta)^{-1}\varepsilon_t. \tag{3.6}$$

Notice that, as is to be expected, in the REE the prediction errors which we denote by $\xi_{t0} = p_{t0} - p_t^* = (1-\beta)^{-1}\varepsilon_t$, satisfy the optimality properties of the unbiasedness and orthogonality discussed in section 2.7.

Suppose now the producers do not know the structural parameters, α_1, α_2, β_1, and β_2 and hence are not able to form (rational) expectations of prices according to (3.5). How are they then likely to form expectations? Clearly in the absence of any definite knowledge about the underlying model, or its parameters, producers have to make an initial guess at what the price will be during the next period. The problem of learning centres on whether there exists an adjustment or a revision rule that producers could use to modify their expectations (every time new evidence comes to light) in such a way as to lead them closer to the RE values, p_{t0}^*, given by (3.5). Under the boundedly rational learning model the problem of learning is approached by assuming that except for its parameters the reduced-form relation, (3.4), and the rule by means of which expectations are revised are 'common knowledge'. That is, every producer knows the reduced form relation and the learning rule, and knows that every other producer knows that too, and etc. *In other words, the way in which information is acquired and processed is taken to be common knowledge* (Aumann, 1976). The learning problem now arises in two ways. Firstly, producers may not know the reduced form parameters $\boldsymbol{\alpha}$ and β, and secondly, they may be unsure of how other producers choose to estimate $\boldsymbol{\alpha}$ and β. The dependence of the equilibrium price in each period upon the expectations errors ξ_t clearly highlights the way producers' collective price forecasts can influence the outcome. A learning rule cannot be specified, even when the reduced form equation (3.4) is assumed to be common knowledge, unless some commonly held hypothesis about the expectations errors ξ_t is also adopted. Producers need to know how other producers forecast prices. The problem of behavioural uncertainty needs to be dealt with before a common learning rule can be arrived at. One possibility which simplifies the analysis substantially is to assume that each producer forecasts the price by setting ξ_t in (3.4) equal to zero. Notice, however, that this represents a paradoxical behaviour. Producers, while learning, assume that the learning process has already converged to the REE. In every period, producers knowingly and in concordance with one another all incorrectly assume that $\xi_t = 0$ and abide by this assumption over the whole period that learning is taking place. Under this paradoxical behavioural pattern the only remaining unknown in the process of expectations formation will be the 'current' estimate used for $\boldsymbol{\alpha}$.

Let $\hat{\boldsymbol{\alpha}}_{t-1,i}$ represent the 'current' estimate of $\boldsymbol{\alpha}$ (i.e. known at time t) of the ith producer based on all the available information up to and including time $t-1$. The relevant information set here is composed of the *current* and the *past* values of $\mathbf{x}_t$, and all the past data on prices and output. That is $\Omega_{t-1} = (\mathbf{x}_t, \mathbf{x}_{t-1}, \ldots; p_{t-1}, p_{t-2}, \ldots; q_{t-1}, q_{t-2}, \ldots)$. Recall that we are assuming

$\mathbf{x}_t$ is known at the time price expectations are formed, and that the information available to all producers is common knowledge. The way $\hat{\boldsymbol{\alpha}}_{t-1,i}$ are computed and then revised subsequently is clearly crucial for the convergence of producers' price expectations $p^*_{ti} = \mathbf{x}_t'\hat{\boldsymbol{\alpha}}_{t-1,i}$ to the RE values $p^*_{t0} = \mathbf{x}_t'\boldsymbol{\alpha}$. There are two general methods that producers can follow in estimating $\boldsymbol{\alpha}$; namely the classical* Bayesian procedures. Under the classical procedure, given the common information set Ω_{t-1} and the assumptions made about $\{\mathbf{x}_t, \varepsilon_t\}$, the best linear unbiased estimator of $\boldsymbol{\alpha}$ is the ordinary least squares (OLS) estimator $\hat{\boldsymbol{\alpha}}_{t-1}$ defined by[8]

$$\hat{\boldsymbol{\alpha}}_{t-1} = \hat{\boldsymbol{\alpha}}_{t-1,i} = \left(\sum_{j=1}^{t-1} \mathbf{x}_j \mathbf{x}_j'\right)^{-1} \left(\sum_{j=1}^{t-1} \mathbf{x}_j p_j\right). \tag{3.7}$$

That is, as classical statisticians, producers all having the same information, i.e. $\{\Omega_{t-1}\}$ arrive at the same estimate of $\boldsymbol{\alpha}$. In the case where all the producers employ the Bayesian method, the situation is more complicated and the parameter estimates depend on the producers' initial prior beliefs about $\boldsymbol{\alpha}$. But as shown by Bray and Savin (1986), under certain reasonable assumptions about prior probability distributions cn $\boldsymbol{\alpha}$, producers' diverse prior beliefs converge, and as $t \to \infty$ they become dominated by the information observed by all the producers. Therefore we focus our attention on the classical method of estimating $\boldsymbol{\alpha}$. To distinguish between the rational price expectations p^*_{t0} and the price expectations *actually* held by producers we denote the latter by p^*_t. Under the above assumptions the model used by all producers in forming their price expectations will be the same and can be written as

$$p^*_t = \mathbf{x}_t'\hat{\boldsymbol{\alpha}}_{t-1}.$$

Notice that so long as $\hat{\boldsymbol{\alpha}}_{t-1} \neq \boldsymbol{\alpha}$ producers' price expectations will differ from the rational expectations solution $p^*_{t0} = \mathbf{x}_t'\boldsymbol{\alpha}$. This has two important implications. Firstly, when learning is incomplete the observed expectations errors, $\xi_t = p_t - p^*_t$, do not satisfy the desired optimality properties of unbiasedness and orthogonality. Secondly, unlike the rational expectations errors $\xi_{t0} = (1-\beta)^{-1}\varepsilon_t$, the observed expectations errors ξ_t will not be stationary even when the processes generating the exogenous variables, $\mathbf{x}_t$, and the disturbances, ε_t, are strictly stationary. The same is also true of p_t, the observed price data. To see this replace $p^*_t = \mathbf{x}_t'\hat{\boldsymbol{\alpha}}_{t-1}$ in the equilibrium price equation (3.4) to obtain

$$p_t = \mathbf{x}_t'\boldsymbol{\alpha} + \beta(1-\beta)^{-1}\mathbf{x}_t'(\boldsymbol{\alpha} - \hat{\boldsymbol{\alpha}}_{t-1}) + (1-\beta)^{-1}\varepsilon_t, \tag{3.8}$$

and

$$\xi_t = (1-\beta)^{-1}\mathbf{x}_t(\boldsymbol{\alpha} - \hat{\boldsymbol{\alpha}}_{t-1}) + (1-\beta)^{-1}\varepsilon_t.$$

Given the path of $\hat{\boldsymbol{\alpha}}_{t-1}$ defined by (3.7), it now readily follows that the

[8] For the OLS estimator $\hat{\boldsymbol{\alpha}}_{t-1}$ to exist it is necessary that t should be at least as large as the number of exogenous variables in $\mathbf{x}_t$.

processes generating p_t and ξ_t are non-stationary even if $\mathbf{x}_t$ and ε_t were generated by stationary processes.[9]

The non-stationary nature of $\{\xi_t\}$ introduces an important degree of technical complexity into studies of the boundedly rational learning processes. Producers need to disentangle the separate effects of $\mathbf{x}_t$ and ξ_t on the observed price movements. That is, for any given systematic change in the price they need to discover the part which is due to a change in the exogenous variables and the part which is due to the systematic effect of incomplete learning on prices. It is only when learning is complete that systematic changes in $\mathbf{x}_t$ and p_t will be perfectly correlated. The non-stationary nature of $\{\xi_t\}$ also invalidates the straightforward application of the classical asymptotic theories to the problem of the convergence of $\hat{\boldsymbol{\alpha}}_{t-1}$ to $\boldsymbol{\alpha}$, or equivalently, the convergence of price expectation p_t^* to the rational expectations, p_{t0}^*. Here, we do not wish to go into the technical details of the various proofs on the convergence of $\hat{\boldsymbol{\alpha}}_t$ that are recently proposed in the literature. See, for example, Fourgeaud et al. (1986), Bray and Savin (1986), and Bowden (1984). But, in order to give readers an idea of the sort of technical problems involved and the type of assumptions that are required for the convergence of the learning process, we rewrite (3.7) in the form of an updating formula.

Denoting the sample moment matrices

$$t^{-1}\left(\sum_{j=1}^{t} \mathbf{x}_j \mathbf{x}_j'\right), \quad \text{and} \quad t^{-1}\left(\sum_{j=1}^{t} \mathbf{x}_j p_j\right)$$

by $\boldsymbol{\Sigma}_t$ and $\mathbf{d}_t$, respectively, (3.7) can also be written as

$$\boldsymbol{\Sigma}_t \hat{\boldsymbol{\alpha}}_t = \mathbf{d}_t. \tag{3.7'}$$

But, by definition

$$\boldsymbol{\Sigma}_t = (1 - t^{-1})\,\boldsymbol{\Sigma}_{t-1} + t^{-1}\mathbf{x}_t\mathbf{x}_t',$$
$$\mathbf{d}_t = (1 - t^{-1})\,\mathbf{d}_{t-1} + t^{-1}\mathbf{x}_t p_t.$$

Therefore,

$$\boldsymbol{\Sigma}_t(\hat{\boldsymbol{\alpha}}_t - \hat{\boldsymbol{\alpha}}_{t-1}) = \mathbf{d}_t - \boldsymbol{\Sigma}_t\hat{\boldsymbol{\alpha}}_{t-1},$$
$$= t^{-1}(\mathbf{x}_t p_t) - t^{-1}(\mathbf{x}_t\mathbf{x}_t')\,\hat{\boldsymbol{\alpha}}_{t-1}. \tag{3.9}$$

Now, substituting p_t from (3.8) in the above result, after some routine algebra, yields[10]

$$\hat{\boldsymbol{\alpha}}_t - \hat{\boldsymbol{\alpha}}_{t-1} = (1-\beta)^{-1}\boldsymbol{\Sigma}_t^{-1}\left(\frac{\mathbf{x}_t\mathbf{x}_t'}{t}\right)(\boldsymbol{\alpha} - \hat{\boldsymbol{\alpha}}_{t-1}) + (1-\beta)^{-1}\boldsymbol{\Sigma}_t^{-1}\left(\frac{\mathbf{x}_t\varepsilon_t}{t}\right), \tag{3.10}$$

[9] The fact that p_t and ξ_t are non-stationary should not, however, be taken to mean that they are necessarily unstable or explosive.

[10] Without loss of generality we assume that $\boldsymbol{\Sigma}_t$ is non-singular. When there are not enough observations available on p_t and $\mathbf{x}_t$, the learning can start with a fixed arbitrary 'guess-estimate' of $\boldsymbol{\alpha}$.

which is a first-order *adaptive learning rule* with varying coefficients. The convergence of the learning process can now be studied by investigating the asymptotic properties of the above stochastic difference equation. It is the time-varying nature of the coefficients of this stochastic difference equation that lies at the heart of the technical difficulties mentioned above. Even in the special case where $\mathbf{x}_t$ is a scalar such that $\mathbf{x}_t = 1$ for all t, the adaptive coefficient still continues to vary with t, and the extent of revision in the estimate of the scalar parameter α is inversely proportional to the number of data sets observed by agents. In this simple scalar case we have

$$\hat{\alpha}_t - \hat{\alpha}_{t-1} = (1-\beta)^{-1} t^{-1} (\alpha - \hat{\alpha}_{t-1}) + (1-\beta)^{-1} t^{-1} \varepsilon_t,$$

which is the univariate version of the learning model examined in some detail in Bray (1983). For this case Bray shows that $\hat{\alpha}_t$ converges almost surely to α if $\beta < 1$ and ε_t are identically, independently distributed random variables.[11] In general, however, the convergence of (3.10) will depend on the true value of β as well as on the stochastic properties of $\{\mathbf{x}_t\}$ and $\{\varepsilon_t\}$.

As yet conditions that are both necessary and sufficient for the convergence of $\hat{\boldsymbol{\alpha}}_t$ to $\boldsymbol{\alpha}$ in the general case are not known. But there are a number of results that give sufficient conditions for the convergence of the $\{\hat{\boldsymbol{\alpha}}_t\}$ sequence. Bray and Savin (1986) show that when $\beta < 1$, the assumption that $\{\mathbf{x}_t, \varepsilon_t\}$ are identically and independently distributed is sufficient. This is a useful result but is of limited value for most applications in economics where the time-series data involved are often highly autocorrelated. The sufficiency conditions given by Fourgeaud et al. (1986) are less restrictive as far as the $\{\mathbf{x}_t\}$ process is concerned but require that $\beta < \frac{1}{2}$. Bowden (1984) approaches the problem of the convergence of $\hat{\boldsymbol{\alpha}}_t$ from the perspective of sequential estimation, and utilizes results originally established by Albert and Gardner (1967). This enables Bowden to deal with the learning problem in a more general context. The Albert–Gardner framework, for example, allows sequential estimation of $\boldsymbol{\alpha}$ by methods other than the OLS procedure. However, it should be pointed out that the Albert–Gardner sufficiency conditions seem rather difficult to verify in practice.

The sequential estimation approach of Albert–Gardner is particularly useful in the study of learning problems, and may hold the key to further developments in this field. For this reason a brief account of it seems to be in order. The basic idea behind the approach involves revision of the parameter estimates in the light of *currently* observed prediction errors. In the case of the cobweb model the revision rule for the unknown parameters $\boldsymbol{\alpha}$ is given by

$$\boldsymbol{\alpha}_t - \boldsymbol{\alpha}_{t-1} = \mathbf{g}_t \xi_t = \mathbf{g}_t (p_t - \mathbf{x}_t' \boldsymbol{\alpha}_{t-1}), \qquad (3.11)$$

---

[11] It is interesting that early experimental evidence on the formation of expectations reported by Rotter (1954, pp. 165–83) do in fact support the time-varying adaptive learning rule. In his experiments Rotter observed that the magnitude of revisions in expectations tended to be inversely proportional to the number of trials already undertaken by the subjects.

where $\boldsymbol{\alpha}_t$ represents the estimator of $\boldsymbol{\alpha}$ at time t, and $\mathbf{g}_t$ is a vector of the same dimension as $\boldsymbol{\alpha}_t$ whose elements define the weights to be attached to the observed prediction errors ξ_t.[12] The sequence $\{\mathbf{g}_t\}$, which is often referred to as the 'gain sequence', is usually formed on the basis of the current and past observations on $\mathbf{x}_t$ and p_t. The choice of the gain sequence $\{\mathbf{g}_t\}$ is clearly crucial if $\boldsymbol{\alpha}_t$ is to converge (almost surely) to $\boldsymbol{\alpha}$.

A comparison of (3.11) and (3.10) reveals the close link that exists between the Albert–Gardner general adaptive scheme and the OLS updating equation. Using the result (3.9), which lies behind (3.10), we have

$$\begin{aligned}\hat{\boldsymbol{\alpha}}_t - \hat{\boldsymbol{\alpha}}_{t-1} &= (t\Sigma_t)^{-1}\mathbf{x}_t(p_t - \mathbf{x}_t'\hat{\boldsymbol{\alpha}}_{t-1}),\\ &= (t\Sigma_t)^{-1}\mathbf{x}_t\xi_t.\end{aligned}$$

Comparing this result with (3.11) now shows that the OLS updating formula (3.10) in fact corresponds to a special case of the Albert–Gardner adaptive scheme, and can be obtained from it when the gain sequence $\mathbf{g}_t$ is specified to be

$$\mathbf{g}_t = (t\Sigma_t)^{-1}\mathbf{x}_t = \left(\sum_{j=1}^{t} \mathbf{x}_j\mathbf{x}_j'\right)^{-1}\mathbf{x}_t.$$

The attraction of the general adaptive scheme (3.11) lies not only in its greater generality, but in the way the problem of learning or revision is set up in a behaviourally plausible manner. Estimates of $\boldsymbol{\alpha}$ are updated only in the light of the currently observed prediction errors. The updating formula is simple and places relatively little demand on agents' analytical ability.

3.5 Cost of Information Acquisition and the REH

The learning models discussed in the previous section focus on the problem of efficient (sequential) processing of information, and assume that learning takes place with negligible resource costs. The assumption of zero information cost is, however, a theoretical abstraction. The acquisition and processing of information can and does involve considerable expenditure of economic resources, and any study of the expectations formation process and learning should take this into account. Whenever information is costly, 'rational' agents (in the sense of profit- or utility-maximizing individuals) face the decision problem of whether the expected benefit of acquiring the information is worth the cost of its acquisition. The amount of information collected and processed by individuals becomes an integral part of the decision-making process. In the case of a single decision-maker, considered in isolation, the economic implications of costly information are relatively straightforward to analyse, and have been discussed in the literature in some detail.[13] The value of information to

---

[12] Notice that in general, $\boldsymbol{\alpha}_t$ differs from $\hat{\boldsymbol{\alpha}}_t$, the OLS estimator of $\boldsymbol{\alpha}$ at time t.

[13] See, for example, McGuire (1972), and Marschak and Radner (1972). This literature has also been recently reviewed by Hirshleifer and Riley (1979).

an individual is measured in terms of the way the acquisition of that information leads the individual to change his/her subjective probability of the occurrence of an event (or events). The important point to note is that the decision-maker, before acquiring the information, cannot know how the acquisition of information will in fact alter his/her subjective probability distribution(s). Acquisition of information generates a probability distribution of a set of messages received by individuals, and not a particular message. As a result, the value of information to individuals will, in general, depend on their *a priori* model of the economy. Obvious instances of information acquisition are: searching amongst sellers for the best buy, surveying land for mineral deposits, or examining students for academic achievement/promise. In all these cases the value of information acquisition to the individual concerned is uncertain, and depends on the view he/she holds about the possible contribution of the acquisition of information to his/her knowledge and, hence to his/her well-being. The dependence of the decision to acquire information on agents' subjective beliefs can be readily seen even in the context of the following simple search problem originally analysed by Stigler (1961).

Consider a consumer who wishes to purchase quantity q of a given commodity, and suppose there are a large number of shops, all equally accessible to the consumer, that sell the commodity at prices $p_1, p_2, p_3, \ldots$. In the absence of *a priori* information on prices at different shops, the consumer has to decide whether to buy the quantity he/she requires from a shop chosen at random, or to search for the best buy. The answer depends on the cost of search, the quantity the consumer wishes to purchase, and the probability distribution of prices $\{p_i\}$ across shops. To obtain a formal solution to this problem let n denote the number of sellers approached by the consumer, and assume that the cost of search is proportional to the number of searches, n. The optimum value of n can now be determined by equating the marginal *expected* benefit from the search to the marginal cost of the search, say c. Even in the case of this simple search model, the consumer needs to know the probability distribution of the asking prices $\{p_i\}$ before he/she can determine the optimum level of information to be acquired. Suppose the consumer believes that prices across shops $p_1, p_2, p_3, \ldots$ are distributed randomly and follow a uniform distribution over the known range $\bar{p} \pm \delta$, where $\bar{p} > 0$ denotes the subjective mean price, and δ, $\bar{p} > \delta > 0$, measures the subjective magnitude of the price dispersion. The subjective cumulative distribution of prices will be given by

$$U(p_i) = \frac{1}{2\delta}(p_i - \bar{p} + \delta), \quad \bar{p} - \delta \leqslant p_i \leqslant \bar{p} + \delta, \quad i = 1, 2, \ldots \tag{3.12}$$

For deriving the optimum solution of the search problem, the consumer requires to compute his/her subjective probability distribution of the most favourable price (i.e. the minimum price) after n searches. Let the cumulative distribution of this price be $F_n(p)$. We have

$$F_n(p) = \text{prob}(p_{\min} < p) = 1 - \text{prob}(p_{\min} > p),$$

where $p_{\min}$ stands for the minimum price after n searches. But

$$\text{prob}(p_{\min} > p) = \text{prob}(p_1 > p, p_2 > p, \ldots, p_n > p),$$

and since by assumption the consumer believes that $p_1, p_2, \ldots, p_n$ are independently distributed, then

$$\text{prob}(p_{\min} > p) = \{1 - U(p)\}^n,$$

where $U(p)$ is given by (3.12). Hence

$$F_n(p) = 1 - \{1 - U(p)\}^n.$$

Using (3.12) in the above result, and differentiating the resultant expression with respect to p, yields

$$f_n(p) = n(2\delta)^{-n}(\delta + \bar{p} - p)^{n-1}, \quad \bar{p} - \delta \leqslant p \leqslant \bar{p} + \delta.$$

From this result it is now easy to compute the consumer's subjective expectation of the minimum asking price conditional on j searches. Denoting this subjective expectations by $E_j(p)$ we have

$$E_j(p) = \bar{p} - \frac{\delta(j-1)}{(j+1)}. \tag{3.13}$$

It is clear that, for $j = 1$, the expected price will be equal to the consumer's subjective mean of the price distribution across shops, and, as the number of searches increases, the subjective expectations of the minimum price will tend closer to the lowest possible price $\bar{p} - \delta$. The expected monetary reward to the consumer after n searches will be[14]:

$$S_n = q\{\bar{p} - E_n(p)\},$$

or, upon using (3.13),

$$S_n = q\delta(n-1)/(n+1).$$

The optimum number of searches, say n^*, can now be ascertained by setting the expected marginal benefit of search equal to the marginal cost of search. With the marginal cost of search fixed at c, the necessary condition for this optimization problem is $\partial S_n/\partial n = c$, which, to the nearest integer, yields

$$n^* = \left[\frac{2q\delta}{c}\right]^{1/2} - 1.$$

It is clear from this result that the optimum number of searches depends on the amount the consumer wishes to purchase, the unit cost of search, and the consumer's subjective view about the range of price variations across shops. Whether the consumer searches for the best buy clearly depends on his/her

[14] It is assumed that the amount of the commodity the consumer is wishing to purchase is not influenced by the outcome of the search activity, that is we assume that $\partial q/\partial n = 0$.

subjective probability distribution of prices. When the consumer believes that the degree of price dispersion, δ, is low relative to q/c, he/she may decide not to search. This, however, has important implications for the consumer's ability to learn the 'true' probability distribution of prices. The fact that the consumer may view searching not to be economically worthwhile, can lead to inadequate accumulation of information on the distribution of prices and a slow learning process. There is, in effect, a kind of vicious circle of ignorance in which the consumer can become trapped. Some of these problems will be mitigated when purchases are repetitive and the probability distribution of prices remains fixed, or change only in an *a priori* known manner. But the basic issue remains. When information acquisition is costly, the decision to collect information, and hence the possibility of learning, can be stifled by agents' *a priori* held subjective beliefs.

3.6 Costly Information and Existence of Informationally Efficient Markets

The issues of information acquisition and learning become more complicated when the effects of advertising, the implications of interaction among consumers, and the possible transmission of information from informed consumers to uninformed consumers through the price system are taken into account. The implications of the interaction amongst economic agents for the existence of informationally efficient markets have been explored in a series of articles by Grossman (1976, 1977, 1978, 1981), and Grossman and Stiglitz (1976, 1980). These studies typically assume that the REH is valid, but concentrate on the problem of the existence of informationally efficient markets. A detailed discussion of these issues is beyond the scope of the present chapter.[15] One thing is, however, clear. When information is costly it is less likely that learning will ever be complete. Given agents' subjective beliefs it may not be worthwhile to learn the 'true' model even if it were in fact possible. As Boland (1982, p. 72) puts it: 'economists might argue that even if induction were logically possible it might not be economical!'. The seemingly plausible view that agents form expectations by acquiring and processing information up to the point where the marginal costs and the marginal *expected* benefits of gathering and processing of information are equated, implicitly assumes that agents already *have* the knowledge necessary to quantify the *expected* benefit of information acquisition. Such an (implicit) assumption, however, begs the main issues that lie behind the problem of expectations formation and learning. When information acquisition is costly, and the expected benefit of information is uncertain, 'rationality' alone cannot save economic agents from making systematic mistakes. Individuals certainly learn from their own past mistakes and the mistakes made by others, but, in general, there is no reason to believe that such a learning process (i.e. learning from *past* mistakes) will

---

[15] A non-technical discussion of the issues involved in studies of asset markets with asymmetrical information can be found in Bray (1985).

necessarily lead individuals to form expectations that possess the optimality properties of unbiasedness and orthogonality that are so central to the policy ineffectiveness propositions of the new classical macroeconomics.

The above discussion also reveals the weakness of the argument often advanced in support of the REH, namely that as long as systematic errors of expectations give rise to opportunities for profitable trading, they will be eliminated. This argument, which is the basic message of the efficient market hypothesis, is nothing but a reiteration of the belief in the efficient functioning of the market mechanism under uncertainty. The view that systematic errors of expectations reveal (without cost) the opportunities for profitable trading is very much related to the view that prices reveal, fully and costlessly, all the private information in the economy. But, as pointed out by Grossman and Stiglitz (1980), this is clearly not possible. If it were true that prices fully and costlessly reflected all the private information in the economy, then there would be no incentive for any agent to acquire information about the profitable trading opportunities that might exist. But if every agent followed this line of argument, no-one would obtain the information, and thus there would be no reason for the profitable opportunities to be identified or eliminated. Some authors have attempted to go round this problem of the lack of existence of informationally efficient markets by assuming that prices reflect the information of informed traders, but only partially. This, together with the assumption that uninformed traders *know* the statistical equilibrium relationship between prices and returns, provides a solution to the existence problem, but considerably weakens the argument that trade will eliminate all systematic errors of expectations. The dilemma faced by efficient market theorists is aptly summarized by Grossman and Stiglitz (1980),[16] p. 404:

> Efficient Markets Theorists seem to be aware that costless information is *sufficient* condition for prices to fully reflect all available information (see Fama, p. 387); they are not aware that it is a *necessary* condition. But this is a *reducta ad absurdum*, since price systems and competitive markets are important only when information is costly (see Fredrick Hayek, p. 452).

The incentive to acquire information and the efficiency with which markets function are in constant conflict.

3.7 Concluding Remarks

The examples of the learning models discussed in this chapter contain a number of important features which are worth emphasizing:

1 Even an apparently irrational behaviour, when adhered to collectively, can produce *limiting* outcomes that are rational. This is not a surprising result and reiterates the importance of self-fulfilling prophesies or

[16] The references in the quotation are to Fama (1970), and to Hayek (1945).

beliefs in economics. The stability of such a limiting outcome, however, crucially depends on the properties of the exogenous variables in the model and on whether the REE that emerges is unique.

2 The REH can be valid only as a limiting property of an evolving dynamic system. It is best suited to characterization of equilibrium phenomenon. During the period that learning is taking place expectations errors need not satisfy any of the optimality properties usually assumed in the rational expectations literature. Only in the tranquillity of complete knowledge (in a probabilistic sense) can we be sure of the optimality of 'rationally' formed expectations.

3 Unless the underlying environment encountered by agents is stationary the convergence of the learning process to the RE solution seems unlikely. This places an important restriction on the REH and robs it of much of its appeal over other rival hypotheses, such as the adaptive expectations hypothesis and especially the augmented adaptive-learning expectations hypothesis to be put forward later, in chapter 9. The major objection to the adaptive expectations hypothesis discussed in section 2.3, namely that it generates systematic expectations errors, will no longer be applicable.

4 The 'common knowledge' assumptions that underlie the cobweb model, and all the other learning models analysed in the literature, in effect rule out that agents can have different information either about the way the economy functions or about the random variables involved. The relaxation of this information homogeneity assumption creates conceptual as well as technical difficulties in rational expectations models. The problem of the existence of the REE and the convergence of the learning process to the REE solution become much more problematic under the heterogeneous information case. (See for example Radner, 1983). The behavioural uncertainty that will be present in such a situation cannot be ignored, or assumed away. The heterogeneity of information across agents necessitates that each agent should adopt rules not only for revision of unknown parameters of the underlying model but also for learning about the private information and the behaviour of other agents in the economy. (On this also see the next chapter.)

5 The results on the convergence of learning processes to the rational expectations solution crucially depend on the assumption that markets clear *in every period*. However, the price formation mechanism which is supposed to bring about such a state of continuous market clearing is left unspecified. Producers are assumed to be price-takers, yet it is not explained how prices actually get set. The assumption of continuous market clearing needed for the proof of convergence of the learning models is rather restrictive, and limits the analysis to certain specific markets such as those in financial assets or markets in non-storable commodities.

6 When information is costly it may not be worthwhile to identify all the profitable opportunities, and there will therefore be no reason for all

systematic errors of expectations to be eliminated through trade. Furthermore, as our search example shows, the decision to collect costly information, and hence the possibility of learning, can be adversely influenced by agents' *a priori* held subjective beliefs. By wrongly believing that it is not worth collecting and processing information, agents may never learn about their mistakes. They can find themselves trapped in what we have called the vicious circle of ignorance.

4 Heterogeneous Information and the Rational Expectations Hypothesis

4.1 The Neoclassical Research Programme and the REH

The discussion in the previous chapter clearly shows that the REH, in the strong sense advanced by Muth, cannot be maintained if it is accepted that individuals do not have, nor are generally able to acquire, the knowledge necessary for forming expectations that satisfy the desired optimality properties of unbiasedness and orthogonality. The fact that complete learning cannot be shown to occur in many situations of interest sheds considerable doubt on the relevance of the Muth version of the REH to the problem of how expectations are actually formed. However, this does not mean that the *idea* of the REH can be dismissed as irrelevant. Most economists who work within the neoclassical paradigm are attracted to the idea of the REH, not necessarily because they think that it represents an 'adequate' description of reality but because the REH can be easily integrated within the basic postulates of the neoclassical economics. Some also view the advent of the REH as an important reinforcement of the neoclassical research programme.[1] Seen from this perspective the REH becomes an indispensable part of a consistent development of the expected-utility-maximization theory of decision-making under uncertainty.[2] In this approach the problem of expectations formation

---

[1] On this point of view see also Boland (1982, ch. 4).

[2] The foundations of the expected-utility-maximization approach to decision-making under uncertainty are discussed in Savage (1954), who builds on the early works of Ramsey (1931), and de Finetti (1937). The viewpoint put forward by Savage does not, however, in general allow an explicit *a priori* distinction between preferences (utilities) and subjective probabilities. It rather assumes that individuals act 'as if' they assign 'probabilities to all possible events and utilities to all possible outcomes'. For an excellent early survey of the alternative approaches to the theory of choice under uncertainty see Arrow (1951). More recent treatments of the subject can be found in Hirschleifer and Riley (1979), Lippman and McCall (1981), and Hey (1984).

arises only in conjunction with the decision-making process. Economic agents will be interested in forming expectations only in so far as expectations are relevant to the optimizing problem they are trying to solve. Thus in the recent developments of the neoclassical theory the emphasis has been on the internal consistency of the expectations formation process, and the problem of decision-making under uncertainty. In many respects this is preferable to Muth's (1961) rather vague notion that 'expectations, since they are informed predictions of future events, are essentially the same as the predictions of the relevant economic theory' (p. 316). The expected-utility-maximization approach gives the REH a micro-foundation firmly based on economic optimization, and thus enables one to see clearly and explicitly the type of assumptions which are needed if the REH is to have the desired optimality properties. In this chapter, by means of simple examples of economic optimization under uncertainty, we examine the conditions under which it is possible to derive the REH directly as a part of the solution to the decision-making problem. We show that the formulation of the REH attempted in the literature, notably by Sargent (1979a) and Hansen and Sargent (1980), is only meaningful if one is prepared to assume that information is homogeneous across firms or households. This assumption is, however, far too restrictive in market economies where decision-making is decentralized, and there is no reason to believe that market prices convey all the private information available in the economy. When the assumption of information homogeneity is abandoned decision-making will be subject to behavioural or strategic uncertainty, and a rigorous derivation of the REH from principles of economic optimization invariably involves the infinite regress problem in expectations originally discussed by Keynes (1936, p. 156). The introduction of heterogeneity of information, itself an inevitable consequence of the decentralization of the decision-making process in market economies, casts serious doubt on the validity of the formulation of the REH along the lines proposed, for example, by Hansen and Sargent (1980).

4.2 Profit Maximization under Uncertainty

Consider the problem of production decisions faced by a firm in an industry. Suppose there are N firms in the industry, each producing a homogeneous, non-storable product under cost conditions that in the short run can be characterized by

$$c_{it}=(1/2\delta_i)q_{it}^2+\eta_{it}q_{it}+\beta_i, \quad \delta_i, \beta_i>0, \quad i=1, 2,\dots, N, \tag{4.1}$$

where c_{it} denotes the ith firm's total cost of producing q_{it} units of output in period t. The parameters δ_i and β_i are intended to capture the differences in capital intensity or in the choice of production techniques that may exist across firms. These parameters can be derived explicitly in terms of input prices, technological coefficients, and the amounts of capital stock held by firms. The random variables η_{it} represent random shocks to the margin cost of firm i at time t, observed by firm i, but unobserved by other firms. We assume that η_{it} have zero means and are distributed independently across firms, but do not rule out the possibility that η_{it} may be serially correlated. Here we also assume that firms can change the level of their output without incurring any adjustment costs. We return to the problem of the adjustment cost in the following section. The use of a quadratic cost function is also intended to simplify the analysis, and has the advantage that it allows an explicit solution to the decision problem. The analysis will be carried out in a partial equilibrium framework with given input prices, but with firms facing output price uncertainty. The output price is uncertain because production decisions in each period must be made before the output price, P_t, is realized in the market. There is no fictitious auctioneer to mediate between firms and consumers. Under market clearing, P_t is determined by the industry demand function, which we assume to be given by the stochastic linear relation

$$P_t = \mathrm{a} - bq_t + \varepsilon_t, \tag{4.2}$$

where q_t is the industry output, and ε_t is a serially uncorrelated process with mean zero and a constant variance. When N is finite, q_t is simply defined as

$$q_t = \sum_{i=1}^{N} q_{it}. \tag{4.3}$$

But in the case of atomistic or competitive market behaviour, where individual firms believe they have no influence on the market beliefs of others and consider their individual contribution to the industry output as being negligible, the appropriate way to define the industry (average) output is by the Lebesque integral $q_t = \int q_{it}\, \mathrm{d}i$ (assuming it is well defined), where i ranges over the closed interval $[0,1]$. In order to avoid unnecessary technical complications, throughout we employ the definition (4.3) even though, strictly speaking, it is not valid for the case of atomistic market behaviour.

Under the above assumptions, and utilizing relations (4.1)–(4.3), the profit function of firm i will be

$$\pi_{it} = q_{it}\left\{\mathrm{a} - b\sum_{j=1}^{N} q_{jt} + \varepsilon_t\right\} - (1/2\delta_i)q_{it}^2 - \eta_{it}q_{it} - \beta_i, \tag{4.4}$$

which is a function of the random shocks to (industry) demand and the technology of firm i (i.e. ε_t and η_{it}), as well as the output decisions of other firms in the industry. It is this latter dependence of the ith firm's profit or pay-off function on the output decisions of other firms, and the implications that it has for the problem of expectations formation, that we wish to emphasize here. For this reason we abstract from the problem of learning already discussed in detail in the previous chapter and assume that every firm knows the true values of a and b and that firm i knows δ_i but not necessarily δ_j $(j \neq i)$. More precisely it will be assumed that the demand function facing the industry and its parameters are 'common knowledge'.[3] Furthermore, we assume that the probability distributions of the random shocks ε_t and η_{it} are invariant to the output decisions of firms, and that this is also common knowledge. Specifically, it will be assumed that

$$E\left(\frac{\partial \varepsilon_t}{\partial q_{it}}\middle|\Omega_{jt}\right)=E\left(\frac{\partial \eta_{jt}}{\partial q_{it}}\middle|\Omega_{jt}\right)=0, \quad \text{for } i,j=1,2,\ldots,N. \tag{4.5}$$

In the terminology of chapter 2, this is equivalent to assuming that for firm i the uncertainty surrounding costs and industry demand is 'exogenous'. The same can not, however, be assumed in general for the effect of changes in q_{it} on the output decisions of other firms. Again in the terminology of chapter 2, the source of uncertainty faced by firm i with respect to the output decision of other firms is 'behavioural'. What follows shows that, in a decentralized market, it is not possible to characterize this latter type of uncertainty by invariant probability distributions, and as a result a solution to the expectations formation problem along the lines of the REH, in general, does not seem to be possible. Only in the case of a fictitious 'representative' firm, or a monopolist, or under the highly restrictive assumption of homogeneous information (across firms), is it possible to derive the REH as the application of the principle of expected-utility-maximization to the decision problem being considered here.

To clarify some of these points let the information available to firm i at time t be denoted by Ω_{it}. In general Ω_{it} differs from the information available to firm j at the same point in time (i.e. $\Omega_{it}\neq\Omega_{jt}$, for $i\neq j$). The exact content of these information sets will be specified shortly. Suppose now that firm i has a well-defined subjective probability distribution over q_{jt} ($j\neq i$), and wishes to choose its output level, q_{it} to maximize its expected utility function conditional on the information set Ω_{it}. Assuming that all firms are risk-neutral (and this is common knowledge), the necessary and sufficient condition for a solution to this optimization problem is given by:[4]

$$E\left(\frac{\partial \pi_{it}}{\partial q_{it}}\middle|\Omega_{it}\right)=0,$$

which upon using relations (4.4), and (4.5) yields the following relation for the determination of the equilibrium value of q_{it} (say q^*_{it})

$$E(p_t|\Omega_{it})-bq^*_{it}E\left(\frac{\partial q_t}{\partial q_{it}}\middle|\Omega_{it}\right)+E(\varepsilon_t|\Omega_{it})=\delta_i^{-1}q^*_{it}+E(\eta_{it}|\Omega_{it}). \tag{4.6}$$

The solution to this equation crucially depends on the exact nature of the information set Ω_{it} available to the firm. It proves useful to decompose Ω_{it}

---

[3]The concept of 'common knowledge', which is originally due to Aumann (1976), is briefly described in chapter 2. A development of this concept can be found in Brandenburger and Dekel (1985).

[4]Notice that, under assumption of risk neutrality, the necessary conditions for the maximization of the expected utility function, and the necessary conditions for the maximization of the expected profit function, are the same.

into two subsets; one subset ψ_t representing the public information available to all firms at time t, and another ϕ_{it} which contains only firm-specific (or private) information. Formally, we assume the following information structure

$$\Omega_{it} = \psi_{t-1} \cup \phi_{it}, \tag{4.7}$$

with the *public information* set given by

$$\psi_t = (P_t, P_{t-1}, \ldots; q_t, q_t, q_{t-1}, \ldots), \tag{4.7a}$$

and, the *private information* set given by

$$\phi_{it} = (\eta_{it}, \eta_{i,t-1}, \ldots; q_{i,t-1}, q_{i,t-2}, \ldots). \tag{4.7b}$$

This specification of the information structure is in accordance with our assumption that firms observe only the production shocks that are specific to them. We are also assuming that firms do not observe the production decisions of other firms. To assume otherwise would be in direct contradiction to the basic tenet of the decentralized decision-making process.

Under the above specification of Ω_{it}, and recalling that ε_t are assumed to be identically and independent distributed with zero means, it then immediately follows that

$$E(\varepsilon_t | \Omega_{it}) = 0,$$

and

$$E(\eta_{it} | \Omega_{it}) = \eta_{it}.$$

Substituting these results in (4.6), and solving for q^*_{it} gives

$$q^*_{it} = (1 + b\delta_i k_{it})^{-1} \delta_i \{E(P_t | \Omega_{it}) - \eta_{it}\}, \tag{4.8}$$

where $E(P_t | \Omega_{it})$ denotes the (subjective) price expectations of firm i, and

$$k_{it} = E\left(\frac{\partial q_t}{\partial q_{it}} \middle| \Omega_{it}\right)$$

represents how firm i expects the industry output to change in response to its own output change. The latter term is known in oligopoly theory as the 'conjectural industry output variation' effect, or 'conjectural variation' for short. Different values of k_{it} correspond to different forms of market behaviour. Under atomistic market behaviour it is assumed that every firm believes that the industry output remains unchanged with respect to its own output decision, and k_{it} will therefore be equal to zero. By contrast, under Nash–Cournot behaviour it is postulated that every firm in the industry believes its own output decision does not induce any change in the output decision of other firms, and as a result every firm rather paradoxically expects that the industry output changes by exactly the same amount as the change in its own output, that is $\partial q_t / \partial q_{it} = 1$, or $k_{it} = 1$. Other types of market behaviour, such as collusive behaviour or Stackelberg behaviour, can also be described in terms of the value of k_{it}. The dependence of the output decision rule (4.8) on k_{it} clearly shows that in general it is not possible for a firm to arrive at a 'rational' decision without knowing how other firms in the industry are likely to react to its own output decision. A detailed analysis of output policy of firms under alternative behavioural assumptions is, however, beyond the scope of this chapter. Here we focus on the case where k_{it} is fixed over time but may vary across firms. Assume that $k_{it}=k_i$, then clearly the cases of atomistic market behaviour where $k_{it}=0$, and Nash–Cournot behaviour where $k_i=1$ can be obtained as special cases of our analysis. With a time-invariant conjectural variation k_i, the decision rule (4.8) simplifies to

$$q^*_{it}=\alpha_i\{E(P_t|\Omega_{it})-\eta_{it}\}, \tag{4.9}$$

where $\alpha_i=\delta_i(1+b\delta_i k_i)^{-1}$.

A complete solution to the decision problem requires formation of expectations about the equilibrium price level, P_t. In the context of the present model a consistent, and therefore a rational, method of expectations formation for each firm would be to form their price expectations on the basis of the market clearing price given by equation (4.2). For this approach to be operational, however, every firm must form expectations of output decisions of all the other firms in the industry. Notice that even under atomistic market behaviour (i.e. $k_{it}=0$) the expectations formation will involve a certain degree of behavioural uncertainty. To form expectations about the output decisions of other firms, each firm must in turn form expectations of other firms' price expectations, and so on, *ad infinitum*. This recursive dependence of output decisions on price expectations, and price expectations on output decisions, results in the problem of infinite regress in expectations implicit in Keynes's example of a beauty contest (see Keynes, 1936, p. 156). The problem of infinite regress in expectations has been recently discussed by Townsend (1978, 1983), and by Phelps, Di Tata, Evans, and Townsend in a conference volume edited by Frydman and Phelps (1983), and is a characteristic of models subject to behavioural uncertainty, and heterogeneous information across agents.[5] The problem can be easily illustrated in the context of our example in the following manner.[6]

Substituting q^*_{it} given by (4.9) in the industry demand function (4.2) yields

$$P_t=\mathrm{a}-b\left\{\sum_{i=1}^{N}\alpha_i E(P_t|\Omega_{it})-\sum_{i=1}^{N}\alpha_i\eta_{it}\right\}+\varepsilon_t,$$

which can be written equivalently as

$$P_t=\mathrm{a}-b\alpha F(P_t)+b\alpha\eta_t+\varepsilon_t, \tag{4.10}$$

where $\alpha=\Sigma\alpha_i$, $\eta_t=(\Sigma\alpha_i\eta_{it})/(\Sigma\alpha_i)$, and $F(P_t)$ stands for the (weighted) average expectations of all firms about the equilibrium price level. We shall refer to

[5] The behavioural uncertainty in the model discussed by Townsend (1978) arises because agents do not share common beliefs about the value of the intercept in the demand function. Otherwise all agents have access to the same information set.

[6] A general analysis of the solution of a simple class of linear RE models with heterogeneous information is given in appendix B.

$F(P_t)$ as the (average) 'market' expectations. The exact expression for it is given by

$$F(P_t) = \alpha^{-1} \sum_{i=1}^{N} \alpha_i E(P_t | \Omega_{it}). \tag{4.11}$$

Equation (4.10) establishes an important relationship between the market expectations of the equilibrium price level and the equilibrium price level itself.

Before proceeding any further with the analysis it is necessary to distinguish between the case where information is homogeneous across firms and the case where it is not. One way of insuring the homogeneity of information across firms is to assume that every firm has access to the private information of every other firm in the industry. This is clearly highly implausible and, as pointed out above, runs counter to the idea of decentralized decision-making. Our purpose in studying this case is, however, expositional; to show the circumstances under which the REH is likely to emerge naturally from the neoclassical theory of decision-making under uncertainty.

4.2.1 Homogeneous Information Case

In this case all firms are assumed to have access to the same information set, Ω_{t-1}, defined as the union of the information sets of all firms in the industry. That is,

$$\Omega_{it} = \Omega_{t-1} = \psi_{t-1} \cup \phi_{1t} \cup \phi_{2t} \ldots \cup \phi_{Nt}, \quad \text{for all } i = 1, 2, \ldots, N.$$

Clearly, under this case there will be no disparities in price expectations across firms, and the 'market' expectations of P_t, given by (4.11) reduce to $E(P_t|\Omega_{t-1})$. Using this result in (4.10) now yields the following first-order linear rational expectations equation

$$P_t = \mathrm{a} - b\alpha E(P_t|\Omega_{t-1}) + b\alpha\eta_t + \varepsilon_t, \tag{4.12}$$

where Ω_{t-1} now contains all the private and public information available in the industry at the time output decisions are made. Therefore, it is possible to derive the REH when there is no private information. As shown in the next chapter, this RE equation has a unique solution which can be obtained by first taking conditional expectations of both sides of (4.12) with respect to the common information set Ω_{t-1}. This yields (assuming that $1 + \alpha b \neq 0$),

$$E(P_t|\Omega_{it}) = E(P_t|\Omega_{t-1}) = (1 + \alpha b)^{-1}(\mathrm{a} + \alpha b\eta_t). \tag{4.13}$$

Using this result in (4.11) now gives

$$F(P_t) = E(P_t|\Omega_{t-1}),$$

which establishes that when firms share the same common information the market expectations and the rational expectations coincide. Furthermore, under homogeneous information expectations will be uniform across firms, which is not borne out by the survey evidence on expectations. As is pointed out by Muth (1961, p. 316) himself, there are considerable cross-sectional differences of opinion in the survey evidence on expectations. The information homogeneity assumption does, however, considerably simplify the analysis of the expectations formation process, and for this reason has been used extensively in the literature.

Given the result (4.13), the optimum output level of firm *i* will be given by

$$q^*_{it} = \alpha_i(1+\alpha b)^{-1}(\mathrm{a}+\alpha b\eta_t) - \alpha_i\eta_{it}.$$

The decision rule of each firm depends on the supply shocks of all the other firms in the industry and highlights the considerable informational demand made on firms under the homogeneous information case. The aggregate output in this case is given by

$$q^*_t = \alpha(1+\alpha b)^{-1}(\mathrm{a}-\eta_t),$$

which if used in the industry demand function (4.2) yields the following expression for the equilibrium price level

$$P^*_t = (1+\alpha b)^{-1}(\mathrm{a}+\alpha b\eta_t) + \varepsilon_t.$$

Therefore, in the case of homogeneous information the error of expectations $\xi_t = P^*_t - E(P^*_t \mid \Omega_{t-1})$ is equal to ε_t, which is, by assumption, a white noise process, and hence establishes that price expectations formed according to (4.13) are Muth-rational and possess the optimal properties of unbiasedness and orthogonality. But we should recall that the expectations formations process (4.13) is only meaningful if all *private* information is costlessly available to all firms, a condition which is extremely unlikely to be satisfied in decentralized markets. The interesting problem is to see whether the derivation of the REH from optimization principles is still possible when the unrealistic information homogeneity assumption is abandoned.

4.2.2 *Heterogeneous Information Case*

The problems arising from the heterogeneity of information across agents are briefly reviewed by Radner (1982). The emphasis in this literature is on the role of market prices in revealing private information; an idea which goes back to, at least, Hayek (1945). But in the present example where there are many firms ($N > 2$) producing the same homogeneous product, market prices cannot be relied upon to reveal the heterogeneous information that may exist across firms producing the same homogeneous product for the same market. For prices to reveal private information there should be at least as many prices as there are private signals (see, for example, Radner, 1982). The imperfect information 'islands' models proposed by Phelps (1970) and utilized extensively in the works of Lucas (1927b, 1973, 1975), Barro (1976) and Townsend (1983) are not relevant here either. In the 'islands' models it is assumed that information is homogeneous across firms in a given market but heterogeneous across markets. The source of heterogeneity of information across markets is due to the fact that markets (or 'islands') are 'imperfectly linked both physically and informationally' (Lucas, 1975, p. 1114). It is merely a parable intended primarily as providing an explanation for the observed cyclical fluctuations in output and employment in an otherwise equilibrium neoclassical model. The problem of the heterogeneity of information across markets in the 'islands' models is solved by means of two important assumptions:

1 All firms observe current equilibrium prices in their local markets.

2 All firms know the true distribution of the disparity between the equilibrium prices in the local markets and the economy-wide average current equilibrium price level.

These assumptions allow an efficient pooling of information from local markets and thus enable firms in each market to extract information about the economy-wide price level.

In our example, firms do not observe current prices, and have to make their output decisions in the light of past public information on prices and output and their own private information. The heterogeneity of information is present in our example simply because firms cannot observe the supply shocks experienced by other firms in the *same* market. As a result, when information is heterogeneous across firms, the solution to equation (4.10) is not a straightforward matter, and involves the infinite regress problem in expectations mentioned above. In this case firms, in arriving at their price expectations, need to form some opinion about the likely magnitude of the supply shocks of other firms. To see why this is so note that under the REH firms attempt to form their price expectations on the basis of the market clearing price equation (4.10). However, this equation, apart from depending on the average market expectations $F(P_t)$ also depends on all the supply shocks of other firms in the industry. In forming its price expectations firm i also needs to form expectations of η_{jt}, for $=1, 2, \ldots, N$. Since firm i observes its own supply shock then $E(\eta_{it}|\Omega_{it})=\eta_{it}$. But in the absence of some *a priori* common knowledge information about the distribution of η_{it}, $j\neq i$, it is unlikely that firm i can form expectations that are rational in the sense of having the orthogonality property. Here we consider the expectations formation problem of the ith firm under two important cases:

Case of Serially Uncorrelated Supply Shocks

In this case we assume it is common knowledge that η_{it} are serially uncorrelated with zero means, but allow for the variances of supply shocks to differ across firms, namely:

$$E(\eta_{jt}|\Omega_{it})=\eta_{it}, \quad \text{for } j=i,$$
$$=0, \quad \text{for } j\neq i,$$

and

$$V(\eta_{jt}|\Omega_{it})=\sigma_j^2, \text{ for all } i \text{ and } j.$$

Taking expectations of both sides of (4.10) with respect to Ω_{it} and using the above results, we obtain (recall also that $E(\varepsilon_t | \eta_{it}) = 0$)

$$E(P_t | \Omega_{it}) = \mathrm{a} - b\alpha E\{F(P_t) | \Omega_{it}\} + b\alpha_i \eta_{it}.$$

The term $E\{F(P_t) | \Omega_{it}\}$ represents the ith firm's (first-order) belief about the (average) market expectations of the equilibrium price. Substituting this result in (4.9), and the resultant output values in the industry demand function (4.2) now gives

$$P_t = \mathrm{a} - \mathrm{a}(b\alpha) + (b\alpha)^2 F^2(P_t) - \mathrm{b}^2 \sum_{i=1}^{N} \alpha_i^2 \eta_{it} + b \sum_{i=1}^{N} \alpha_i \eta_{it} + \varepsilon_t,$$

where

$$F^2(P_t) = \alpha^{-1} \sum_{i=1}^{N} \alpha_i E\{F(P_t) | \Omega_{it}\},$$

is the second-order market expectations of the equilibrium price level, or in Keynes's terminology, $F^2(P_t)$ is what the average opinion expects the average opinion to be. If this regressive process in expectations formation is continued up to the rth order, one finally obtains

$$P_t = \mathrm{a} \sum_{j=0}^{r-1} (-b\alpha)^j + (-b\alpha)^r F^r(P_t) - \sum_{j=1}^{r} \sum_{i=1}^{N} (-\alpha_i b)^j \eta_{it} + \varepsilon_t, \quad (4.14)$$

where $F^r(P_t)$ is the rth-order average market expectations of the equilibrium price level, and satisfies the following recursive relation

$$F^{r+1}(P_t) = \alpha^{-1} \sum_{i=1}^{N} \alpha_i E\{F^r(P_t) | \Omega_{it}\}.$$

Therefore, at least in principle, the infinite regress problem in this case has a solution. Assuming that $|\alpha b| < 1$, and that $F^r(P_t)$ remains bounded as r (the order of the regressive process in expectations) tends to infinity, the expression in (4.14) for P_t converges to[7]:

$$P_t = \frac{\mathrm{a}}{1 + \alpha b} - \sum_{r=1}^{\infty} \sum_{s=1}^{N} (-\alpha_s b)^r \eta_{st} + \varepsilon_t,$$

or

$$P_t = \frac{\mathrm{a}}{1 + \alpha b} + b \sum_{i=1}^{N} \left(\frac{\alpha_i \eta_{it}}{1 + \alpha_i b} \right) + \varepsilon_t. \quad (4.15)$$

If we now assume further that the true value of $\alpha = \Sigma \alpha_i$ is common knowledge (which is clearly a restrictive assumption), the above reduced-form equation

[7] The requirement $|\alpha b| < 1$ is the familiar condition for the stability of cobweb models.

can be utilized by any of the firms in the industry to form its subjective expectations of the equilibrium price level. For firm i, taking conditional expectations of both sides of (4.15) with respect to Ω_{it}, we have[8]:

$$E(P_t|\Omega_{it}) = \frac{\mathrm{a}}{1+\alpha b} + \frac{b\alpha_i\eta_{it}}{1+\alpha_i b}. \tag{4.16}$$

This solution is still based on a number of restrictive assumptions, but is certainly more plausible than the expectations formation equation (4.13) which is based on homogeneity of information across agents. The solution (4.16) has a number of interesting features that are not present in the homogeneous information case and are worth emphasizing:

1 There will be disparities in price expectations across firms which do not disappear even if all firms had the same cost functions and entertained the same value for the conjectural variation parameter k_i. This is because of the existence of firm-specific shocks that are observed only by the firm which experiences the shocks.

2 To an econometrician who does not observe the realizations η_{1t}, $\eta_{2t}, \ldots, \eta_{Nt}$, the price expectations across firms will follow a stochastic process with the same mean $\mathrm{a}/(1+\alpha b)$, but with variances $b^2\alpha_i^2\sigma_i^2/(1+\alpha_i b)^2$, that in general differ across firms. This result is particularly relevant to the problem of the conversion of qualitative survey data on price expectations to quantitative measures to be discussed in chapter 8.

3 The price level given by (4.15) and obtained by a 'mental process' as a strategic solution to the infinite regress problem in expectations, is in fact the equilibrium price that will be realized in the market. Starting with the individual firms' price expectations in (4.16), the optimal output of firm i will be

$$q_{it}^* = \alpha_i\left\{\frac{\mathrm{a}}{1+\alpha b} - \frac{\eta_{it}}{1+\alpha_i b}\right\},$$

which yields the following expression for the industry aggregate supply

$$q_t^* = \frac{\alpha \mathrm{a}}{1+\alpha b} - \sum_{i=1}^{N}\left(\frac{\alpha_i\eta_{it}}{1+\alpha_i b}\right).$$

Hence, using this result in the demand function (4.2), one obtains the equilibrium price level

$$P_t^* = \frac{\mathrm{a}}{1+\alpha b} + b\sum_{i=1}^{N}\left(\frac{\alpha_i\eta_{it}}{1+\alpha_i b}\right) + \varepsilon_t, \tag{4.17}$$

which is exactly the same as the infinite regress solution given by (4.15).

[8] Recall that, by assumption, $E(\varepsilon_t|\Omega_{it}) = 0$, and that $E(\eta_{st}|\Omega_{it}) = 0$ for $s \neq i$.

4 Price expectations formed by an individual firm satisfy the optimality properties of unbiasedness and orthogonality with respect to the information set available to that firm. Let ξ_{it} denote the expectations errors of firm i, then using (4.17), it immediately follows that

$$\begin{aligned}\xi_{it} &= P_t^* - E(P_t^* | \Omega_{it}),\\ &= b \sum_{\substack{s=1\\ s\neq i}}^{N} \left(\frac{\alpha_s \eta_{st}}{1+\alpha_s b} \right) + \varepsilon_t. \end{aligned} \tag{4.18}$$

On the assumption that $E(\eta_{jt}|\Omega_{it}) = 0$, for $j \neq i$ it is easily seen that $E(\xi_{it}) = 0$, and $E(\xi_{it}|\Omega_{it}) = 0$, which establish the optimality of price expectations formed by firm i, with respect to its own information set, Ω_{it}. The result in (4.18) also shows that unless $N=2$ firms cannot extract the information about the supply shocks experienced by other firms from the knowledge of their own expectations errors. They cannot separate the effect of the demand shock from those of the supply shocks on their expectations errors.

5 The heterogeneity of price expectations across firms also means that only an average expectations concept, such as the market expectations function, $F(P_t)$, given by (4.11) is meaningful at the industry level. Such an average concept is particularly relevant to empirical studies of expectations formation that employ aggregate time-series data. (See chapters 8 and 9.) The market expectations corresponding to individual firm expectations (4.16) are given by[9]:

$$F(P_t^*) = \frac{\mathrm{a}}{1+\alpha b} + b\alpha^{-1} \sum_{j=1}^{N} \left(\frac{\alpha_j^2 \eta_{jt}}{1+\alpha_j b} \right), \tag{4.19}$$

and the corresponding expectations errors will be[10]:

$$\begin{aligned}\xi_t &= P^* - F(P_t^*),\\ &= (b/\alpha) \sum_{j=1}^{N} \left(\frac{(\alpha-\alpha_j)\,\alpha_j \eta_{jt}}{1+\alpha_j b} \right) + \varepsilon_t. \end{aligned} \tag{4.20}$$

Notice that, unlike the homogeneous information case, the error in average market expectations ξ_t is not orthogonal to the information set of individual firms in the industry. That is

$$E(\xi_t|\Omega_{it}) = (b\alpha_i/\alpha)(\alpha-\alpha_i)\,\eta_{it}/(1+\alpha_i b),$$

---

[9] Notice that the weight α_i/a attached to the price expectations of firm i is in fact equal to $E(q_{it}^*)/E(q_t^*)$ which is the share of the ith firm mean output in the mean output of the industry. Therefore $F(P_t)$ aggregates price expectations of different firms according to their (average) market shares.

[10] Using results (4.18) and (4.20), it is also easily established that $\xi_t = \alpha^{-1}\Sigma\alpha_i\xi_{it}$, which simply states that market expectations errors are equal to a weighted average of expectations errors of individual firms.

which in general will be different from zero. However, ξ_t is orthogonal to the *intersection* of the information sets. That is $E(\xi_t|\psi_{t-1})=0$, where

$$\psi_{t-1}=\Omega_{1t}\cap\Omega_{2t}\ldots\cap\Omega_{Nt}=(P_{t-1},P_{t-2},\ldots;q_{t-1},q_{t-2},\ldots).$$

The orthogonality condition $E(\xi_t|\psi_{t-1})=0$ simply states that commonly observed data on past prices and past (industry) outputs will be used efficiently in the formation of market expectations. More specifically

$$E(\xi_t|P_{t-1},P_{t-2},\ldots;q_{t-1},q_{t-2},\ldots)=0.$$

This is an important testable implication of the 'rationality' hypothesis for aggregate data, to which we shall return in later chapters.

6 Under the homogeneous information case it is possible to aggregate the output decision rules of all the firms in the industry to obtain the familiar industry supply curve

$$q_t^s=\alpha E(P_t|\Omega_{t-1})-\alpha\eta_t,$$

which when combined with the demand function

$$P_t=\mathrm{a}-bq_t^d+\varepsilon_t,$$

and the market clearing condition $q_t^d=q_t^s=q_t$ leads to the rational expectations cobweb model originally analysed by Muth (1961). However, such a simple cobweb structure cannot be arrived at when there are disparities in information across firms. Under the heterogeneous information case the industry supply curve can be obtained by aggregating the output decision rules in (4.9), which gives

$$q_t^s=\alpha F(P_t)-\alpha\eta_t.$$

The price expectations variable in this supply curve is the average price expectations of the market participants, and in general will be different from the rational expectations solution $E(P_t|\Omega_{t-1})$, derived for the homogeneous information case in (4.13). Consequently, a straightforward application of the REH to models with heterogeneous information in general will not be valid.

Case of Serially Correlated Supply Shocks

Consider now the more complicated situation where it is known that supply shocks experienced by individual firms may be serially correlated. For the sake of concreteness suppose η_{it} follow an AR(1) process with parameter ϕ_i. That is

$$\eta_{it}=\phi_i\eta_{i,t-1}+v_{it},\quad i=1,2,\ldots,Nn \tag{4.21}$$

where v_{it} are white noise processes. We further assume that v_{it} are distributed independently across firms and that η_{it} are observable to firm i but not to other firms in the industry. The information structure facing firm i is defined by (4.7) from which it follows that

$$E(\eta_{it}|\Omega_{it})=\eta_{it}.$$

But to form rational expectations of P_t, firm i also needs to form expectations of the supply shocks (η_{jt}) experienced by other firms. This introduces an important subjective factor into the process of expectations formation for which an objective basis does not seem to exist. The public information available at time t (i.e. ψ_{t-1}) will not be sufficient for individual firms to obtain information on past supply shocks of other firms. As a result the *a priori* knowledge that η_{it} may be serially correlated will not be of much help to firms when forming their price expectations. To see this take the relatively simple case where $\phi_i = \phi$. Then aggregating (4.21) across firms we have

$$\eta_t = \phi\eta_{t-1} + v_t,$$

where,

$$\eta_t = \alpha^{-1} \sum_{i=1}^{N} \alpha_i \eta_{it}$$

and

$$v_t = \alpha^{-1} \sum_{i=1}^{N} \alpha_i v_{it}.$$

Using this result in (4.10) and taking conditional expectations with respect to Ω_{it} yields

$$E(P_t|\Omega_{it}) = b - b\alpha E\{F(P_t)|\Omega_{it}\} + b\alpha\phi E(\eta_{t-1}|\Omega_{it}) + b\alpha_i v_{it},$$

where $E(\eta_{t-1}|\Omega_{it})$ stands for what firm i believes at time t to have been the average supply shocks to the industry in the previous period. It is now easy to show that even in this simple case where $\phi_i = \phi$, the method of infinite regress in expectations discussed above will not lead to a determinate solution of the expectations formation problem. This follows because it is not possible to eliminate the unknown expectational variable $E(\eta_{t-1}|\Omega_{it})$ from the price expectations formation process of the ith firm. Clearly the problem will admit a determinate solution if it is assumed that past average realizations of supply shocks to the industry are common knowledge. In such a case $E(\eta_{t-1}|\Omega_{it}) = \eta_{t-1}$, and the application of the infinite regress method yields

$$E(P_t|\Omega_{it}) = \frac{\text{a}}{1+\alpha b} + \left(\frac{b\alpha_i}{1+\alpha_i b}\right) v_{it} + \frac{\alpha b\phi}{1+\alpha b}\eta_{t-1},$$

which is a generalization of (4.16). It seems, however, unlikely for the past values of η_t to become public information in a decentralized market economy. (Also see example B.2 in appendix B.)

These results show that when we explicitly recognize the existence of heterogeneous information, even in simple examples and under strong common knowledge assumptions, it may not be possible to derive the REH, in the strong sense advanced by Muth, from the principles of economic optimality alone.

We now turn to a more complicated example where in addition to uncertainty firms also face adjustment costs. We again show that it is not possible to derive the REH from the principles of economic optimization, unless one makes the rather strong assumption that information is homogeneous across firms.

4.3 Profit Maximization under Adjustment Costs

The problem of employment or output decision of a firm under adjustment costs and uncertainty has been extensively analysed in the literature, notably by Kennan (1979), Sargent (1978, 1979a), and Hansen and Sargent (1980). These studies show that in the case of a 'representative' firm with a quadratic cost function the optimal decision rule will in fact be a linear rational expectations model. These examples of economic optimizations are often regarded as a demonstration of how, in the case of a 'representative' firm, the REH can be derived rigorously from principles of economic optimization. It is not, however, explained what is exactly meant by a 'representative' firm. Marshall originally employed the concept as a sort of 'average' firm to abstract from abnormal variations in conditions of demand and production that different firms in the industry may encounter in the course of running their business (Marshall, 1964, pp. 264–5). In the rational expectations literature, where exogenous shocks to the firm are explicitly modelled, the idea of a 'representative' firm along the lines envisaged by Marshall is rather difficult to rationalize when information is heterogeneous across firms. It is therefore important to re-examine the analysis and the conclusions of these studies in the context of a model where information across firms is heterogeneous, such as the one set out in the previous section. In this way it will be possible to shed further light on the conditions needed for a rigorous derivation of the REH from the principles of economic optimization, when the decision-making is subject to adjustment costs.

We adopt the model of the previous section but assume that firms incur costs in adjusting the level of their outputs. These costs may be due to hiring and firing costs of labour, or may arise because of the technical difficulties associated with output changes, or may simply be due to inertia in the organization of production. To quantify the adjustment costs we follow the usual practice and add a quadratic term in $\Delta q_{it} = q_{it} - q_{i,t-1}$ to the cost function (4.1). The cost function of firm i will now be

$$c_{it} = (1/2\delta_i) q_{it}^2 + \eta_{it} q_{it} + \tfrac{1}{2}\theta_i (q_{it} - q_{i,t-1})^2 + \beta_i, \tag{4.1'}$$

where θ_i measures the importance of the adjustment costs, relative to the other production costs, incurred by firm i. We assume that θ_i is fixed and is strictly positive. Other notations are as before. The industry demand is given by (4.2), and it will be assumed that η_{it} are observed by firm i, but not by other firms in the industry. In the presence of adjustment costs we assume that firm i chooses its output level q_{it} to maximize its expected present value of future streams of profits

$$\lim_{T \to \infty} E\left(\sum_{j=0}^{T} \gamma_i^j \pi_{i,t+j} \,|\, \Omega_{it} \right), \tag{4.22}$$

with respect to the information set, Ω_{it}, available to firm i at time t. The fixed parameter $\gamma_i (0<\gamma_i<1)$ represents the ith firm subjective discount factor.[11] The profit function π_{it} is given by

$$\pi_{it} = P_t q_{it} - c_{it}, \tag{4.23}$$

where c_{it} is specified by (4.1′). Here to make the analysis manageable we focus on atomistic market behaviour and also assume that $E\{\partial q_{t+s}/\partial q_{i,t+j} | \Omega_{it}\} = 0$, for all t and all $s \geqslant j$. This assumption extends the 'static' atomistic market behaviour to dynamic situations. Firms do not expect their output decisions to have any effect on the level of industry output either in the current period or in future periods. Under these assumptions the necessary first-order conditions for the solution to the above discrete-time optimization problem can be obtained by differentiating the objective function (4.22) with respect to $q_{i,t+j}$, for $j=0, 1, \ldots, T-1$, and setting the derivatives equal to zero.[12] Since only the profit functions $\pi_{i,t+j}$, and $\pi_{i,t+j+1}$, depend on $q_{i,t+j}$, it follows that

$$E\left(\gamma_i^j \frac{\partial \pi_{i,t+j}}{\partial q_{i,t+j}} + \gamma_i^{j+1} \frac{\partial \pi_{i,t+j+1}}{\partial q_{i,t+j}} \middle| \Omega_{it}\right) = 0, \tag{4.24a}$$

for $j=0, 1, 2, \ldots, T-1$. Differentiating (4.22) with respect to $q_{i,t+T}$ gives the following condition for the terminal period

$$\lim_{T\to\infty} E\left(\gamma_i^T \frac{\partial \pi_{i,t+T}}{\partial q_{i,t+T}} \middle| \Omega_{it}\right) = 0. \tag{4.24b}$$

The conditions (4.24) are also known as the stochastic Euler equations, because of the analogy that exists between the above solution method and the classical method of calculus of variations.[13] The terminal condition (4.24b) is known as the 'transversality condition', and plays a crucial role in the solution of a certain class of linear rational expectations models (see chapter 5).

Using the profit function (4.23), and recalling that by assumption $E(\varepsilon_t | \Omega_{it}) = 0$, the stochastic Euler equations become,[14]

---

[11] The discount factor γ_i is defined by $1/(1+r_i)$, where r_i is the subjective rate of discount of the ith firm.

[12] Sargent (1979a, ch. 14) provides a clear exposition of this solution method and demonstrates its application to a number of economic problems.

[13] A brief review of the method of calculus of variations, accessible to economists, can be found in Lancaster (1968, pp. 376–84).

[14] Notice that

$$\frac{\partial \pi_{i,t+j}}{\partial q_{t+j}} = P_{t+j} - \delta_i^{-1} q_{i,t+j} - \theta_i \Delta q_{i,t+j} - \eta_{i,t+j},$$

and

$$\frac{\partial \pi_{i,t+j+1}}{\partial q_{t+j}} = \theta_i \Delta q_{i,t+j+1}.$$

$$E_{it}(q_{i,t+j}) = \mu_i E_{it}(P_{t+j} - \eta_{i,t+j}) + \mu_i \theta_i E_{it}(q_{i,t+j-1}) + \mu_i \theta_i \gamma_i E_{it}(q_{i,t+j+1}),$$
$$\text{for } j = 0, 1, 2, \ldots \qquad (4.25a)$$

where

$$\mu_i = \delta_i / \{1 + \theta_i \delta_i (1 + \gamma_i)\}, \qquad (4.26)$$

and $E_{it}(\cdot)$ stands for $E(\cdot | \Omega_{it})$, the conditional mathematical expectations taken with respect to the information set Ω_{it}. The transversality condition (4.24b) also simplifies to

$$\lim_{T \to \infty} \gamma_i^T E_{it} \; \{P_{t+T} - \eta_{i,t+T} - (\delta_i^{-1} + \theta_i) q_{i,t+T} + \theta_i q_{i,t+T-1}\} = 0. \qquad (4.25b)$$

The solution of the above Euler equations is not a straightforward matter and depends on the *i*th firm's expectations of equilibrium prices, not only in the current period but also in all the future periods. To see this more clearly we first write down the output decision rule for the current period, t. Noting that by assumption $E_{it}(\eta_{it}) = \eta_{it}$, and using (4.25a) for $j = 0$, it follows that

$$q_{it} = \mu_i E_{it}(P_t) + \mu_i \theta_i q_{i,t-1} + \mu_i \theta_i \gamma_i E_{it}(q_{i,t+1}) - \mu_i \eta_{it}. \qquad (4.27)$$

The fact that the current output decision of firm i depends on its next period output decision means that to solve for its current output decision firm i must form expectations of equilibrium prices not only in the current period, but also in all periods in the future. Under the REH, using the industry demand function (4.2), $E_{it}(P_t)$ are given by,

$$E_{it}(P_t) = \mathrm{a} - bE_{it}(q_t). \qquad (4.28)$$

But to form expectations of industry output, $E_{it}(q_t)$, firm i must first solve the Euler equations (4.25) for q_{jt}, $j = 1, 2, \ldots, N$. Then it must aggregate these solutions (assuming that they are unique) to arrive at its expectations of the industry output. However, since the solution of the Euler equations depends on price expectations, the solution to the expectations formation problem involves terms such as $E_{it}\{E_{jt}(P_{t+s})\}$, $E_{it}[E_{jt}\{E_{rt}(P_{t+s})\}]$, and so on. That is, firm i must form expectations of the jth firm's price expectations in the current, and in all future, periods. This is the problem of infinite regress in expectations that we have already encountered in the case of the static model of the previous section. But in the present example, because of the dynamic nature of the problem, a convergent solution to the infinite regress problem in expectations seems rather unlikely. To see this we first need to obtain a solution of the Euler equations (4.25). The alternative methods of solving such equations (i.e. rational expectations models with future expectations) will be reviewed in the next chapter (see section 5.3). There we show that equations such as (4.27) possess a unique stationary solution assuming that the processes generating P_t and η_{it} are stationary, and that one of the two roots of the quadratic equation

$$(\mu_i \theta_i \gamma_i) z^2 - z + \mu_i \theta_i = 0, \qquad (4.29)$$

falls outside the unit circle, and the other falls inside the unit circle. The assumption that P_t and η_{it} are stationary, can be relaxed, and be replaced by the transversality condition (4.25b). But given that the process generating $\{P_t\}$ itself depends on firms' output decisions, it is difficult to see how such an *a priori* assumption concerning $\{P_t\}$ can be justified. The assumptions on the roots of (4.29) are, however, satisfied (given plausible parameter values) in the present example.[15] As is shown in chapter 5 (section 5.3.4), the unique stationary solution of (4.27) is given by

$$q_{it} = \rho_i q_{i,t-1} + (\rho_i/\theta_i) \sum_{j=0}^{\infty} (\gamma_i \rho_i)^j E_{it}(P_{t+j} - \eta_{i,t+j}), \tag{4.30}$$

where ρ_i denotes the root of (4.29) that falls within the unit circle.

This result is the dynamic analogue of the static decision rule given by (4.9) for the case of atomistic market behaviour where $k_i = 0$. In fact it is easily seen that setting $k_i = 0$ and $\theta_i = 0$ reduces (4.30) to (4.9), as it should. However, when $\theta_i \neq 0$, firm i in deciding upon its output policy needs to form expectations of P_t and η_{it} not only for the current period, but also for all future periods. To obtain future expectations of the production shocks, we adopt a simple data generation process, and assume that η_{it} are serially independent for all i. That is

$$\begin{aligned} E_{it}(\eta_{i,t+j}) &= \eta_{it}, \quad \text{for } j = 0, \\ &= 0, \quad \text{For } j = 1, 2, \ldots \end{aligned}$$

Substituting this result in (4.30) we obtain

$$q_{it} = \rho_i q_{i,t-1} + \lambda_i \sum_{j=0}^{\infty} (\gamma_i \rho_i)^j E_{it}(P_{t+j}) - \lambda_i \eta_{it}, \tag{4.31}$$

where $\lambda_i = \rho_i/\theta_i$. The formation of price expectations $E_{it}(P_{t+j})$ is, however, a far more complicated problem. This is because the process generating P_t is not exogenous to the behaviour of firms and depends on their output deci-

---

[15] Denote the two roots of equation (4.29) by ρ_i and ρ_i'. Firstly, since

$$\rho_i \rho_i' = \gamma_i^{-1} = (1 + r_i) > 1,$$

then at least one of the two roots should fall outside the unit circle. But we also have

$$\begin{aligned} (\rho_i - 1)(\rho_i' - 1) &= \rho_i \rho_i' - (\rho_i + \rho_i') + 1, \\ &= \gamma_i^{-1} - (\mu_i \theta_i \gamma_i)^{-1} + 1, \end{aligned}$$

which in view of (4.26) gives

$$(\rho_i - 1)(\rho_i' - 1) = -(\delta_i \theta_i \gamma_i)^{-1} < 0.$$

Hence it is not possible for both roots to fall outside the unit circle. Therefore the roots of (4.29) satisfy the regularity conditions necessary for (4.27) to have a unique stationary solution.

sions. The aggregation of (4.31) over firms gives the following industry supply function,

$$q_t = \sum_{i=1}^{N} \rho_i q_{i,t-1} + \sum_{j=0}^{\infty} \sum_{i=1}^{N} \lambda_i (\gamma_i \rho_i)^j E_{it}(P_{t+j}) - \sum_{i=1}^{N} \lambda_i \eta_{it}, \tag{4.32}$$

which depends on price expectations of all firms in the current, as well as in the future, periods. The equilibrium market price can now be obtained in terms of price expectations and past output levels at the point of intersection of the above aggregate supply function (4.32), and the aggregate demand function given by (4.2). We have

$$P_t = \mathrm{a} - b \sum_{i=1}^{N} \rho_i q_{i,t-1} - b \sum_{j=0}^{\infty} \sum_{i=1}^{N} \lambda_i (\gamma_i \rho_i)^j E_{it}(P_{t+j}) + b \sum_{i=1}^{N} \lambda_i \eta_{it} + \varepsilon_t. \tag{4.33}$$

This is analogous to equation (4.10) but cannot be used in the same way to obtain $E_{it}(P_{t+j})$. Firstly, to use the above price equation, firm *i* requires information on past output policies of each firm in the industry separately. Secondly, firm *i* needs to know the parameters that enter the decision rules of the other firms. Thirdly, and most importantly, the use of (4.33) requires firm *i* to form expectations of what other firms' price expectations are, not only in the current period, but also in all periods in the future. This in turn leads to the infinite regress problem encountered before, but now in an 'infinite' number of periods! In fact there seems to be no solution to this infinite regress problem, and firms are unlikely to have the analytic ability and the *a priori* knowledge required to form Muth-rational price expectations in the case of the present model. Even if all firms were identical, a convergent solution to the infinite regress problem may not be available to individual firms as long as each firm experiences different production shocks, unobserved by other firms.

4.3.1 *Case of Identical Firms with Heterogeneous Information*

Under the common knowledge assumption that all firms are identical, namely that, $\theta_i = \theta$, $\gamma_i = \gamma$, $\rho_i = \rho$, and $\lambda_i = \lambda$, for all *i*, using (4.32), the aggregate supply function may be written as

$$q_t = \rho q_{t-1} + (N\rho/\theta) \sum_{j=0}^{\infty} (\gamma\rho)^j F_t(P_{t+j}) - \lambda N \eta_t, \tag{4.32'}$$

where $\eta_t = N^{-1}\Sigma_{i=1}^{N} \eta_{it}$, and $F_t(P_{t+j})$ is the average 'market' expectations of the equilibrium price level in period $t+j$ formed at time t, and is defined by

$$F_t(P_{t+r}) = N^{-1} \sum_{i=1}^{N} E_{it}(P_{t+r}). \tag{4.34}$$

The equilibrium price level in period t will now be

$$P_t = \mathrm{a} - b\rho q_{t-1} - (Nb\rho/\theta) \sum_{j=0}^{\infty} (\gamma\rho)^j F_t(P_{t+j}) + Nb\lambda\eta_t + \varepsilon_t, \qquad (4.33')$$

which can be used by firm i to form expectations of the current market price. That is

$$E_{it}(P_t) = \mathrm{a} - b\rho q_{t-1} - (Nb\rho/\theta) \sum_{j=0}^{\infty} (\gamma\rho)^j E_{it}\{F_t(P_{t+j})\} + b\lambda\eta_{it}.$$

But, to arrive at its output decision (via equation (4.31)) firm i must also form expectations of equilibrium prices at all periods in the future. To arrive at a rational expectations solution some common knowledge assumptions about the industry demand and the industry cost conditions in the future will also be needed. Under the rather strong assumptions that the industry demand function (4.2) and the cost function of firms are expected by all firms to remain unchanged through time the market clearing condition for period $t+1$ can be written as (see (4.33′))

$$P_{t+1} = \mathrm{a} - b\rho q_t - (Nb\rho/\theta) \sum_{j=0}^{\infty} (\gamma\rho)^j F_{t+1}(P_{t+j+1}) + Nb\lambda\eta_{t+1} + \varepsilon_{t+1}.$$

Taking expectations with respect to Ω_{it}, and recalling that ε_t and η_{it} are assumed to be serially uncorrelated, we obtain

$$E_{it}(P_{t+1}) = \mathrm{a} - b\rho E_{it}(q_t) - (Nb\rho/\theta) \sum_{j=0}^{\infty} (\gamma\rho)^j E_{it}\{F_{t+1}(P_{t+j+1})\}. \qquad (4.35)$$

But using (4.34) and noting that $E_{it}\{E_{i,t+1}(P_{t+r})\} = E_{it}(P_{t+r})$, we also have

$$E_{it}\{\mathrm{F}_{t+1}(\mathrm{P}_{t+j+1})\} = E_{it}\{\mathrm{F}_t(\mathrm{P}_{t+j+1})\}.$$

Therefore (4.35) can also be written as

$$E_{it}(P_{t+1}) = a - b\rho E_{it}(q_t) - (Nb\rho/\theta) L_{it,1}, \qquad (4.36)$$

where

$$L_{it,s} = \sum_{j=0}^{\infty} (\gamma\rho)^j E_{it}\{F_t(P_{t+j+s})\}, \quad \text{for } s = 0, 1, 2, \ldots$$

This result shows the dependence of expectations of future prices on the current output expectations, $E_{it}(q_t)$. The latter can be obtained using (4.32′). That is

$$E_{it}(q_t) = \rho q_{t-1} + (N\rho/\theta) L_{it,0} - \lambda\eta_{it}.$$

Replacing this result in (4.36) now yields

$$E_{it}(P_{t+1}) = \mathrm{a} - b\rho^2 q_{t-1} - (Nb\rho/\theta)\{L_{it,1} + \rho L_{it,0}\} + b\lambda\rho\eta_{it}.$$

Repeating the above derivations recursively for $P_{t+2}, P_{t+3}\ldots$ we arrive at the following expression for price expectations of the ith firm in all periods in the future

$$E_{it}(P_{t+r}) = \mathrm{a} - \mathrm{b}\rho^{r+1}q_{t-1} - (Nb\rho/\theta)\sum_{s=0}^{r}\rho^{r-s}L_{it,s} + b\lambda\rho^{r}\eta_{it},$$

$$\text{for } r = 0, 1, 2, \ldots. \qquad (4.37)$$

The price of expectations of individual firms therefore depends on what they expect the market expectations of equilibrium prices are in *all* future periods. Substituting the above result in (4.31) now yields the output decision of firm i at the second stage in the process of obtaining a RE solution to the infinite regress problem. Like the simple static example of the previous section, this regressive process in expectations formation can be followed *ad infinitum*, and if convergent leads one to the RE solution. It is nevertheless important to note that in the present dynamic example the conditions needed for the convergence of the regressive process are particularly strong, and the problem does not seem to us worth pursuing any further. It is difficult to imagine firms forming second-and higher-order expectations of what the market expects prices to be in an infinite number of periods in the future. The assumption of 'identical' firms on its own is not therefore sufficient for the derivation of the REH from the principles of economic optimization. To derive the REH, in the sense of Muth, we also need the assumption of homogeneity of information across firms.

4.3.2 *Case of Identical Firm with Homogeneous Information*

When firms are identical and all have access to the same information, we have $\Omega_{it} = \Omega_{t-1} = \psi_{t-1} \cup \phi_{1t} \cup \phi_{2t} \ldots \cup \phi_{Nt}$, and the Euler equation (4.27) becomes:[16]

$$q_{it} = \mu E(P_t|\Omega_{t-1}) + \mu\theta q_{i,t-1} + \mu\theta\gamma E(q_{i,t+1}|\Omega_{t-1}) - \mu\eta_{it}, \qquad (4.38)$$

for $i = 1, 2, \ldots, N$. The fact that all firms are identical and have the same information does not necessarily imply that they will all produce the same amount of output. This is because different firms may experience different shocks to their marginal costs. One possible way of dealing with these random differences amongst firms would be to employ the Marshallian concept of the 'representative' firm. In the context of the present example a representative firm is an average firm which experiences the average production shock $\eta_t = N^{-1}\Sigma_{i=1}^{N}\eta_{it}$. Notice, however, that this formalization of the concept of 'representative' firm is not meaningful if information happens to be heterogeneous across firms.

It is now a straightforward matter to derive a standard linear rational expectations model (in the strong sense advanced by Muth) from the Euler equa-

---

[16] That is $\Omega_{it} = \Omega_{t-1}$, for all i, where the information sets ψ_{t-1}, and ϕ_{it} are already defined by (4.7).

tions (4.38). Aggregating these equations over all firms in the industry yields the following dynamic industry supply function

$$q_t = N\mu E(P_t|\Omega_{t-1}) + \mu\theta q_{t-1} + \mu\theta\gamma E(q_{t+1}|\Omega_{t-1}) - N\mu\eta_t. \tag{4.39}$$

This supply function together with the industry demand function (4.2) provide a complete system of equations, and can be solved for the equilibrium value of q_t, and hence the price expectations, $E(P_t|\Omega_{t-1})$. From the industry demand function we have

$$E(P_t|\Omega_{t-1}) = \mathrm{a} - bE(q_t|\Omega_{t-1}),$$

which if substituted back in (4.39) gives

$$q_t = \mathrm{N}a\mu + \mu\theta q_{t-1} - N\mu bE(q_t|\Omega_{t-1}) + \mu\theta\gamma E(q_{t+1}|\Omega_{t-1}) - N\mu\eta_t. \tag{4.40}$$

This is still a relatively complicated linear rational expectations model which contains both current and future expectational variables. The next chapter will review alternative methods that are available for solving this and other linear rational expectations models. At this point, however, we wish to stress that the rational expectations solution implicit in (4.40) crucially depends on the validity of the information homogeneity assumption.

4.4 Concluding Remarks

This chapter, by means of simple examples of economic optimization, has shown how and under what conditions the REH can be derived rigorously from the principles of expected utility maximization. The examples looked at clearly demonstrate how the usual derivations of the REH from the principles of economic optimization depend crucially on the assumption that information is homogeneous across firms, even if attention is confined to atomistic market behaviour where each firm regards its output decision as having negligible impact on output decisions of other firms. The assumption of information homogeneity is, however, perhaps the most difficult assumption to justify in the context of a market economy. The assumption that every firm in an industry knows the random shocks experienced by every other firm in the industry is in direct contradiction to the idea of a decentralized competitive system of decision-making. Many studies in the rational expectations literature that obtain rational expectations models directly as solutions to the problems of economic optimization base their derivations on behaviour under uncertainty of a 'representative' firm or a 'representative' consumer, without fully setting out the assumptions that are implicit in such an approach. The use of the notion of a 'representaive' agent effectively allows these researchers to by-pass the important problem of information heterogeneity which is at the heart of decentralized systems of decision-making. By means of relatively simple examples, the chapter demonstrated that the idea of a representative firm is meaningful if we are prepared to assume that information is homogeneous across firms. Under heterogeneous information decision-making will be subject to behavioural uncertainty, and a rigorous derivation of the rational expectations models from principles of economic optimization generally will not be possible. Only in situations where the source of uncertainty is exogenous can we hope to derive the REH rigorously and consistently from the principles of economic optimization. This, however, considerably limits the application of the REH in economics, even if we are prepared, for the sake of theoretical consistency, to ignore the learning problems discussed in the previous chapter.

Part II

Econometric Considerations

5 Solution of Linear Rational Expectations Models

5.1 Introduction

So far this volume has emphasized the severe informational requirement of the REH, and has argued that save in trivial cases it is extremely unlikely that the economic agents can ever obtain the information necessary for the formation of rational expectations along the lines advanced by Muth. We now turn our attention to the econometric problems that arise in empirical analysis of rational expectations (RE) models. This chapter reviews the techniques proposed in the literature for the solution of a variety of linear rational expectations (LRE) models with known coefficients, and examines the issue of the non-uniqueness of the solution of rational expectations models with future expectations of the endogenous variable. The problems of identification, estimation and hypothesis testing in LRE models will be addressed in subsequent chapters. Study of non-linear RE models poses a number of further technical problems that fall outside the scope of the present volume.

There are now a large number of techniques available in the literature for solving LRE models, some of which are reviewed in the following sections. In its most general form a single-equation LRE model can be written as

$$y_t = \sum_{i=1}^{m} \lambda_i y_{t-i} + \sum_{i=0}^{r} \sum_{j=1}^{s} \alpha_{ij} E(y_{t+j-i} | \Omega_{t-i}) + \omega_t, \tag{5.1}$$

where ω_t is the exogenous process which drives the model. The information set Ω_t represents a non-decreasing set (i.e. $\Omega_t \supset \Omega_{t-1} \supset \Omega_{t-2} \ldots$), and contains all the information available at time t. We assume that the content of the information set Ω_t is given by current and past values of $\{y_t, \omega_t\}$, that is

$$\Omega_t = (y_t, y_{t-1}, \ldots ; \omega_t, \omega_{t-1}, \ldots).$$

But it is possible to expand Ω_t to include information on variables other than those that appear in (5.1). In most cases the exogenous process ω_t is decomposed into a systematic component $\gamma' \mathbf{x}_t$, and a stochastic component u_t, where $\mathbf{x}_t$ stands for a vector of observable exogenous variables, and u_t for the unobservable disturbance term. Current and/or future expectations of the exogenous variables can also be included in the model via the $\{\omega_t\}$ process. The term $E(y_{t+j-i}|\Omega_{t-i})$, $(j\geqslant 0)$ stands for the conditional mathematical expectations of y_{t+j-i} with respect to the information set Ω_{t-j}.[1]

All the LRE models discussed in the literature can be obtained from (5.1) as special cases. For example, setting

$$\alpha_{ij}=0, \quad \text{for } i\neq j,$$
$$=\beta_j, \quad \text{for } i=j=1, 2, \ldots, s,$$

yields the models considered by Aoki and Canzoneri (1979), Visco (1981, 1984a), and Broze and Szafarz (1984). Under the above restrictions (5.1) reduces to

$$y_t=\sum_{i=1}^{m}\lambda_i y_{t-i}+\sum_{i=1}^{s}\beta_i E(y_t|\Omega_{t-i})+\omega_t, \tag{5.2}$$

which is a LRE model *without* expectations of future endogenous variables.[2] We have already encountered a simple example of (5.2) in the previous chapter. This is given by equation (4.12) where $\omega_t=\mathrm{a}+ba\eta_t+\varepsilon_t$, $\beta_1=-ba$, $\beta_i=0\ (i\geqslant 2)$, and $\lambda_i=0\ (i\geqslant 1)$.

Another important class of LRE models is the class of models that contains only future expectations of the endogenous variables. This type of model has been studied extensively by, amongst others, Blanchard (1979), Blanchard and Kahn (1980), Gourieroux et al. (1982), McCallum (1983), Sargan (1983), Shiller (1978), Pesaran (1981, appendix), Taylor (1977), and Whiteman (1983). As will be shown later, an important feature of the RE models with future expectations is that information on the past history of y_t in general is not sufficient for the determination of a unique solution. A simple example of this type of model is given by the partial adjustment equation (4.40) derived in the previous chapter. A general specification of RE models containing only future expectations of the endogenous variable can be obtained from (5.1) by setting $\alpha_{0j}=\alpha_j$, and $\alpha_{ij}=0$ for all $i>0$. We have

$$y_t=\sum_{i=1}^{m}\lambda_i y_{t-i}+\sum_{j=1}^{s}\alpha_j E(y_{t+j}|\Omega_t)+\omega_t. \tag{5.3}$$

Other LRE models can also be obtained from (5.1). For example, equation (4.40) corresponds to the case where $\omega_t=N\mu(\mathrm{a}-\eta_t)$, $\lambda_1=\mu\theta$, $\lambda_i=0\ (i\geqslant 2)$, $\alpha_{ij}=0$, except for $\alpha_{11}=-N\mu b$, and $\alpha_{12}=\mu\theta\gamma$. The exchange rate overshooting models (Dornbusch, 1976; Buiter and Miller, 1983), the staggered contracts models (Taylor, 1980; Fischer, 1977), and Cagan's (1956) hyperinflation model all involve solution of LRE models that are special cases of

---

[1] The definition and certain key properties of the conditional mathematical expectations are briefly reviewed in appendix A.

[2] Equations such as (5.2) are also known in the literature as 'withholding equations' (see Whiteman, 1983, p. 29).

equations (5.2) or (5.3). Clearly models that are linear combinations of (5.2) and (5.3) are also encountered in practice. But by use of simple transformations of y_t's, such mixed current–future expectations models can be reduced to models of type (5.3). Here, we shall not deal with mixed expectations models as a separate category; although at the end of this chapter we discuss a generalization of Muth's speculative inventory model which involves both current and future expectations of prices. A solution technique which is directly applicable to the mixed current–future expectations model (5.1) has been recently proposed by Broze et al. (1985), and we shall briefly review it later in this chapter. But for pedagogical purposes it is more convenient to consider the problem of obtaining solutions of the RE models (5.2), and (5.3) separately. This is because unlike the models with future expectations of the endogenous variable, the RE models with only current expectations of the endogenous variable (except in degenerate cases) have a unique solution.

The plan of this chapter is as follows. The problem of solving LRE models with only current expectations of the endogenous variable will be covered fully in the next section. Section 5.3 deals with the solution of RE models with future expectations of the endogenous variable where five different solution techniques proposed in the literature will be reviewed. There we also examine the problem of non-uniqueness of the solution of LRE models with future expectations, and discuss the alternative criteria proposed in the literature for selecting a unique solution. We argue that 'deeper theorizing' does not generally resolve the non-uniqueness problem, and the application of the REH to models with future expectations requires making further *a priori* common knowledge assumptions, which are difficult to reconcile with the neoclassical individualistic formulation of the hypothesis. This chapter also includes analysis of the solution of three important examples of LRE models frequently encountered in the literature, namely the new classical macroeconomic model, Taylor's (1977) macroeconomic model, and a generalization of Muth's (1961) inventory speculation model.

5.2 Solution of LRE Models with Current Expectations

Solutions of LRE models such as (5.2) which only contain current expectations of the endogenous variable formed on the basis of information available at different points in time in the past, have been derived by Aoki and Canzoneri (1979), Visco (1981, 1984a), and Broze and Szafarz (1984). These authors show that, save for a number of degenerate cases, equation (5.2) admits a unique solution. The solution method adopted by Visco employs the projection technique which uses the law of iterated conditional expectations (property P4 in appendix A), while Broze and Szafarz (1984) employ a martingale theorem due to Doob (1953). The method used by Broze and Szafarz is relatively simple, but requires the assumption that the processes $\{\omega_t\}$ and $\{y_t\}$ are integrable.[3] Visco's method is based on a slightly weaker assump-

[3] A process $\{y_t\}$ is said to be integrable if $E(y_t)$ is finite for all t.

tion. It only requires that the conditional mathematical expectations of y_t and ω_t with respect to $\{\Omega_{t-i}, i=1, 2, \ldots, s\}$ exist. Here we follow Visco's procedure, and without any loss of generality set $m=1$. Notice that by appropriate transformation of y_t and its lagged values it is always possible to rewrite equation (5.2) as a first-order autoregression in y_t. To see this let

$$z_{1t}=y_t,$$
$$z_{2t}=z_{1,t-1},$$
$$z_{3t}=z_{2,t-1},$$
$$\vdots$$
$$z_{mt}=z_{m-1,t-1}.$$

Then (5.2) can be written as

$$\mathbf{z}_t=\Lambda\mathbf{z}_{t-1}+\sum_{i=1}^{s} A_i E(\mathbf{z}_t|\Omega_{t-i})+\boldsymbol{\omega}_t \tag{5.2$'$}$$

where $\mathbf{z}_t'=(z_{1t}, z_{2t}, \ldots, z_{mt})$, $\boldsymbol{\omega}_t'=(\omega_t, 0, 0, \ldots, 0)$, and

$$\Lambda=\begin{bmatrix}\lambda_1 & \lambda_2 & \ldots & \lambda_{m-1} & \lambda_m\\ 1 & 0 & \ldots & 0 & 0\\ \vdots & \vdots & & \vdots & \vdots\\ 0 & 0 & \ldots & 1 & 0\end{bmatrix}, \quad A_i=\begin{bmatrix}\alpha_i & 0 & \ldots & 0\\ 0 & 0 & \ldots & 0\\ \vdots & \vdots & & \vdots\\ 0 & 0 & \ldots & 0\end{bmatrix}.$$

Notice that since $\mathbf{z}_t'=(y_t, y_{t-1}, \ldots, y_{t-m+1})$, then the information set Ω_t will also include current and past values of $\mathbf{z}_t$ and $\boldsymbol{\omega}_t$. That is we have $\Omega_t=(\mathbf{z}_t, \mathbf{z}_{t-1}, \ldots; \boldsymbol{\omega}_t, \boldsymbol{\omega}_{t-1}, \ldots)$. The above reformulation of equation (5.2) is in fact more general than it appears at first sight. It readily allows for the inclusion of terms such as $E(y_{t-j}|\Omega_{t-i})$, $s>i>j>0$. One needs simply to replace the appropriate non-zero elements of the matrix A_i by the coefficients of $E(y_{t-j}\ |\Omega_{t-i})$.

The solution of equation (5.2) can in principle be obtained, albeit tediously, by the repeated application of the 'projection technique'. The basic idea behind this technique is easily demonstrated in the simple case where $s=1$. In this case (5.2$'$) reduces to

$$\mathbf{z}_t=\Lambda\mathbf{z}_{t-1}+AE(\mathbf{z}_t|\Omega_{t-1})+\boldsymbol{\omega}_t, \tag{5.2$''$}$$

where for simplicity of exposition we have suppressed the subscript of matrix A_i. Taking conditional mathematical expectations of both sides of the above equation with respect to Ω_{t-1} we have

$$E(\mathbf{z}_t|\Omega_{t-1})=\Lambda\mathbf{z}_{t-1}+AE(\mathbf{z}_t|\Omega_{t-1})+E(\boldsymbol{\omega}_t|\Omega_{t-1}),$$

which assuming that the matrix $I-A$ is non-singular yields

$$E(\mathbf{z}_t|\Omega_{t-1})=(I-A)^{-1}\Lambda\mathbf{z}_{t-1}+(I-A)^{-1}E(\boldsymbol{\omega}_t|\Omega_{t-1}).$$

Now substituting this result in (5.2″), and noting that

$$I + A(I-A)^{-1} = (I-A)^{-1},$$

we obtain the following unique solution of $\mathbf{z}_t$ (in terms of its past history)

$$\mathbf{z}_t = (I-A)^{-1}\Lambda\mathbf{z}_{t-1} + A(I-A)^{-1}E(\boldsymbol{\omega}_t|\Omega_{t-1}) + \boldsymbol{\omega}_t.$$

In the degenerate case where $I-A$ is singular, the solution of (5.2″) will be indeterminate.

A straightforward application of the projection technique to the general equation (5.2′) is, however, rather tedious. Below we provide alternative solution techniques and appropriate uniqueness theorems for the general case both when the equation under consideration contains lagged dependent variables and when it does not.

5.2.1 *Case of* $\Lambda = 0$ *(Models Without Lagged Dependent Variables)*

We first prove the following theorem which establishes the uniqueness of the solution (when it exists) in the case of LRE models with only current expectations of the endogenous variable.

Theorem 5.1 Suppose that matrices

$$Q_j = I - \sum_{i=1}^{j} A_i, \quad j = 1, 2, \ldots s,$$

are non-singular. Then the LRE equation

$$\mathbf{z}_t = \sum_{i=1}^{s} A_i E(\mathbf{z}_t|\Omega_{t-i}) + \boldsymbol{\omega}_t, \tag{5.4}$$

has a unique solution.

Proof Let $\mathbf{z}_t^0$ and $\mathbf{z}_t^1$ be two different solutions of (5.4). We show that this is impossible. If $\mathbf{z}_t^0$ and $\mathbf{z}_t^1$ were in fact two different solutions of (5.4) we would have

$$\mathbf{x}_t = \mathbf{z}_t^0 - \mathbf{z}_t^1 = \sum_{i=1}^{s} A_i E(\mathbf{x}_t|\Omega_{t-i}). \tag{5.5}$$

Taking conditional expectations of (5.5) with respect to Ω_{t-1} gives:[4]

$$E(\mathbf{x}_t|\Omega_{t-s}) = \left(\sum_{i=1}^{s} A_i\right) E(\mathbf{x}_t|\Omega_{t-s}),$$

[4] Notice that $E\{E(x_t|\Omega_{t-i})|\Omega_{t-j}\} = E(x_t|\Omega_{t-j}), \quad \text{for } j \geqslant i.$

or

$$Q_s E(\mathbf{x}_t | \Omega_{t-s}) = 0.$$

Now write (5.5) as

$$\mathbf{x}_t = \sum_{i=1}^{j} A_i E(\mathbf{x}_t | \Omega_{t-i}) + \sum_{i=j+1}^{s} A_i E(\mathbf{x}_t | \Omega_{t-i}),$$

and take conditional expectations with respect to Ω_{t-j}, for $j < s$, then one obtains

$$Q_j E(\mathbf{x}_t | \Omega_{t-j}) = \sum_{i=j+1}^{s} A_i E(\mathbf{x}_t | \Omega_{t-i}), \quad j = 1, 2, \ldots, s-1.$$

But since by assumption, $\{Q_j, j = 1, 2, \ldots, s\}$ are non-singular, using the above results iteratively from $j = s-1, s-2, \ldots, 1$, it readily follows that

$$E(\mathbf{x}_t | \Omega_{t-j}) = 0, \quad j = 1, 2, \ldots, s,$$

which if used in (5.5) establishes that $\mathbf{x}_t = \mathbf{z}_t^0 - \mathbf{z}_t^1 = 0$. QED

Assuming the condition of the above theorem is satisfied, the unique solution of (5.4) can be obtained by successive applications of the projection technique. Taking mathematical expectations of (5.4) conditional on Ω_{t-s} yields

$$Q_s E(\mathbf{z}_t | \Omega_{t-s}) = E(\boldsymbol{\omega}_t | \Omega_{t-s}),$$

which if used in (5.4) results in a RE equation of order $s-1$. This process can be continued until the unique solution of $\mathbf{z}_t$ in terms of $\boldsymbol{\omega}_t$, $E(\boldsymbol{\omega}_t | \Omega_{t-1}), \ldots,$ and $E(\boldsymbol{\omega}_t | \Omega_{t-s})$ is obtained. This solution method, however, can be rather tedious, especially when s is moderately large. An alternative approach would be to adopt Muth's method of 'undetermined coefficients'. This method has been used extensively in the literature for solving simple LRE models with future expectations of the endogenous variable. It involves making a conjecture about the general form of the solution. In the case of equation (5.4) the general solution form is given by

$$\mathbf{z}_t = \sum_{j=0}^{s} B_j E(\boldsymbol{\omega}_t | \Omega_{t-j}), \tag{5.6}$$

and since the solution is unique we should be able to obtain the matrices B_j uniquely in terms of the structural matrices A_j. The usual practice is first to substitute $\mathbf{z}_t$ from (5.6) in (5.4), and then derive B_j by setting the coefficients of $E(\boldsymbol{\omega}_t | \Omega_{t-j})$ in the resultant expression equal to zero. In the case of the present problem this procedure is rather tedious to apply. A simpler alternative would be to use (5.4) to eliminate $\boldsymbol{\omega}_t$ from (5.6). Using (5.4) we have

$$E(\boldsymbol{\omega}_t | \Omega_{t-j}) = Q_j E(\mathbf{z}_t | \Omega_{t-j}) - \sum_{i=j+1}^{s} A_i E(\mathbf{z}_t | \Omega_{t-i}), \quad \text{for } j = 1, 2, \ldots, s,$$

where as before $Q_j = I - \sum_{i=1}^{j} A_i$. Substituting these results in (5.6) now yields

$$\mathbf{z}_t = B_0\left(\mathbf{z}_t - \sum_{i=1}^{s} A_i E(\mathbf{z}_t|\Omega_{t-i})\right) + \sum_{j=1}^{s} B_j Q_j E(\mathbf{z}_t|\Omega_{t-j})$$

$$- \sum_{j=1}^{s} B_j \sum_{i=j+1}^{s} A_i E(\mathbf{z}_t|\Omega_{t-i}),$$

or

$$(I - B_0)\mathbf{z}_t = \sum_{j=1}^{s}\left(B_j Q_j - \left(\sum_{i=0}^{j-1} B_i\right) A_j\right) E(\mathbf{z}_t|\Omega_{t-j}).$$

Hence we arrive at the following recursive relations for the determination of B_j

$$B_0 = I$$

$$B_j Q_j = \left(\sum_{i=0}^{j-1} B_i\right) A_j, \quad j = 1, 2, \ldots, s.$$

The unique solution of B_j can now be easily obtained as long as Q_j are non-singular. Let

$$P_j = \sum_{i=0}^{j} B_i, \quad j = 0, 1, 2, \ldots$$

Then $B_j = P_j - P_{j-1}$, and therefore, noting that $A_j = Q_{j-1} - Q_j$, the above recursive relations can also be written as

$$P_j Q_j = P_{j-1} Q_{j-1}, \quad j = 1, 2, \ldots$$

But $P_0 Q_0 = B_0 = I$, hence $P_j Q_j = 1$ for $j \geqslant 0$. It therefore follows that

$$P_j = Q_j^{-1}, \quad \text{for } j = 0, 1, 2, \ldots, s,$$

and hence

$$B_j = P_j - P_{j-1} = Q_j^{-1} - Q_{j-1}^{-1}.$$

The general solution of (5.4) can now be written as

$$\mathbf{z}_t = \boldsymbol{\omega}_t + \sum_{j=1}^{s} (D_j - D_{j-1}) E(\boldsymbol{\omega}_t|\Omega_{t-j}), \tag{5.7}$$

where $D_j = Q_j^{-1}$. From this result it readily follows that when the process generating $\{\boldsymbol{\omega}_t\}$ is serially uncorrelated, the RE equation (5.4) will also have a serially uncorrelated solution. Notice also that the above solution technique is applicable irrespective of whether the process generating $\boldsymbol{\omega}_t$ is stationary or not. It is only required that the conditional mathematical expectations $E(\boldsymbol{\omega}_t|\Omega_{t-i})$, $i = 1, 2, \ldots, s$ exist.

5.2.2 *Case of $\Lambda \neq 0$ (Models with Lagged Dependent Variables)*

We now extend the above results to the general case where the equation under consideration contains lagged dependent variables. For this purpose we adopt the general matrix formulation given by (5.2′).

Theorem 5.2 Suppose that matrices Q_j, $j=1, 2, \ldots, s$ defined in theorem 5.1 are non-singular and all the eigenvalues of the matrix $H_s = Q_s^{-1}\Lambda$ fall inside the unit circle, then the general LRE equation (5.2′) has a unique solution, irrespective of the past history of $\mathbf{z}_t$.

Proof As in the proof of theorem 5.1, let $\mathbf{z}_t^0$ and $\mathbf{z}_t^1$ be two different solutions of (5.2′). Then

$$\mathbf{x}_t = \mathbf{z}_t^0 - \mathbf{z}_t^1 = \Lambda \mathbf{x}_{t-1} + \sum_{i=1}^{s} A_i E(\mathbf{x}_t \mid \Omega_{t-i}). \tag{5.8}$$

Taking conditional expectations of both sides of (5.8) with respect to Ω_{t-s} yields

$$Q_s E(\mathbf{x}_t \mid \Omega_{t-s}) = \Lambda E(\mathbf{x}_{t-1} \mid \Omega_{t-s}).$$

Similarly, following Visco (1984a), for $j < s$ we have

$$Q_j E(\mathbf{x}_t \mid \Omega_{t-j}) = \Lambda E(\mathbf{x}_{t-1} \mid \Omega_{t-j}) + \sum_{i=j+1}^{s} A_i E(\mathbf{x}_t \mid \Omega_{t-i}), \tag{5.9}$$

$$Q_j E(\mathbf{x}_t \mid \Omega_{t-j-1}) = \Lambda E(\mathbf{x}_{t-1} \mid \Omega_{t-j-1}) + \sum_{i=j+1}^{s} A_i E(\mathbf{x}_t \mid \Omega_{t-i}). \tag{5.10}$$

Subtracting (5.10) from (5.9) and noting that by assumption Q_j are non-singular gives

$$\xi_{tj} = H_j \xi_{t-1,j-1}, \quad \text{for } j = 1, 2, \ldots, s, \tag{5.11}$$

where

$$\xi_{tj} = E(\mathbf{x}_t \mid \Omega_{t-j}) - E(\mathbf{x}_t \mid \Omega_{t-j-1}), \tag{5.12}$$

and

$$H_j = Q_j^{-1}\Lambda, \quad \text{for } j = 1, 2, \ldots, s. \tag{5.13}$$

Now employing (5.11) recursively we have

$$\xi_{t1} = H_1 \xi_{t-1,0},$$

$$\xi_{t2} = H_2 \xi_{t-1,1} = H_2 H_1 \xi_{t-2,0},$$

$$\vdots$$

$$\xi_{tj} = (H_j H_{j-1} \ldots H_1) \xi_{t-j,0}, \quad \text{for } j = 1, 2, \ldots, s. \tag{5.14}$$

But by (5.12)

$$\xi_{t-j,0} = E(\mathbf{x}_{t-j}|\Omega_{t-j}) - E(\mathbf{x}_{t-j}|\Omega_{t-j-1}),$$
$$= \mathbf{x}_{t-j} - E(\mathbf{x}_{t-j}|\Omega_{t-j-1}).$$

Using (5.8) we also have

$$E(\mathbf{x}_{t-j}|\Omega_{t-j-1}) = \mathbf{x}_{t-j}, \quad \text{for } j=0, 1, 2, \ldots$$

Therefore $\xi_{t-j,0}=0$, which in the light of (5.14) establishes that $\xi_{tj}=0$, for $j=1, 2, \ldots, s$. This in turn implies that

$$\mathbf{x}_t = E(\mathbf{x}_t|\Omega_{t-j}), \quad \text{for } j=1, 2, \ldots, s.$$

Substituting these results in (5.8) now gives

$$\mathbf{x}_t = H_s\mathbf{x}_{t-1},$$

which is a first-order vector autoregression process with the coefficient matrix H_s. The solution of this equation in terms of the initial values $\mathbf{x}_{-N}(N>0)$ is given by

$$\mathbf{x}_t = H_s^{t+N}\mathbf{x}_{-N},$$

and since by assumption all the eigenvalues of H_s fall within the unit circle, then

$$\lim_{N\to\infty}(\mathbf{x}_t) = \lim_{N\to\infty}(\mathbf{z}_t^0 - \mathbf{z}_t^1) = 0,$$

irrespective of the initial values $\mathbf{x}_{-N}$. QED

Notice that the above proof of the uniqueness of the solution of (5.2′) does not require the process $\{\boldsymbol{\omega}_t\}$ to be stationary. Moreover, even if the roots of H_s are not all within the unit circle, the reduced form solution of (5.2′) in terms of $\mathbf{z}_{t-1}$ will still be unique.

The unique solution of (5.2′) can now be obtained by the method of undetermined coefficients when the order s is relatively small ($s=1$ or 2). But for values of $s>2$ the methods proposed by Visco (1981, 1984a), and Broze and Szafarz (1984) are more suitable. Here we briefly describe Visco's solution technique. Consider the revision in the expectations of $\mathbf{z}_t$ made between the periods $t-j-1$ and $t-j$, and, denote this revision by χ_{tj}, that is

$$\chi_{tj} = E(\mathbf{z}_t|\Omega_{t-j}) - E(\mathbf{z}_t|\Omega_{t-j-1}).$$

Then it is easily seen that

$$\mathbf{z}_t = \sum_{j=0}^{s-1}\chi_{tj} + E(\mathbf{z}_t|\Omega_{t-s}). \tag{5.15}$$

The expectations revision terms such as χ_{tj}, which also form the basis of the solution method proposed by Broze et al. (1985), have the important orthogonality property

$$E(\chi_{tj}|\Omega_{t-j-1}) = 0, \tag{5.16}$$

from which it also follows that $E(\chi_{tj})=0$, for all t and j. Visco's method utilizes (5.16), and involves deriving appropriate recursive relations for χ_{ti} in terms of the revisions in the expectations of the exogenous process $\{\boldsymbol{\omega}_t\}$. That is,

$$\eta_{tj}=E(\boldsymbol{\omega}_t|\Omega_{t-j})-E(\boldsymbol{\omega}_t|\Omega_{t-j-1}).$$

To implement this method we need first to take conditional expectations of (5.2′) with respect to Ω_{t-j} and Ω_{t-j-1}. Applying the chain rule properties of conditional mathematical expectations for $j<s$ we have

$$Q_jE(\mathbf{z}_t|\Omega_{t-j})=\Lambda E(\mathbf{z}_{t-1}|\Omega_{t-j})+\sum_{i=j+1}^{s}A_iE(\mathbf{z}_t|\Omega_{t-i})+E(\boldsymbol{\omega}_t|\Omega_{t-j}).$$

Similarly,

$$Q_jE(\mathbf{z}_t|\Omega_{t-j-1})=\Lambda E(\mathbf{z}_{t-1}|\Omega_{t-j-1})+\sum_{i=j+1}^{s}A_iE(\mathbf{z}_t|\Omega_{t-i})+E(\boldsymbol{\omega}_t|\Omega_{t-j-1}).$$

Subtracting the above two results from one another and pre-multiplying both sides by $D_j=Q_j^{-1}$ now yields the recursive relations

$$\chi_{tj}=H_j\chi_{t-1,j-1}+D_j\eta_{tj},\quad \text{for } j=1, 2, \ldots, s, \tag{5.17}$$

where H_j is already defined by (5.13). To obtain the appropriate expression for $E(\mathbf{z}_t|\Omega_{t-s})$, we need first to take the conditional expectations of (5.2′) with respect to Ω_{t-s}. This gives

$$E(\mathbf{z}_t|\Omega_{t-s})=H_sE(\mathbf{z}_{t-1}|\Omega_{t-s})+D_sE(\boldsymbol{\omega}_t|\Omega_{t-s}).$$

But we also have

$$E(\mathbf{z}_{t-1}|\Omega_{t-s})=\mathbf{z}_{t-1}-\sum_{j=1}^{s-1}\chi_{t-1,j-1}.$$

Therefore

$$E(\mathbf{z}_t|\Omega_{t-s})=H_s\left(\mathbf{z}_{t-1}-\sum_{j=1}^{s-1}\chi_{t-1,j-1}\right)+D_sE(\boldsymbol{\omega}_t|\Omega_{t-s}).$$

Using this result in (5.15) and rearranging terms we finally obtain

$$\mathbf{z}_t=H_s\mathbf{z}_{t-1}+\chi_{t0}+\sum_{j=1}^{s-1}(\chi_{tj}-H_s\chi_{t-1,j-1})+D_sE(\boldsymbol{\omega}_t|\Omega_{t-s}),\ s\geqslant 1. \tag{5.18}$$

The derivation of χ_{tj} in terms of the revisions in the expectations of the exogenous variables $\{\eta_{tj}\}$ can be carried out by means of the recursive relations (5.17). For $j=1$ we have

$$\chi_{t1}=H_1\chi_{t-1,0}+D_1\eta_{t1}, \tag{5.19}$$

and for $j=2$

$$\chi_{t2}=H_2\chi_{t-1,1}+D_2\eta_{t2},$$

which using (5.19) gives

$$\chi_{t2}=H_2H_1\chi_{t-2,0}+H_2D_1\eta_{t-1,1}+D_2\eta_{t2}.$$

In general we have

$$\chi_{tj}=F_{j1}\chi_{t-j,0}+\sum_{i=2}^{j}F_{ji}D_{i-1}\eta_{t+i-j-1,i-1}+D_j\eta_{tj}, \quad \text{for } j=1,2,\ldots,s, \tag{5.20}$$

where

$$F_{ji}=H_jH_{j-1}\ldots H_i, \quad \text{for } i\leqslant j=1,2,\ldots,s.$$

The initial values $\chi_{t-j,0}$ are given by:[5]

$$\begin{aligned}\chi_{t-j,0}&=\eta_{t-j,0},\\&=\boldsymbol{\omega}_{t-j}-E(\boldsymbol{\omega}_{t-j}|\Omega_{t-j-1}).\end{aligned}$$

With the help of the above results the general solution given by (5.18) can now be written down explicitly in terms of the conditional expectations of $\{\boldsymbol{\omega}_t\}$. Notice again that the solution (5.18) is valid irrespective of whether $\{\boldsymbol{\omega}_t\}$ is stationary or not.

The above solution has the important property that it will always contain a moving-average error component of order $s-1$, even if $\{\boldsymbol{\omega}_t\}$ is a serially uncorrelated process. To see this suppose that $\{\boldsymbol{\omega}_t\}$ is a white-noise process. Then

$$\begin{aligned}\eta_{ti}&=\boldsymbol{\omega}_t, &&\text{for } i=0,\\&=0, &&\text{for } i>0,\end{aligned}$$

and the recursive relations in (5.20) simplifies to $\chi_{tj}=F_{j1}\chi_{t-j,0}$. But $\chi_{t-j,0}=\eta_{t-j,0}$, hence

$$\begin{aligned}\chi_{tj}&=F_{j1}\eta_{t-j,0},\\&=F_{j1}\boldsymbol{\omega}_{t-j}. \quad j=1,2,\ldots\end{aligned}$$

Using these results in (5.19) now yields

$$\mathbf{z}_t=H_s\mathbf{z}_{t-1}+\boldsymbol{\omega}_t+\sum_{j=1}^{s-1}(F_{j1}-H_sF_{j-1,1})\boldsymbol{\omega}_{t-j}.$$

---

[5] Notice that by definition

$$\chi_{t-j,0}=\mathbf{z}_{t-j}-E(\mathbf{z}_{t-j}|\Omega_{t-j-1}),$$

and using (5.2′) we have

$$\mathbf{z}_{t-j}-E(\mathbf{z}_{t-j}|\Omega_{t-j-1})=\boldsymbol{\omega}_{t-j}-E(\boldsymbol{\omega}_{t-j}|\Omega_{t-j-1}).$$

or

$$\mathbf{z}_t = H_s \mathbf{z}_{t-1} + \boldsymbol{\omega}_t + \sum_{j=1}^{s-1} (H_j - H_s) F_{j-1,1} \boldsymbol{\omega}_{t-j}, \quad s \geqslant 1, \tag{5.21}$$

which establishes that the solution (5.18) contains a moving-average component of order $s-1$ even if $\{\boldsymbol{\omega}_t\}$ is a white-noise process. The presence of a moving-average component in the solution is, however, primarily due to the fact that the RE equation under consideration contains lagged values of the exogenous variable. As shown in section 5.2.1, the moving-average component disappears if the equation contains no lagged values of the endogenous variable, but there will always be a moving-average error component whenever $s > 1$ and $\Lambda \neq 0$.

Example 5.1 Lucas's Surprise Supply Function

A simple example of equation (5.2) arises in the 'new classical' macroeconomics. The aggregate supply function, Lucas's so-called surprise supply function, in its general form, is specified by

$$y_t^s - \bar{y}_t = \sum_{i=1}^{m} \mu_i (y_{t-i} - \bar{y}_{t-i}) + \gamma \{p_t - E(p_t | \Omega_{t-1})\} + \varepsilon_{ty}, \quad \gamma > 0, \tag{5.22}$$

where y_t^s is the logarithm of aggregate supply, y_t and $\bar{y}_t$ are the market clearing level of output and its 'natural' level (in logarithm) at time t, and p_t is the logarithm of the general level of prices. The disturbance term ε_{ty} is assumed to be a white-noise process. The aggregate demand function is usually specified using an IS–LM framework. A particularly simple formulation of the aggregate demand function is given by the following quantity theory equation written in a logarithmic form.

$$y_t^d + p_t = v_t + m_t, \tag{5.23}$$

where y_t^d is the logarithm of aggregate demand, and m_t and v_t are the logarithms of the money supply and its circulation velocity. An important feature of the new classical model is the assumption that markets clear instantaneously. That is

$$y_t^d = y_t^s = y_t. \tag{5.24}$$

Other major assumptions of the new classical approach are that processes generating m_t and v_t are exogenous to the determination of output and prices, and that the natural level of output $\bar{y}_t$ is exogenously given and is known to agents at time $t-1$, {i.e. $E(\bar{y}_t | \Omega_{t-1}) = \bar{y}_t$}. These assumptions are clearly restrictive, and are discussed in Pesaran (1984a), where a critical account of the new classical theories and propositions can be found. But here we adopt them in order to show how the solution techniques of this section can be applied to concrete problems that are encountered in the literature.

Suppose m_t and v_t are generated according to the following general feedback rules

$$m_t = \sum_{i=1}^{a} a_i m_{t-i} + \sum_{i=1}^{b} b_i \tilde{y}_{t-i} + \varepsilon_{tm}, \tag{5.25}$$

$$v_t = \sum_{i=1}^{c} c_i m_{t-i} + \sum_{i=1}^{d} d_i \tilde{y}_{t-i} + \varepsilon_{tv}, \tag{5.26}$$

where $\tilde{y}_t = y_t - \bar{y}_t$, and $\{\varepsilon_{tm}\}$ and $\{\varepsilon_{tv}\}$ are white-noise processes. The system of equations given by (5.22)–(5.26) can now be reduced to an equation of type (5.2). Using (5.24) and (5.23) in (5.22), and noting from (5.25) and (5.26) that

$$m_t - E(m_t | \Omega_{t-1}) = \varepsilon_{tm}, \text{ and } v_t - E(v_t | \Omega_{t-1}) = \varepsilon_{tv},$$

we obtain:[6]

$$\tilde{y}_t = \sum_{i=1}^{m} \lambda_i \tilde{y}_{t-i} + \beta E(\tilde{y}_t | \Omega_{t-1}) + \omega_t,$$

where

$$\tilde{y}_t = y_t - \bar{y}_t,$$
$$\omega_t = \beta(\varepsilon_{tm} + \varepsilon_{tv}) + (1+\gamma)^{-1}\varepsilon_{ty},$$
$$\beta = (1+\gamma)^{-1}\gamma,$$

and

$$\lambda_i = (1+\gamma)^{-1}\mu_i, \quad i = 1, 2, \ldots, m.$$

Since $\{\omega_t\}$ in this example is composed of white-noise processes $\{\varepsilon_{tm}\}$, $\{\varepsilon_{tv}\}$, and $\{\varepsilon_{ty}\}$, the solution (5.21) with $s=1$ is directly applicable. The unique solution for $\tilde{y}_t$ is given by:[7]

$$\tilde{y}_t = (1-\beta)^{-1} \sum_{i=1}^{m} \lambda_i \tilde{y}_{t-i} + \omega_t,$$

or in more detail

$$\tilde{y}_t = \sum_{i=1}^{m} \mu_i \tilde{y}_{t-i} + (1+\gamma)^{-1}\gamma(\varepsilon_{tm} + \varepsilon_{tv}) + (1+\gamma)^{-1}\varepsilon_{ty}. \tag{5.27}$$

Therefore in the new classical model the deviation of (equilibrium) level of output from its ‘natural’ level follows an autoregressive scheme and is only affected by *unanticipated* changes in the quantity of money and the velocity of

---

[6] Notice that by assumption Ω_{t-1} also includes information on $\bar{y}_t$.
[7] Notice that $\beta \neq 1$ for all finite values of γ.

its circulation. In most empirical tests of this proposition, it is assumed that $\varepsilon_{tv} = 0$, and therefore it is argued that only the unanticipated component of the quantity of money has any influence on the level of output and employment. This assumption is, however, unlikely to be valid in practice. Even if the velocity of circulation is constant in the 'long run' there is no reason to believe that its short-run movements can be predicted perfectly by economic agents.

5.3 Solution of LRE Models with Future Expectations

There now exists a sizeable literature on the solution of LRE models containing future expectations of the endogenous variables, where different solution techniques have been adopted by different authors. Broadly speaking the solution techniques proposed can be grouped into five categories:

1 *The method of undetermined coefficients*. This method was first introduced by Muth (1961) and has since been used extensively by many investigators including Lucas (1972b, 1973), Taylor (1977), Blanchard (1979), and McCallum (1983). This solution method is most suitable in situations where an infinite moving-average representation or an autoregressive representation of the solution is desired. As will be shown shortly, this method suffers from the major shortcoming that it often leads one to overlook a large class of possible solutions.

2 *The operator or the z-transform method*. This is a variant of the method of undetermined coefficients and utilizes the polynomial operator technique familiar in the study of ordinary difference equations. This solution technique has been used for example by Shiller (1978), and Sargent (1979a). A detailed account of this solution method is given by Whiteman (1983).

3 *The forward recursive substitution method*. This procedure was first employed by Sargent and Wallace (1973) and provides a solution of the RE equation recursively in terms of future expected values of the exogenous processes, and the expected terminal value of the endogenous variable formed conditional on the available information set Ω_t. This method is similar to the backward recursive procedure used in solving difference equations. Wallis (1980), and Revankar (1980), also employ this method to obtain their solutions.

4 *The martingale method*. This solution method has been proposed by Gourieroux et al. (1982) and Pesaran (1981), and allows a general characterization of all the solutions in terms of martingales.[8]

5 *The martingale difference method*. This method is a variant of the martingale approach and has been recently proposed by Broze et al. (1985) as

[8] Process $\mathcal{M}_t$ is said to be a 'martingale' with respect to the increasing sequence of information sets Ω_t if its mean exists and if it has the property that $E(\mathcal{M}_t | \Omega_{t-1}) = \mathcal{M}_{t-1}$. A random walk is a simple example of such a process. See appendix A for further details.

a general approach to the solution of LRE models. The basic idea behind this method is the representation of the general solution of the RE equation in terms of revision processes that appear in the procedure for updating expectations.

5.3.1 Cagan's Hyper-inflation Model–the First-order Case

Before dealing with the general problem of the characterization of all the possible solutions of LRE models with future expectations we shall first demonstrate the above five solution strategies by applying them to Cagan's (1956) familar hyper-inflation model. The demand for money in Cagan's model is given by

$$m_t - p_t = \gamma\{E(p_{t+1}|\Omega_t) - p_t\},$$

where p_t is the logarithm of the price level at time t, m_t is the logarithm of the money stock, and Ω_t is the information set available at time t. In this model it is assumed that money markets clear instantaneously and that the process generating the stock of money is given exogenously. The above equation can also be written as

$$y_t = \alpha E(y_{t+1}|\Omega_t) + \omega_t, \tag{5.28}$$

where $\alpha = \gamma/(\gamma - 1)$, $y_t = p_t$, and $\omega_t = -m_t/(\gamma - 1)$. Equation (5.28) is the first-order case of the general specification (5.3), and can be obtained from it by setting $m = 0$, and $s = 1$. In order to allow for the possibility of multiple solutions, we do not impose any *a priori* restrictions on the sign of γ.

The Method of Undetermined Coefficients

To apply this method a conjecture about the general form of the solution of (5.28) is needed. One possible solution form, frequently employed in the literature, is the (backward) infinite moving-average representation:

$$y_{tB} = \sum_{i=1}^{\infty} d_i \omega_{t-i}. \tag{5.29}$$

The method of undetermined coefficients then involves obtaining the unknown coefficients d_i in such a way that y_{tB} verifies equation (5.28) as a solution. Leading equation (5.29) once and taking expectations on both sides with respect to the information set Ω_t we have

$$E(y_{t+1,B}|\Omega_t) = d_1\omega_t + \sum_{i=1}^{\infty} d_{i+1}\omega_{t-i}. \tag{5.30}$$

Replacing (5.30) and (5.29) in (5.28), and collecting terms now yields

$$(\alpha d_1 + 1)\omega_t + \sum_{i=1}^{\infty}(d_i - \alpha d_{i+1})\omega_{t-i} = 0.$$

Therefore for y_{tB} to be a solution of (5.28) we should have

$$d_{i+1} = \alpha^{-1} d_i, \quad i = 1, 2, \ldots$$

with the initial value $d_1 = -\alpha^{-1}$. This is a simple first-order difference equation with the unique solution

$$d_i = -\alpha^{-i}, \quad i = 1, 2, \ldots$$

Using this result in (5.29) gives the so-called *backward solution*

$$y_{tB} = -\sum_{i=1}^{\infty} \alpha^{-i} \omega_{t-i}, \tag{5.31}$$

which is based solely on past values of ω_t (or the money stock).[9]

The backward solution is not, however, the only solution of (5.28). An alternative solution can be obtained by making the reasonable conjecture that the price depends on current and expected future values of the money stock. The general form of this solution, often referred to as the *forward solution*, can be written as

$$y_{tF} = \sum_{i=0}^{\infty} c_i E(\omega_{t+i} | \Omega_t). \tag{5.32}$$

As before we have

$$E(y_{t+1,F} | \Omega_t) = E\left(\sum_{i=0}^{\infty} c_i E(\omega_{t+i+1} | \Omega_{t+1}) | \Omega_t \right),$$

which by the law of iterated conditional expectations (see property P4 in appendix A) simplifies to

$$E(y_{t+1,F} | \Omega_t) = \sum_{i=0}^{\infty} c_i E(\omega_{t+i+1} | \Omega_t).$$

Hence, for (5.32) to be a solution of (5.28) we should have

$$c_i = \alpha c_{i-1}, \quad i = 1, 2, \ldots$$

with $c_0 = 1$. The specific form of the forward solution will then be

$$y_{tF} = \sum_{i=0}^{\infty} \alpha^i E(\omega_{t+i} | \Omega_t). \tag{5.33}$$

Other solutions can also be obtained by adopting different conjectures about the general solution form of (5.28). In fact, as will be seen shortly, equation (5.28) admits an infinite number of solutions. Clearly by its very nature the

---

[9] Here we are assuming that the infinite sum in (5.31) converges. The conditions necessary for the convergence of the sum clearly depend on the magnitude of α and the nature of the process generating ω_t.

method of undetermined coefficients, being based on a conjecture, may fail to reveal all the possible solutions of the LRE equations with future expectations.

The Operator or the z-Transform Method

We now turn to the application of the operator method to equation (5.28). This method, explained in detail by Whiteman (1983), seeks a *linear* solution in the case where $\{\omega_t\}$ is a univariate, zero-mean covariance stationary process with the infinite moving-average representation

$$\omega_t = \sum_{i=0}^{\infty} f_i \varepsilon_{t-i} = \left(\sum_{i=0}^{\infty} f_i L^i\right) \varepsilon_t = F(L)\varepsilon_t, \tag{5.34}$$

where $\Sigma_{i=0}^{\infty} f_i^2 < \infty$, and $\varepsilon_t = \omega_t - E(\omega_t | \Omega_{t-1})$ are the innovations of the $\{\omega_t\}$ process. The function $F(z)$ must be analytic on the unit circle ($|z| < 1$), and L stands for the lag operator ($L^j \varepsilon_t = \varepsilon_{t-j}$). The solution form considered in this approach is

$$y_t = \sum_{i=0}^{\infty} g_i \varepsilon_{t-i} = \left(\sum_{i=0}^{\infty} g_i L^i\right) \varepsilon_t = G(L)\varepsilon_t, \tag{5.35}$$

where again it is assumed that $\Sigma_{i=0}^{\infty} g_i^2 < \infty$, and $G(z)$ is analytic on the unit circle.[10] The solution strategy is to obtain the operator function $G(z)$ in terms of $F(z)$ and the parameters of the RE equation. As before, leading equation (5.35) once, and taking conditional expectations with respect to Ω_t gives[11]

$$\begin{aligned} E(y_{t+1} | \Omega_t) &= g_1 \varepsilon_t + g_2 \varepsilon_{t-1} + \ldots, \\ &= L^{-1}(g_1 \varepsilon_{t-1} + g_2 \varepsilon_{t-2} + \ldots), \\ &= L^{-1}\{G(L) - g_0\} \varepsilon_t, \end{aligned} \tag{5.36}$$

Substituting relations (5.34)–(5.36) in (5.28) now yields

$$G(L)\varepsilon_t = \alpha\{G(L) - g_0\} L^{-1} \varepsilon_t + F(L)\varepsilon_t,$$

or in terms of z-transforms

$$(1 - \alpha z^{-1}) G(z) = F(z) - \alpha g_0 z^{-1}. \tag{5.37}$$

In general the solution of $G(z)$ is not unique and depends on the unknown parameter g_0. But given the *a priori* restrictions that the functions $G(z)$ and $F(z)$ must be analytic on the unit circle, the value of g_0 can be determined when $|\alpha| < 1$. Under this case, for $G(z)$ to be analytic on $|z| < 1$, the residue of $G(z)$ at α should be zero.[12] That is we should have

$$\lim_{z \to \alpha} (1 - \alpha z^{-1}) G(z) = \lim_{z \to \alpha} \{F(z) - \alpha g_0 z^{-1}\} = 0,$$

---

[10] The functions $F(z)$ and $G(z)$ are viewed as functions of the complex variable z.
[11] Notice that by assumption $E(\varepsilon_{t+1} | \Omega_t) = 0$, and $E(\varepsilon_{t-i} | \Omega_t) = \varepsilon_{t-i}$, for $i \geqslant 0$.
[12] See, for example, Ahlfors (1966, chapter 4).

which gives $g_0 = F(\alpha)$. Therefore, when $|\alpha| < 1$, the unique linear stationary solution of (5.28) will be

$$y_t = \left(\frac{LF(L) - \alpha F(\alpha)}{L - \alpha} \right) \varepsilon_t, \quad |\alpha| < 1. \tag{5.38a}$$

In the case where $|\alpha| \geqslant 1$, the function $G(z)$ is analytic for all values of g_0 and hence the requirement that $G(z)$ and $F(z)$ should be analytic does not lead to a particular value for g_0. In other words under $|\alpha| \geqslant 1$, equation (5.28) has a large number of linear stationary solutions, indexed by the parameter g_0, and given by

$$y_t = \left(\frac{g_0 - \alpha^{-1} LF(L)}{1 - \alpha^{-1} L} \right) \varepsilon_t, |\alpha| \geqslant 1. \tag{5.38b}$$

In the case where $|\alpha^{-1}| < 1$ the above solution can also be written as

$$y_t = \alpha^{-1} y_{t-1} - \alpha^{-1} \omega_{t-1} + g_0 \varepsilon_t, \tag{5.38b$'$}$$

or,

$$y_t = \alpha^{-1} y_{t-1} - \alpha^{-1} \omega_{t-1} + g_0 \{\omega_t - E(\omega_t | \Omega_{t-1})\}. \tag{5.38b$''$}$$

This last solution form is particularly convenient for estimation purposes.

The Forward Recursive Substitution Method

The application of the 'forward recursive substitution method' to equation (5.28) proceeds along the following lines. Rewriting (5.28) for $t+1$, and then taking expectations conditional on Ω_t yields

$$E(y_{t+1} | \Omega_t) = \alpha E\{E(y_{t+2} | \Omega_{t+1}) | \Omega_t\} + E(\omega_{t+1} | \Omega_t).$$

However, since Ω_t is a non-decreasing set, using the property P4 in appendix A we have

$$E\{E(y_{t+2} | \Omega_{t+1}) | \Omega_t\} = E(y_{t+2} | \Omega_t),$$

and

$$E(y_{t+1} | \Omega_t) = \alpha E(y_{t+2} | \Omega_t) + E(\omega_{t+1} | \Omega_t).$$

Substituting this result for $E(y_{t+1} | \Omega_t)$ in (5.28) now yields

$$y_t = \alpha^2 E(y_{t+2} | \Omega_t) + \omega_t + \alpha E(\omega_{t+1} | \Omega_t).$$

Repeating the above process for $t+2, t+3, \ldots$ and recursively using the results to eliminate $E(y_{t+2} | \Omega_t)$, $E(y_{t+3} | \Omega_t)$, and so on we finally obtain

$$y_t = \alpha^N E(y_{t+N} | \Omega_t) + \sum_{i=0}^{N-1} \alpha^i E(\omega_{t+i} | \Omega_t). \tag{5.39}$$

This expression for y_t can be regarded as a unique solution of (5.28) if the terminal conditional expectations $E(y_{t+N} | \Omega_t)$ is known for some $N > 0$. This solution procedure in effect requires one to start from a known point in the future and then to work backwards to the present. But expectations about the future, unlike observations about the past, are rarely given, and (5.39) can be regarded as a solution of (5.28) if the terminal solution $E(y_{t+N}|\Omega_t)$ turns out to have no influence on the current value of y_t. This can happen if $|\alpha|<1$. Under this parametric restriction, if we are prepared to assume that y_t will grow slowly enough so that $\alpha^N E(y_{t+N}|\Omega_t)$ approaches zero as N tends to infinity, then the forward recursive substitution method yields the forward solution y_{tF} given by (5.33). The condition

$$\lim_{N\to\infty} \alpha^N E(y_{t+N}|\Omega_t)=0, \tag{5.40}$$

in an optimization context is often referred to as the 'transversality condition'. Clearly, the assumption that y_t will not explode too fast in the future may not be appropriate. What is important, however, is to note that a unique rational expectations solution for (5.28) does not seem possible unless some *a priori* assumption concerning the *future* course of y_t is made.

The Martingale Method

The nature of multiplicity of solutions of (5.28) can be more fully explored by the martingale method. As is shown in appendix C, a general solution of (5.28) which is valid for *all* $\{\omega_t\}$ processes and *all* non-zero values of α may be written as:[13]

$$y_t=\alpha^{-t}\mathscr{M}_t-\sum_{i=1}^{t-1}\alpha^{-i}\omega_{t-i}, \quad \text{for } t\geqslant 1 \tag{5.41}$$

where $\{\mathscr{M}_t\}$ represents an arbitrary martingale process, i.e. $E(\mathscr{M}_t|\Omega_{t-1})=\mathscr{M}_{t-1}$. In the first instance the above solution appears to be very different from the solutions obtained above. This is, however, solely due to the presence of the martingale process $\{\mathscr{M}_t\}$ in the solution. As there are an infinite number of stochastic processes that have a martingale representation, the solution (5.41) is not unique and can be used to generate a large number of apparently different, but basically equivalent, solutions of equation (5.28). It is indeed possible to write (5.41) in many different ways. Assuming that the mathematical expectations of the infinite sum $\Sigma_{i=1}^{\infty}\alpha^i\omega_i$ conditional on the information available at time t exist,[14] then $\{\mathscr{F}_t\}$ defined as

$$\mathscr{F}_t=\mathscr{M}_t-E\left(\sum_{i=1}^{\infty}\alpha^i\omega_i|\Omega_t\right), \tag{5.42}$$

will also be a martingale process. This is because

[13] For $\alpha=0$, the solution of (5.28) is trivially given by $y_t=\omega_t$.

[14] The existence of $\Sigma_{i=1}^{\infty}\alpha^i E(\omega_i|\Omega_t)$ is ensured if $|\alpha|<1$, and $\{\omega_t\}$ is stationary, although neither of these two conditions are necessary.

$$E(\mathscr{F}_{t+1}|\Omega_t)=E(\mathscr{M}_{t+1}|\Omega_t)-E\left(\sum_{i=1}^{\infty}\alpha^i E(\omega_i|\Omega_{t+1})|\Omega_t\right),$$

$$=\mathscr{M}_t-\sum_{i=1}^{\infty}\alpha^i E\{E(\omega_i|\Omega_{t+1})|\Omega_t\},$$

$$=\mathscr{M}_t-\sum_{i=1}^{\infty}\alpha^i E(\omega_i|\Omega_t),$$

$$=\mathscr{F}_t.$$

If we now substitute $\mathscr{M}_t$ from (5.42) in (5.41) we obtain

$$y_t=\alpha^{-t}\mathscr{F}_t+\sum_{i=0}^{\infty}\alpha^i E(\omega_{t+i}|\Omega_t), \quad \text{for } t\geqslant 1, \tag{5.43}$$

or

$$y_t=\alpha^{-t}\mathscr{F}_t+y_{tF}.$$

Therefore, apart from the martingale component $\mathscr{F}_t$, this gives the forward solution y_{tF} defined by (5.33), and exists if and only if

$$E\left(\sum_{i=1}^{\infty}\alpha^i\omega_i|\Omega_t\right)$$

exists. But we should not overlook the fact that the results (5.41) and (5.43) are different ways of writing down the same general solution.

The backward solution y_{tB} defined by (5.31) can also be obtained from (5.41) if the infinite sum $\Sigma_{i=0}^{\infty}\alpha^{-i}\omega_{-i}$ exists. Let

$$\mathscr{B}_t=\mathscr{M}_t+\sum_{i=1}^{\infty}\alpha^{-i}\omega_{-i}.$$

Then it is easily seen that $\mathscr{B}_t$ is also a martingale. Using this result, solution (5.41) can alternatively be written as

$$y_t=\alpha^{-t}\mathscr{B}_t-\sum_{i=1}^{\infty}\alpha^{-i}\omega_{t-i}, \quad t\geqslant 1, \tag{5.44}$$

or

$$y_t=\alpha^{-t}\mathscr{B}_t+y_{tB}.$$

In short the forward and the backward solutions obtained by the method of undetermined coefficients are special cases of the general solution (5.41) and exist if certain infinite sums converge.

In general it is easy to show that when y_t^0 is a solution of (5.28) so will $y_t^1=y_t^0+\alpha^{-t}\mathscr{M}_t$, where $\mathscr{M}_t$ is a martingale process. Starting with the first expression in the right-hand side of (5.28) we have

$$\alpha E(y^1_{t+1} \mid \Omega_t) = \alpha E(y^0_{t+1} + \alpha^{-t-1}\mathcal{M}_{t+1} \mid \Omega_t),$$
$$= \alpha E(y^0_{t+1} \mid \Omega_t) + \alpha^{-t} E(\mathcal{M}_{t+1} \mid \Omega_t),$$

and since $\mathcal{M}_t$ is a martingale process then

$$\alpha E(y^1_{t+1} \mid \Omega_t) = \alpha E(y^0_{t+1} \mid \Omega_t) + \alpha^{-t}\mathcal{M}_t.$$

But since y^0_t is a solution of (5.28) it also follows that

$$\alpha E(y^1_{t+1} \mid \Omega_t) = y^0_t - \omega_t + \alpha^{-t}\mathcal{M}_t,$$
$$= y^1_t - \omega_t.$$

Thus

$$y^1_t = \alpha E(y^1_{t+1} \mid \Omega_t) + \omega_t,$$

which establishes that y^1_t will also be a solution of (5.28). In fact for any particular solution y^0_t, the general solution of (5.28) can be written as $y^0_t + \alpha^{-t}\mathcal{M}_t$. Despite the apparent similarity that exists between this solution and the general solution of ordinary difference equations, in the case of RE models the knowledge of past history of y_t and ω_t is not sufficient for the determination of the martingale process that enters the solution. Some knowledge of the value of y_t or its trajectory in the future is needed.

The Martingale Difference Method

We now finally come to the martingale difference method recently proposed by Broze et al. (1985). The basis of this method is the revision processes that enter the updating of expectations from one period to the next. These authors consider successive expectations of the variable y_{t+j} formed at time $t-1$ and t. They refer to the difference $E(y_{t+j} | \Omega_t) - E(y_{t+j} | \Omega_{t-1})$ as the revision error in the expectations of y_{t+j} between $t-1$ and t. Denoting this revision in expectations by ε^j_t, it is easily seen that ε^j_t has a zero mean and is orthogonal to all past information:

$$E(\varepsilon^j_t | \Omega_{t-i}) = E\{[E(y_{t+j} | \Omega_t) - E(y_{t+j} | \Omega_{t-1})] | \Omega_{t-i}\},$$
$$= E(y_{t+j} | \Omega_{t-i}) - E(y_{t+j} | \Omega_{t-i}) = 0, \quad \text{for } j \geqslant 0, \text{ and } i > 0.$$

It follows, therefore, that $\{\varepsilon^j_t\}$ is a martingale difference process.[15] To obtain a solution of (5.28) by the martingale difference method, first note that

$$\varepsilon^0_{t+1} = y_{t+1} - E(y_{t+1} \mid \Omega_t).$$

Now substituting $E(y_{t+1} \mid \Omega_t)$ from the above relation in (5.28), the general solution results

$$y_t = \alpha(y_{t+1} - \varepsilon^0_{t+1}) + \omega_t,$$

---

[15] Suppose that $\mathcal{M}_t$ is a martingale process, then $\mathcal{M}_t - \mathcal{M}_{t-1}$ is a martingale difference process.

which can also be written equivalently as

$$y_t = \alpha^{-1} y_{t-1} - \alpha^{-1} \omega_{t-1} + \varepsilon_t^0. \tag{5.45}$$

To see the relationship that exists between this solution and the solution (5.41) obtained by the martingale method, write (5.41) as

$$\mathscr{M}_t = \alpha^t y_t + \alpha^t \sum_{i=1}^{t-1} \alpha^{-i} \omega_{t-i}.$$

Subtracting this relation from the same relation for $t-1$, now yields

$$y_t = \alpha^{-1} y_{t-1} - \alpha^{-1} \omega_{t-1} + \alpha^{-t} \Delta \mathscr{M}_t. \tag{5.46}$$

The exact equivalence of the solutions (5.41) and (5.45) now readily follows from the fact that if $\Delta \mathscr{M}_t$ is a martingale difference process so will $\alpha^{-t} \Delta \mathscr{M}_t$.

The above solutions, which represent different ways of expressing the same mathematical formula, clearly highlight the fact that in models with future expectations of the endogenous variable the REH generally does not yield a unique answer to the problem of how expectations are actually formed.

5.3.2 *The Non-uniqueness Problem*

The problem of non-uniqueness of the solution of the LRE models with future expectations of the endogenous variable has attracted a great deal of attention in the literature. Some authors have suggested that this non-uniqueness problem represents a fundamental indeterminacy in modelling of rational expectations, while others have dismissed it as 'empirically irrelevant', and which can be disposed of by 'deeper theorizing'. Here we argue that in general 'deeper theorizing' does not resolve the non-uniqueness problem, and the application of the REH to models with future expectations inevitably involves making further *a priori*, often non-testable, restrictions.

The problem of how to select a solution from the infinite set of solutions available in the case of the LRE models with future expectations has been discussed by Taylor (1977), Gourieroux et al. (1982), McCallum (1983), and Evans (1985). These authors consider alternative selection criteria, although none provide a satisfactory account of the economic rationale that may lie behind the particular selection criteria that they advocate. These selection criteria can be grouped into the following categories:[16]

1 economic optimality,
2 stationarity (boundedness in mean),
3 minimum variance,
4 minimal use of state variables.

We shall briefly review these selection criteria and comment on their appropriateness.

---

[16] Recently, Evans (1986) has also proposed a selection criterion based on the concept of 'expectational stability'.

Criterion of Economic Optimality
The criterion of economic optimality can be invoked when the RE equation is derived as a necessary condition for the solution of an optimization problem faced by economic agents. In a large number of cases where the RE equation under consideration is a part of a 'macroeconomic' model and the underlying optimization problems for individual agents are not specified, the criterion of economic optimality for selecting a unique solution cannot be applied. Even in situations where the underlying optimization problems are fully specified, the criterion of economic optimality leads to a unique solution only when agents have infinite planning horizons. In these circumstances the 'transversality conditions' associated with the optimization problems usually give the terminal conditions needed for the determination of a unique non-explosive solution. However, appeal to economic optimization cannot resolve the non-uniqueness problem when agents have finite planning horizons. A prominent example of this case is the overlapping generations models discussed for example in Blanchard (1979). Furthermore, in examples of economic optimization where information across agents is not homogeneous, it is difficult to imagine that all the economic agents will necessarily choose the same solution amongst the many solutions available to them. In these situations one needs to augment the REH with strong common knowledge assumptions about the selection criterion chosen by agents in the economy. This, however, requires a kind of collective rationality on the part of agents, which does not seem to be compatible with the neoclassical individualistic formulation of the REH.

Criterion of Stationarity
In situations where $\{\omega_t\}$ is stationary, one reasonable selection criterion would be to consider only stationary solutions of (5.28). The extent to which the use of this selection criterion narrows down the set of feasible solutions is analysed in Gourieroux et al. (1982). They show that the criterion of stationarity, or the less demanding criterion of boundedness in mean, when applied to equation (5.28) yields a unique stationary solution only when $|\alpha|<1$. A proof of this uniqueness property can be obtained along the following lines. Suppose y_t^0 and y_t^1 are two distinct solutions of (5.28) that are bounded in mean. We show that this is not possible if $|\alpha|<1$. Since y_t^0 and y_t^1 are both solutions of (5.28), then

$$x_t = y_t^0 - y_t^1 = \alpha^{-t}\mathcal{M}_t,$$

and

$$E|x_t| = |\alpha|^{-t} E|\mathcal{M}_t|. \tag{5.47}$$

But, since $\mathcal{M}_t$ is a martingale, by property P8 in appendix A, we have $E|\mathcal{M}_t| \leqslant E|\mathcal{M}_{t+1}| \leqslant E|\mathcal{M}_{t+2}| \leqslant \dots$ Therefore, with $|\alpha|<1$, the right-hand side of (5.47) will increase without bound as t increases, which contradicts the premise that y_t^0 and y_t^1 are both bounded in mean. The only choice of $\mathcal{M}_t$ for which $E|x_t|$ is bounded is $\mathcal{M}_t=0$, almost surely for all t. But this implies that $y_t^0 = y_t^1$, almost surely.

Consider now the case where $|\alpha|>1$, and suppose that y_t^0 is a solution bounded in mean. Then it is easily seen that there will be an infinite number of such solutions. Take the example where $\{\omega_t\}$ is a white-noise process. Since $|\alpha|>1$, the backward solution y_{tB} given by (5.31) exists and is stationary. But $y_{tF}=\omega_t$ is also a stationary solution of (5.28), and any convex linear combinations of y_{tB} and y_{tF} will also be a stationary solution of (5.28). The fact that the stationarity criterion does not lead to a unique solution when $|\alpha|>1$, is also apparent from the dependence of the general linear stationary solution (5.38b) on the arbitrary parameter g_0.

Notice that this multiplicity of the stationary solutions discussed above in the case of $|\alpha|>1$ is not due to 'bubbles' or 'boot-strap' effects, and arise even if these effects are ruled out. The 'speculative bubble' phenomenon occurs if the expectation of its occurrence ensures that it will in fact occur. For example, suppose $\{u_t\}$ is an arbitrary white-noise process distinct from $\{\omega_t\}$ whose current and past realizations are included in the information set Ω_t. Then it is easily verified that when $|\alpha|>1$, and $\{\omega_t\}$ is a white-noise process

$$y_t=\mu_1 y_{tB}+(1-\mu_1)\omega_t+\mu_2\sum_{i=0}^{\infty}\alpha^{-i}u_{t-i}, \tag{5.48}$$

is also a stationary solution of (5.28) for $0\leqslant\mu_1\leqslant 1$, and for all values of μ_2. The 'speculative bubble' effect in this solution is given by

$$\sum_{i=0}^{\infty}\alpha^{-i}u_{t-i},$$

and occurs in the solution because it is expected to occur! Excluding speculative bubbles, i.e. setting $\mu_2=0$ in the above solution, substantially restricts the sets of possible stationary solutions of (5.28), but does not resolve the non-uniqueness problem. There still remains a large number of linear stationary solutions, corresponding to different values of μ_1, from which to choose.

The stationarity criterion, therefore, leads to a unique solution only under $|\alpha|<1$. In this case, not surprisingly, all the five solution methods discussed above lead to the same unique stationary solution, given by the forward solution. In situations where $\{\omega_t\}$ is a mean-zero stationary process with an infinite moving-average representation, the forward solution y_{tF} can also be written as (5.38a), the unique stationary solution obtained by the z-transform method. (A simple proof of this result can be found in appendix D.)

Minimum Variance Criterion

Since the imposition of the stationary criterion does not lead to a unique solution when $|\alpha|>1$, a number of authors have considered more stringent selection criteria. In particular Taylor (1977) has suggested choosing the solution with the minimum variance.[17] The argument advanced in support of

[17] A related selection principle is discussed in Gourieroux et al. (1982), where the criterion of predictive power is suggested. The minimum variance criterion is a limiting case of the predictive power criterion.

this criterion is the rather strong assumption that people prefer outcomes that are less variable, and this is 'common knowledge'. As Taylor himself points out the use of this criterion requires some kind of collective rationality on the part of the agents. The assumption that agents all choose the solution with the least variance in effect rules out the possibility of bubbles or bootstrap effects, a phenomenon which can, and does, occur in practice. (See, for example, Flood and Garber (1980).)

The application of the minimum variance criterion to the stationary solutions (5.48) is a straightforward matter. Firstly, because the extraneous variables u_t are assumed to be distributed independently of $\{\omega_t\}$, it follows that the variance of $\{y_t\}$ will attain its minimum only if $\mu_2=0$. Furthermore, since it is assumed that $\{\omega_t\}$ is a white-noise process, then $\{\omega_t\}$, and $\{y_{tB}\}$ in (5.48) will be statistically uncorrelated and we have

$$V(y_t)=\mu_1^2 V(y_{tB})+(1-\mu_1)^2 V(\omega_t),$$

where $V(\cdot)$ stands for the variance operator. The value of μ_1 which minimizes $V(y_t)$ is given by

$$\mu_1^*=\frac{V(\omega_t)}{V(\omega_t)+V(y_{tB})}.$$

But

$$V(y_{tB})=V(\omega_t)\sum_{i=1}^{\infty}\alpha^{-2i}$$

$$=\alpha^{-2}V(\omega_t)/(1-\alpha^{-2}).$$

Therefore, $\mu_1^*=1-\alpha^{-2}$, and the following unique minimum variance solution results

$$y_{tM}=(1-\alpha^{-2})\sum_{i=1}^{\infty}\alpha^{-i}\omega_{t-i}+\alpha^{-2}\omega_t,\quad |\alpha|>1. \tag{5.49}$$

Notice that when $\{\omega_t\}$ is a white-noise process the unique stationary solution under $|\alpha|<1$ is given by $y_{tF}=\omega_t$, which differs from the unique minimum variance solution y_{tM}, obtained above. Clearly, the choice between the two solutions y_{tM} and y_{tF} depends on the sign of $|\alpha|-1$.

In the case where $\{\omega_t\}$ has the general infinite moving-average representation (5.34), the set of bubble-free stationary solutions (indexed by the arbitrary parameter g_0) is given by (5.38b). Assuming that $\{\varepsilon_t\}$ is a white-noise process and using (5.35), the variance of y_t is given by

$$V(y_t)=\left(\sum_{i=0}^{\infty}g_i^2\right)\sigma_\varepsilon^2<\infty, \tag{5.50}$$

where σ_ε^2 stands for the common variance of ε_t, and g_i are the coefficients in the infinite series expansion of

$$G(L)=\frac{g_0-\alpha^{-1}LF(L)}{1-\alpha^{-1}L} \quad |\alpha|>1.$$

Post-multiplying both sides by $(1-\alpha^{-1}L)$

$$G(L)=g_0+\alpha^{-1}\{LG(L)-LF(L)\},$$

and replacing $G(L)$ and $F(L)$ by their infinite series expansion yields

$$g_i=\alpha^{-1}(g_{i-1}-f_{i-1}), \quad i=1,2,\ldots$$

where g_0 can take any arbitrary value. The solution to the above deterministic difference equation is given by

$$g_i=\alpha^{-i}g_0-\theta_i, \quad i=0,1,2,\ldots \tag{5.51}$$

where $\theta_0=0$, and

$$\theta_i=\sum_{j=0}^{i-1}\alpha^{-j-1}f_{i-j-1}, \quad i=1,2,\ldots \tag{5.52}$$

Substituting g_i from (5.51) in (5.50) now gives

$$V(y_t)=\left(\sum_{i=0}^{\infty}(\alpha^{-i}g_0-\theta_i)^2\right)\sigma_\varepsilon^2.$$

The first-order condition for the minimization of $V(y_t)$ in terms of g_0 is

$$\sum_{i=0}^{\infty}\alpha^{-i}(\alpha^{-i}g_0^*-\theta_i)=0,$$

or

$$g_0^*=(1-\alpha^{-2})\sum_{i=0}^{\infty}\alpha^{-i}\theta_i.$$

Using (5.52), and recalling that $\theta_0=0$, the expression for g_0^* can be further simplified to

$$g_0^*=\alpha^{-2}F(\alpha^{-1}), \tag{5.53}$$

which exists for $|\alpha|>1$. The unique minimum variance solution in this case is given by (5.38b″), with g_0 replaced by g_0^* given above. That is

$$y_t=\alpha^{-1}y_{t-1}-\alpha^{-1}\omega_{t-1}+\alpha^{-2}F(\alpha^{-1})\{\omega_t-E(\omega_t|\Omega_{t-1})\}. \tag{5.54}$$

In the simple case where $\{\omega_t\}$ is a white-noise process, $F(\alpha^{-1})=1$, $E(\omega_t|\Omega_{t-1})=0$, and using (5.54), the following expression for the minimum variance solution results

$$y_t=\alpha^{-1}y_{t-1}+\alpha^{-2}(\omega_t-\alpha\omega_{t-1}), \quad |\alpha|>1$$

which is a *restricted* ARMA(1,1) process, and is easily seen to be the same as the solution (5.49) already obtained for this case. The minimum variance solution (5.54) represents a general result and can be employed under a variety of specifications generating $\{\omega_t\}$. For example, when ω_t follows an AR(1) process with parameter $\rho(|\rho|<1)$, we have

$$F(\alpha^{-1})=\frac{1}{1-\alpha^{-1}\rho}, \quad |\alpha^{-1}\rho|<1,$$

$$E(\omega_t|\Omega_{t-1})=\rho\omega_{t-1},$$

and the unique stationary minimum-variance solution will be

$$y_t=\alpha^{-1}y_{t-1}+\left(\frac{\alpha^{-2}}{1-\alpha^{-1}\rho}\right)(\omega_t-\alpha\omega_{t-1}),$$

which is again a restricted ARMA(1,1) process.

The minimum variance criterion is a natural extension of the stationarity assumption and has the advantage that it involves a testable parametric restriction when $\{\omega_t\}$ is stationary, and it is known *a priori* that $|\alpha|>1$. The relevant restriction is given by (5.53), and can be tested via equations such as (5.54). Unfortunately, the uniqueness property of the above minimum variance solutions does not carry over to higher-order RE models. This is because the minimum variance criterion in effect imposes only one parametric restriction on the solutions and therefore in general will not be enough to yield a unique solution in circumstances where the stationary solutions depend on two or more arbitrary parameters.

Minimal Use of State Variables

This criterion is suggested by McCallum (1983), and considers solutions (irrespective of whether they are stationary or not) that are based on a minimal set of state or predetermined variables. The argument behind this criterion is that agents economize in the use of state variables in forming their expectations, and that this is 'common knowledge'. The application of this criterion does not, however, yield a unique solution in all cases. Consequently, McCallum has suggested supplementing this criterion by a further *ad hoc* requirement that the solution formulae should be valid for all 'admissible' parameter values. We demonstrate the McCallum solution procedure in the case of the first-order equation (5.28). We assume that

$$\omega_t=\beta x_t+u_t,$$

where u_t is a white-noise process, and $\{x_t\}$ follows the AR(2) process

$$x_t+\rho_1x_{t-1}+\rho_2x_{t-2}=v_t. \tag{5.55}$$

The minimal set of state variables for this problem is $\{u_t, x_t, x_{t-1}\}$, which defines the following general solution form

$$y_t=\pi_0u_t+\pi_1x_t+\pi_2x_{t-1}.$$

Application of the technique of undetermined coefficients to this solution form now yields

$$\pi_0 = 1,$$

$$\pi_1 = \alpha\rho_2\pi_2,$$

$$\pi_2 = (\alpha\rho_1 + \alpha^2\rho_2)\pi_2 + \beta.$$

Hence, assuming that α is not a root of the characteristic equation of the AR(2) process, we arrive at the following solution

$$y_t = u_t + \beta(1+\phi_0)^{-1}(1-\phi_1 L)x_t, \tag{5.56}$$

where:[18]

$$\phi_j = \sum_{i=j+1}^{2} \rho_i \alpha^{i-j}, \quad j=0, 1.$$

But it is easily seen that this solution is in fact the unique stationary forward solution y_{tF} given by (5.33) which exists only if $|\alpha|<1$. To see this first note that since $\{u_t\}$ is a white-noise process then

$$y_{tF} = u_t + \beta \sum_{i=0}^{\infty} \alpha^i E(x_{t+i}|\Omega_t), \quad |\alpha|<1.$$

Using result (D.7) in appendix D we have

$$\sum_{i=0}^{\infty} \alpha^i E(x_{t+i}|\Omega_t) = (1+\phi_0)^{-1}(1-\phi_1 L)x_t,$$

which establishes the equivalence of y_{tF} and the minimal-state-variable solution (5.56), when $|\alpha|<1$. The exact equivalence of the minimum-state-variable solution and the forward solution when $|\alpha|<1$ is hardly surprising, and follows directly from the fact that in this case equation (5.28) has a unique stationary solution. McCallum, however, argues that solution (5.56) is still appropriate even when $|\alpha|>1$. Whether (5.56) is a meaningful solution under $|\alpha|>1$ is, however, debatable. For example, consider the case where $\omega_t = \beta x_t$, $(\beta>0)$, and $x_t = \rho x_{t-1} + v_t$, $(\rho>0)$. Then the minimum-state-variable solution of (5.28) is given by $y_t = \{\beta/(1-\alpha\rho)\}x_t$. When $\alpha>1$ this solution can clearly result in $y_t<0$ for all t, even when the exogenous input, βx_t in (5.28), exerts a positive influence on y_t. The fact that $y_t = \{\beta/(1-\alpha\rho)\}x_t$ verifies (5.28) does not necessarily mean that it provides a meaningful solution of (5.28). This point can be more readily seen in the context of ordinary difference equations. Consider the first-order difference equation

$$y_t = \lambda y_{t-1} + \kappa,$$

---

[18] See also result D.8 in appendix D.

where $\lambda > 1$, and $\kappa > 0$. It is well known that for $\lambda > 1$ the above difference equation does not have a *stable* solution, although it is not difficult to show that $y_t = \kappa/(1-\lambda)$, still verifies it. When $\lambda > 1$ the solution $y_t = \kappa/(1-\lambda)$ is not meaningful. Similarly, the fact that there exists a unique minimum-state-variable solution that satisfies (5.28) does not mean that this is a meaningful or a sensible solution when $|\alpha| > 1$.

Another difficulty surrounding the use of selection criteria such as the minimal-state-variable criterion, or the minimum variance criterion, lies in the fact that in general they lead to different, albeit *a priori* plausible, solutions. This poses a further problem for the application of the REH to models with future expectations. Which one of these two solutions should be chosen? Evidently, the REH on its own does not yield a complete specification of the expectations formation process, and has to be complemented with strong 'common knowledge' assumptions about the choice of a selection criteria for obtaining a unique solution.

Example 5.2 Taylor's Macroeconomic Model

Here we consider the application of the martingale method to the macroeconomic model discussed by Taylor (1977). As argued above, the main advantage of the martingale method lies in the fact that it gives a general characterization of all the solutions of the model. Taylor considers a simple stochastic macroeconomic model composed of the aggregate demand function

$$y_t = -\gamma_1\{r_t - E(P_{t+1} - P_t \mid \Omega_{t-1})\} + \gamma_2(m_t - P_t) + \varepsilon_{1t}, \quad \gamma_1, \gamma_2 > 0$$

depending negatively on the real rate of interest, $r_t - E(P_{t+1} - P_t \mid \Omega_{t-1})$, and positively on real money balances, $m_t - P_t$. The aggregate supply function

$$y_t = \phi_0 + \phi_1(m_t - P_t) + \varepsilon_{2t}, \quad \phi_1 > 0,$$

which is assumed to depend positively on the level of real balances. For the money demand equation the following standard specification is adopted

$$m_t = y_t + P_t - \alpha_1 r_t + \alpha_2(m_t - P_t) + \varepsilon_{3t}, \quad \alpha_1 > 0, 1 \geqslant \alpha_2 > 0,$$

which postulates that the money demand varies positively with nominal income, negatively with the nominal rate of interest, and positively with the real money balances. The disturbances ε_{t1}, ε_{t2}, ε_{t3} are assumed to be serially independent, with zero means. All variables, except for the nominal rate of interest (r_t), are measured in logarithms. The market clearing level of prices (in logarithm) is denoted by P_t, and the logarithm of output is represented by y_t. The logarithm of money supply (assumed to be equal to the demand for money) is fixed at $m_t = m$. Solving the above equation system for prices yields the following LRE equation (see Taylor, 1977)

$$E(P_{t+1} \mid \Omega_{t-1}) = E(P_t \mid \Omega_{t-1}) + \delta_1 P_t + \delta_0 + u_t, \quad (5.57)$$

where

$$\delta_1 = \alpha_1^{-1}(1-\alpha_2) + \gamma_2\gamma_1^{-1} - \phi_1(\alpha_1^{-1} + \gamma_1^{-1}),$$
$$\delta_0 = \phi_0(1+\alpha_1\gamma_1)^{-1} - \delta_1 m,$$

and

$$u_t = \varepsilon_{1t} - \alpha_1\gamma_1^{-1}\varepsilon_{2t} + (1+\alpha_1\gamma_1^{-1})\varepsilon_{3t}.$$

Now taking conditional expectations of both sides of (5.57) with respect to Ω_{t-1} and solving for $E(P_t|\Omega_{t-1})$ gives

$$E(P_t|\Omega_{t-1}) = (1+\delta_1)^{-1}E(P_{t+1}|\Omega_{t-1}) - (1+\delta_1)^{-1}\delta_0.$$

Substituting this result back in (5.57) yields

$$P_t = (1+\delta_1)^{-1}E(P_{t+1}|\Omega_{t-1}) + \omega_t, \tag{5.58}$$

where

$$\omega_t = -\delta_0(1+\delta_1)^{-1} - \delta_1 u_t.$$

Equation (5.58) is the same as (5.28) except that expectations of P_{t+1} are taken with respect to Ω_{t-1} instead of Ω_t. The general solution of (5.58) is given by result (C.7) in appendix C. Since by assumption $\{\varepsilon_{ti}\}$ are serially independent with zero means, then $\{\omega_t\}$ will also be serially independent with a constant mean equal to $-\delta_0(1+\delta_1)^{-1}$. Thus

$$\omega_t - E(\omega_t|\Omega_{t-1}) = -\delta_0^{-1}u_t,$$

and solution of (5.58) reduces to

$$P_t = (1+\delta_1)^t\mathcal{M}_{t-1} - \delta_1^{-1}u_t - \sum_{j=1}^{t-1}(1+\delta_1)^j\omega_{t-j}, \tag{5.59}$$

where $\mathcal{M}_{t-1}$ is a martingale process. In the case where $\delta_1 > 0$ the unique stationary solution is given by the forward solution (see (5.33) with Ω_t replaced by Ω_{t-1})

$$P_{tF} = -\delta_1^{-1}u_t + \sum_{i=0}^{\infty}(1+\delta_1)^{-i}E(\omega_{t+i}|\Omega_{t-1}),$$

which upon using ω_t defined above becomes

$$P_{tF} = -\delta_1^{-1}u_t + \sum_{i=0}^{\infty}(1+\delta_1)^{-i}\{-\delta_0(1+\delta_1)^{-1}\},$$

or

$$P_{tF} = -\delta_1^{-1}u_t - \delta_1^{-1}\delta_0, \quad \text{for } \delta_1 > 0. \tag{5.60}$$

The case $\delta_1 < 0$ leads to multiplicity of stationary solutions. Result (5.59) can also be written in the quasi-difference form

$$P_t = (1+\delta_1)P_{t-1} + \delta_0 - \delta_1^{-1}u_t + 2\left(\frac{1+\delta_1}{\delta_1}\right)u_{t-1} + \varepsilon_t^1, \tag{5.61}$$

which is the general form of the stationary solutions obtained by Taylor (1977). In this solution

$$\varepsilon_t^1 = (1+\delta_1)^t \Delta \mathscr{M}_{t-1},$$

is an arbitrary martingale difference process, such that $E(\varepsilon_t^1 | \Omega_{t-2}) = 0$. A result similar to (5.61) can also be derived by the martingale difference method proposed by Broze et al. (1985). The set of stationary solutions considered by Taylor corresponds to the values of ε_t^1 defined by the equation

$$\varepsilon_t^1 + 2(1+\delta_1)\delta_1^{-1}u_t = \{g_0 + (1+\delta_1)\delta_1^{-1}\}u_{t-1},$$

or

$$\varepsilon_t^1 = \{g_0 - (1+\delta_1)\delta_1^{-1}\}u_{t-1},$$

where, clearly $E(\varepsilon_t^1 | \Omega_{t-2}) = 0$ for all values of g_0. Setting the martingale difference process $\{\varepsilon_t^1\}$ in (5.60) equal to the above expression yields Taylor's set of stationary solutions (indexed by g_0):[19]

$$P_t = (1+\delta_1)P_{t-1} + \delta_0 - \delta_1^{-1}u_t + \{g_0 + (1+\delta_1)\delta_1^{-1}\}u_{t-1}, \quad \delta_1 < 0.$$

It is now easily seen that the minimum-variance solution obtains at $g_0 = 0$, which results in the same stationary solution (5.60) derived for the case of $\delta_1 > 0$. But as pointed out above, this is not a general result and usually the minimum-variance solution differs from the unique stationary solution.

5.3.3 *Higher-order Cases (Models with No Lagged Dependent Variables)*

The solution of higher-order LRE models with future expectations can be carried out by a straightforward (albeit rather tedious) extension of the solution methods discussed above. Here we focus our attention on the martingale solution method which allows a complete characterization of all the solutions. Initially we consider the problem of solving the general LRE equation (5.3) when no lagged values of the endogenous variable appear in the model. That is

$$y_t = \sum_{i=1}^{s} \alpha_i E(y_{t+i} | \Omega_t) + \omega_t. \tag{5.62}$$

---

[19] Note that there is a typographical error in the solution given by Taylor. In his equation (12) the term $(1+\delta_1)\delta_1^{-1}$ should have a positive instead of a negative sign.

Let

$$z_{t1} = y_t,$$
$$z_{t2} = E(y_{t+1} \mid \Omega_t),$$
$$\vdots \quad \vdots$$
$$z_{ts} = E(y_{t+s-1} \mid \Omega_t).$$

Then equation (5.62) will be the first equation in the following first-order multivariate LRE equation[20]

$$\mathbf{z}_t = \mathrm{A}E(\mathbf{z}_{t+1} \mid \Omega_t) + \boldsymbol{\omega}_t, \tag{5.63}$$

where $\mathbf{z}_t' = (z_{t1}, z_{t2}, \ldots, z_{ts})$, $\boldsymbol{\omega}_t' = (\omega_t, 0, 0, \ldots 0)$, and

$$A = \begin{bmatrix} \alpha_1 & \alpha_2 & \ldots & \alpha_{s-1} & \alpha_s \\ 1 & 0 & \ldots & 0 & 0 \\ \vdots & \vdots & & \vdots & \vdots \\ 0 & 0 & \ldots & 1 & 0 \end{bmatrix}. \tag{5.64}$$

Now following the martingale solution method set out in appendix C, the general solution of (5.63) can be written as[21]

$$\mathbf{z}_t = A^{-t}\mathcal{M}_t - \sum_{i=1}^{t-1} A^{-i}\boldsymbol{\omega}_{t-i}, \quad \text{for } t \geqslant 1, \tag{5.65}$$

where $\mathcal{M}_t$ is a martingale vector process with s arbitrary martingale components such that $E(\mathcal{M}_{t+1} \mid \Omega_t) = \mathcal{M}_t$.

As in the univariate first-order case the forward solution of (5.63) exists if *all* the eigenvalues of matrix A fall within the unit circle. When this condition is satisfied by analogy with (5.43) we obtain

$$\mathbf{z}_{tF} = A^{-t}\mathcal{F}_t + \sum_{i=0}^{\infty} A^i E(\boldsymbol{\omega}_{t+i} \mid \Omega_t), \tag{5.66}$$

where $\mathcal{F}_t$ is an $s \times 1$ martingale vector process. Similarly the backward solution is given by

$$\mathbf{z}_{tB} = A^{-t}\mathcal{B}_t - \sum_{i=1}^{\infty} A^{-i}\boldsymbol{\omega}_{t-i}, \tag{5.67}$$

and exists if *all* the eigenvalues of A fall outside the unit circle.

The nature of multiplicity of solutions of (5.62) is more explicitly established by the following theorem.

---

[20] Note that $E(z_{t+1,i} \mid \Omega_t) = E\{E(y_{t+i} \mid \Omega_{t+1}) \mid \Omega_t\} = E(y_{t+i} \mid \Omega_t)$, for $i = 1, 2, \ldots, s$.

[21] Note that matrix A is non-singular for all values of $\alpha_s \neq 0$.

Theorem 5.3 Suppose y_t^0 is a (special) solution of (5.62), then

$$y_t^1 = y_t^0 + \sum_{j=1}^{s} \mathscr{M}_{tj}\mu_j^{-t}, \tag{5.68}$$

will also be a solution of (5.62) where $\{\mathscr{M}_{tj}, i=1, 2, \ldots, s\}$ represent s distinct martingale processes, and $\mu_1, \mu_2, \ldots \mu_s$ are the s distinct eigenvalues of matrix A defined in (5.64).

Proof Since y_t^0 is a solution of (5.62) then

$$y_t^1 - \sum_{j=1}^{s} \mathscr{M}_{tj}\mu_j^{-t}$$

$$= \sum_{i=1}^{s} \alpha_i E(y_{t+i}^1 | \Omega_t) - \sum_{i,j=1}^{s} \alpha_i \mu_j^{-(t+i)} E(\mathscr{M}_{t+i,j} | \Omega_t) + \omega_t,$$

and y_t^1 will also be a solution if

$$\sum_{j=1}^{s} \mathscr{M}_{tj}\mu_j^{-t} = \sum_{i,j=1}^{s} \alpha_i \mu_j^{-(t+j)} E(\mathscr{M}_{t+i,j} | \Omega_t). \tag{5.69}$$

However, since $\{\mathscr{M}_{tj}\}$ are distinct martingale processes, then

$$E(\mathscr{M}_{t+i,j} | \Omega_t) = \mathscr{M}_{tj}, \quad \text{for } i \geqslant 0$$

and the condition (5.69) reduces to

$$\sum_{j=1}^{s} \mathscr{M}_{tj}\mu_j^{-t} = \sum_{j=1}^{s} \left(\sum_{i=1}^{s} \alpha_i \mu_j^{-(t+i)} \right) \mathscr{M}_{tj}.$$

Equating coefficients of $\mathscr{M}_{tj}$ we have

$$\mu_j^{-t} = \sum_{i=1}^{s} \alpha_i \mu_j^{-(t+i)}, \quad \text{for } j = 1, 2, \ldots, s,$$

which establishes that $\mu_1, \mu_2, \ldots, \mu_s$ should be the distinct roots of the polynomial equation

$$\sum_{i=1}^{s} \alpha_i \mu^{-i} = 1. \tag{5.70}$$

It is now easy to show that (5.70) is in fact the same as the characteristic equation of matrix A.

The above theorem can also be extended to cases where the characteristic roots of A are not distinct. Suppose $\mu_1, \mu_2, \ldots, \mu_h$ $(h \leqslant s)$ are the distinct roots of (5.70), and μ_j is repeated precisely n_j times. Then if y_t^0 is a solution of (5.62) so will

$$y_t^1 = y_t^0 + \sum_{j=1}^{h} \mu_j^{-t} \sum_{i=0}^{n_j - 1} t^i \mathscr{M}_{jit},$$

where for each j and i the process $\{\mathscr{M}_{jit}\}$ is a martingale.[22] This result can now be used to show that the imposition of the criterion of stationarity results in a unique solution only when all the eigenvalues of A lie inside the unit circle.

When all the eigenvalues of A are within the unit circle, the unique stationary solution of (5.62) can be obtained from (5.66) and is given by

$$y_{tF} = \sum_{i=0}^{\infty} c_i E(\omega_{t+i} \mid \Omega_t),$$

where c_i is the first element in the matrix A^i. When $\{\omega_t\}$ has the non-deterministic moving-average representation (5.34), the forward solution can be obtained more easily by the z-transform method (see Whiteman (1983), for details). In situations where some of the roots of A are outside the unit circle, there are an infinite number of stationary solutions. The extent of these multiplicities depends on the number of roots that fall outside the unit circle and the number of times that each of these roots is repeated. For example if the characteristic equation of A has two roots outside the unit circle each repeated twice, then the stationary solutions of (5.62) depend on four distinct arbitrary martingale processes. This considerably complicates the task of selecting a unique stationary solution. The criterion of minimum variance no longer leads to a unique solution when more than one eigenvalue of matrix A falls on or outside the unit circle. To obtain a unique solution one needs to augment the REH with further restrictions. The number of different restrictions needed is determined by the number of roots of equation (5.70) that lie on or outside the unit circle.

5.3.4 *Higher-order Cases (Models with Lagged Dependent Variables)*

The simplest LRE model containing future expectations as well as lagged values of the endogenous variable may be written as

$$y_t = \lambda y_{t-1} + \alpha E(y_{t+1} \mid \Omega_t) + \omega_t, \tag{5.71}$$

where as before ω_t can be any function of exogeneous variables or their future expectations. This type of model arises frequently in the RE literature on adjustment costs, and has been extensively studied for example by Kennan (1979), Hansen and Sargent (1980), and Sargan (1984).[23] Equation (5.71) also occurs in the staggered contract models discussed, for example, in Taylor (1980). In these models the contract wage-rate, y_t, depends on the future expected wage, $E(y_{t+1} \mid \Omega_t)$, because firms and workers take into account the

---

[22] This generalization of theorem 5.3 was supplied to me by Peter Hall of the Australian National University, to whom I am extremely grateful. A proof can be obtained from the author on request.

[23] See also section 4.3 for a discussion of the type of assumptions needed if an equation such as (5.71) is to be derivable from the principle of economic optimization.

wage set by firms and other workers. The lagged wage-rate appears in the model because contracts are assumed to last two periods. To characterize all the solutions of this model we first transform (5.71) into an equation of type (5.28), and then apply the martingale method to the transformed equation.

Set

$$y_t = \tilde{y}_t + \mu y_{t-1}, \tag{5.72}$$

where μ is an arbitrary (possibly complex) parameter to be determined shortly. Then

$$E(y_{t+1} \mid \Omega_t) = E(\tilde{y}_{t+1} \mid \Omega_t) + \mu \tilde{y}_t + \mu^2 y_{t-1}.$$

Substituting this result together with (5.72) in (5.71) now yields

$$\tilde{y}_t = \alpha(1-\alpha\mu)^{-1} E(\tilde{y}_{t+1} \mid \Omega_t) + (1-\alpha\mu)^{-1}\omega_t, \tag{5.73}$$

where μ is a root of the quadratic equation

$$\lambda z^{-1} + \alpha z = 1. \tag{5.74}$$

The general solution of (5.73) can now be obtained, for example, by the martingale method described in section 5.3.1. We have

$$\tilde{y}_t = \left(\frac{1-\alpha\mu}{\alpha}\right)^t \mathcal{M}_t - (1-\alpha\mu)^{-1} \sum_{i=1}^{t-1} \left(\frac{1-\alpha\mu}{\alpha}\right)^t \omega_{t-i},$$

or upon using (5.72)

$$y_t = \mu y_{t-1} + \left(\frac{1-\alpha\mu}{\alpha}\right)^t \mathcal{M}_t - (1-\alpha\mu)^{-1} \sum_{i=1}^{t-1} \left(\frac{1-\alpha\mu}{\alpha}\right)^t \omega_{t-i}.$$

This provides a complete characterization of all the solutions of (5.71), in terms of the arbitrary martingale process $\{\mathcal{M}_t\}$. The nature of these solutions crucially depends on the roots of the auxiliary equation (5.74). Denote these roots by μ_1 and μ_2. Then $\alpha^{-1} = \mu_1 + \mu_2$, and

$$\alpha^{-1}(1-\alpha\mu_1) = \alpha^{-1} - \mu_1 = \mu_2,$$

similarly

$$\alpha^{-1}(1-\alpha\mu_2) = \alpha^{-1} - \mu_2 = \mu_1.$$

Therefore, in terms of μ_1 and μ_2, the general solution of y_t may also be written as

$$y_t = \mu_2 y_{t-1} + \mu_1^t \mathcal{M}_t - (\alpha\mu_1)^{-1} \sum_{i=1}^{t-1} \mu_1^i \omega_{t-i}. \tag{5.75}$$

It is now clear that if both roots μ_1, and μ_2 fall outside the unit circle then no stationary solution will be possible. For stationarity at least one of the roots (say, μ_2) should fall inside the unit circle. But when both roots fall inside the unit circle there will be an infinite number of stationary solutions to choose from. This situation is described by Sargan (1983, 1984), as the 'irregular' case, and arises because with $|\mu_1|<1$ it is always possible to choose an arbitrary martingale process $\{\mathcal{M}_t\}$ such that $\{\mu_1^t \mathcal{M}_t\}$ is a stationary process. There can be a unique stationary solution only in the situation where one of the roots (i.e. μ_2) falls inside and the other (i.e. μ_1) falls outside the unit circle. This case is referred to by Sargan as the 'regular' case, and yields the following unique stationary forward solution (assuming, of course, that $\{\omega_t\}$ is stationary):[24]

$$y_t=\mu_2 y_{t-1}+(\alpha\mu_1)^{-1}\sum_{i=0}^{\infty}\mu_1^{-i}E(\omega_{t+i}|\Omega_t). \tag{5.76}$$

This is the solution which is employed in econometric applications by, for example, Sargent (1978) and Kennan (1979), and is based on the assumption that μ_1 and μ_2 are real and, $|\mu_2|<1$, and $|\mu_1|>1$.

In the 'irregular' case where both roots fall inside the unit circle it is often more helpful to write the general solution given by (5.75) in the form of a second-order autoregression in y_t. Pre-multiplying both sides of (5.75) by μ_1^{-t} and taking first differences yields

$$y_t=(\mu_1+\mu_2)y_{t-1}-\mu_1\mu_2 y_{t-2}-\alpha^{-1}\omega_{t-1}+\mu_1^t\,\Delta\mathcal{M}_t,$$

which in view of $\mu_1+\mu_2=\alpha^{-1}$ and $\mu_1\mu_2=\lambda/\alpha$ gives

$$y_t=\alpha^{-1}y_{t-1}-\alpha^{-1}\lambda y_{t-2}-\alpha^{-1}\omega_{t-1}+\varepsilon_t^0, \tag{5.77}$$

where $\varepsilon_t^0=\mu_1^t\Delta\mathcal{M}_t$ is a martingale difference process with respect to Ω_t. That is $E(\varepsilon_t^0|\Omega_{t-1})=0$. This solution form is a straightforward generalization of the result (5.46) which was obtained for the first-order case with no lagged dependent variables. Solution (5.77) can also be obtained via the method proposed by Broze et al. (1985). It is now clear that different stationary solutions can be obtained from (5.77) for different choices of the martingale difference process $\{\varepsilon_t^0\}$. One only needs to choose martingale difference processes that have a finite variance. One obvious choice for $\{\varepsilon_t^0\}$ is the bubble-free linear specification

$$\varepsilon_t^0=g_0\{\omega_t-E(\omega_t|\Omega_{t-1})\},$$

where g_0 is an arbitrary parameter. But even if it is known *a priori* that (y_t, ω_t) follow a bubble-free covariance stationary process, the problem of which of the two stationary solutions (5.76) or (5.77) should be employed in practice still remains.

Consider now the general autoregressive rational expectations model (5.3). In this case the solution depends on s arbitrary martingale processes, and m initial values. The general martingale solution for this case is derived in

[24] Note that the assumption that $\{\omega_t\}$ is stationary is sufficient but not necessary for y_t in (5.76) to be stationary. For example, when ω_t follows an AR(1) process with parameter ρ, the necessary condition for $\{y_t\}$ to be stationary is given by $|\rho|<|\mu_1|$.

appendix C and is given by (C.18). This solution is a straightforward generalization of (5.75). The solution method is similar to that employed in section 5.3.3. We first write (5.3) in the form of a first-order multivariate LRE, and then obtain the solution by the martingale method. The details are given in appendix C. The various selection criteria discussed above can now be applied to these solutions. Here we only consider the criterion of stationarity. Application of other selection criteria is either intractable or leads to a unique solution only under very special circumstances. The characterization of the stationary solutions of (5.3) depends on the roots of the characteristic equation

$$\sum_{i=1}^{m} \lambda_i z^{-i} + \sum_{i=1}^{s} \alpha_i z^i = 1. \tag{5.78}$$

This is a generalization of (5.74) and follows from (C.19) by setting $z = \rho^{-1}$. There exists a unique stationary solution only if the above polynomial equation has exactly s roots outside the unit circle, with the remaining m roots falling strictly inside the unit circle. If this condition on the roots is satisfied the unique stationary solution for any stationary $\{\omega_t\}$ process is given by the 'autoregressive-forward solution'

$$y_t = \sum_{j=1}^{m} \theta_j y_{t-j} + \sum_{j=1}^{s} \delta_j \left\{ \sum_{i=0}^{\infty} \mu_j^{-i} E(\omega_{t+i} | \Omega_t) \right\}, \tag{5.79}$$

where $\mu_1, \mu_2, \ldots, \mu_s$ are those roots of (5.78) that fall outside the unit circle. This solution is a generalization of (5.76). The parameters θ_j and δ_j can be obtained from the results given in appendix C. For example, in the simple case of $m = s = 1$, we have $\theta_1 = \mu_2$, and $\delta_1 = (\alpha\mu_1)^{-1}$. If (5.78) has more than s roots outside the unit circle the autoregressive part of the solution will be unstable and the RE equation will have no stationary solution. Finally, when the characteristic equation has less than s roots outside the unit circle there will be an infinite number of stationary solutions.[25] In this 'irregular' case all the stationary solutions can be readily characterized by the martingale difference solution method proposed by Broze et al. (1985). As an example consider the case of $m = s = 2$, and suppose that all the four roots of the characteristic equation fall inside the unit circle. Introduce the following martingale difference processes,

$$\varepsilon_t^0 = y_t - E(y_t | \Omega_{t-1}),$$

and

$$\varepsilon_t^1 = E(y_{t+1} | \Omega_t) - E(y_{t+1} | \Omega_{t-1}).$$

Notice that $E(\varepsilon_t^0 | \Omega_{t-1}) = E(\varepsilon_t^1 | \Omega_{t-1}) = 0$. Then

$$E(y_{t+1} | \Omega_t) = y_{t+1} - \varepsilon_{t+1}^0,$$

[25] For a proof, in the case where $\{\omega_t\}$ has the stationary infinite moving-average representation (5.34), see Whiteman (1983, chapter IV).

and

$$E(y_{t+2}|\Omega_t)=E(y_{t+2}|\Omega_{t+1})-\varepsilon_{t+1}^1,$$
$$=y_{t+2}-\varepsilon_{t+2}^0-\varepsilon_{t+1}^1.$$

Using these results in (5.3) to eliminate the expectational variables yields

$$y_t=\lambda_1 y_{t-1}+\lambda_2 y_{t-2}+\alpha_1 y_{t+1}+\alpha_2 y_{t+2}+v_t,$$

where

$$v_t=\omega_t-\alpha_1\varepsilon_{t+1}^0-\alpha_2[\varepsilon_{t+2}^0+\varepsilon_{t+1}^1].$$

When all the roots of (5.78) (for $m=s=2$) fall inside the unit circle the autoregressive part of the above solution will be stationary, and for all arbitrary stationary martingale difference processes $\{\varepsilon_t^0\}$ and $\{\varepsilon_t^1\}$, the resultant solutions will also be stationary. When attention is confined to *linear* stationary solutions of the type given by (5.35), it is possible to obtain ε_t^0 and ε_t^1 in terms of the innovations $\varepsilon_t=\omega_t-E(\omega_t|\Omega_{t-1})$. Using (5.35) it is easily seen that

$$\varepsilon_t^0=y_t-E(y_t|\Omega_{t-1})=g_0\varepsilon_t,$$

and similarly

$$\varepsilon_t^1=E(y_{t+1}|\Omega_t)-E(y_{t+1}|\Omega_{t-1})=g_1\varepsilon_t.$$

Therefore

$$v_t=\omega_t-(\alpha_1 g_0+\alpha_2 g_1)\varepsilon_{t+1}-\alpha_2 g_0\varepsilon_{t+2}=\omega_t-\kappa_0\varepsilon_t-\kappa_1\varepsilon_{t-1}$$

where g_0 and g_1 (or κ_0 and κ_1) are arbitrary parameters. The set of bubble-free linear stationary solutions can now be written as

$$y_t=-\alpha_2^{-1}\alpha_1 y_{t-1}+\alpha_2^{-1}y_{t-2}-\alpha_2^{-1}\lambda_1 y_{t-3}-\alpha_2^{-1}\lambda_2 y_{t-4}$$
$$-\alpha_2^{-1}\omega_{t-2}+\kappa_0\varepsilon_t+\kappa_1\varepsilon_{t-1}, \quad (5.80)$$

where κ_0, and κ_1 are arbitrary constants, and ε_t are innovations of the $\{\omega_t\}$ process. The parameters κ_0 and κ_1 can be uniquely determined only if the characteristic equation has exactly two roots outside the unit circle. When only one of the roots of the AR part of (5.80) falls outside the unit circle the requirement of stationarity places only one restriction on κ_0 and κ_1, and is not enough to give a unique value for these parameters.

The chapter concludes with an application of the martingale solution technique to a generalized version of Muth's inventory model, where the equilibrium price level depends on its past, as well as on its current and future expected values. This application helps to demonstrate how the techniques reviewed here can be utilized in the case of models with a mixture of current and future expectations of the endogenous variable.

Example 5.3 An Extension of Muth's Model of Inventory Speculation

This is a generalization of the cobweb model already discussed in section 3.4 in connection with the learning problem, and allows for the possibility of storage and inventory speculation. The supply and demand functions (3.1) and (3.2) are supplemented by a speculative inventory demand function and a new market clearing condition which does not require the equality of production and consumption in every period. Muth derives the speculative inventory demand function by a expected-utility-maximization approach assuming that storage and interest costs are negligible. An exact derivation of this demand function, in a slightly more general setting, follows.

Suppose that the real costs of transactions and storage per unit of output is equal to c, and the real rate of interest during period t is r, then the real profit, π_t, during t will be given by

$$\pi_t = \{P_{t+1} - (1+r)P_t - c\} I_t, \tag{5.81}$$

where I_t is the level of speculative inventory to be held at the end of the period t, and P_t is the price of the commodity in question deflated by the general level of prices. Suppose further that P_t are normally distributed and that the utility function of speculators can be approximated by the constant absolute risk-aversion utility function

$$U(\pi_t) = K_1 - K_2 \exp(-\kappa\pi_t), \quad K_1 \geqslant K_2 > 0,$$

where $\kappa > 0$ denotes the Arrow–Pratt index of absolute risk-aversion. Then conditional on Ω_t, the information set available to all speculators at time t, π_t will also be normally distributed and we obtain:[26]

$$E\{U(\pi_t) | \Omega_t\} = K_1 - K_2 \exp\{-\kappa E(\pi_t | \Omega_t) + \tfrac{1}{2}\kappa^2 V(\pi_t | \Omega_t)\}, \tag{5.82}$$

where $V(\cdot|\cdot)$ stands for the conditional variance operator.[27] But using (5.81) we have

$$E(\pi_t | \Omega_t) = I_t\{E(P_{t+1} | \Omega_t) - (1+r)P_t - c\},$$

$$V(\pi_t | \Omega_t) = I_t^2 V(P_{t+1} | \Omega_t).$$

Substituting these results in (5.82), and taking the derivative of $E\{U(\pi_t) | \Omega_t\}$ with respect to I_t yields the following speculative inventory demand function

$$I_t = \{\kappa V(P_{t+1} | \Omega_t)\}^{-1}\{E(P_{t+1} | \Omega_t) - (1+r)P_t - c\}.$$

The optimal level of inventory demand therefore depends directly on the expectations of the gain from speculation on the margin, and indirectly on the degree of risk-aversion augmented by the expected variability of prices. Notice that in this model it is not possible to separate the effects of changes in risk-aversion and expected price variability upon the inventory demand. In general higher expected price variability and/or higher degrees of aversion to risk results in a reduction for speculative inventory.

The cobweb model of section 3.4 can now be modified to take account of inventory changes. The complete model will be

$$q_t^s = \mathbf{x}_{t1}'\boldsymbol{\alpha}_1 + \beta_1 E(P_t | \Omega_{t-1}) + \varepsilon_{t1}, \tag{5.83}$$

---

[26] It is well known that when $x \sim N(\mu, \sigma^2)$, then $E\{\exp(\lambda x)\} = \exp\{\lambda\mu + \tfrac{1}{2}\lambda^2\sigma^2\}$.

[27] More specifically, $V(\pi_t | \Omega_t) = E(\pi_t^2 | \Omega_t) - \{E(\pi_t | \Omega_t)\}^2$.

$$q_t^d = \mathbf{x}'_{t2}\boldsymbol{\alpha}_2 - \beta_2 P_t + \varepsilon_{t2}, \tag{5.84}$$

$$I_t = \delta_t\{E(P_{t+1} \mid \Omega_t) - (1+r)P_t - c\}, \tag{5.85}$$

$$q_t^s - q_t^d = I_t - I_{t-1}, \tag{5.86}$$

where $\delta_t = \{\kappa V(P_{t+1} \mid \Omega_t)\}^{-1}$. The last equation represents the market clearing condition and states that in equilibrium changes in inventories $(I_t - I_{t-1})$, must be equal to the excess of current supply (q_t^s) over current consumption demand (q_t^d). Other notations are as in section 3.4. The vectors $\mathbf{x}_{t1}$, and $\mathbf{x}_{t2}$ contain the exogenous variables affecting supply and demand, and ε_{t1} and ε_{t2} are the random shocks assumed to be white-noise processes.[28] This model generalizes Muth's speculative inventory model in two respects. Firstly, it explicitly allows for the effect of exogenous variables such as income, and factor prices on demand and supply decisions, and secondly it extends the analysis to the case of a non-zero real rate of interest.

As it stands, because of the dependence of I_t on the conditional variance of future prices, the model is subject to an important type of non-linearity with which it is difficult to deal. Muth avoids this problem by assuming that $V(P_{t+1} \mid \Omega_t)$ is constant and that δ_t can be treated as a fixed arbitrary parameter, say equal to δ. This assumption clearly ignores the fact that under the REH, $\{P_t\}$ and hence $V(P_{t+1} \mid \Omega_t)$ are endogenously determined. But without such an assumption it is difficult to see how the model can be solved in general. Setting $\delta_t = \delta$, and eliminating q_t^s, q_t^d, and I_t from the equations (5.83)–(5.86) yield the following LRE equation in prices:[29]

$$P_t = \lambda P_{t-1} + \beta E(P_t \mid \Omega_{t-1}) + \alpha E(P_{t+1} \mid \Omega_t) + \omega_t, \tag{5.87}$$

where

$$\left.\begin{aligned} &\lambda = d^{-1}\delta(1+r), \quad \beta = -(\beta_1 + \delta)d^{-1}, \quad \alpha = \delta d^{-1}, \\ &\omega_t = d^{-1}(\varepsilon_{t2} - \varepsilon_{t1}) + d^{-1}(\mathbf{x}'_{t2}\boldsymbol{\alpha}_2 - \mathbf{x}'_{t1}\boldsymbol{\alpha}_1), \\ &d = \beta_2 + \delta(1+r) \end{aligned}\right\} \tag{5.88}$$

The above RE equation can now be solved by any of the five solution methods reviewed in this section. But the application of the z-transform method, or the method of undetermined coefficients to (5.87) requires that the processes generating $\mathbf{x}_{t1}$, and $\mathbf{x}_{t2}$ are stationary. Here we consider the application of the martingale solution method by means of which it is possible to obtain all the solutions of (5.87) without imposition of any restriction on the $\{\mathbf{x}_{t1}\}$ and $\{\mathbf{x}_{t2}\}$ processes. To this end set

$$P_t = z_t + \mu P_{t-1}. \tag{5.89}$$

---

[28] Notice that for P_t to be normally distributed we need to assume that $\mathbf{x}_{t1}$, $\mathbf{x}_{t2}$, ε_{t1} and ε_{t2} are also normally distributed. Recall that the exact derivation of (5.85) was based on the assumption that P_t are normally distributed.

[29] Notice that under $\delta_t = \delta$, the path of prices does not depend on the average transaction or storage costs, c.

Then

$$E(P_t|\Omega_{t-1})=E(z_t|\Omega_{t-1})+\mu P_{t-1},$$
$$E(P_{t+1}|\Omega_t)=E(z_{t+1}|\Omega_t)+\mu z_t+\mu^2 P_{t-1}.$$

Substituting these results in (5.87) gives (assuming that $\alpha\mu\neq 1$),

$$z_t=(1-\alpha\mu)^{-1}\beta E(z_t|\Omega_{t-1})+(1-\alpha\mu)^{-1}\alpha E(z_{t+1}|\Omega_t)+\omega_t, \tag{5.90}$$

where μ is a root of the quadratic equation

$$\alpha\mu^2-(1-\beta)\mu+\lambda=0. \tag{5.91}$$

Consider now the transformation

$$z_t=y_t+\left(\frac{\beta}{1-\alpha\mu}\right)E(z_t|\Omega_{t-1}), \tag{5.92}$$

then,

$$E(z_t|\Omega_{t-1})=\left(\frac{1-\alpha\mu-\beta}{1-\alpha\mu}\right)E(y_t|\Omega_{t-1}),$$

$$E(z_{t+1}|\Omega_t)=\left(\frac{1-\alpha\mu-\beta}{1-\alpha\mu}\right)E(y_{t+1}|\Omega_t),$$

and assuming that $1-\alpha\mu-\beta\neq 0$, equation (5.90) can be written as the following first-order equation

$$y_t=\left(\frac{\alpha}{1-\alpha\mu-\beta}\right)E(y_{t+1}|\Omega_t)+\left(\frac{\omega_t}{1-\alpha\mu}\right),$$

the general solution of which is given by (5.41), or by (5.43) if the forward solution exists. The general solution of (5.87) can now be obtained by observing from (5.89) and (5.92) that

$$P_t=\mu P_{t-1}+y_t+\left(\frac{\beta}{1-\alpha\mu-\beta}\right)E(y_t|\Omega_{t-1}).$$

More specifically when the forward solution exists we have

$$P_t=\mu_2^t\{\mathscr{F}_t+(\beta/\alpha\mu_2)\mathscr{F}_{t-1}\}+\mu_1 P_{t-1}+X_t+(\beta/\alpha\mu_2)E(X_t|\Omega_{t-1}), \tag{5.93}$$

where

$$X_t=(1-\alpha\mu_1)^{-1}\sum_{i=0}^{\infty}\mu_2^{-i}E(\omega_{t+i}|\Omega_t), \tag{5.94}$$

μ_1 and μ_2 are the roots of (5.91), and as before $\{\mathscr{F}_t\}$ represents a martingale process with respect to Ω_t.[30] The solution of the speculative inventory model crucially depends on the roots of the quadratic equation (5.91). In terms of the structural parameters, these roots are given by

$$\mu_1 = 1 + \tfrac{1}{2}(\gamma + r) - \tfrac{1}{2}\{(\gamma + r)^2 + 4\gamma\}^{1/2},$$
$$\mu_2 = 1 + \tfrac{1}{2}(\gamma + r) + \tfrac{1}{2}\{(\gamma + r)^2 + 4\gamma\}^{1/2},$$

where $\gamma = (\beta_1 + \beta_2)/\delta$. Therefore, for *a priori* plausible values of the parameters (i.e. β_1, β_2, δ, $r > 0$), both roots are real with $\mu_1 < 1$, and $\mu_2 > 1$. Consequently the speculative inventory model will have a unique stationary solution whenever $\{X_t\}$ defined by (5.94) exists and is stationary. This unique stationary solution is obtained by setting the coefficient of the explosive root μ_2^t in (5.93) equal to zero. That is[31,32]

$$P_t = \mu_1 P_{t-1} + X_t - \left(\frac{\delta + \beta_1}{\delta \mu_2}\right) E(X_t \mid \Omega_{t-1}). \tag{5.95}$$

The particular model studied by Muth corresponds to the situation where $r = 0$, and $\omega_t = -(\beta_2 + \delta)^{-1}\varepsilon_{t1}$. In this special case we have

$$E(\omega_{t+i} \mid \Omega_t) = -(\beta_2 + \delta)^{-1}\varepsilon_{t1}, \quad \text{for } i = 0,$$
$$= 0, \quad \text{for } i > 0.$$

Substituting these results in (5.94) yields

$$X_t = -(\beta_2 + \delta)^{-1}(1 - \alpha\mu_1)^{-1}\varepsilon_{t1},$$

or using (5.88)

$$X_t = -\{\beta_2 + \delta(1 - \mu_1)\}^{-1}\varepsilon_{t1}.$$

Hence the unique stationary solution of Muth's own version of the speculative inventory model is

$$P_t = \mu_1 P_{t-1} - \{\beta_2 + \delta(1 - \mu_1)\}^{-1}\varepsilon_{t1}.$$

The advantage of the general stationary solution form (5.95) lies in the fact that it is applicable to all versions of the speculative inventory model so long as the processes generating $\mathbf{x}_{t1}$, $\mathbf{x}_{t2}$, ε_{t1}, and ε_{t2} ar such that $\{X_t\}$ defined by (5.94) exists and is stationary. For example, consider the case where $\mathbf{x}_{t1}$ and $\mathbf{x}_{t2}$ are scalars and follow the first order autoregressive processes:

$$x_{t1} = \rho_1 x_{t-1,1} + \eta_{t1},$$
$$x_{t2} = \rho_2 x_{t-2,2} + \eta_{t2},$$

---

[30] Notice that, using (5.91) we have

$$(1 - \alpha\mu_1 - \beta)/\alpha = (1 - \beta)/\alpha - \mu_1 = (\mu_1 + \mu_2) - \mu_1 = \mu_2.$$

[31] See appendix D for a derivation of infinite sums such as X_t, in terms of the parameters of the processes generating ω_t.

[32] Notice that using (5.88), it is easily seen that $(\beta/\alpha\mu_2) = -(\delta + \beta_1)/\delta\mu_2$.

with $|\rho_i| < \mu_2$, $i=1, 2$.[33] Using (5.94), and noting that ω_t is defined in (5.88) it now readily follows that

$$\{\beta_2+\delta(1+r-\mu_1)\}X_t=\varepsilon_{t2}-\varepsilon_{t1}+\left(\frac{\alpha_2\mu_2}{\mu_2-\rho_2}\right)x_{t2}-\left(\frac{\alpha_1\mu_2}{\mu_2-\rho_1}\right)x_{t1}.$$

Hence

$$\{\beta_2+\delta(1+r-\mu_1)\}E(X_t|\Omega_{t-1})=\left(\frac{\alpha_2\mu_2\rho_2}{\mu_2-\rho_2}\right)x_{t-1,2}-\left(\frac{\alpha_1\mu_2\rho_1}{\mu_2-\rho_1}\right)x_{t-1,1},$$

where μ_1 and μ_2 are the roots of (5.91) that fall inside and outside the unit circle respectively. Substituting these results in (5.95) gives the unique stationary solution path of the equilibrium price level in the speculative inventory model under the assumption that $\{x_{ti}\}$ follow AR(1) processes with parameters ρ_i, $i=1,2$. This solution will be consistent with our theoretical derivation of the speculative inventory demand function (5.85) if P_t is normally distributed and if $V(P_{t+1}|\Omega_t)$ is time-invariant. The latter follows if the disturbances of the model, namely ε_{t1}, ε_{t2}, η_{t1}, and η_{t2} are homoscedastic. The former requirement will be fulfilled if it is further assumed that these disturbances are normally distributed.

5.4 Concluding Remarks

This chapter has provided what we believe to be a comprehensive analysis of the solution of linear univariate rational expectations models. In the case of models with future expectations of the endogenous variables it was shown how the martingale solution method can be used to obtain *general* solution forms in a variety of circumstances. The non-uniqueness problem that arises in the case of these models is also discussed in some detail. The review of the various criteria proposed in the literature (i.e. economic optimality, stationarity, minimum variance and the minimal use of state variables) for selecting a unique solution shows that the application of these criteria generally either fails to lead to a unique solution, or that they are *ad hoc* and lack a proper economic rationale.

Although this chapter has focused primarily on the solution of univariate models, most of the techniques discussed can be easily adapted to deal with some important multivariate linear rational expectations models. The general solution of a first-order multivariate model is given in appendix C, where using the martingale method it is shown how the form of the solution crucially depends on whether the coefficient matrix of the expectational variables is invertible or not.

---

[33] Notice that since $\mu_2>1$, the condition $|\rho_i|<\mu_2$ does not necessarily mean that $\{\mathbf{x}_{ti}\}$ should be stationary. Although stationarity of $\{\mathbf{x}_{ti}\}$ will be sufficient for the existence and the stationarity of $\{X_t\}$.

Despite the important technical advances made over the past 5 years in the area of solution of rational expectations models there still remain important gaps with respect to the solution of dynamic multivariate models with future expectations and non-linear rational expectations models. Another important topic not covered in the present chapter is the solution of rational expectations models with heterogenous information. Simple examples of such a model are discussed in chapter 4 and appendix B, but a more general formulation of the problem and the characterization of its solutions will have to be the subject of future research.

6 Identification of Linear Rational Expectations Models

6.1 Introduction

Identification is a fundamental prerequisite to the empirical analysis of structural models. Unless a model is identified it will not be possible to give a meaningful interpretation to its parameter estimates. The conditions for the identifiability of systems of simultaneous equations have been extensively studied in the econometric literature (cf. Fisher, 1966; Wegge, 1965; Rothenberg, 1971; and Bowden, 1973). But in the context of RE models, where direct observations on expectational variables are not available, the identification problem acquires a new dimension. The familiar rank and order conditions for the identifiability of simultaneous equation models will no longer be applicable. In the case of RE models the identification problem presents itself at two levels: first, at the level of a single equation, the substitution of unobserved expectational variables by functions of observables poses the problem of whether the unknown parameters can be identified from the knowledge of observables; second, at a simultaneous equation level where, apart from the difficulty of unobserved expectations, there is also the additional problem of identifying the structural parameters from the (pseudo-) reduced-form parameters. This chapter investigates the rank and order conditions needed for the identifiability of LRE models at both levels. These conditions play a crucial role in the estimation and testing of RE models, and should be examined before embarking upon an empirical analysis of the RE models.

The first part of the chapter will be primarily concerned with the order conditions for identification of different types of single-equation RE models under alternative stochastic specifications of the exogenous variables and the disturbances. In the case of RE models with forward-looking or future expectations we discuss the identification problem both when the RE model under consideration has a unique stationary solution (the regular case) and when it has an infinite number of stationary solutions (the irregular case). The chapter will show that identification in the regular case can be viewed as a specialization of the identification problem in the irregular case. In general, however, it is shown that, in the absence of *a priori* restrictions on the processes generating the exogenous variables and the disturbances, the RE and general distributed lag models will be 'observationally equivalent' and therefore the extrapolative and the rational methods of expectations formations, in general, cannot be distinguished from one another.[1] The chapter shows this observational equivalence problem in the context of the proposed tests of the natural rate-rational expectations hypothesis, and the efficient market hypothesis.

The second part of the chapter considers the identifiability conditions for systems of simultaneous equations containing rational expectational variables. This problem has been studied in the literature by Wallis (1980), Pesaran (1981), and Wegge and Feldman (1983a). In the case of LRE models containing only current expectations of the endogenous variables, Wallis obtains necessary and sufficient rank conditions in terms of the reduced form parameters assuming that expectations of the exogenous variables are given. This analysis does not allow for the presence of perfectly predictable variables, such as lagged variables or fixed constants amongst the predetermined variables of the model. Here a more general framework is adopted, and the relevant rank and order conditions for the global identification of linear RE models with current expectations of the endogenous variables are derived explicitly in terms of the structural parameters and the general homogeneous linear identifying restrictions. The chapter also considers the problem of identification of LRE models containing lagged values of the exogenous and the endogenous variables, and emphasizes the importance of distinguishing between the variables that can, and those that cannot, be forecast perfectly for the identification of these models.

In the case of LRE models with the forward-looking expectations of the endogenous variables, because of the 'non-uniqueness' problem discussed in the previous chapter, the identification involves additional, often quite arbitrary, restrictions. Moreover, due to the presence of intractable non-linearities, the derivation of usable necessary and sufficient conditions for the identification of future RE models does not seem to be possible. The rank condition obtained in theorem 6.2 for identification of RE models with future expectations contains reduced-form parameters that are highly non-linear functions of the structural parameters, and as a result it is very difficult to apply in practice. There is clearly scope for further analysis of the identification problem in the context of models with future expectations and in mixed models containing both current and future expectations of the endogenous variables formed at different points in time. Other topics of interest not covered in this chapter include the problem of system identification under non-linear identifying restrictions, and identification by means of restrictions on higher-order moments. Readers interested in these topics are advised to consult the paper by Wegge and Feldman (1983a).

Two important conclusions emerge from the analysis of this chapter that are worth emphasizing here: the more informed economic agents are about

---

[1] For a definition of the extrapolative and the rational methods of expectations formation see chapter 2. A detailed review of the extrapolative models can be found in chapter 9.

the future course of the exogenous variables at the time they are making their decisions, the less likely is it that an outside observer (econometrician) will be able to discover the structural relations that underlie the agents' decision rules. In the extreme case where agents have perfect foresight, it will be *impossible* for the outside econometrician to identify the underlying structure. The second major conclusion of the chapter has a direct bearing on the debate between the Keynesian and the new classical explanations of output and employment, and was first emphasized by Sargent (1976b), and later discussed by Nelson (1979), McCallum (1979) and Sargent (1979b). Put in general terms it is concluded that in the absence of *a priori* information concerning the order of lags in economic relations or *a priori* restrictions on the processes generating the exogenous variables and the disturbances, RE and non-RE linear dynamic models will be observationally equivalent, and therefore cannot be distinguished from each other on empirical grounds. This general under-identification of LRE models casts serious doubts on the soundness of the attempts by Sargent (1976a), Barro (1977, 1978) and others, which purport to provide empirical evidence favouring the proposition that monetary and fiscal policies are incapable of influencing the path of real output and employment, even in the short run.

6.2 Identification: Basic Concepts

Identification is a fundamental concept in the empirical analysis of structural models and precedes the problem of estimation and hypothesis testing. For a formalization of the concept of identification it is convenient to make a distinction between a *model* and its possible *structures*. Suppose the purpose of modelling is to explain the observations $\mathbf{y}_t=(y_{t1}, y_{t2}, \ldots, y_{tg})'$ for $t=1, 2, \ldots, n$ on the g-dimensional vector of endogenous variables $\mathbf{y}$ conditional on the occurrence of the k-dimensional exogenous variable $\mathbf{x}$. Then the model for $\mathbf{y}$ is defined by the joint probability distribution function of $Y=(\mathbf{y}_1, \mathbf{y}_2, \ldots, \mathbf{y}_n)$ conditional on $X=(\mathbf{x}_1, \mathbf{x}_2, \ldots, \mathbf{x}_n)$, namely $f(Y|X, \theta)$ for all *admissible* values of the p-dimensional unknown parameter vector θ. The set of admissible values of θ, generally known as the *parameter space*, will be denoted by Θ. A structure $S(\theta_0)$ is defined by $f(Y|X, \theta_0)$ where θ_0 is a *particular* point in the parameter space Θ. In effect, a structure represents the *complete* probability law generating the endogenous variables conditional on a particular point in the parameter space and a particular realization of the processes generating the exogenous variables. Clearly it is also possible to define a model as the set of all admissible structures $S(\theta)$, $\theta\in\Theta$.

In the context of the model $f(Y|X, \theta)$, two structures $S(\theta_0)$ and $S(\theta_1)$ are said to be *observationally equivalent if* $f(Y|X, \theta_0)=f(Y|X, \theta_1)$ for all values of Y and X. A structure $S(\theta_0)$ is said to be *globally identified* if there is no other $\theta\in\Theta$ such that $f(Y|X, \theta)=f(Y|X, \theta_0)$ for all Y and X. When none of the structures of a model are identified the model is said to be *under-identified*. Therefore global identification of a model requires that all its possible structures are globally identified. It is, however, quite possible for a substructure of a model to be identified even though the model as a whole is under-identified. This can arise when only a subset of θ or a certain function of θ can be identified. In certain situations it is also desirable to consider the weaker notion of local identifiability where the identification of a structure $S(\theta_0)$ is considered on an open neighbourhood containing θ_0. A structure $S(\theta_0)$ is said to be *locally identified* if there exists an open neighbourhood containing θ_0 such that there is no other θ in that neighbourhood at which $f(Y|X, \theta_0)$. The concept of local identifiability is useful in the context of non-linear models and we shall have occasion to employ it in section 6.6 where the problem of the identification of RE models with future expectations will be considered.[2]

In the case of econometric models the identification problem is usually studied in terms of the first- and the second-order moments of the underlying probability distributions only, and information on higher-order moments is ignored. This is clearly justified when the endogenous variables have multivariate normal distributions. In other circumstances identifiability conditions obtained on the basis of the first- and the second-order moments may very well be too restrictive. This chapter follows the literature, and considers the first- and second-order moments. Models that can be identified only on the basis of the higher-order moments of their underlying probability distributions are likely to provide only a weak basis for empirical analysis in econometrics and will not be covered here.

A: Single-equation Models

6.3 Identification of Single-equation RE Models with Current Expectations

Consider the model

$$y_t = \beta y_t^* + \sum_{i=0}^{s} \gamma_i' \mathbf{x}_{t-i} + u_t, \tag{6.1}$$

where y_t^* stands for the expectations of the endogenous variable y_t formed at time $t-1$, $\mathbf{x}_t$ is the $k\times 1$ vector of the explanatory variables, and u_t is the unobservable disturbance term. Under the REH the expectations y_t^* will be given by

$$y_t^* = E(y_t|\Omega_{t-1}), \tag{6.2}$$

[2] The concepts of observational equivalence and identification can also be generalized to cover situations when two or more different parametric models are under consideration. For a formalization of the notion of observational equivalence in these circumstances see Pesaran (1987).

where as before Ω_t denotes the set of all the observations available at time t. Here we assume that

$$\Omega_t = \{y_t, y_{t-1}, \ldots; \mathbf{x}_t, \mathbf{x}_{t-1}, \ldots\},$$
$$= \{\Omega_{ty}; \Omega_{tx}\}.$$

Situations where Ω_t contains information on variables other than those appearing in (6.1), can be easily covered by imposing zero restrictions on the appropriate elements of the parameter vectors γ_i.

In the case of model (6.1) it is the identification of the structural parameters $(\beta, \gamma_0, \gamma_1, \ldots, \gamma_s)$ which is of interest. Since direct observations on expectations are not available, we first need to solve for y_t^* in terms of the observables. Utilizing the solution techniques reviewed in the previous chapter (see section 5.2) and assuming that $\beta \neq 1$, it is easily seen that

$$y_t = \mu\gamma_0'\mathbf{x}_t^* + \gamma_0'\mathbf{x}_t + (1+\mu)\sum_{i=1}^{s}\gamma_i'\mathbf{x}_{t-i} + \xi_t, \tag{6.3}$$

where

$$\mathbf{x}_t^* = E(\mathbf{x}_t|\Omega_{t-1}), \quad \mu = (1-\beta)^{-1}\beta,$$

and

$$\xi_t = \mu E(u_t|\Omega_{t-1}) + u_t. \tag{6.4}$$

The above solution still contains expectations of the explanatory variables that are in general unobservable. The application of the REH to the structural model (6.1) has in effect enabled us to pass the problem of expectations formation of the endogenous variable y_t^*, on to the problem of formation of expectations of the explanatory variables $\mathbf{x}_t^*$. We are still left with the task of modelling expectations of the $\mathbf{x}_t$ variables, and unless they are directly observable, any discussion of the identification of the parameters of the structural model (6.1) will inevitably be conditional on the process generating $\{\mathbf{x}_t\}$. For this reason solution (6.3) is best regarded as a *pseudo-reduced form* or a *pseudo-structural form* of the structural model (6.1).

In considering the identifiability of model (6.1) we initially assume that $\{u_t\}$ is a non-autocorrelated process. In this case $E(u_t|\Omega_{t-1}) = 0$ and, by virtue of (6.4), $\xi_t = u_t$. Therefore the disturbances of the pseudo-reduced form equation (6.3) will also be serially uncorrelated, and only the first-order moments of y_t enter the conditions necessary for the identification of (6.1). When all the components of $\mathbf{x}_t^*$ are directly observable and it is not possible to express them as exact linear functions of $\mathbf{x}_t, \mathbf{x}_{t-1}, \ldots, \mathbf{x}_{t-s}$ the structural parameters β, $\gamma_0, \gamma_1, \ldots, \gamma_s$ are clearly identifiable if we further assume that u_t and $\mathbf{x}_t$ are contemporaneously uncorrelated. Under these assumptions the structural parameters can be consistently estimated by the direct application of the least squares method to (6.3). But, in general, the identification of (6.1) crucially depends on the possibility of using information contained in $\mathbf{x}_t^*$. For example, when the current values of $\mathbf{x}_t$ do not appear in (6.1) (i.e. $\gamma_0 = 0$), knowledge of

$\mathbf{x}_t^*$ will be irrelevant and the remaining structural parameters $\beta, \gamma_1, \gamma_2, \ldots, \gamma_s$ will be under-identified. The problem of under-identification of (6.1) will also arise if $\gamma_0 \neq 0$, but $\mathbf{x}_t$ are *perfectly* predictable, i.e. $\mathbf{x}_t^* = E(\mathbf{x}_t | \Omega_{t-1}) = \mathbf{x}_t$. In this perfect foresight case, (6.3) simplifies to

$$y_t = (1+\mu) \sum_{i=0}^{s} \gamma_i' \mathbf{x}_{t-i} + \xi_t,$$

and model (6.1) will be observationally equivalent to a general distributed lag relation between y_t and $\mathbf{x}_t$. As we shall see, this under-identification of RE models under perfect foresight assumptions on the process generating the predetermined variables carries over to models with future expectations and simultaneous equation models. The precision with which μ (and hence β) can be estimated clearly depends on the additional information contained in $\mathbf{x}_t^*$ not already available in the predetermined variables included in the model.

In practice it is unlikely that all components of $\mathbf{x}_t$ are perfectly predictable at time $t-1$, and therefore the identification of the RE model (6.1) cannot be ruled out. A useful approach would be to classify the components of $\mathbf{x}_t$ into those that can be predicted perfectly (such as fixed constants and lagged values of y_t) and those that cannot be. Accordingly, partition $\mathbf{x}_t$ into $\mathbf{x}_{1t}$ with k_1 components, and $\mathbf{x}_{2t}$ with k_2 components, $(k_1 + k_2 = k)$, and assume that $\mathbf{x}_{1t}^* \neq \mathbf{x}_{1t}$, but $\mathbf{x}_{2t}^* = {}_{2t}$. Partitioning $\gamma_0 = (\gamma_{01}', \gamma_{02}')'$ conformable to $\mathbf{x}_t = (\mathbf{x}_{1t}', \mathbf{x}_{2t}')$, relation (6.3) can now be written

$$y_t = \mu \gamma_{01}' \mathbf{x}_{1t}^* + \gamma_{01}' \mathbf{x}_{1t} + (1+\mu) \gamma_{02}' \mathbf{x}_{2t} + (1+\mu) \sum_{i=1}^{s} \gamma_i' \mathbf{x}_{t-i} + u_t. \tag{6.3$'$}$$

In this formulation direct observations on $\mathbf{x}_{1t}^*$, if available, can be employed to estimate all the structural parameters. In this case, assuming zero correlations between $\mathbf{x}_{1t}^*$ and u_t, the model will be over-identified if $k_1 > 1$, the number of over-identifying restrictions being equal to $k_1 - 1$. This is because variables $\mathbf{x}_{2t}$ that are perfectly predictable at time $t-1$ do not contribute to the identification of the RE models.

Consider now the more realistic situation where $\mathbf{x}_{1t}^*$ are unobservable. In order to form rational expectations of $\mathbf{x}_{1t}$ conditional on Ω_{t-1} we employ the following generalized vector autoregressive formulation

$$\mathbf{x}_{1t} = \sum_{i=1}^{r} R_i \mathbf{x}_{t-i} + \mathbf{v}_{1t}, \tag{6.5}$$

where $\mathbf{v}_{1t}$ is a $k_1 \times 1$ vector of random disturbances distributed independently of $\mathbf{x}_{t-1}, \ldots, \mathbf{x}_{t-r}$ and of u_t with zero means, and R_i are parameter matrices of order $k_1 \times k$ each. The specification (6.5) is more general than it may appear at first. Since at time $t-1$, $\{y_{t-i}, i \geqslant 1\}$ are known exactly, lagged values of y_t can therefore be included as elements of $\mathbf{x}_{2t}$ (or $\mathbf{x}_t$) without in any way altering the pseudo-reduced form equation given by (6.3′). The inclusion of $\{y_{t-i}, i \geqslant 1\}$ as elements of $\mathbf{x}_t$ also means that (6.5) can be regarded as an equation system with feedbacks, where $\mathbf{x}_{1t}$ are determined not only by their own past but also by the past history of the endogenous variable, y_t. Thus, general linear policy rules with feedbacks may be considered within the present framework without any need for further notational elaborations. Note also that when none of the explanatory variables are exactly predictable, then $\mathbf{x}_{1t}=\mathbf{x}_t$ and (6.5) is equivalent to assuming that $\mathbf{x}_t$ follows an rth-order vector autoregressive (AR(r)) process. By letting r tend to infinity and placing suitable restrictions on R_i, more general stationary and linear specifications of the $\mathbf{x}_t$ process such as autoregressive moving average (ARMA) schemes can also be specified.

Using (6.5), the rational expectations solution for $\mathbf{x}_{1t}$ is given by

$$\mathbf{x}_{1t}^{*}=E(\mathbf{x}_{1t}|\Omega_{t-1})=\sum_{i=1}^{r} R_i\mathbf{x}_{t-i}, \tag{6.6}$$

which is also the best linear predictor of $\mathbf{x}_{1t}$ relative to the information set Ω_{t-1}.

The identification of the structural parameters can now be examined directly in terms of the joint probability distribution of $(y_t, \mathbf{x}_{1t})$ conditional on $\mathbf{x}_{2t}, \mathbf{x}_{t-1}, \mathbf{x}_{t-2}, \dots$. Using (6.6) in (6.3′) we obtain

$$y_t=\sum_{i=0}^{\max(r,s)} \theta_i'\mathbf{x}_{t-i}+u_t, \tag{6.7}$$

where

$$\theta_0=(\theta_{01}', \theta_{02}')'=(\gamma_{01}', (1+\mu)\gamma_{02}')', \tag{6.8a}$$

$$\theta_i=\mu R_i'\gamma_{01}+(1+\mu)\gamma_i, \quad i=1, 2, \dots, s, \tag{6.8b}$$

$$\theta_i=\mu R_i'\gamma_{01}, \quad i=s+1, \dots, r. \tag{6.8c}$$

Since by assumption $\mathbf{x}_{t-i}$ are distributed independently of u_t, then the least squares regression of y_t on $\mathbf{x}_t, \mathbf{x}_{t-1}, \dots, \mathbf{x}_{t-m}$ yields consistent estimates of θ_0, $\theta_1, \dots, \theta_m$, where $m=\max(r,s)$. From this, and using (6.8a), it immediately follows that γ_{01} which is equal to θ_{01} is identifiable. But the identification of the other structural parameters depends on whether $r>s$. When $r\leqslant s$, relations (6.8c) cannot be written down and even if R_i, $i=1, 2, \dots, r\leqslant s$ are known, the key parameter μ (and hence β) cannot be identified. In these circumstances only the structural parameters γ_{01} can be identified. None of the other parameters are identifiable when the order of lags of the process generating $\mathbf{x}_{1t}$ in (6.5) is less than that of $\mathbf{x}_t$ in the structural equation (6.1). Clearly, some *a priori* restrictions on the orders of lags in the economic relations are required if the RE model is to be identified. As will be seen below, this is a general result and survives the various generalizations of the RE model (6.1) which will be considered in this chapter. When the necessary condition for identification is satisfied (i.e. $r>s$), relations (6.8c) provide us with the total of $k(r-s)-1$ over-identifying restrictions. These over-identifying restrictions are known in the literature as cross-equation parametric restrictions, and play an important role in the indirect tests of the REH (see section 7.5).

The results obtained so far can be summarized by the following proposition.

Proposition 6.1 The RE model (6.1), with current expectations and with serially uncorrelated disturbances will be identified if

(a) there are variables in the model such that their values at time t cannot be anticipated perfectly at time $t-1$; and if
(b) the order of the process generating $\{\mathbf{x}_{1t}\}$, the variables that cannot be anticipated perfectly, is strictly greater than the order of the distributed lag function assumed for the predetermined variables of the model.

Condition (b), although necessary, is not clearly sufficient for the identification of the RE model (6.1). It is also important to note that the above proposition is not robust to particular changes in the specification of the RE model. In what follows we re-examine the identification problem under three possible extensions/specializations of (6.1).

6.3.1 *Models with Current Expectations of the Endogenous and the Exogenous Variables*

Consider the following extension of (6.1)

$$y_t = \beta y_t^* + \sum_{i=0}^{s} \gamma_i' \mathbf{x}_{t-i} + \delta' \mathbf{x}_t^* + u_t,$$

and suppose that none of the variables in $\mathbf{x}_t$ are perfectly predictable. Then under the assumption that the disturbances u_t are serially uncorrelated, the pseudo-reduced form equation of this model is easily seen to be

$$y_t = (1-\beta)^{-1}(\beta\gamma_0 + \delta)'\mathbf{x}_t^* + \gamma_0\mathbf{x}_t + (1-\beta)^{-1}\sum_{i=1}^{s} \gamma_i'\mathbf{x}_{t-i} + u_t,$$

which is indistinguishable from the pseudo-reduced form equation of (6.1) given by (6.3). Therefore, a RE equation with only current expectations which contains both an expected and a realized value of the same exogenous variable cannot be identified. This result does not necessarily hold in models with future expectations.

6.3.2 *Models with Autocorrelated Disturbances*

Consider now the case where the disturbances u_t follow the stationary ARMA(p,q) process

$$\rho(L)u_t = \phi(L)\varepsilon_t, \tag{6.9}$$

where

$$\rho(L)=1+\rho_1 L+\rho_2 L^2+\ldots+\rho_p L^p, \tag{6.10a}$$

$$\phi(L)=1+\phi_1 L+\phi_2 L^2+\ldots+\phi_q L^q, \tag{6.10b}$$

and L is the one-period lag operator (i.e. $Lu_t=u_{t-1}$). In this case the disturbances ξ_t of the pseudo-reduced form equation (6.3), is still given by (6.4), but $E(u_t|\Omega_{t-1})$ is no longer equal to zero. From (6.9) we have[3]

$$\begin{aligned} E(u_t|\Omega_{t-1}) &= (\phi_1 L+\phi_2 L^2+\ldots+\phi_q L^q)\,\varepsilon_t-(\rho_1 L+\rho_2 L^2+\ldots+\rho_p L^p)\,u_t, \\ &= \{\phi(L)-1\}\,\varepsilon_t-\{\rho(L)-1\}\,u_t, \\ &= u_t-\varepsilon_t. \end{aligned}$$

Using this result in (6.4) it now follows that

$$\xi_t=(1+\mu)\,u_t-\mu\varepsilon_t,$$

or upon substituting for u_t from (6.9)

$$\rho(L)\,\xi_t=\psi(L)\,\varepsilon_t,$$

where $\psi(L)=(1+\mu)\phi(L)-\mu\rho(L)$. That is, the pseudo-reduced form disturbances ξ_t will be autocorrelated and will follow a stationary ARMA$\{p, \max(p,q)\}$ process. The coefficients of the polynomial lag operator $\psi(L)$ are given by

$$\begin{aligned} &\psi_0=1, \\ &\psi_i=(1+\mu)\,\phi_i-\mu\rho_i, \quad i=1,2,\ldots,q \\ &\psi_i=-\mu\rho_i. \quad\quad\quad\quad\ i=q+1,q+2,\ldots,p \end{aligned}$$

Therefore the presence of autocorrelation amongst the disturbances of the RE model (6.1) will help identification by imposing further restrictions on the coefficient of the expectational variable (i.e. β) whenever the order of the autoregressive part of the error process is strictly greater than the order of its moving-average part (i.e. $p>q$).

6.3.3 *Exclusion Restrictions*

Identification of the RE model (6.1) can also be achieved if some of the variables in Ω_t that are included in the $\mathbf{x}_{1t}$-process can be excluded *a priori* from the RE model itself. Suppose that

$$\mathbf{x}_{1t}=\sum_{i=1}^{r} R_i \mathbf{x}_{t-i}+G'\mathbf{z}_{t-1}+\mathbf{v}_{1t}, \tag{6.11}$$

---

[3] Notice that under the REH the values of ε_{t-i}, $i=1,2,\ldots$ are all implied by the information set Ω_{t-1}, and knowledge of the equations (6.1) and (6.9). That is $E(\varepsilon_{t-i}|\Omega_{t-1})=\varepsilon_{t-i}$, for $i=1,2,\ldots$

where $\mathbf{z}_t$ represents an $h \times 1$ vector of observations on the variables in Ω_t not included in the model (6.1), and G' is a $k_1 \times h$ parameter matrix. Then assuming that u_t are serially uncorrelated the (observable) reduced-form equation corresponding to (6.1) and (6.11) will be

$$y_t = \sum_{i=0}^{\max(r,s)} \theta_i' \mathbf{x}_{t-i} + \mu \gamma_{01}' G' \mathbf{z}_{t-1} + u_t, \tag{6.12}$$

where θ_i are the same as those already given in relations (6.8). Since γ_{01} is identifiable irrespective of whether $r > s$ or not, it follows that μ (and hence other structural parameters) can be identified through the coefficients of $\mathbf{z}_{t-1}$ in (6.12). Since G can be estimated consistently using (6.11), and given that we only need an estimate of μ in order to identify the remaining structural parameters, the *a priori* exclusion of $\mathbf{z}_{t-1}$ from (6.1) provides us with $h-1$ overidentifying restrictions. It is perhaps worth noting that the necessary order condition for identification stated in proposition 6.1, namely $r > s$, can be regarded as a special case of the exclusion restrictions. When $r > s$ there are in effect variables in the specification of the $\mathbf{x}_{1t}$-process that are excluded from the RE model (6.1). Whether such exclusion restrictions can be justified on *a priori* grounds is difficult to ascertain, and crucially depends on the economic interpretation that is given to the RE model.

Important examples of the identification of RE models by means of exclusion restrictions are provided in the empirical literature on tests of the neutrality of the anticipated monetary policy. Even the approach by Neftci and Sargent (1978), and Bean (1984), whereby the identification of the new classical output equation is achieved by utilizing information concerning structural breaks, falls under the category of identification by exclusion restrictions. This is because the structural breaks in the policy regime can be specified by suitable choice of variables in $\mathbf{z}_{t-1}$ which are then excluded from the output equation.

Example 6.1 Identification of the Lucas Aggregate Supply Function

Tests of the natural rate–rational expectations (NR–RE) hypothesis attempted in the literature, for example by Lucas (1973), Barro (1977, 1978), and Mishkin (1982, 1983), presuppose that the underlying RE model is identified. Here we consider the identification of the general form of Lucas's aggregate supply function already discussed in some detail in example 5.1, and derive the necessary order conditions for its identification. The pseudo-reduced form equation of the aggregate supply function (5.22) is given by (5.27), which we write as

$$\tilde{y}_t = \sum_{i=1}^{s} \mu_i \tilde{y}_{t-i} + \beta(m_t - m_t^*) + u_t, \tag{6.13}$$

where $\beta = (1+\gamma)^{-1}\gamma$, $m_t^* = E(m_t \mid \Omega_{t-1})$, $\mu_t = (1+\gamma)^{-1}\varepsilon_{ty}$, and for simplicity of exposition we have assumed that the velocity of circulation of money is constant (i.e. $\varepsilon_{tv}=0$).[4] All the other notations are defined in example 5.1. It is clear that when the movements of the money supply are perfectly predictable (i.e. $m_t^*=m_t$), the key parameter γ will be unidentified. In the case that m_t is not perfectly predictable but is known to follow the general feedback policy rule given by (5.25), the best linear predictor of m_t relative to the information set $\Omega_{t-1}=(y_{t-1}, y_{t-2}, \ldots; m_{t-1}, m_{t-2}, \ldots)$ will be

$$m_t^* = \sum_{i=1}^{a} a_i m_{t-i} + \sum_{i=1}^{b} b_i \tilde{y}_{t-i}. \tag{6.14}$$

In view of the general discussion of the identification problem above, it is now easily seen that since lagged values of the (logarithm) of the money supply m_{t-i} ($i \geqslant 1$) are excluded from (6.13) but are included in the policy rule (5.25), the Lucas aggregate supply function is (globally) identifiable. In general the model, as specified in (5.22), will be over-identified. The number of over-identifying restrictions is determined by the orders of lags on m_t and on y_t in the policy feedback rule (i.e. a and b respectively), and the order of lags on $\tilde{y}_t = y_t - \bar{y}_t$ in the supply function (i.e. s). When $s \geqslant b$, the number of over-identifying restrictions is equal to $a-1$.

The above identification problem has also been studied by Sargent (1976b, 1979b), Nelson (1979), and McCallum (1979). These authors consider the case where s, a, and b, the orders of the distributed lag relations in (6.13) and (6.14) are all infinitely large. In such a circumstance, as is shown by McCallum (1979), there will be an infinite number of over-identifying restrictions linking the distributed lag coefficients a_i in the policy rules (5.25) or (6.14) to the coefficients of m_{t-i}, $i \geqslant 1$ in a freely estimated distributed lag relation between y_t, its past values, and current and lagged values of m_t. This result, however, crucially depends on the assumption that current and lagged values of m_t do not enter the aggregate supply function. This assumption clearly renders the new classical supply function identifiable, but will be of limited value if the new classical model is to be confronted with a viable Keynesian alternative. To see this consider the following alternative specification of the aggregate supply function which allows for the possibility of a 'Keynesian' effect of changes in money supply on the deviation of output from its natural level

$$\tilde{y}_t = \sum_{i=1}^{s} \mu_i \tilde{y}_{t-i} + \sum_{i=0}^{c} c_i m_{t-i} + \beta(m_t - m_t^*) + u_t. \tag{6.15}$$

Under the new classical model $c_i=0$, for $i=0, 1, \ldots, c$. We now consider the problem of identification of c_i. Replacing m_t^* from (6.14) in the above specification we obtain

$$\tilde{y}_t = \sum_{i=1}^{\max(s,b)} \theta_i \tilde{y}_{t-i} + \sum_{i=0}^{\max(c,a)} \delta_i m_{t-i} + u_t.$$

[4] Notice that the restriction $\varepsilon_{tv}=0$ would also follow if we assume that the velocity of circulation is not constant but that its movements can be predicted perfectly.

The precise relationships between the reduced form parameters θ_i and δ_i and the structural parameters μ_i, c_i and β depend on the signs of $s-b$ and $c-a$. When $b>s$ and $a>c$ we have

$$\begin{aligned} \theta_i &= \mu_i - \beta b_i, && \text{for } i=1,2,\ldots,s, \\ \theta_i &= -\beta b_i, && \text{for } i=s+1,\ldots,b, \\ \delta_0 &= c_0+\beta, && \\ \delta_i &= c_i - \beta a_i, && \text{for } i=1,2,\ldots,c, \\ \delta_i &= -\beta a_i, && \text{for } i=c+1,\ldots,a. \end{aligned}$$

In this case all the structural parameters, including c_i, are globally identifiable and there will be a total number of $(a+b)-(c+s)-1$ over-identifying restrictions. The order condition for identification of the parameters of the generalized aggregate supply function (6.15) is given either by $a>c$ or $b>s$. Neither of these conditions is clearly satisfied if the orders of lags in the supply function are infinitely large. Therefore, unless some *a priori* restrictions are placed on the orders of the distributed lag relations in the supply function it is not possible to empirically distinguish between a 'Keynesian' and a new classical model within the present linear framework. In other words, in the absence of *a priori* restrictions on the orders of the lag distributions the 'Keynesian' and the new classical models will be observationally equivalent. As can be seen from the following example, a similar result will also be obtained if the Lucas aggregate supply function (5.22) is replaced by the version popularized in the literature by Barro's empirical work.[5]

Example 6.2 Identification of Models with Lagged Unanticipated Effects

Consider the pseudo-reduced form rational expectations model

$$y_t = \sum_{i=0}^{s} \mathbf{c}_i'(\mathbf{x}_{t-i} - \mathbf{x}_{t-i}^{*}) + \sum_{i=0}^{s} \mathbf{a}_i'\mathbf{x}_{t-i}^{*} + u_t, \tag{6.16}$$

$$\mathbf{x}_{t-i}^{*} = E(\mathbf{x}_{t-i} \mid \Omega_{t-i-1}), \tag{6.17}$$

$$\mathbf{x}_t = B'\mathbf{z}_{t-1} + \mathbf{v}_t, \tag{6.18}$$

where y_t is a scalar endogenous variable, $\mathbf{x}_t$ is a $k\times 1$ vector of explanatory variables, $\mathbf{z}_{t-1}$ is an $h\times 1$ vector of the pre-determined variables known at time $t-1$, and $\mathbf{x}_{t-i}^{*}$ denote the rational expectations of $\mathbf{x}_{t-i}$ formed at time $t-i-1$ relative to the information set Ω_{t-i-1}. The information set Ω_t is assumed to contain all the information available at time t, that is $\Omega_t = (y_t, y_{t-1}, \ldots; \mathbf{x}_t, \mathbf{x}_{t-1}, \ldots; \mathbf{z}_t, \mathbf{z}_{t-1}, \ldots)$. The random variables u_t and $\mathbf{v}_t$ represent the

[5] A critical evaluation of Barro's empirical work can be found in Pesaran (1982).

unobservable disturbances of the model and under the REH will be orthogonal to the information set Ω_{t-1}. That is

$$E(u_t|\Omega_{t-1})=0, \tag{6.19a}$$

$$E(\mathbf{v}_t|\Omega_{t-1})=0. \tag{6.19b}$$

These orthogonality conditions ensure that u_t and $\mathbf{v}_t$ have zero means and are uncorrelated with their own past values and all the past values of y_t, $\mathbf{x}_t$ and $\mathbf{z}_t$. More specifically, setting $\boldsymbol{\xi}_t=(u_t, \mathbf{v}_t')'$ and $\mathbf{f}_t=(y_t, \mathbf{x}_t', \mathbf{z}_t')'$, we have

$$E(\boldsymbol{\xi}_t)=0,$$

$$E(\boldsymbol{\xi}_t\boldsymbol{\xi}_{t-i}')=0, \quad \text{for } i=1, 2, \ldots$$

$$E(\boldsymbol{\xi}_t\mathbf{f}_{t-i}')=0, \quad \text{for } i=1, 2, \ldots$$

and

$$E(\mathbf{x}_{t-i}|\Omega_{t-i-1})=\mathbf{x}_{t-i}^*=B'\mathbf{z}_{t-i-1}.$$

But since current and future values of $\mathbf{f}_t$ are not in Ω_{t-1}, then in general

$$E(\boldsymbol{\xi}_t\mathbf{f}_{t+i}')\neq 0, \quad \text{for } i=0, 1, 2, \ldots$$

The above model forms the basis of a large number of empirical investigations in the RE literature and, in one form or another, has been employed for testing the market efficiency hypothesis, the NR–RE hypothesis and the REH using *direct* observations on expectations.[6] Here we shall first discuss the problem of identification in the relatively simple but important case where $s=0$. Most tests of the market efficiency hypothesis are based on the model of this simple case.

From (6.17) and (6.18) it is firstly clear that $\mathbf{x}_t^*=B'\mathbf{z}_{t-1}$, which if substituted in (6.16) yields the following reduced-form equation

$$y_t=\mathbf{c}_0'\mathbf{x}_t+\boldsymbol{\theta}_0'\mathbf{z}_{t-1}+u_t, \tag{6.20}$$

where

$$\boldsymbol{\theta}_0=B(\mathbf{a}_0-\mathbf{c}_0). \tag{6.21}$$

Given the orthogonality condition (6.19a) it is clear that the parameter matrix B is identified and can be estimated consistently by the OLS regressions of $\mathbf{x}_t$ on $\mathbf{z}_{t-1}$. The same is not, however, true of the parameters of (6.20). The correlation between u_t and $\mathbf{v}_t$ causes $\mathbf{x}_t$ and u_t to be correlated and since *all* the variables in (6.18) also appear as regressors in (6.20) then in general it will not be possible to identify the parameters $\mathbf{c}_0$ and $\boldsymbol{\theta}_0$. In empirical applications the identification is achieved by assuming a zero correlation between u_t and $\mathbf{v}_t$, which is equivalent to assuming that the explanatory variables in (6.16) are exogenous with respect to the error term u_t. Under this identifying restriction, $\mathbf{c}_0$ and $\boldsymbol{\theta}_0$ can be consistently estimated by the OLS regression of y_t on $\mathbf{x}_t$ and

[6] For a discussion of the use of this model in econometric applications and relevant references to the literature see Abel and Mishkin (1983), and Mishkin (1983).

$\mathbf{z}_{t-1}$ and the relations in (6.21) can then be used to obtain a consistent estimate of the remaining structural parameters, namely $\mathbf{a}_0$. When u_t and $\mathbf{v}_t$ are contemporaneously uncorrelated the necessary and sufficient condition for identification of $\mathbf{a}_0$ is that matrix B should be of full rank. From this it follows that the necessary order condition for identification is $h \geqslant k$, which if satisfied yields $h-k$ over-identifying restrictions given by (6.21).

Although the identification of $\mathbf{c}_0$ and $\mathbf{a}_0$ requires the *a priori* imposition of zero correlations between u_t and $\mathbf{v}_t$, it is still possible to carry out statistical tests of certain hypotheses involving the parameter vector $\mathbf{a}_0$ even when u_t and $\mathbf{v}_t$ are correlated. To see this suppose we are interested in testing $\mathbf{a}_0=0$ in (6.16) when $s=0$. Since in this case $\mathbf{c}_0$ cannot be identified, one possibility would be to use (6.17) and (6.18) to write (6.16) as

$$y_t = \boldsymbol{\phi}_0' \mathbf{z}_{t-1} + \xi_t, \tag{6.22}$$

where

$$\xi_t = u_t + \mathbf{c}_0' \mathbf{v}_t, \tag{6.23}$$

$$\boldsymbol{\phi}_0 = B\mathbf{a}_0. \tag{6.24}$$

Notice that since ξ_t and $\mathbf{z}_{t-1}$ are uncorrelated then (6.22) is a 'true' reduced-form equation, and the parameters $\boldsymbol{\phi}_0$ can be consistently estimated by the OLS regression of y_t on $\mathbf{z}_{t-1}$. A test of $\mathbf{a}_0=0$ can now be carried out by testing the hypothesis $\boldsymbol{\phi}_0=0$ in (6.22). This is because by virtue of (6.24), the restrictions $\mathbf{a}_0=0$ imply $\boldsymbol{\phi}_0=0$ and a test of the latter can be implemented by testing for zero correlations between y_t and $\mathbf{z}_{t-1}$, which is the same as testing the orthogonality condition $E(y_t|S_{t-1})=0$, where

$$S_t = (\mathbf{z}_t, \mathbf{z}_{t-1}, \ldots), \text{ with } S_t \subset \Omega_t.$$

The fact that it is possible to test for implications of $\mathbf{a}_0=0$, does not, however, mean that $\mathbf{a}_0$ itself is identifiable. The above test of the orthogonality hypothesis can be given other interpretations. Consider the alternative model defined by equations

$$y_t = \mathbf{c}_0'(\mathbf{x}_t - \mathbf{x}_t^*) + u_t,$$

and

$$\mathbf{x}_t^* = \bar{B}\mathbf{z}_{t-1},$$

where $\mathbf{x}_t$ is generated according to (6.18), and $\bar{B} \neq B$. In this model the neutrality hypothesis (i.e. the hypothesis that perfectly anticipated changes in $\mathbf{x}_t$ have no effect on y_t) is maintained but the REH is violated. The reduced form of the above model is still given by (6.22) but the parameter vector $\boldsymbol{\phi}_0$ is now defined by $(B-\bar{B})\mathbf{c}_0$. The test of the orthogonality hypothesis $E(y_t|S_{t-1})=0$ can therefore be interpreted either as a test of the REH when the neutrality hypothesis is maintained or a test of the neutrality (as in (6.16) with $s=0$) when the REH is maintained. In view of the above discussion, the orthogonality test is best regarded as a *joint* test of the rational expectations and the neutrality hypotheses (see also section 7.5).

The question that now remains is whether the above results carry over to the general case where $s \geqslant 1$. More specifically, can the neutrality hypothesis $\mathbf{a}_i = 0$, $i = 0, 1, 2, \ldots, s$ be tested when u_t and $\mathbf{v}_t$ are correlated? Use (6.17) and (6.18) in (6.16) to obtain

$$y_t = \sum_{i=0}^{s} \boldsymbol{\phi}_i' \mathbf{z}_{t-i-1} + \xi_t, \tag{6.25}$$

in which ξ_t is now given by

$$\xi_t = u_t + \sum_{i=0}^{s} \mathbf{c}_i' \mathbf{v}_{t-i},$$

and

$$\boldsymbol{\phi}_i = B a_i, \quad i = 0, 1, 2, \ldots, s.$$

As before, a test of $\{\mathbf{a}_i = 0,\ i = 0, 1, 2, \ldots, s\}$ can be carried out by testing $\{\boldsymbol{\phi}_i = 0,\ i = 0, 1, 2, \ldots, s\}$ in the reduced-form equation (6.25). But this presupposes that the reduced-form parameters $\boldsymbol{\phi}_i$ can be identified. To identify $\boldsymbol{\phi}_i$ we either need zero correlations between $\mathbf{z}_{t-i-1}$ and ξ_t or there should exist (instrumental) variables orthogonal to ξ_t that are excluded from $\mathbf{z}_{t-i-1}$, $i = 0, 1, 2, \ldots, s$. However, because of the serial correlation which is now present in the reduced-form disturbances ξ_t $(s > 0)$, for $\mathbf{z}_{t-i-1}$ to be orthogonal to ξ_t, the correlations between $\mathbf{v}_{t-i}$ and $\mathbf{z}_{t-j-1}$ should be zero for all $i, j = 0, 1, 2, \ldots, s$. This requires that $\mathbf{v}_t$ should be orthogonal to future as well as to past information on $\mathbf{z}_t$, which is clearly a much more restrictive assumption than is warranted under the REH. Therefore, unlike the case where $s = 0$, a test of $\mathbf{a}_i = 0$ in general cannot be carried out by resort to a standard orthogonality test. We need to rely on the existence of variables orthogonal to $\mathbf{v}_{t-i}$, $i = 0, 1, 2, \ldots, s$ which are at the same time excluded from $(\mathbf{z}_{t-1}, \mathbf{z}_{t-2}, \ldots, \mathbf{z}_{t-s-1})$. This is an equally demanding requirement, especially when s is relatively large.

6.4 Identification of Single-equation RE Models with Forward-looking Expectations

As compared with models of the previous section, the study of identification of RE models with forward-looking expectations involves further complications that primarily arise from the non-linear nature of the identifying restrictions and the non-uniqueness of the solution of these models discussed in chapter 5. A comprehensive discussion of identification of general RE models with forward-looking or future expectations is beyond the scope of the present volume and involves a number of as yet unresolved technical problems. Initially we restrict our analysis to first order models and in particular focus on the identification of

$$y_t = \alpha E(y_{t+1} | \Omega_t) + w_t, \tag{6.26}$$

where

$$w_t = \sum_{i=0}^{s} \gamma_i' \mathbf{x}_{t-i} + u_t. \tag{6.27}$$

All the notations are the same as before, but here we initially assume that the $k \times 1$ vector $\mathbf{x}_t$ does not contain lagged values of y_t and treat it strictly as a vector of exogenous variables.

From the discussion in chapter 5 it should be clear that, in the absence of suitable restrictions on the parameter α and/or on the content of the information set Ω_t, there will be an infinite number of solutions to choose from. Therefore, in general, without some *a priori* restrictions, the identification of (6.26) from observed data does not seem to be possible. One important type of *a priori* restriction is to impose the condition that (apart from deterministic components) the process $\{y_t\}$ is stationary. This considerably narrows down the set of feasible solutions and allows a fruitful analysis of the identification problem in the case of RE models with future expectations of the endogenous variables. Although when $|\alpha| > 1$ the stationarity assumption does not resolve the non-uniqueness problem, it nevertheless provides an appropriate starting point for the identification problem in this case. Accordingly, we investigate the identification problem on the assumption that the solution of (6.26) is stationary, and treat the two cases where $|\alpha| < 1$ and $|\alpha| > 1$ separately. For want of a better terminology we follow Sargan (1983) and refer to these as the 'regular' and the 'irregular' cases respectively.

6.4.1 *Identification in the Regular Case, $|\alpha| < 1$*

If it is known *a priori* that $|\alpha| < 1$, then the stationary solution of (6.26) is unique and is given by

$$y_t = \sum_{j=0}^{\infty} \alpha^j E(w_{t+j} | \Omega_t). \tag{6.28}$$

The details of the derivation of this solution can be found in section 5.3. Substituting w_t from (6.27) in the above solution and denoting $\Sigma_{i=0}^{s} \gamma_i' \mathbf{x}_{t-i}$ by g_t we have

$$y_t = \sum_{j=0}^{\infty} \alpha^j E(g_{t+j} | \Omega_t) + \sum_{j=0}^{\infty} \alpha^j E(u_{t+j} | \Omega_t). \tag{6.29}$$

In the case where $\{u_t\}$ is a white-noise process the second term in the above expression will be equal to u_t. But, as is demonstrated in appendix D, under the assumption that u_t follows a stationary ARMA(p,q) process, the disturbances of (6.29) will follow an ARMA$(p,p+q-1)$ process with $p-1$ parametric restrictions linking, in a highly non-linear manner, the parameters of the autoregressive part to those of the moving average part. To simplify the exposition we confine our attention to the case where u_t are serially uncorrelated.

A complete specification of the reduced-form equation (6.29) also requires modelling the future expectations of the exogenous variables $\mathbf{x}_t$. As before, we need to distinguish between those elements of $\mathbf{x}_t$ which can be forecast perfectly and those which cannot. Here, to keep the notations simple, we assume that none of the elements of $\mathbf{x}_t$ can be forecast perfectly and suppose that $\mathbf{x}_t$ is generated according to the following stationary AR(r) process

$$\mathbf{x}_t = \sum_{i=1}^{r} R_i \mathbf{x}_{t-i} + \mathbf{v}_t. \tag{6.5'}$$

Notice that in this specification $\mathbf{v}_t$ represents a $k \times 1$ white-noise process distributed independently of u_t, and R_i are $k \times k$ parameter matrices. Therefore R_i can be consistently estimated by the OLS regressions of $\mathbf{x}_t$ on $\mathbf{x}_{t-1}$, $\mathbf{x}_{t-2}, \ldots, \mathbf{x}_{t-r}$. Now the best linear predictor of $\mathbf{x}_{t+j}$ relative to the information set Ω_t may be written as[7]:

$$\mathbf{x}^*_{t+j} = \sum_{i=0}^{r-1} R_{ij} \mathbf{x}_{t-i}, \quad j = 1, 2, \ldots \tag{6.30}$$

where $R_{i1} = R_{i+1}$, for $i = 0, 1, 2, \ldots, r-1$, and $\{R_{ij}, j > 1\}$ are $k \times k$ parameter matrices that can be obtained, in a recursive manner, in terms of the autoregression matrices $R_1, R_2, \ldots, R_r$. In the simplest case when $\{\mathbf{x}_t\}$ follows an AR(1) scheme with the parameter matrix R (i.e. $R_{01} = R_1 = R$), we have

$$R_{0j} = R^j, \quad j = 1, 2, \ldots$$
$$R_{ij} = 0, \quad \forall i, j \geqslant 1.$$

Under the assumption that the disturbances u_t are non-autocorrelated, using (6.29) we have

$$y_t = \sum_{j=0}^{\infty} \alpha^j \sum_{i=0}^{s} \gamma_i' \mathbf{x}^*_{t+j-i} + u_t,$$

or equivalently,

$$y_t = \sum_{i=0}^{s} \left\{ \sum_{j=0}^{i} \alpha^j \gamma_i' \mathbf{x}^*_{t-i+j} + \sum_{j=i+1}^{\infty} \alpha^j \gamma_i' \mathbf{x}^*_{t+j-i} \right\} + u_t.$$

But since $\mathbf{x}^*_{t-i+j} = \mathbf{x}_{t-i+j}$ for $j = 0, 1, 2, \ldots, s$ and for all $j \leqslant i$, after some algebraic manipulations we obtain

$$y_t = \sum_{i=1}^{s} \delta_i' \mathbf{x}_{t-i} + \delta_0' \mathbf{z}^*_t + u_t, \tag{6.31}$$

[7] In this section $\mathbf{x}^*_{t+j}$, $j \geqslant 1$ stand for the mathematical expectations of $\mathbf{x}_{t+j}$ relative to the information set Ω_t and not Ω_{t-1} as assumed in the previous section.

where

$$\mathbf{z}_t^* = \sum_{j=0}^{\infty} \alpha^j \mathbf{x}_{t+j}^*,$$

and

$$\delta_i = \sum_{j=i}^{s} \alpha^{j-i} \gamma_j, \quad i = 0, 1, 2, \ldots, s, \tag{6.32}$$

or in a backward recursive form

$$\delta_{s-i} = \alpha \delta_{s-i+1} + \gamma_{s-i}, \quad i = 1, 2, \ldots, s, \tag{6.32'}$$

with $\delta_s = \gamma_s$.

The solution given by (6.31) has two important features: firstly it involves all the future expected values of the exogenous variables; and secondly it depends on the structural parameters α and $(\gamma_0, \gamma_1, \ldots, \gamma_s)$ in a highly non-linear manner. The unobserved values $\mathbf{x}_{t+i}^*$ can be eliminated from the solution if, for example, it is assumed that $\{\mathbf{x}_t\}$ follows the stationary AR(r) process given by (6.5′). In such a case using results (D.14) derived in appendix D, an expression for $\mathbf{z}_t^*$ can be obtained explicitly in terms of the parameters of the $\mathbf{x}_t$-process, R_i. We have

$$\mathbf{z}_t^* = (I + \Phi_0)^{-1} (I_k - \sum_{j=1}^{r-1} \Phi_j L^j) \mathbf{x}_t,$$

where I_k represents an identity matrix of order k, and

$$\Phi_j = - \sum_{i=j+1}^{r} \alpha^{i-j} R_i, \quad j = 0, 1, 2, \ldots, r-1.$$

This result can also be written in the form of the following backward recursive relations

$$\Phi_i = \alpha(\Phi_{i+1} - R_{i+1}), \quad i = r-2, r-3, \ldots, 1, \tag{6.33}$$

where $\Phi_{r-1} = -\alpha R_r$. Substituting $\mathbf{z}_t^*$, given above, in relation (6.31) now yields

$$y_t = \sum_{i=0}^{\max(s, r-1)} \theta_i' \mathbf{x}_{t-i} + u_t, \tag{6.31'}$$

where

$$\theta_0 = (I_k + \Phi_0')^{-1} \delta_0, \tag{6.34a}$$

$$\theta_i = \delta_i - \Phi_i'(I_k + \Phi_0')^{-1} \delta_0, \quad i = 1, 2, \ldots, s \tag{6.34b}$$

$$\theta_i = -\Phi_i'(I_k + \Phi_0')^{-1} \delta_0, \quad i = s+1, \ldots, r-1. \tag{6.34c}$$

Under the assumption that $\mathbf{x}_t$ are exogenously determined with respect to u_t, the reduced-form parameters θ_i are globally identified and can be estimated consistently by the OLS regression of y_t on $\mathbf{x}_t, \mathbf{x}_{t-1}, \ldots, \mathbf{x}_{t-m}$, where $m = \max(s, r-1)$.

The system of equations in (6.34) can now be used to obtain the structural parameters α, $\gamma_0, \gamma_1, \ldots, \gamma_s$ in terms of the estimates of $\theta_0, \theta_1, \ldots, \theta_m$; and those of $R_1, R_2, \ldots, R_r$.[8] The necessary condition for this system of equations to have a solution is given by $r > s+1$; otherwise there will be more unknowns than there are equations in (6.34). When $r > s+1$, parameter α can be estimated consistently using any one of the relations in (6.34c), or equivalently using any one of the following $k(r-s-1)$ equations

$$\theta_{s+1} = \alpha(R'_{s+2}\theta_0 + \theta_{s+2}),$$
$$\theta_{s+2} = \alpha(R'_{s+3}\theta_0 + \theta_{s+3}),$$
$$\vdots$$
$$\theta_{r-2} = \alpha(R'_{r-1}\theta_0 + \theta_{r-1}),$$
$$\theta_{r-1} = \alpha R'_r\theta_0.$$

These equations can be obtained by utilizing (6.33) and (6.34a) in (6.34c), and provide us with a total number of $k(r-s-1)-1$ over-identifying restrictions. The RE model will be exactly identified if and only if $r = s+2$ and $k = 1$. Given a consistent estimate of α, parameters Φ_i, defined recursively by (6.33), and hence $\delta_0, \delta_1, \ldots, \delta_s$ can be estimated consistently using (6.34a) and (6.34b). The structural parameters γ_i can then be obtained in a backward recursive fashion by means of relations (6.32′).

The above discussion now allows us to state

Proposition 6.2 When $|\alpha| < 1$ the necessary order condition for identification of (6.26) is that the order of the autoregressive process generating $\mathbf{x}_t$ should be strictly greater than one plus the order of the distributed lag function of $\mathbf{x}_t$ in the RE model.[9]

It is interesting to recall from the analysis of the previous section that in the case of RE models with current expectations of the endogenous variables, the necessary condition for the identification of the structural parameters was less restrictive (i.e. $r > s$ instead of $r > s+1$). This is, however, solely due to the different information sets assumed to be available at the time expectations of the current and the future endogenous variables are formed. If in (6.26) expectations of y_{t+1} were formed conditional on Ω_{t-1} instead of Ω_t, then the necessary condition for identification of the RE model (6.26) would have also been $r > s$. It is also interesting to note that when it is known *a priori* that $|\alpha| < 1$, and that the current and future expectational variables in models (6.1) and (6.26) are formed on the basis of the information set, Ω_{t-1}, then these RE

---

[8] Recall that R_i can be consistently estimated by the OLS regressions of $\mathbf{x}_t$ on $\mathbf{x}_{t-1}, \ldots, \mathbf{x}_{t-r}$.

[9] As will be shown later, in section 7.7.2, this proposition holds even for higher-order RE models with lagged dependent variables.

models will be observationally equivalent. This result holds even if $r>s$. When $r \leqslant s$ the observational equivalence of (6.1) and (6.26) follows trivially from the fact that when Ω_t in (6.26) is replaced by Ω_{t-1}, both models will be observationally equivalent to the non-RE model $y_t = \Sigma_{i=0}^{s} \gamma_i' \mathbf{x}_{t-i} + u_t$.

Example 6.3 The Efficient Market Hypothesis

An important example of a RE model with future expectations arises in the application of the efficient market hypothesis to the determination of security prices traded on the stock market. The efficient market hypothesis, like the new classical version of the natural rate hypothesis, is composed of two parts: the market clearing hypothesis and the rational expectations hypothesis. Broadly speaking, the efficient market hypothesis postulates that the error in forecasting the rate of return from holding securities traded on stock markets or foreign exchange markets is orthogonal to the 'costlessly' available information at the time forecasts are made. Let y_{t+1} denote the rate of return on holding a particular security between time t and time $t+1$. Considering the speculative nature of trade in securities, y_{t+1} will be equal to the sum of dividend payments and capital gains or losses. That is

$$y_{t+1} = \underbrace{(d_{t+1}/P_t)}_{\text{Dividend payments}} + \underbrace{(P_{t+1} - P_t)/P_t}_{\text{Capital gains}}, \tag{6.35}$$

where P_t is the price of the security at time t and d_{t+1} is the dividend payments received on holding the security for one period between time t and time $t+1$. Under a number of special conditions the efficient market hypothesis postulates that[10]

$$E(y_{t+1} - \bar{y}_{t+1} | \Omega_t) = 0, \tag{6.36}$$

where $\bar{y}_{t+1}$ is the market equilibrium value of y_{t+1} and Ω_t is the information (or a subset of the information) available at time t. There are different equilibrium models for the determination of $\bar{y}_{t+1}$. However, in most applications of the efficient market hypothesis the equilibrium rate of return $\bar{y}_{t+1}$ is assumed to be constant, $\bar{y}_{t+1} = \bar{y}$. In this simple case the orthogonality condition (6.36) simply states that $\bar{y}$ is the best predictor of the rate of return. The condition $E(\bar{y}_{t+1} | \Omega_t) = \bar{y}$ also forms the basis of most tests of market efficiency implemented in the literature as reviewed, for example, by Fama (1970, 1976). To test the market efficiency hypothesis, one possibility would be to test the hypothesis of $\phi_0 = 0$ in the context of the following OLS regression

$$y_{t+1} = \text{cons.} + \phi_0' \mathbf{z}_t + \varepsilon_{t+1},$$

[10] The equation (6.36) assumes that agents operate in a competitive market environment, have time-separable utility functions, are risk neutral, and do not face distortionary taxes.

where $\mathbf{z}_t$ is a vector of observations on the variables in the information set Ω_t and $E(\varepsilon_{t+1}|\Omega_t)=0$. An alternative method of testing the market efficiency hypothesis would be to focus on security prices rather than on rates of return, and to test the predictions of the hypothesis against an alternative model for the determination of security prices. By considering this alternative approach we will be able to shed light on the necessary conditions for the identification of the parameters of the RE model which underlie the orthogonality condition (6.36).

Substituting y_{t+1} from (6.35) in (6.36) and recalling that by assumption $\bar{y}_{t+1}=\bar{y}$, we have

$$P_t = \alpha E(P_{t+1}|\Omega_t) + \alpha E(d_{t+1}|\Omega_t), \tag{6.37}$$

where $\alpha=(1+\bar{y})^{-1}$ represents the discount factor. In situations where the equilibrium rate of return $\bar{y}$ is positive (a case usually assumed in the literature), then $0<\alpha<1$ and the above equation has a unique stationary solution, although non-stationary solutions containing 'speculative bubbles' of the type discussed in section 5.3.2 cannot be ruled out (for examples of non-stationary bubbles in the context of the present problem see Blanchard and Watson, 1982). Confining ourselves to bubble-free solutions, the unique stationary solution of (6.37) is given by (cf. Shiller, 1981, eq. 2):

$$P_t = \sum_{i=1}^{\infty} \alpha^i E(d_{t+i}|\Omega_t), \tag{6.38}$$

which restates the efficiency market hypothesis in the alternative fundamental form (that is in equilibrium security prices are equal to the discounted value of expected future dividends). This representation of the orthogonality condition which focuses on the determination of security prices also forms the basis of the 'volatility' tests developed by LeRoy and Porter (1981) and Shiller (1981).

Consider now the following more general model for the determination of security prices as an alternative to (6.37)

$$P_t = \alpha E(P_{t+1}|\Omega_t) + \beta E(d_{t+1}|\Omega_t) + \sum_{i=0}^{s} \gamma_i d_{t-i} + u_t, \tag{6.39}$$

where μ_t obeys the orthogonality condition $E(\mu_t|\Omega_{t-1})=0$, with a constant variance σ_u^2, and γ_i are scalar constants. In the context of this general model the test of the market efficiency hypothesis can be carried out by testing the joint hypothesis of $\alpha=\beta$; $\gamma_i=0$, for $i=0, 1, 2, \ldots, s$; and $\sigma_u^2=0$. A prerequisite for the implementation of such a test is the identification of the structural parameters α, β, γ_0, γ_1, ..., γ_s, and σ_u^2. Under the hypothesis that dividend payments d_t follow an AR(r) process, the result stated in proposition 6.2 suggests that unless $r>s+1$ these structural parameters cannot be identified. Even when this condition is satisfied it may not be possible to identify all the structural parameters. Suppose $s=0$, and d_t follows the second-order process (i.e. $r=2$)

$$d_t = \rho_1 d_{t-1} + \rho_2 d_{t-2} + \varepsilon_t, \tag{6.40}$$

where ε_t is a white-noise process. In this case the alternative model (6.39) simplifies to

$$P_t = \alpha E(P_{t+1}|\Omega_t) + (\beta\rho_1 + \gamma_0)d_t + \beta\rho_2 d_{t-1} + u_t,$$

which yields the following unique stationary solution (assuming that $0 < \alpha < 1$)

$$P_t = (\beta\rho_1 + \gamma_0)\sum_{i=0}^{\infty} \alpha^i d^*_{t+i} + \beta\rho_2 \sum_{i=0}^{\infty} \alpha^i d^*_{t+i-1} + u_t,$$

where $d^*_{t+i} = E(d_{t+i}|\Omega_t)$. Now using results derived in appendix D we have

$$\sum_{i=0}^{\infty} \alpha^i d^*_{t+i} = \frac{1}{1-\alpha\bar{\rho}}(d_t + \alpha\rho_2 d_{t-1}),$$

where $\bar{\rho} = \rho_1 + \alpha\rho_2$. Similarly

$$\sum_{i=0}^{\infty} \alpha^i d^*_{t+i-1} = d_{t-1} + \alpha \sum_{i=0}^{\infty} \alpha^i d^*_{t+i},$$

$$= \frac{1}{1-\alpha\bar{\rho}}\{\alpha d_t + (1-\alpha\rho_1)d_{t-1}\}.$$

Substituting these results in the above solution we obtain

$$P_t = \left(\frac{\gamma_0 + \beta\bar{\rho}}{1-\alpha\bar{\rho}}\right) d_t + \frac{\rho_2(\alpha\gamma_0 + \beta)}{(1-\alpha\bar{\rho})} d_{t-1} + u_t, \tag{6.41}$$

where $\bar{\rho} = \rho_1 + \alpha\rho_2$. It is clear from this reduced-form equation that only the variance of u_t can be identified. None of the other structural parameters are identifiable, and a test of the efficient market hypothesis is only possible with respect to the variance of u_t. In this special case the hypothesis $\sigma_u^2 = 0$ can be tested by means of instrumental variable regression of P_t on d_t and d_{t-1} using $d_{t-2}, d_{t-3}, \ldots$ or other variables in the information set as instruments. This is an extremely powerful test and most likely will lead to the rejection of the market efficiency hypothesis.

The test of $\sigma_u^2 = 0$ in (6.41) is similar to the 'volatility' test mentioned above. This test is based on the result that under the efficient market hypothesis security prices should be less volatile than the perfect foresight prices. Denoting the latter by $\tilde{P}_t$ and using (6.38) we have

$$\tilde{P}_t = \sum_{i=1}^{\infty} \alpha^i d_{t+i},$$

which upon using (6.40) yields

$$\tilde{P}_t = \frac{\alpha\bar{\rho}}{1-\alpha\bar{\rho}} d_t + \frac{\alpha\rho_2}{1-\alpha\bar{\rho}} d_{t-1} + \eta_t,$$

where

$$\eta_t = (1 - \alpha\bar{\rho})^{-1} \sum_{i=1}^{\infty} \alpha^i \varepsilon_{t+i}.$$

But under the efficient market hypothesis, using the expected present value formula we have[11]:

$$P_t = \frac{\alpha\bar{\rho}}{1 - \alpha\bar{\rho}} d_t + \frac{\alpha\rho_2}{1 - \alpha\bar{\rho}} d_{t-1}.$$

Hence

$$\tilde{P}_t = P_t + \eta_t,$$

and as is required the 'volatility' condition $\mathrm{var}(\tilde{P}_t) \geqslant \mathrm{var}(P_t)$ follows. Therefore the volatility test can also be interpreted as a test of $\sigma_u^2 = 0$, in (6.39).

6.4.2 *Identification in the Irregular Case, $|\alpha| > 1$*

In this case the RE equation (6.26) admits an infinite number of stationary solutions. Following Broze et al. (1985), these solutions can be written down in terms of the arbitrary martingale difference process $\{\varepsilon_t^0\}$ with respect to the information set Ω_{t-1}, (see section 5.3 for further details). A complete characterization of the stationary solutions of (6.26) is already given by (5.45). Substituting w_t from (6.27) in (5.45) now yields

$$y_t = \alpha^{-1} y_{t-1} - \alpha^{-1} \sum_{i=0}^{s} \gamma_i' \mathbf{x}_{t-i-1} - \alpha^{-1} u_{t-1} + \varepsilon_t^0 \qquad (6.42)$$

where $E(\varepsilon_t^0 | \Omega_{t-1}) = 0$. The identification and estimation of the parameters of the above reduced-form equation now crucially depend on the specific choice of ε_t^0 and the content of the information set Ω_t. Different assumptions concerning ε_t^0 and Ω_t can lead to different identifiability requirements. Here we assume that ε_t^0 has a constant variance and that Ω_t contains observations on the variables y_t, $\mathbf{x}_t$, u_t and their lagged values. The assumption that u_t is included in Ω_t is justifiable in a decision-making context where the 'representative' agent observes the realization of u_t at the time y_t is decided upon. Although the (observing) econometrician does not observe u_t, it is assumed that he/she knows the information set and the form of the decision rule employed by the representative agent.[12] The econometrician's objective is to identify the structural parameters α, γ_0, γ_1, ..., γ_s, and σ_u^2 from the available time-series data on y_t and $\mathbf{x}_t$. The key to the identification of these parameters lies in a proper utilization of the correlation of ε_t^0 and the innovations in the variables included in the information set Ω_t. Under the assumption that Ω_t

---

[11] This result can also be obtained from (6.41) by setting $\beta = \alpha$, $\gamma_0 = 0$, and $\sigma_u^2 = 0$.

[12] See example 7.2 in the next chapter for more details.

contains only the variables y_t, $\mathbf{x}_t$, u_t and their lagged values, the correlations between ε_t^0 and the innovations in $\mathbf{x}_t$ and u_t can be characterized in terms of the following linear regression[13]

$$\varepsilon_t^0 = \delta_x'(\mathbf{x}_t - \mathbf{x}_t^*) + \delta_u(u_t - u_t^*) + \varepsilon_t,$$

where ε_t is a white-noise process with variance σ_ε^2 distributed independently of the innovations in $\mathbf{x}_t$ and u_t.[14] δ_x, δ_u and σ_ε^2 will be referred to as auxiliary parameters. Substituting this result in (6.42), and noting that when u_t are serially uncorrelated $u_t^* = E(u_t|\Omega_{t-1}) = 0$, we have

$$y_t = \alpha^{-1}y_{t-1} - \alpha^{-1}\sum_{i=0}^{s}\gamma_i'\mathbf{x}_{t-i-1} + \delta_x'(\mathbf{x}_t - \mathbf{x}_t^*) + \xi_t, \tag{6.43}$$

where

$$\xi_t = \delta_u u_t - \alpha^{-1}u_{t-1} + \varepsilon_t. \tag{6.44}$$

This composite disturbance term has the same serial correlation pattern as a first order moving-average process. We can therefore write

$$\xi_t = \nu_t + \phi\nu_{t-1} \tag{6.44'}$$

in which ν_t is a white-noise process with mean zero and a constant variance σ_ν^2. The new parameters ϕ and σ_ν^2 are related to the structural and auxiliary parameters in the following manner:

$$(1+\phi^2)\sigma_\nu^2 = \sigma_u^2(\delta_u^2 + \alpha^{-2}) + \sigma_\varepsilon^2, \tag{6.45a}$$

$$\phi\sigma_\nu^2 = -\alpha^{-1}\delta_u\sigma_u^2. \tag{6.45b}$$

It is now clear that estimation of (6.43) subject to an MA(1) error process at most yields consistent estimates for α, γ_i, δ_x, ϕ and σ_ν^2, and does not allow the identification of δ_u, σ_u^2 and σ_ε^2 (and hence u_t) irrespective of whether direct observations on $\mathbf{x}_t^*$ are available or not. One important implication of this result is that bootstrap or bubbles effects represented by ε_t in solution (6.43) cannot be identified.[15] Lack of identification of u_t also means that future expectations of y_t defined by

$$E(y_{t+1}|\Omega_t) = \alpha^{-1}y_t - \alpha^{-1}\sum_{i=0}^{s}\gamma_i'\mathbf{x}_{t-i} - \alpha^{-1}u_t,$$

---

[13] The assumption that the regression of ε_t^0 on the innovations of $\mathbf{x}_t$ and u_t is linear can be justified in situations where linear models are employed as a first approximation or when it is known that y_t, $\mathbf{x}_t$ and u_t have a covariance stationary multivariate normal distribution. (For a proof see section 7.7.2.)

[14] As will be shown in section 7.7.2, ε_t may also be viewed as innovations in variables representing bootstrap or bubbles effects, assuming of course that observations on these variables are allowed to enter the information set Ω_t.

[15] This is a general result and holds for higher-order RE models. The problem of identification of bubbles effects in RE models is recently discussed by Hamilton and Whiteman (1985).

will not be identifiable either.[16] Despite this, all the other structural parameters $\alpha, \gamma_0, \gamma_1, \ldots, \gamma_s$ can in general be identified using (6.43) and noting that ξ_t have an MA(1) representation. In the case that $\mathbf{x}_t$ follows the AR(r) process (6.5′) the reduced-form equation of the model can be obtained by replacing $\mathbf{x}_t^* = \Sigma_{i=1}^r R_i \mathbf{x}_{t-i}$ in (6.43). We have

$$(1-\alpha^{-1}L)y_t = \left(\sum_{i=0}^{\max(s+1,r)} \beta_i' L^i\right)\mathbf{x}_t + (1+\phi L)v_t, \tag{6.46}$$

where $\xi_t = (1+\phi L)v_t$ is already defined by (6.44′). Hence

$$\beta_0 = \delta_x, \tag{6.47a}$$

$$\beta_i = -\{\alpha^{-1}\gamma_{i-1} + R_i'\beta_0\}, \quad \text{for } i = 1, 2, \ldots, s+1, \tag{6.47b}$$

$$\beta_i = -R_i'\beta_0, \quad \text{for } i = s+2, \ldots, r. \tag{6.47c}$$

These results show that the structural parameters $\alpha, \gamma_0, \gamma_1, \ldots, \gamma_s$, and the auxiliary parameters δ_x are identifiable irrespective of whether $r > s+1$ or not. There is, however, one important qualification that should be borne in mind: there should not exist a common factor between the lag structures on y_t, $\mathbf{x}_t$ and ξ_t. When this condition is not satisfied, by eliminating the common factor $(1-\alpha^{-1}L)$ from both sides of (6.46), once again we obtain (if $|\alpha| < 1$) the reduced-form equation (6.31′) and, as already demonstrated, the identification of the structural parameters in this case can be achieved if and only if $r > s+1$. Seen from this perspective the unique solution (6.31′) obtained for the regular case is nested within the set of solutions characterized by (6.46). The reduced-form equation of the regular case can always be derived from (6.46) by imposition of suitable parametric restrictions on the auxiliary parameters δ_x, δ_u and σ_ε^2, so that (6.46) has the common factor $(1-\alpha^{-1}L)$. In the case of the present problem the relevant restrictions are given by

$$\sum_{i=0}^{\max(s+1,r)} \beta_i' \alpha^i = 0,$$

and

$$1 + \alpha\phi = 0.$$

Now using the results (6.47) in the first of the above two restrictions it is easily seen that

$$\delta_x = \left(I_k - \sum_{i=1}^{r} \alpha^i R_i'\right)^{-1} \left(\sum_{i=0}^{s} \alpha^i \gamma_i\right). \tag{6.48a}$$

[16] The expression for $E(y_{t+1}|\Omega_t)$ given in the text can be obtained using (6.43) and noting from (6.44) that $E(\xi_{t+1}|\Omega_t) = -\alpha^{-1}u_t$.

Similarly replacing $\phi = -\alpha^{-1}$ in (6.45) and solving for σ_ε^2 and δ_u we obtain

$$\sigma_\varepsilon^1 = \sigma_u^2(1-\delta_u)(\delta_u - \alpha^{-2}), \tag{6.48b}$$

$$\delta_u = \sigma_u^2/\sigma_v^2. \tag{6.48c}$$

Under the restrictions (6.48) the general solution (6.46) will have the common factor $(1-\alpha^{-1}L)$ and can be written as

$$y_t = \sum_{i=0}^{\max(s,r-1)} \theta_i' x_{t-i} + v_t,$$

where v_t is a white-noise process and[17]

$$(1-\alpha^{-1}L)\sum_{i=0}^{\max(s,r-1)} \theta_i' L^i = \sum_{i=0}^{\max(s+1,r)} \beta_i' L^i.$$

Now using relations (6.47) in the above result we obtain the following recursive relations for the derivation of θ_i:

$$\theta_0 = \delta_x = \left(I_k - \sum_{i=1}^{r} \alpha^i R_i'\right)^{-1}\left(\sum_{i=0}^{s} \alpha^i \gamma_i\right), \tag{6.49a}$$

$$\theta_i = \alpha^{-1}(\theta_{i-1} - \gamma_{i-1}) - R_i'\theta_0, \quad \text{for } i = 1, 2, \ldots, s+1, \tag{6.49b}$$

$$\theta_i = \alpha^{-1}\theta_{i-1} - R_i'\theta_0, \quad \text{for } i = s+2, \ldots, r-1. \tag{6.49c}$$

These recursive relations will give exactly the same values for θ_i as those defined by (6.34) and (6.32′). They are, however, easier to use in practice.

6.4.3 *Extensions to RE Models with Lagged Endogenous Variables and Future Expectations*

Another important advantage of the above approach to the derivation of the reduced-form equation for the regular case lies in the fact that the approach can be easily extended to the RE models with lagged endogenous variables and future expectations. To see this, consider the following generalization of (6.26)

$$y_t = \sum_{i=1}^{m} \lambda_i y_{t-i} + \alpha E(y_{t+1}|\Omega_t) + \sum_{i=0}^{s} \gamma_i' \mathbf{x}_{t-i} + u_t, \tag{6.50}$$

which covers many important examples in the literature of rational expectations (Kennan, 1979; Hansen and Sargent, 1980, 1982; and Sargan, 1984).

---

[17] Notice in the regular case where $|\alpha| < 1$, v_t defined by $(1-\alpha^{-1}L)v_t = (\delta_u - \alpha^{-1}L)u_t + \varepsilon_t$ can represent a stationary process if and only if $\delta_u = 1$ and $\sigma_\varepsilon^2 = 0$ (see 6.48b). In this case we have $v_t = u_t$, which also establishes the uniqueness of the stationary solution of (6.26) in the regular case.

Substituting the unobserved expectational variable $E(y_{t+1}|\Omega_t)$ by $y_{t+1}-\varepsilon^0_{t+1}$, and rearranging the resultant equation we have (see section 5.3.4)

$$y_t=\alpha^{-1}y_{t-1}-\alpha^{-1}\sum_{i=1}^{m}\lambda_i y_{t-i-1}-\alpha^{-1}\sum_{i=0}^{s}\gamma_i'\mathbf{x}_{t-i-1}+\varepsilon^0_t-\alpha^{-1}u_{t-1}. \qquad (6.51)$$

Again for identification we assume that the solution of the model is linear and the variables y_t, $\mathbf{x}_t$, u_t have a stationary multivariate distribution (apart from deterministic components). Under these assumptions, as before, we can write ε^0_t as a linear function of the innovations in $\mathbf{x}_t$ and u_t, and write (6.51) as[18]

$$\lambda(L)y_t=\gamma(L)\mathbf{x}_t+\xi_t, \qquad (6.52)$$

where ξ_t is defined by (6.44) and

$$\lambda(L)=1-\alpha^{-1}L+\alpha^{-1}\sum_{i=1}^{m}\lambda_i L^{i+1}, \qquad (6.53a)$$

$$\gamma(L)=-\alpha^{-1}\sum_{i=0}^{s}\gamma_i'L^{i+1}+\delta_x'(I_k-\sum_{i=1}^{r}R_iL^i). \qquad (6.53b)$$

For these solutions to be stationary we need to assume that all the roots of the characteristic equation $\lambda(z^{-1})=0$ fall inside the unit circle. The general distributed lag equation (6.52) characterizes all the stationary solutions of the irregular case indexed by the auxiliary parameters δ_x, δ_u and σ^2_ε. Suppose now that exactly one root of $\lambda(z^{-1})=0$, say μ, falls outside the unit circle.[19] A unique stationary solution for (6.50) can now be obtained by eliminating the unstable factor $(1-\mu L)$ from both sides of the general solution (6.52). For this to be possible we need to impose the restrictions $\sigma^2_\varepsilon=0$, $\gamma(\mu^{-1})=0$, and $\delta_u=(\alpha\mu)^{-1}$. Under these restrictions the unique stationary solution of (6.50) will be given by

$$y_t=\sum_{i=1}^{m}\psi_i y_{t-i}+\sum_{i=0}^{\max(s,r-1)}\theta_i'\mathbf{x}_{t-i}+(\alpha\mu)^{-1}u_t. \qquad (6.54)$$

where ψ_i and θ_i are defined by

$$(1-\mu L)\left(\sum_{i=1}^{m}\psi_i L^i\right)=\lambda(L), \qquad (6.55a)$$

and

$$(1-\mu L)\left(\sum_{i=0}^{\max(s,r-1)}\theta_i L^i\right)=\gamma(L). \qquad (6.55b)$$

---

18 The innovations in $\mathbf{x}_t$ are derived under the assumption that $\mathbf{x}_t$ follows the AR(r) process (6.5′) on p. 135.

19 In situations where $\lambda(z^{-1})=0$ has more than one root outside the unit circle, the RE model (6.50) does not possess a stationary solution.

From (6.55a) it easily follows that

$$\psi_1 = \alpha^{-1} - \mu, \tag{6.56a}$$

$$\psi_i = \alpha^{-1}\lambda_{i-1} - \mu\psi_{i-1}, \quad \text{for } i = 2,3, \ldots, m. \tag{6.56b}$$

The recursive relations for θ_i can also be easily obtained from (6.55b) and in effect provide a generalization of the recursive relations (6.49). We have

$$\theta_0 = \delta_x \tag{6.57a}$$

$$\theta_i = \mu\theta_{i-1} - \alpha^{-1}\gamma_{i-1} - R_i'\theta_0, \quad \text{for } i = 1, 2, \ldots, s+1 \tag{6.57b}$$

$$\theta_i = \mu\theta_{i-1} - R_i'\theta_o, \quad \text{for } i = s+1, \ldots, r-1, \tag{6.57c}$$

where, as before, the expression for δ_x can be derived using the common factor restriction, $\gamma(\mu^{-1}) = 0$. Using (6.53b) we obtain

$$\delta_x = (\alpha\mu)^{-1}\left(I_k - \sum_{i=1}^{r} \mu^{-i} R_i'\right)^{-1}\left(\sum_{i=9}^{s} \mu^{-i}\lambda_i\right), \tag{6.48a'}$$

which generalizes the earlier expression for δ_x given by (6.48a). Therefore, in the regular case using results (6.56), (6.57) and (6.48a'), the reduced-form parameters ψ_i and θ_i can be obtained in terms of the structural parameters in a simple recursive manner. Only the computation of μ, the unstable root of $\lambda(z^{-1}) = 0$, is required. As will be seen in the next chapter (see section 7.7.2), this considerably simplifies the computations involved for the efficient estimation of the structural parameters of forward-looking RE models with lagged dependent variables. The above results also show that the identification conditions obtained earlier for the regular and the irregular cases remain valid when the RE model (6.26) is generalized to include lagged dependent variables.

B: Simultaneous Equation Models[20]

6.5 Identification of Simultaneous RE Models with Current Expectations

In this and the following section the analysis of the identification of single equation models to simultaneous equation models is extended. The chapter will primarily be concerned with identification of a single equation from a system of simultaneous equations under a set of homogeneous linear restrictions. The problem of system identification will not be dealt with here, nor will the chapter comprehensively address the problem of identification involving

[20] The results presented in this part are based on Pesaran (1981). Here I take the opportunity to correct the errors in that paper (arising from an incorrect computation of the rank of a block-triangular matrix), one instance of which has already been pointed out by Wegge and Feldman (1983b).

restrictions on the second-order moments of the endogenous variables.

Consider the following linear multivariate RE model

$$B\mathbf{y}_t + \Gamma_0\mathbf{x}_t + C\mathbf{y}_t^* = \mathbf{u}_t, \tag{6.58}$$

where $\mathbf{y}_t$ and $\mathbf{y}_t^*$ are $m \times 1$ vectors of the *observable* actual and the *unobservable* expected values of the m endogenous variables, respectively, at time t; $\mathbf{x}_t$ is a $k \times 1$ vector of the current observable values of the exogenous variables and $\mathbf{u}_t$ is a $m \times 1$ vector of unobservable disturbances. The structural parameters of interest are given by the $m \times m$ elements of B, the $m \times k$ elements of Γ_0, and the $m \times m$ elements of C. In the event that expectations of one or more of the endogenous variables are absent from the model, the corresponding columns of C will contain zeros only.[21]

In this section it will be assumed that current expectations (whether of endogenous or of exogenous variables) are perceived by the public 'rationally' with the information available at time $t-1$. Therefore, $\mathbf{y}_t^* = E(\mathbf{y}_t|\Omega_{t-1})$ and $\mathbf{x}_t^* = E(\mathbf{x}_t|\Omega_{t-1})$, where, as before, Ω_t denotes the set of available observations on all the endogenous and exogenous variables up to and including time t. More specifically, $\Omega_t = \{\mathbf{y}_t, \mathbf{y}_{t-1}, \ldots; \mathbf{x}_t, \mathbf{x}_{t-1}, \ldots\}$. We now make the following assumptions:

Assumption 6.1 The matrices B and $B + C$ are both non-singular.
Assumption 6.2 The disturbances $\mathbf{u}_t$ are non-autocorrelated.
Assumption 6.3 The disturbances $\mathbf{u}_t$ are distributed independently of the stochastic process generating $\mathbf{x}_t$ and have a zero mean and a finite variance-covariance matrix.

Given assumptions 6.1 and 6.2, taking conditional mathematical expectations of both sides of (6.58) with respect to the information set Ω_{t-1} and solving for $\mathbf{y}_t^*$, yields

$$\mathbf{y}_t^* = -(B + C)^{-1}\Gamma_0\mathbf{x}_t^*, \tag{6.59}$$

which if used in (6.58) gives the following pseudo-reduced form model

$$B\mathbf{y}_t + \Gamma_0\mathbf{x}_t - C(B + C)^{-1}\Gamma_0\mathbf{x}_t^* = \mathbf{u}_t. \tag{6.60}$$

As in the univariate case, we first observe that when all values of the exogenous variables in $\mathbf{x}_t$ are known at time $t-1$, or can be predicted perfectly at time $t-1$ the above pseudo-reduced form model will be observationally equivalent to the non-RE model $B\mathbf{y}_t + \Gamma\mathbf{x}_t = \mathbf{u}_t$, and in general the RE model (6.58) will be unidentifiable. Notice also that the observational equivalence of the RE model (6.58) and the standard econometric model $B\mathbf{y}_t + \Gamma\mathbf{x}_t = \mathbf{u}_t$ in the case where $\mathbf{x}_t^* = \mathbf{x}_t$ will not be affected by rewriting (6.58) as

$$B_0\mathbf{y}_t - C(\mathbf{y}_t - \mathbf{y}_t^*) + \Gamma_0\mathbf{x}_t = \mathbf{u}_t, \tag{6.61}$$

---

[21] When discussing the identification problem both Wallis (1980) and Revankar (1980) prefer to employ a truncated form of matrix C with all its zero columns removed. We found formulation (6.58) analytically more convenient to work with.

which is the form employed in the various attempts to test the new classical policy neutrality propositions.[22] The equation systems (6.58) and (6.61) are equivalent algebraically, and the latter can be obtained from the former by setting $B = B_0 - C$. Therefore, contrary to what Pudney (1982, p. 117) states, setting $B = B_0 - C$ in (6.58) does not necessarily involve additional identifying restrictions on the parameters of the RE model. The reason for Pudney's conclusion that the non-zero elements of C cannot be identified rests not with the particular form of (6.59) (as compared with (6.58)), but because he assumes that the vector $\mathbf{x}_t$ contains exogenous variables whose values are *all* known at the time expectations $\mathbf{y}_t^*$ are formed. But in general only some of the variables in $\mathbf{x}_t$, such as time trends, seasonal dummies or lagged variables, are known at time $t-1$, and the identification of the RE model with current expectations, whether written as (6.58) or (6.61), cannot be ruled out.

Let $\mathbf{x}_t$ be partitioned into $\mathbf{x}_{1t}$ with $k_1 \times 1$ elements whose values cannot be forecast perfectly, and a $k_2 \times 1$ vector $\mathbf{x}_{2t}$, $(k_1 + k_2 = k)$ whose values are perfectly predictable at time $t-1$ (i.e. $\mathbf{x}_{2t}^* = \mathbf{x}_{2t}$). Partitioning $\Gamma_0 = (\Gamma_{01}, \Gamma_{02})$ conformable to $\mathbf{x}_t' = (\mathbf{x}_{1t}', \mathbf{x}_{2t}')$, (6.60) can be written as

$$B\mathbf{y}_t + \Gamma_{01}\mathbf{x}_{1t} - C(B+C)^{-1}\Gamma_{01}\mathbf{x}_{1t}^* + \{I_m - C(B+C)^{-1}\}\Gamma_{02}\mathbf{x}_{2t} = \mathbf{u}_t, \tag{6.62}$$

and its pseudo-reduced form as

$$\mathbf{y}_t = \Pi_0\mathbf{x}_{1t} + \Pi_1\mathbf{x}_{1t}^* + \Pi_2\mathbf{x}_{2t} + \mathbf{v}_t, \tag{6.63}$$

where $\mathbf{v}_t = B^{-1}\mathbf{u}_t$, I_m is an identity matrix of order m and

$$\begin{cases} \Pi_0 = -B^{-1}\Gamma_{01}, & (6.64a) \\ \Pi_1 = B^{-1}C(B+C)^{-1}\Gamma_{01}, & (6.64b) \\ \Pi_2 = -B^{-1}\{I_m - C(B+C)^{-1}\}\Gamma_{02}. & (6.64c) \end{cases}$$

We now proceed to study the identification problem in two cases; when direct observations on $\mathbf{x}_{1t}^*$ (i.e. those elements of $\mathbf{x}_t$ that cannot be forecast perfectly) are available, and when $\mathbf{x}_{1t}^*$ are estimated on the basis of linear feedback relations such as (6.6).

6.5.1 *Case of Known* $\mathbf{x}_{1t}^*$

Here we treat $\mathbf{x}_{1t}^*$ as given or observable and make the following further assumption:

Assumption 6.4 The vectors $\mathbf{x}_t$ and $\mathbf{x}_{1t}^*$ are such that it is not possible to express any one of their components as a non-trivial linear function of the remaining components, for all t.

This assumption in effect rules out the possibility of exact multicollinearities among the explanatory variables of (6.63) and, together with

[22] The identification of a special bivariate form of (6.61) is discussed by Buiter (1983), where the problem of observational equivalence of the new classical model is examined in some detail.

assumptions 6.2 and 6.3, enables us to estimate the reduced-form parameters Π_0, Π_1 and Π_2 consistently. The identification of the structural parameters will then depend on whether it is possible to get estimates of (B, Γ_0, C) from those of the reduced-form parameters.

Without any loss of generality we concentrate on the identification of the parameters of the first equation in (6.58). No restrictions on the variance–covariance matrix of the disturbance vector, $\mathbf{u}_t$, will be assumed. Let $a' = (b', \gamma_{01}', \gamma_{02}', c')$ be the first row of matrix $A = (B, \Gamma_{01}, \Gamma_{02}, C)$ and consider the following l homogeneous linear *a priori* restrictions on the elements of a,

$$a'\Phi = 0, \tag{6.65}$$

where Φ is a $(2m+k)\times l$ matrix of known constants. It will prove convenient to rewrite these restrictions also in the following partitioned form

$$b'\Phi_b + \gamma_{01}'\Phi_{\gamma_{01}} + \gamma_{02}'\Phi_{\gamma_{02}} + c'\Phi_c = 0, \tag{6.66}$$

with $\Phi' = (\Phi_b', \Phi_{\gamma_{01}}', \Phi_{\gamma_{02}}', \Phi_c')$. We shall now prove the following theorem.

Theorem 6.1 Under assumptions 6.1 to 6.4, and the identifying restrictions (6.65), the structural parameters of the first equation of the RE model (6.58) will be identified up to a scalar constant if, and only if,

$$\text{Rank}\begin{pmatrix} A\Phi & 0 \\ B(\Phi_b - \Phi_c) & \Gamma_{01} \end{pmatrix} = 2m - 1.$$

Proof Since

$$B^{-1}C(B+C)^{-1} = B^{-1}(B+C-B)(B+C)^{-1} = B^{-1} - (B+C)^{-1},$$

relations (6.64) can be written as

$$B\Pi_0 + \Gamma_{01} = 0, \tag{6.64a$'$}$$

$$B\Pi_1 + C(\Pi_0 + \Pi_1) = 0, \tag{6.64b$'$}$$

$$(B+C)\Pi_2 + \Gamma_{02} = 0. \tag{6.64c$'$}$$

Then the equations relevant to the estimation of the structural parameters of the first equation in (6.58) become:

$$b'\Pi_0 + \gamma_{01}' = 0, \tag{6.67a}$$

$$b'\Pi_1 + c'(\Pi_0 + \Pi_1) = 0, \tag{6.67b}$$

$$b'\Pi_2 + \gamma_{02}' + c'\Pi_2 = 0. \tag{6.67c}$$

Relations (6.66) together with (6.67) form a linear homogeneous system of equations in vector a, which admits a non-trivial unique solution up to a scalar constant if, and only if, the rank of Q is $2m+k-1$, where

$$Q = \begin{bmatrix} \Phi_b & \Pi_0 & \Pi_2 & \Pi_1 \\ \Phi_{\gamma_{01}} & I_{k_1} & 0 & 0 \\ \Phi_{\gamma_{02}} & 0 & I_{k_2} & 0 \\ \Phi_c & 0 & \Pi_2 & \Pi_0 + \Pi_1 \end{bmatrix},$$

and I_{k_1} and I_{k_2} are unit matrices of order k_1 and k_2 respectively. Now pre-multiplying Q by the matrix

$$T=\begin{bmatrix} B & \Gamma_{01} & \Gamma_{02} & C \\ 0 & I_{k_1} & 0 & 0 \\ 0 & 0 & I_{k_2} & 0 \\ 0 & 0 & 0 & -(B+C) \end{bmatrix},$$

and using the results given in (6.64′), it is then easily established that

$$TQ=\begin{bmatrix} A\Phi & 0 & 0 & 0 \\ \Phi_{\gamma_{01}} & I_{k_1} & 0 & 0 \\ \Phi_{\gamma_{02}} & 0 & I_{k_2} & 0 \\ -(B+C)\Phi_c & 0 & \Gamma_{02} & \Gamma_{01} \end{bmatrix}.$$

But under assumption 6.1, T is non-singular and Rank(Q) = Rank(TQ). Since the rank of a matrix is invariant under elementary row or column operations, then it is easily seen that the rank of TQ will be the same as the rank of

$$\begin{bmatrix} A\Phi & 0 & 0 & 0 \\ \Phi_{\gamma_{01}} & 0 & I_{k_1} & 0 \\ \Phi_{\gamma_{02}} & 0 & 0 & I_{k_2} \\ -(B+C)\Phi_c & \Gamma_{01} & 0 & \Gamma_{02} \end{bmatrix},$$

which in turn will have the same rank as

$$\begin{bmatrix} A\Phi & 0 & 0 & 0 \\ 0 & 0 & I_{k_1} & 0 \\ 0 & 0 & 0 & I_{k_2} \\ \psi & \Gamma_{01} & 0 & 0 \end{bmatrix},$$

where

$$\psi = -(B+C)\Phi_c - \Gamma_{02}\Phi_{\gamma_{02}}.$$

Hence the rank of Q will be equal to $k = k_1 + k_2$ plus the rank of matrix

$$\begin{bmatrix} A\Phi & 0 \\ \psi & \Gamma_{01} \end{bmatrix}.$$

This result can be further simplified by noting that

$$\begin{bmatrix} I_m & 0 \\ I_m & I_m \end{bmatrix}\begin{bmatrix} A\Phi & 0 \\ \psi & \Gamma_{01} \end{bmatrix}\begin{bmatrix} I_l & 0 \\ -\Phi_{\gamma_{01}} & I_{k_1} \end{bmatrix}=\begin{bmatrix} A\Phi & 0 \\ B(\Phi_b-\Phi_c) & \Gamma_{01} \end{bmatrix},$$

where I_m, and I_l stand for identity matrices of orders m and I respectively. Therefore,

$$\text{Rank}(Q)=\begin{bmatrix} A\Phi & 0 \\ B(\Phi_b-\Phi_c) & \Gamma_{01} \end{bmatrix}+k,$$

and the identification condition, $\text{Rank}(Q)=2m+k-1$ will imply the following rank condition in terms of the structural parameters and the constants of the identifying restrictions

$$\text{Rank}\begin{bmatrix} A\Phi & 0 \\ B(\Phi_b-\Phi_c) & \Gamma_{01} \end{bmatrix}=2m-1.$$

QED

Theorem 6.1 is a generalization of the familiar rank condition for the identification of the simultaneous systems originally derived by Koopmans et al. (1950). The following order condition for the identification of (6.58) can also be proved.

Proposition 6.3 When $\mathbf{x}_{1t}^*$ are known, the necessary (though not sufficient) condition for the identification of a given equation in RE model (6.58) is that the total number of exogenous (or predetermined) variables plus the number of exogenous variables that cannot be exactly predicted should be greater than or equal to the total number of variables included in the equation minus one.

Proof Since matrix Q is $(2m\times k)\times(l+k+k_1)$, for it to have rank $2m+k-1$ it is necessary that $l+k_1\geqslant 2m-1$. Denoting the number of endogenous, exogenous (whether perfectly predictable or not) and expectational endogenous variables that are included in the ith equation by $\bar{m}$, $\bar{k}$ and $\bar{h}$ respectively, then $l=(m-\bar{m})+(k-\bar{k})+(m-\bar{h})$ and the order condition for identification of this equation becomes

$$k+k_1\geqslant(\bar{m}+\bar{h}+\bar{k})-1. \tag{6.68}$$

QED

Notice that the above order condition is valid for 'exclusion restrictions'. In the general case where the parameters are subject to linear homogeneous restrictions the relevant order condition for identification is $l+k_1\geqslant 2m-1$.

6.5.2 *Case of Unknown* $\mathbf{x}_{1t}^*$

We now drop the unrealistic assumption that $\mathbf{x}_{1t}^*$ are given, and at the same time generalize (6.58) to include lagged values of $\mathbf{x}_t$. That is

$$B\mathbf{y}_t+\sum_{i=0}^{s}\Gamma_i\mathbf{x}_{t-i}+C\mathbf{y}_t^*=\mathbf{u}_t. \tag{6.69}$$

As before, solving for y_t^* and writing (6.69) in terms of the exogenous variables we get

$$B\mathbf{y}_t+\Gamma_0\mathbf{x}_t-C(B+C)^{-1}\Gamma_0\mathbf{x}_t^*+\sum_{i=1}^{s}\{I_m-C(B+C)^{-1}\}\Gamma_i\mathbf{x}_{t-i}=\mathbf{u}_t.$$

Again partitioning $\mathbf{x}_t$ into those elements that cannot be predicted exactly (i.e. $\mathbf{x}_{1t}$) and those that are perfectly predictable (i.e. $\mathbf{x}_{2t}$), the above relation may be written as

$$B\mathbf{y}_t+\Gamma_{01}\mathbf{x}_{1t}-C(B+C)^{-1}\Gamma_{01}\mathbf{x}_{1t}^*+\{\Gamma_{02}-C(B+C)^{-1}\Gamma_{02}\}\mathbf{x}_{2t}$$
$$+\sum_{i=1}^{s}\{I_m-\mathrm{C(B+C)}^{-1}\}\Gamma_i\mathbf{x}_{t-i}=\mathbf{u}_t, \qquad (6.70)$$

where $\Gamma_0=(\Gamma_{01}, \Gamma_{02})$ is partitioned so that it is conformable to $\mathbf{x}_t'=(\mathbf{x}_{t1}', \mathbf{x}_{t2}')$. Since $\mathbf{x}_{1t}^*$ are unknown we also need to replace them by a suitable estimate of $E(\mathbf{x}_{1t}|\Omega_{t-1})$. For this purpose we assume that $\mathbf{x}_{1t}$ follow a general linear feedback rule and adopt (6.6) as the best linear predictor of $\mathbf{x}_{1t}$ relative to the information set Ω_{t-1}. Therefore, for given values of R_i (obtainable, say, from the regression of $\mathbf{x}_{1t}^*$ on $\mathbf{x}_{t-1}, \mathbf{x}_{t-2}, \ldots, \mathbf{x}_{t-r}$), substituting $\mathbf{x}_{1t}^*$ from (6.6) in (6.70) we obtain the following reduced form equation,[23]

$$\mathbf{y}_t=\Pi_0\mathbf{x}_{1t}+\Pi_1\mathbf{z}_t+\Pi_2\mathbf{x}_{2t}+\sum_{i=1}^{s}\Pi_{i+2}\mathbf{x}_{t-i}+\mathbf{v}_t, \qquad (6.71)$$

where (assuming $r>s$)

$$\begin{cases}\Pi_0=-B^{-1}\Gamma_{01}, & (6.72a)\\ \Pi_1=B^{-1}C(B+C)^{-1}\Gamma_{01}, & (6.72b)\\ \Pi_2=-B^{-1}\{I_m-C(B+C)^{-1}\}\Gamma_{02}, & (6.72c)\\ \Pi_{i+2}=-B^{-1}\{\Gamma_i-C(B+C)^{-1}\Gamma_i-C(B+C)^{-1}\Gamma_{01}R_i\}, & (6.72d)\end{cases}$$

$$\text{for } i=1, 2, \ldots, s,$$

$$\mathbf{z}_t=\sum_{i=s+1}^{r}R_i\mathbf{x}_{t-i},$$

and $\mathbf{v}_t=B^{-1}\mathbf{u}_t$. From these results it is firstly clear that unless $\mathbf{z}_t\neq 0$, the RE model given by (6.69) and the simultaneous distributed lag model specified by $B\mathbf{y}_t+\Sigma_{i=0}^{s}\Gamma_i\mathbf{x}_{t-i}=\mathbf{u}_t$ will be observationally equivalent and the structural parameters of the RE model cannot be identified. For $\mathbf{z}_t$ to be non-zero it is necessary that $r>s$. Therefore we have the following generalization of the proposition 6.1 that we obtained for the univariate case in section 6.3.

[23] Notice that in this model it is possible to allow for lagged values of $\mathbf{y}_t$ by including them in $\mathbf{x}_{2t}$, or more generally in $\mathbf{x}_{t-i}$, $i=1, 2, \ldots, s$.

Proposition 6.4 For RE model (6.69) to be identifiable, the order of the autoregressive scheme assumed for the $\mathbf{x}_t$ process should be strictly greater than the order of the distributed lag relation specified between the exogenous and the endogenous variables of the model (that is $r > s$).

Although it is possible to consider high enough values for r so that $r > s$, this will not enable us to obtain consistent estimates of Π_1 in (6.71) if the true order of the $\{\mathbf{x}_t\}$ process is in fact equal to or less than s. Moreover, there is no reason why s should be kept fixed when r is allowed to increase. In the absence of *a priori* information concerning the true values of r and s it will be impossible to distinguish between the RE and the non-RE infinite distributed lag models.

Clearly, $r > s$ (or more strictly a non-zero $\mathbf{z}_t$) is a necessary but not a sufficient condition for the identification of (6.69), and other restrictions will be needed. Derivation of other necessary and sufficient conditions can be achieved by adopting exactly the same method used to prove theorem 6.1. We first rewrite (6.72) as:

$$\begin{cases} B\Pi_0 + \Gamma_{01} = 0, & (6.72a') \\ B\Pi_1 + C(\Pi_1 + \Pi_0) = 0, & (6.72b') \\ (B + C)\Pi_2 + \Gamma_{02} = 0, & (6.72c') \\ (B + C)(\Pi_{i+2} - \Pi_1 R_i) + \Gamma_i = 0, \quad \text{for } i = 1, 2, \ldots, s. & (6.72d') \end{cases}$$

Concentrating on the identification of the first equation of (6.69) we again consider homogeneous linear restrictions on the elements of the first row of matrix A, which we now define as $A = (B, \Gamma_{01}, \Gamma_{02}, \Gamma_1, \ldots, \Gamma_s, C)$. Then *given* $r > s$, the necessary and sufficient condition for identification of the first equation of (6.69) is easily seen to be

$$\text{Rank}\begin{pmatrix} A\Phi & 0 \\ B(\Phi_b - \Phi_c) & \Gamma_{01} \end{pmatrix} = 2m - 1,$$

where Φ is now the $\{2m + (s+1)k\} \times l$ matrix of l homogeneous linear restrictions on the parameters of the first equation of (6.69). It is interesting to note that this rank condition is exactly the same as that obtained for the simple case where $s = 0$. This is hardly surprising, and stems from the fact that the RE model with lagged values of $\mathbf{x}_t$ can always be rewritten in the form of the simple model (6.58), by writing all the lagged variables (whether endogenous or exogenous) as a part of $\mathbf{x}_{2t}$, the variables whose values can be perfectly predicted at time $t-1$.

The order condition for this case may also be written as (assuming that $r > s$)

$$K + k_1 \geqslant (\bar{m} + \bar{h} + \bar{K}) - 1,$$

where k_1, $\bar{m}$ and $\bar{h}$ are defined as before, $\bar{K}$ stands for the number of predetermined variables (current as well as lagged values of the exogenous variables) that are included in the equation under consideration, and $K=(s+1)k$. The addition of lagged values of the exogenous or the endogenous variables to the RE model has a mixed effect for the identification of the model. An increase in s helps fulfil the order condition $(s+1)k+k_1 \geqslant (\bar{m}+\bar{h}+\bar{K})-1$, but at the same time it may result in the violation of the condition $r>s$.

Example 6.4 Identification of Taylor's Macroeconomic Model of the US Economy

As an application of theorem 6.1, consider the following simple macroeconomic model of the US economy, an extended version of which has been used by Taylor (1979) in his analysis of optimal monetary policy rules under the REH.

$$q_t=\alpha_1 q_{t-1}+\alpha_2(m_t-p_t)+\alpha_3\pi_t^*+u_{t1}, \tag{6.73}$$

$$\pi_t=\beta_1\pi_{t-1}+\beta_2 q_t^*+u_{t2}, \tag{6.74}$$

where q_t is the logarithm of real expenditures measured relative to a known trend, p_t is the logarithm of the general price level, $\pi_t=p_t-p_{t-1}$ is the rate of inflation, m_t is the logarithm of the money supply, and u_{t1} and u_{t2} are serially uncorrelated random disturbances with zero means and an unconstrained covariance matrix. The above model represents the reduced form of a conventional IS–LM system combined with an inflation equation which can be rationalized in a number of different ways. It can be regarded as an expectations-augmented Phillips curve with the lagged inflation rate π_{t-1} acting as a proxy for inflation expectations, or it can be derived from a two-period model of staggered pricing with overlapping multi-period contracts. The latter interpretation is favoured by Taylor on the grounds that under the REH the inflation expectations $\pi_t^*=E(\pi_t|\Omega_{t-1})$ are determined in terms of all the variables and the particular specification of the model as a whole and not just π_{t-1}.

To apply theorem 6.1 we need first to write the equations (6.73) and (6.74) in the form of (6.58). That is

$$B\mathbf{y}_t+\Gamma_0\mathbf{x}_t+C\mathbf{y}_t^*=\mathbf{u}_t,$$

where $\mathbf{y}_t'=(q_t,\pi_t)$, $\mathbf{x}_t'=(m_t, q_{t-1}, p_{t-1}, \pi_{t-1})$, $\mathbf{u}_t'=(u_{t1}, u_{t2})$, and

$$B=\begin{pmatrix}1 & \alpha_2\\ 0 & 1\end{pmatrix}, \qquad C=\begin{pmatrix}0 & -\alpha_3\\ -\beta_2 & 0\end{pmatrix},$$

$$\Gamma_{01}=\begin{pmatrix}-\alpha_2\\ 0\end{pmatrix}, \qquad \Gamma_{02}=\begin{pmatrix}-\alpha_1 & \alpha_2 & 0\\ 0 & 0 & -\beta_1\end{pmatrix},$$

with $\Gamma_0=(\Gamma_{01}, \Gamma_{02})$. If we now follow Taylor and assume that m_t can be predicted perfectly at time $t-1$ we have $k_1=1$, $k_2=4$ (hence $k=5$), and $m=2$. Consider now the identification of equation (6.73). It is easily seen that this equation is subject to four homogeneous linear restrictions and one normalization restriction. In terms of the notations in (6.65) we have

$$\Phi_b = \begin{pmatrix} 0 & 0 & 0 & 0 \\ 1 & 1 & 0 & 0 \end{pmatrix}, \quad \Phi_c = \begin{pmatrix} 0 & 0 & 0 & 1 \\ 0 & 0 & 0 & 0 \end{pmatrix},$$

and

$$\Phi_{\gamma_0} = \begin{bmatrix} 1 & 0 & 0 & 0 \\ 0 & 0 & 0 & 0 \\ 0 & -1 & 0 & 0 \\ 0 & 0 & 1 & 0 \end{bmatrix}, \quad \Phi = \begin{bmatrix} \Phi_b \\ \Phi_{\gamma_0} \\ \Phi_c \end{bmatrix},$$

which yields[24]

$$A\Phi = \begin{bmatrix} 0 & 0 & 0 & 0 \\ 1 & 1 & -\beta_1 & -\beta_2 \end{bmatrix},$$

$$B(\Phi_b - \Phi_c) = \begin{bmatrix} \alpha_2 & \alpha_2 & 0 & -1 \\ 1 & 1 & 0 & 0 \end{bmatrix}.$$

Therefore the rank condition of theorem 6.1 in the case of this example can be written as

$$\text{Rank} \begin{bmatrix} 0 & 0 & 0 & 0 & 0 \\ 1 & 1 & -\beta_1 & -\beta_2 & 0 \\ \alpha_2 & \alpha_2 & 0 & -1 & -\alpha_2 \\ 1 & 1 & 0 & 0 & 0 \end{bmatrix} = 3.$$

It is now easily established that, except for special parameter values $\beta_1 = \beta_2 = 0$, and $\alpha_2 = \beta_1 = 0$, this rank condition is satisfied and all the parameters of the equation (6.73) are identifiable. The application of the order condition to this equation also reveals that for values of $\beta_1 \neq 0$ there are two over-identifying restrictions that can be tested. This is because with $k_1 = 1$ and $m = 2$ the order condition $l + k_1 \geqslant 2m - 1$ will be satisfied with two (linear) restrictions, while (apart from the normalization restriction) the number of parametric restrictions imposed on the output equation is equal to four. A similar exercise with respect to the inflation equation also shows that it is subject to three over-identifying restrictions.

---

[24] Recall that $A = (B, \Gamma_0, C)$.

6.6 Identification of Simultaneous RE Models with Forward-looking Expectations

Consider now the problem of identification of the following general linear model containing forward-looking or future expectations of the endogenous variables

$$B\mathbf{y}_t + \sum_{i=0}^{s} \Gamma_i \mathbf{x}_{t-i} + CE(\mathbf{y}_{t+1}|\Omega_t) = \mathbf{u}_t. \tag{6.75}$$

The notations are as before, but in this formulation the $k \times 1$ vector $\mathbf{x}_t$ is assumed to contain only current values of the exogenous variables and that these variables cannot be forecast perfectly at time $t-1$. We shall, however, continue to maintain the assumptions 6.1–6.3.

The above model, although it covers a number of important applications in the literature, is nevertheless restrictive as it does not allow for the inclusion of lagged values of $\mathbf{y}_t$ amongst the explanatory variables. But it still provides a convenient starting point for highlighting the special problems that arise in studying the identification of simultaneous equation models with future expectations.

In situations where C, the coefficient matrix of the expectational variables, is non-singular the solution and identification of (6.75) do not pose any new problems, and the martingale difference procedures discussed in section 6.4 for the identification of the univariate models with forward-looking expectations can be readily generalized to the multivariate case under consideration. But in most applications the coefficient matrix C is likely to contain many zero elements and may not be invertible, and therefore other solution methods should be sought (see appendix C). Here we assume that C may not be invertible but concentrate on the regular case where the model possesses a unique stationary solution. We also make the following additional assumptions:

Assumption 6.5 All the non-zero eigenvalues of $B^{-1}C$ fall inside the unit circle.

Assumption 6.6 The processes generating $\mathbf{x}_t$ and $\mathbf{u}_t$ are covariance stationary.

The assumption 6.5 also implies that the matrices $B-C$ and $B+C$ are non-singular. In this regular case, as is shown in appendix C, the unique stationary solution of (6.75) is given by

$$\mathbf{y}_t = \sum_{j=0}^{\infty} D^j E(\mathbf{w}_{t+j}|\Omega_t), \tag{6.76}$$

where $D = -B^{-1}C$, and

$$\mathbf{w}_t = B^{-1}\left[-\sum_{i=0}^{s} \Gamma_i \mathbf{x}_{t-i} + \mathbf{u}_t\right].$$

This is the familiar stationary 'forward solution', and is also obtainable by the forward recursive substitution method used, among others, by Shiller (1978, pp. 29–33).

Recalling that, under assumption 6.2, the $\mathbf{u}_t$ are non-autocorrelated, then

$$E(\mathbf{w}_{t+j}|\Omega_t) = -B^{-1}\sum_{i=0}^{s}\Gamma_i\mathbf{x}_{t-i} + B^{-1}\mathbf{u}_t, \quad \text{for } j=0,$$

$$= -B^{-1}\sum_{i=0}^{s}\Gamma_i\mathbf{x}^*_{t+j-i}, \quad \text{for } j \geqslant 1.$$

Using these results in (6.76) we obtain

$$\mathbf{y}_t = -\sum_{j=0}^{\infty} D^j \sum_{i=0}^{s} B^{-1}\Gamma_i\mathbf{x}^*_{t+j-i} + \mathbf{v}_t,$$

where $\mathbf{v}_t$ is defined as before ($\mathbf{v}_t = B^{-1}\mathbf{u}_t$), but unlike in the previous section, $\mathbf{x}^*_{t+j-i}$ now stands for the mathematical expectations of $\mathbf{x}_{t+j-i}$ relative to the information set Ω_t and not Ω_{t-1}. Furthermore, since $\mathbf{x}^*_{t-i+j} = \mathbf{x}_{t-i+j}$ for $i=0, 1, 2, \ldots, s$ and for all $j \leqslant i$, the above reduced form relation may also be written as

$$\mathbf{y}_t = \sum_{j=0}^{s} \Delta_j\mathbf{x}_{t-j} + \sum_{j=1}^{\infty} D^j\Delta_0\mathbf{x}^*_{t+j} + \mathbf{v}_t, \tag{6.77}$$

where

$$\Delta_j = -\sum_{i=j}^{s} D^{i-j}B^{-1}\Gamma_i, \quad \text{for } j=0, 1, 2, \ldots, s. \tag{6.78}$$

The above result is a multivariate generalization of the pseudo-reduced form equation (6.31).

Important features of this result are the highly non-linear way that the structural parameters enter the reduced form, and the dependence of $\mathbf{y}_t$ upon all the future expectations of the exogenous variables. Clearly if dummy variables and time trends are included among the exogenous variables, a partitioning of $\mathbf{x}_t$ and $\mathbf{x}^*_{t+j}$, similar to that considered in the case of current RE models, should be made before the conditions for the identification of (6.75) can be obtained. But, in order to make the analysis manageable, we ignore this complication and proceed with the pseudo-reduced form equation (6.77) as it stands.

Assuming all future expectations of the exogenous variables are known, using (6.77) it can be shown that RE models with future expectations are identified if, and only if, for given future expectations of the endogenous variables {i.e. $E(\mathbf{y}_{t+1}|\Omega_t)$} their underlying structures are identified.[25] We do not propose to go into the details of this extremely unlikely case. The situation is

---

[25] This result does not, however, hold in the case of current RE models where the relevant rank condition for identification is given in theorem 6.1.

different when $\mathbf{x}^*_{t+j}$ are not known, in which case, as to be expected, the identification will critically depend upon the characterization of the $\mathbf{x}_t$ process.

Assuming $\mathbf{x}_t$ follows the multivariate AR(r) process specified by (6.5′) on p. 135, the values of $\mathbf{x}^*_{t+j}$ can be obtained in terms of $\mathbf{x}t$, $\mathbf{x}_{t-1}, \ldots, \mathbf{x}t-r$ in a recursive manner. Using (6.30) in (6.77) now yields the following 'empirically observable' reduced-form equation

$$\mathbf{y}_t = \sum_{i=0}^{\max(s,r-1)} \Pi_i \mathbf{x}_{t-i} + \mathbf{v}_t, \tag{6.79}$$

where, assuming $r > s+1$

$$\begin{cases} \Pi_i = \Delta_i + \sum_{j=1}^{\infty} D^j \Delta_0 R_{ij}, & \text{for } i = 0, 1, \ldots, s, \quad (6.80a) \\ \Pi_i = \sum_{j=1}^{\infty} D^j \Delta_0 R_{ij}, & \text{for } i = s+1, \ldots, r-1, \quad (6.80b) \end{cases}$$

and Δ_i are given by (6.78) with $D = -B^{-1}C$.

Despite the highly non-linear nature of the relations that exist between the structural parameters $(B, \Gamma_0, \Gamma_1, \ldots, \Gamma_s, C, R_1, R_2, \ldots, R_r)$, and the reduced-form parameters $\Pi_0, \Pi_1, \ldots, \Pi_{r-1}$ (if $r > s+1$) it is clear from the above results that the necessary order condition is still given by $r > s+1$. This is a straightforward generalization of the condition obtained for the univariate case in section 6.4.1. In particular it shows that, even if the rational expectations model specified by (6.75) does not include any lagged exogenous variables, its identification requires the specification of at least a second-order autoregressive process for $\mathbf{x}_t$. Furthermore, as in the univariate case, if Ω_t in (6.75) is replaced by Ω_{t-1}, under assumptions 6.1 to 6.6, the RE models with future expectations will be observationally equivalent to the RE models with current expectations when $\mathbf{x}_t$ is represented by an AR process. This result holds irrespective of whether $r > s$ or not.

Suppose now it is known *a priori* that $r > s+1$. What other conditions are necessary if (6.75) is to be identified? Due to the non-linearities that are present in relations (6.80), the derivation of rank conditions for the *global* identification of the structural parameters from these relations is not possible. They can, however, be written in recursive forms that are linear in structural parameters, but non-linear in the reduced-form parameters which allow derivation of the relevant rank conditions for local identification. Such recursive relations for Π_i may be obtained by substituting the solution (6.79) back in the RE model (6.75). Since $\mathbf{x}_t$ is assumed to follow the multivariate AR(r) process (6.5′), we first note that

$$\begin{aligned} E(\mathbf{y}_{t+1} | \Omega_t) &= \Pi_0 E(\mathbf{x}_{t+1} | \Omega_t) + \sum_{i=1}^{r-1} \Pi_i \mathbf{x}_{t-i+1}, \\ &= \sum_{i=0}^{r-1} H_{i+1} \mathbf{x}_{t-i}, \end{aligned} \tag{6.81}$$

where

$$H_i = \Pi_0 R_i + \Pi_i, \quad \text{for } i = 1, 2, \ldots, r-1, \tag{6.82a}$$

$$H_i = \Pi_0 R_i, \quad \text{for } i = r. \tag{6.82b}$$

Using (6.79) and (6.81) in (6.75) now yields the following recursive relations in Π_i, $(r > s+1)$[26]

$$B\Pi_i + \Gamma_i + CH_{i+1} = 0, \quad \text{for } i = 0, 1, 2, \ldots, s \tag{6.83a}$$

$$B\Pi_i + CH_{i+1} = 0, \quad \text{for } i = s+1, \ldots, r-1. \tag{6.83b}$$

If we now introduce $a'\Phi = 0$ as the $1 \times l$ *a priori* linear homogeneous restrictions on the parameters of the first equation of (6.75) where, as before, a' stands for the first row of the $m \times \{2m + k(s+1)\}$ matrix, $A = (B, \Gamma_0, \Gamma_1, \ldots, \Gamma_s, C)$ and using (6.83), identification of the $\{2m + k(s+1)\} \times 1$ vector a requires that $\text{Rank}(Q) = 2m + k(s+1) - 1$, where

$$Q = \begin{bmatrix} \Phi_b & \Pi_0 & \Pi_1 & \cdots & \Pi_{s-1} & \Pi_s & \Pi_{s+1} & \cdots & \Pi_{r-1} \\ \Phi_{\gamma_0} & I_k & 0 & \cdots & 0 & 0 & 0 & \cdots & 0 \\ \vdots & & & & & & & & \vdots \\ \Phi_{\gamma_s} & 0 & 0 & \cdots & 0 & I_k & 0 & \cdots & 0 \\ \Phi_c & H_1 & H_2 & \cdots & H_s & H_{s+1} & H_{s+2} & \cdots & H_r \end{bmatrix},$$

and $\Phi' = (\Phi'_b, \Phi'_{\gamma_0}, \ldots, \Phi'_{\gamma_s}, \Phi'_c)$.

Pre-multiplying the matrix Q by the non-singular matrix T

$$T = \begin{bmatrix} B & \Gamma_0 & \Gamma_1 & \cdots & \Gamma_s & C \\ 0 & I_k & 0 & \cdots & 0 & 0 \\ \vdots & & & & & \vdots \\ 0 & \cdots\cdots & & 0 & I_k & 0 \\ 0 & \cdots\cdots & & & 0 & I_m \end{bmatrix},$$

we obtain

$$TQ = \begin{bmatrix} A\Phi & 0 & 0 \\ \Phi_\gamma & I_K & 0 \\ \Phi_c & \mathbf{H}_1 & \mathbf{H}_2 \end{bmatrix},$$

where $\Phi'_\gamma = (\Phi'_{\gamma_0}, \Phi'_{\gamma_1}, \ldots, \Phi'_{\gamma_s})$, $\mathbf{H}_1 = (H_1, H_2, \ldots, H_{s+1})$, $\mathbf{H}_2 = (H_{s+2}, H_{s+3}, \ldots, H_r)$, and I_K is an identity matrix of order $K = (s+1)k$. By means of elementary

[26] Notice that the recursive equations (6.83) in Π_i, have a unique solution which is given by (6.80). Recall that R_{ij} in (6.80) can be obtained uniquely from R_i in a recursive fashion.

row and column operations similar to those performed in the proof of theorem 6.1, it is easily shown that

$$\text{Rank}(Q) = \text{Rank}(TQ) = \text{Rank}\begin{bmatrix} A\Phi & 0 \\ \Phi_c - \mathbf{H}_1\Phi_\gamma & \mathbf{H}_2 \end{bmatrix} + K.$$

The above result allows us to state the following theorem.

Theorem 6.2 Under assumptions 6.1 to 6.6 and the identifying restrictions $a'\Phi = 0$, the unknown parameter vector a, containing the structural parameters of the first equation of the RE model (6.75), will be (locally) identified up to a scalar constant if, and only if,

$$\text{Rank}\begin{pmatrix} A\Phi & 0 \\ \Phi_c - \mathbf{H}_1\Phi_\gamma & \mathbf{H}_2 \end{pmatrix} = 2m - 1, \tag{6.84}$$

where $\mathbf{H}_1 = (H_1, H_2, \ldots, H_{s+1})$, $\mathbf{H}_2 = (H_{s+2}, H_{s+3}, \ldots, H_r)$, and the $m \times k$ matrices H_i are defined by relations (6.82).[27]

Despite its apparent simplicity, the above theorem is difficult to apply in practice, since it involves the reduced-form parameters Π_i that are highly non-linear functions of the structural parameters. Nevertheless it can be employed to obtain a number of important order conditions. From the rank condition (6.84) it follows that the order condition for identification is given by

$$l + (r - s - 1)k \geqslant 2m - 1,$$

where l is the number of homogeneous restrictions on the parameters of the structural equation under consideration. This order condition can also be written as

$$K + (r - s - 1)k \geqslant (\bar{m} + \bar{K} + \bar{h}) - 1,$$

which states that the total number of predetermined variables in the model {i.e. $K = (s+1)k$} plus $(r - s - 1)k$ should be at least as large as the total number of included endogenous variables, $\bar{m}$, predetermined variables, $\bar{K}$, and expectational variables, $\bar{h}$, in the equation minus one.

6.7 Concluding Remarks

The rank and order conditions obtained in this chapter clearly demonstrate the importance of *a priori* information on the order of lags in economic relations for the identification of RE models, and give further support to the view that the REH is 'more deeply subversive of identification than has yet been recognized' (Sims, 1980, p. 7). Whether economic theory can be relied on to

[27] This theorem corrects the errors in the results given on pages 393–4 of Pesaran (1981).

provide us with such *a priori* restrictions on lag-lengths is a doubtful matter. But if one is prepared to impose *a priori* restrictions on lag-lengths, the REH need not be subversive of identification, and in certain circumstances can even contribute towards the identification of structural models. I am personally doubtful that we have the knowledge on the lag-lengths required to empirically distinguish linear RE models from linear non-RE models and vice-versa. This is unfortunate for macroeconomic policy analysis, as RE models with Walrasian characteristics happen to imply strikingly different policy prescriptions as compared with non-RE macroeconomic models.

7 Estimation and Hypothesis Testing in Rational Expectations Models

7.1 Introduction

This chapter will consider the problems of estimation and hypothesis testing in a variety of rational expectations models, assuming that the conditions necessary for the identification of these models are satisfied. There already exists a large number of different procedures for the estimation of linear rational expectations models. The main difference between these procedures lies in the extent to which information concerning the processes generating the exogenous variables of the model is utilized. The 'full-information' methods proposed, for example, by Wallis (1980), Revanker (1980), Chow (1980), Sargan (1984), Dagli and Taylor (1984), and Watson (1986) require a complete characterization of all the stochastic processes involved, while the instrumental variables or the general method of moments estimators proposed by McCallum (1976), Wickens (1982), Hansen (1982), Cumby et al. (1983), and Hayashi and Sims (1983) are based on the *a priori* availability of a sufficient set of instruments or moment conditions. This latter category of estimators is usually referred to as 'limited-information' estimators, to highlight the fact that a complete characterization of all the stochastic processes involved is not needed, or that it is not used in the estimation process. The limited-information estimators by their very nature can be less efficient than their full-information counterparts. However, they have two important advantages: firstly, they are generally more robust than the full-information estimators to certain types of mis-specifications; and secondly, they are computationally less demanding. This chapter considers the application of both methods to a number of rational expectations models used especially in tests of rationality of forecasts, efficiency of foreign exchange and capital markets, costs of adjustment models, and the neutrality propositions of the new classical macroeconomics. Part A of the chapter deals with models containing only current or past expectations, and Part B is devoted to models with future expectations.

Section 7.2 sets up the basic model, surveys the various estimators proposed in the literature, and discusses their relative asymptotic efficiency. In particular it shows that the errors-in-variables method (EVM) and the substitution method (SM) discussed in Wickens (1982) lead exactly to the same likelihood function, and therefore establish that, as far as full-information maximum likelihood estimation of RE models is concerned, there is little to choose between these two estimation methods. Sections 7.3 and 7.4 deal with extensions of the basic model and allow for the presence of current and lagged expected and unexpected effects amongst the regressors. We show that when the RE model contains only current expected and unexpected effects, the results obtained for the basic model by and large remain applicable, though the situation is completely different when *lagged* expected or unexpected effects are included in the model. In this more general case not only are two-step and instrumental variable (IV) estimators asymptotically inefficient, but the computation of their asymptotic variance matrix (needed for making inferences) is also rather complicated and requires special computer programs. In view of this, section 7.4.3 argues that the estimation of RE models with lagged expected or unexpected effects is best approached in the full-information maximum likelihood (FIML) framework. In this respect the two-step asymptotically efficient estimator proposed by Pagan (1986), which is based on the first iteration of the scoring algorithm for the computation of ML estimators, is especially convenient from a computational viewpoint. Part A ends with a discussion of the problems connected with the use of cross-equation tests as tests of the REH. In particular we reiterate the fact that cross-equation tests are valid as tests of the REH if the model within which the REH is embodied is correctly specified. We also examine the relationship between Granger non-causality tests and the joint tests of the neutrality and rationality propositions that are central to the new classical macroeconomics. We show that the two tests are equivalent only if the specified aggregate supply function does not contain lagged expected or unexpected effects.

Part B first considers problems of estimation and hypothesis testing in the context of rational expectations models of exchange rate determination, and then turns to more general RE models with lagged dependent variables and future expectations of the endogenous variables of arbitrary orders. Estimators proposed by Hansen (1982), Cumby et al. (1983), and Hayashi and Sims (1983) are reviewed, and show the importance of distinguishing between the case when the model under consideration has a unique solution (the 'regular' case), and the case when it has a multiplicity of stationary solutions (the 'irregular case'), for the consistent and efficient estimation of RE models. This distinction also allows us to explore explicitly the relationships that exist between the identification conditions derived in the previous chapter and the problem of consistent estimation of RE models with future expectations. By means of a simple example we demonstrate the pitfalls inherent in indiscriminately applying the IV method to RE models with future expectations, an issue which is often overlooked in the literature. We also show that fully efficient estimation of RE models with future expectations invariably requires some *a priori* knowledge of the number of unstable roots of the model. Our formulation also allows a simple analysis of the problem of testing for boot-strap effects or self-fulfilling expectations in RE models recently discussed by Hamilton and Whiteman (1985).

A: Models with Current and Lagged Expectations

7.2 The Basic Model

We start our review of the estimation of RE models with the following simple model analysed in detail by Pagan (1984), and more recently by Turkington (1985):

$$y_t = a_1 x_t^* + \mathbf{a}_2' \mathbf{w}_t + u_t, \tag{7.1}$$

$$x_t = \mathbf{b}' \mathbf{z}_t + v_t, \tag{7.2}$$

$$x_t^* = E(x_t | \Omega_{t-1}), \tag{7.3}$$

where y_t and x_t are scalar endogenous variables, $\mathbf{w}_t$ a $p \times 1$ vector of exogenous or predetermined variables, and $\mathbf{z}_t$ an $h \times 1$ vector of predetermined variables which are either known at time $t-1$ or are perfectly predictable, such as time trends or seasonal dummies. Under the REH x_t^* is given by (7.3), where $E(x_t | \Omega_{t-1})$ represents the rational expectations of x_t formed at time $t-1$ relative to the information set Ω_{t-1}, which is assumed to include observations on at least the variables $\mathbf{z}_t$ as well as on the past values of y_t, x_t, $\mathbf{w}_t$ and $\mathbf{z}_t$. In particular we have $E(\mathbf{z}_t | \Omega_{t-1}) = \mathbf{z}_t$.

For the purpose of estimating the unknown parameters a_1, $\mathbf{a}_2$ and $\mathbf{b}$, and in order to compare the asymptotic efficiency of the alternative estimators of these parameters, in this part we make the following standard assumptions

Assumption 7.1 Conditional on the information set Ω_{t-1}, the disturbances $\boldsymbol{\xi}_t = (u_t, v_t)'$ are normally distributed with zero means and the non-singular variance matrix

$$\Sigma = \begin{pmatrix} \sigma_{uu} & \sigma_{uv} \\ \sigma_{uv} & \sigma_{vv} \end{pmatrix}. \tag{7.4}$$

Assumption 7.2 For the predetermined/exogenous variables of the model $\mathbf{f}_t = (\mathbf{z}_t', \mathbf{w}_t')'$, the following probability limits exist:

$$n^{-1} \sum_{t=1}^{n} \mathbf{f}_t \mathbf{f}_t' \xrightarrow{p} \Sigma_{ff} = \begin{pmatrix} \Sigma_{zz} & \Sigma_{zw} \\ \Sigma_{wz} & \Sigma_{ww} \end{pmatrix}, \tag{7.5}$$

$$n^{-1}\sum_{t=1}^{n}\mathbf{f}_t\boldsymbol{\xi}_t' \xrightarrow{p} 0, \tag{7.6}$$

where Σ_{ff} is a finite positive semi-definite matrix.

Assumption 7.3 for the regressors of (7.1), namely $\mathbf{h}_t^* = (x_t^*, \mathbf{w}_t')' = (\mathbf{z}_t'\mathbf{b}, \mathbf{w}_t')'$, the following probability limit exists and is non-singular

$$n^{-1}\sum_{t=1}^{n}\mathbf{h}_t^*\mathbf{h}_t^{*\prime} \xrightarrow{p} \Sigma_{h^*h^*} = \begin{pmatrix}\mathbf{b}'\Sigma_{zz}\mathbf{b} & \mathbf{b}'\Sigma_{zw}\\ \Sigma_{wz}\mathbf{b} & \Sigma_{ww}\end{pmatrix}. \tag{7.7}$$

Assumption 7.4 The matrix Σ_{zz} is non-singular.

The assumption that, conditional on Ω_{t-1}, the disturbances are normally distributed is needed for the derivation of the ML estimators, and can be dispensed with in derivation of the asymptotic distribution of the alternative estimators. The assumption that the matrix Σ_{ff} is positive semi-definite allows for all or some columns of $\mathbf{w}_t$ to be exact linear functions of the columns of $\mathbf{z}_t$. As will be seen below, this is an important consideration for the comparison of the asymptotic efficiency of the alternative estimators of a_1 *and* $\mathbf{a}_2$. Assumptions 7.2 and 7.4 ensure that the parameter vector $\mathbf{b}$ is identified, while for a given value of $\mathbf{b}$, assumption 7.3 ensures the identification of a_1 *and* $\mathbf{a}_2$. Assumption 7.3 also implies that $\mathbf{b}'\Sigma_{zz}\mathbf{b}$ and Σ_{ww} are non-singular, and rules out the trivial case where $\mathbf{b}=0$. The orthogonality condition $E(\boldsymbol{\xi}_t|\Omega_{t-1})=0$, implicit in assumption 7.1, also ensures that $\boldsymbol{\xi}_t$ has zero mean (unconditionally) and is uncorrelated with its past values and all the current and past values of $\mathbf{f}_t$. Notice, however, that under the REH, $\boldsymbol{\xi}_t$ is not necessarily uncorrelated with future values of $\mathbf{f}_t$. Specifically, we have

$$E(\boldsymbol{\xi}_t)=0, \tag{7.8}$$

$$E(\boldsymbol{\xi}_t\boldsymbol{\xi}_{t-i}')=0, \quad \text{for } i=1,2,\ldots \tag{7.9}$$

$$E(\boldsymbol{\xi}_t\mathbf{f}_{t-i}')=0, \quad \text{for } i=0,1,\ldots \tag{7.10}$$

$$E(x_t|\Omega_{t-1})=x_t^*=\mathbf{b}'\mathbf{z}_t, \tag{7.11}$$

but

$$E(\boldsymbol{\xi}_t\mathbf{f}_{t+i}' \neq 0, \quad \text{for } i=1,2,\ldots$$

This last result is particularly important when we consider models with lagged values of unanticipated variables such as $(x_{t-i}^* - x_{t-i})$.

Writing (7.1) and (7.2) in matrix notation, and noting from (7.11) that under the REH, $x_t^*=\mathbf{b}'\mathbf{z}_t$, we have

$$\mathbf{y}=a_1\mathbf{x}^*+W\mathbf{a}_2+\mathbf{u}, \tag{7.12}$$

$$\mathbf{x}=Z\mathbf{b}+\mathbf{v}=\mathbf{x}^*+\mathbf{v}, \tag{7.13}$$

where W and Z are $n\times p$ and $n\times h$ matrices of observations on $\mathbf{w}_t$ and $\mathbf{z}_t$; $\mathbf{y}$

and $\mathbf{x}$ are the $n \times 1$ vectors of observations on y_t and x_t, and $\mathbf{u}$ and $\mathbf{v}$ are the $n \times 1$ vectors of disturbances.

7.2.1 The ML Estimators

The estimation of the parameters of the above model can now be carried out either by full-information or limited-information methods. The application of the full-information maximum likelihood method to the present problem is straightforward but involves iterative numerical calculations. Under assumption 7.1 the log likelihood function of the model is given by[1]:

$$l(\boldsymbol{\theta}) \propto -\frac{n}{2}\log|\Sigma| - \tfrac{1}{2}\boldsymbol{\xi}'(\Sigma^{-1}\otimes I_n)\boldsymbol{\xi}, \tag{7.14}$$

where I_n is an identity matrix of order n, $\boldsymbol{\theta} = (\mathbf{a}', \mathbf{b}', \boldsymbol{\sigma}')'$, $\mathbf{a}' = (a_1, \mathbf{a}_2')$, $\boldsymbol{\sigma}$ is the 3×1 column vector containing the distinct elements of Σ, namely $\boldsymbol{\sigma}' = (\sigma_{uu}, \sigma_{uv}, \sigma_{vv})$, and

$$\boldsymbol{\xi} = \begin{bmatrix} \mathbf{y} - a_1(Z\mathbf{b}) - W\mathbf{a}_2 \\ \mathbf{x} - Z\mathbf{b} \end{bmatrix}. \tag{7.15}$$

The ML estimators can now be obtained by maximizing $l(\boldsymbol{\theta})$ in (7.14) with respect to $\boldsymbol{\theta}$. Let $\hat{\boldsymbol{\gamma}}_{\text{ML}}$ and $\hat{\boldsymbol{\sigma}}_{\text{ML}}$ be the ML estimators of $\boldsymbol{\gamma} = (\mathbf{a}', \mathbf{b}')'$, and $\boldsymbol{\sigma}$, respectively. Then it is easily seen that $\hat{\boldsymbol{\gamma}}_{\text{ML}}$ and $\hat{\boldsymbol{\sigma}}_{\text{ML}}$ are independently distributed asymptotically and that $\sqrt{n}(\hat{\boldsymbol{\gamma}}_{\text{ML}} - \boldsymbol{\gamma})$ has a limiting normal distribution. The asymptotic variance matrix of ML estimators is given by

$$V(\sqrt{n}\hat{\mathbf{a}}_{\text{ML}}) = [\sigma^{uu}\Sigma_{h^*h^*} + (\sigma_{ee}^{-1} - \sigma^{uu})\Sigma_{h^*z}\Sigma_{zz}^{-1}\Sigma_{zh^*}]^{-1}, \tag{7.16}$$

where $\Sigma_{h^*h^*}$ is already defined in (7.7), and

$$\Sigma_{zh^*} = (\Sigma_{zz}\mathbf{b}, \Sigma_{zw}), \tag{7.17}$$

$$\sigma^{uu} = \sigma_{vv}/(\sigma_{uu}\sigma_{vv} - \sigma_{uv}^2), \tag{7.18}$$

$$\sigma_{ee} = V(u_t - a_1 v_t) = \sigma_{uu} - 2a_1\sigma_{uv} + a_1^2\sigma_{vv}. \tag{7.19}$$

The first term in the square brackets in (7.16) represents the sampling error of estimating $\mathbf{a}$ for a known value of $\mathbf{b}$, while the second term represents the sampling error of estimating $\mathbf{b}$. The ML estimator of $V(\sqrt{n}\hat{\mathbf{a}}_{\text{ML}})$, can be obtained from (7.16) and is given by

$$\hat{V}(\hat{\mathbf{a}}_{\text{ML}}) = \hat{\sigma}_{ee}\begin{bmatrix} \hat{\mathbf{b}}_{\text{ML}}'(Z'Z)\hat{\mathbf{b}}_{\text{ML}} & \hat{\mathbf{b}}_{\text{ML}}'Z'W \\ W'Z\hat{\mathbf{b}}_{\text{ML}} & W'W + \hat{\mu}W'M_zW \end{bmatrix}, \tag{7.20}$$

where $M_z = I - Z(Z'Z)^{-1}Z'$, $\hat{\sigma}_{ee}$ represents the ML estimator of σ_{ee}, and $\hat{\mu}$ is the ML estimator of μ defined by[2]:

$$\mu = (\sigma_{uu} - a_1\sigma_{vv})^2/(\sigma_{uu}\sigma_{vv} - \sigma_{uv}^2) > 0.$$

---

[1] The operation $\Sigma^{-1}\otimes I_n$ represents the Kronecker product of matrices Σ^{-1} and I_n.

[2] Result (7.20) is directly comparable with the one given in Turkington (1985, p. 508).

7.2.2 *Two-step Estimators*

Two-step estimators of RE models are based on the substitution method, whereby in the first step consistent (but not necessarily efficient) estimates of the expectational variables are computed, and these are then substituted back into the RE model in the second step to obtain consistent estimates of the parameters. In the second step the parameters of the RE model are computed as if the estimates of the expectational variables from the first step are given data, and are therefore free from sampling variations.

In the case of the simple RE model (7.12), a consistent estimate of $\mathbf{x}^*$ is obtained in the first step by the OLS regression of $\mathbf{x}$ on Z, yielding $\hat{\mathbf{x}}^*$, where

$$\hat{\mathbf{x}}^* = Z(Z'Z)^{-1}Z'\mathbf{x} = P_z\mathbf{x}. \tag{7.21}$$

In the second step the parameters a_1 and $\mathbf{a}_2$ are then estimated by the OLS regression of $\mathbf{y}$ on $\hat{\mathbf{x}}^*$ and W.
Denoting the two-step estimator of $\mathbf{a}$ by $\hat{\mathbf{a}}_{2S}$, we have

$$\hat{\mathbf{a}}_{2S} = (\hat{H}_*'\hat{H}_*)^{-1}\hat{H}_*'\mathbf{y}, \tag{7.22}$$

where $\hat{H}^* = (\hat{\mathbf{x}}^*, W) = (P_z\mathbf{x}, W)$. To derive the asymptotic variance matrix of $\hat{\mathbf{a}}_{2S}$ we first note that (7.12) can be rewritten as

$$\mathbf{y} = \hat{H}_*\mathbf{a} + \boldsymbol{\varepsilon}, \tag{7.23}$$

where

$$\boldsymbol{\varepsilon} = \mathbf{u} - a_1 P_z\mathbf{v}. \tag{7.24}$$

Hence, unlike $\mathbf{u}$, the variance matrix of the compound disturbance vector $\boldsymbol{\varepsilon}$ is not spherical, being given by

$$\Sigma_{\varepsilon\varepsilon} = V(\boldsymbol{\varepsilon}) = \sigma_{uu}I_n + (\sigma_{ee} - \sigma_{uu})P_z, \tag{7.25}$$

where σ_{ee} is already defined by (7.19). Now substituting (7.23) in (7.22) and using (7.25), we obtain the following expression for the asymptotic variance matrix of $\hat{\mathbf{a}}_{2S}$:

$$V(\sqrt{n}\hat{\mathbf{a}}_{2S}) = \sigma_{uu}\Sigma_{h^*h^*}^{-1} + (\sigma_{ee} - \sigma_{uu})\Sigma_{h^*h^*}^{-1}\Sigma_{h^*z}\Sigma_{zz}^{-1}\Sigma_{zh^*}\Sigma_{h^*h^*}^{-1}, \tag{7.26}$$

which can be estimated consistently by

$$\hat{V}(\hat{\mathbf{a}}_{2S}) = \hat{\sigma}_{uu}(\hat{H}_*'\hat{H}_*)^{-1} + (\hat{\sigma}_{ee} - \hat{\sigma}_{uu})(\hat{H}_*'\hat{H}_*)^{-1}\hat{H}_*'P_z\hat{H}_*(\hat{H}_*'\hat{H}_*)^{-1}. \tag{7.27}$$

From this result it immediately follows that the standard errors computed using standard computer packages in the second step of the two-step estimators are inconsistent, and any inference based on them will be invalid even asymptotically. (See also Mishkin, 1982; Pagan, 1984; Newey, 1984; and Murphy and Topel, 1985.) This result is hardly surprising, stemming from the fact that the disturbances $\boldsymbol{\varepsilon}$ in (7.23) have a non-spherical variance matrix.

7.2.3 *IV Estimators*

Instrumental variable (IV) estimators of $\mathbf{a}$ are based on the errors-in-variables method of solving and estimating RE models first suggested by McCallum

(1976), and more recently by Wickens (1982). Since under the REH, $\mathbf{x}^* = \mathbf{Zb} = \mathbf{x} - \mathbf{v}$, then equations (7.12) and (7.13) can also be written as

$$\mathbf{y} = H\mathbf{a} + \mathbf{e}, \tag{7.28}$$

$$\mathbf{x} = \mathbf{Zb} + \mathbf{v}, \tag{7.29}$$

where $H = (\mathbf{x}, W)$, and

$$\mathbf{e} = \mathbf{u} - a_1\mathbf{v}. \tag{7.30}$$

In this representation of the RE model, H and $\mathbf{e}$ will be correlated irrespective of whether $\sigma_{uv} = 0$ or not. An obvious method of dealing with this problem would be to apply the IV procedure to (7.28) using all the predetermined variables of the model, namely $F = (Z, W)$, as instruments. Denoting the resultant IV estimator of $\mathbf{a}$ by $\hat{\mathbf{a}}_{IV}$, we have

$$\hat{\mathbf{a}}_{IV} = (H'P_f H)^{-1} H'P_f\mathbf{y},$$

where $P_f = F(F'F)^{-1}F'$. Moreover, in view of (7.30), since the variance matrix of $\mathbf{e}$ is given by $\sigma_{ee}I_n$, the relevant expression for the asymptotic variance of $\hat{\mathbf{a}}_{IV}$ is given by

$$V(\sqrt{n}\hat{\mathbf{a}}_{IV}) = \sigma_{ee}\Sigma_{h^*h^*}^{-1}, \tag{7.31}$$

which can be estimated consistently by

$$\hat{V}(\hat{\mathbf{a}}_{IV}) = \hat{\sigma}_{ee}(H'P_f H)^{-1} \tag{7.32}$$

where $\hat{\sigma}_{ee}$ now represents the IV estimator of σ_{ee} given by

$$\hat{\sigma}_{ee} = n^{-1}(\mathbf{y} - H\hat{\mathbf{a}}_{IV})'(\mathbf{y} - H\hat{\mathbf{a}}_{IV}).$$

7.2.4 A Comparison of the Alternative Estimators

Comparing the asymptotic variance matrices of $\hat{\mathbf{a}}_{ML}$, $\hat{\mathbf{a}}_{2S}$ and $\hat{\mathbf{a}}_{IV}$ given by (7.16), (7.26) are (7.31), respectively, it is easily seen that, *in general, the two-step and the IV estimators are less efficient than the ML estimators.* The asymptotic inefficiency of the two-step estimator of $\mathbf{a}$ relative to the ML estimators can be traced to the fact that in deriving $\hat{\mathbf{a}}_{2S}$ no allowance is made for the fact that the variance of $\boldsymbol{\varepsilon}$ in (7.24) is non-spherical. A two-step estimator of $\mathbf{a}$ which takes account of the specific structure of $V(\boldsymbol{\varepsilon}) = \Sigma_{\varepsilon\varepsilon}$ can be obtained by applying the generalized least squares method to (7.23). The resultant estimator

$$\hat{\mathbf{a}}_{GLS} = (\hat{H}_*'\Sigma_{\varepsilon\varepsilon}^{-1}\hat{H}_*)^{-1}\hat{H}_*'\Sigma_{\varepsilon\varepsilon}^{-1}\mathbf{y} \tag{7.33}$$

will not, however, be of much practical value, since its computation is complicated and requires an *a priori* estimate of a_1 *and* $\Sigma_{\varepsilon\varepsilon}$. (The expression for $\Sigma_{\varepsilon\varepsilon}$ is defined in (7.25) and depends on a_1, σ_{uu}, σ_{uv} and σ_{vv}).

It is interesting to note that in the special case where W is contained in Z (or $W \subset Z$), the two-step estimator $\hat{\mathbf{a}}_{2S}$ and the generalized least squares estimator $\hat{\mathbf{a}}_{GLS}$ will be algebraically idential. To see this, note that when $W \subset Z$

then $P_z\hat{H}_* = \hat{H}_*$, and using (7.25)

$$\Sigma_{\varepsilon\varepsilon}\hat{H}_* = \sigma_{ee}\hat{H}_*,$$

or

$$\Sigma_{\varepsilon\varepsilon}^{-1}\hat{H}_* = \sigma_{ee}^{-1}\hat{H}_*.$$

Substituting this back in (7.33) now yields the required result, namely $\hat{\mathbf{a}}_{2S} = \hat{\mathbf{a}}_{GLS}$.

To see the reason for the asymptotic inefficiency of the IV estimator, note that since $\hat{\mathbf{a}}_{IV}$ can also be viewed as the two-stage least squares (TSLS) estimator of $\mathbf{a}$ in the simultaneous equation system (7.28) and (7.29), then in general it will be less efficient than the corresponding three-stage least squares or the full-information maximum-likelihood estimators. The exact equivalence of the ML estimators of $\mathbf{a}$ and $\mathbf{b}$ in equations (7.12) and (7.13), and in equations (7.28) and (7.29), will be established below.

The three estimators, $\hat{\mathbf{a}}_{ML}$, $\hat{\mathbf{a}}_{2S}$ and $\hat{\mathbf{a}}_{IV}$ will, however, be equally efficient asymptotically if either

(i) $a_1 = 0$, and $\sigma_{uv} = 0$,

or

(ii) $W \subset Z$.

In case (i), the asymptotic variance matrices of all the three estimators collapse to $\sigma_{uu}\Sigma_{h^*h^*}^{-1}$, and when $W \subset Z$, then $\Sigma_{h^*h^*} = \Sigma_{h^*z}\Sigma_{zz}^{-1}\Sigma_{zh^*}$ and all the three variance matrices reduce to the expression $\sigma_{ee}\Sigma_{h^*h^*}^{-1}$.

As far as two-step and IV estimators are concerned, it is not generally possible to rank them according to their asymptotic variance matrices. But in the special case where $\mathbf{u}$ and $\mathbf{v}$ are uncorrelated, it is easily seen that two-step estimators are asymptotically more efficient than the IV estimators. Using (7.26) and (7.31) we have

$$V(\sqrt{n}\hat{\mathbf{a}}_{IV}) - V(\sqrt{n}\hat{\mathbf{a}}_{2S}) = (\sigma_{ee} - \sigma_{uu})\Sigma_{h^*h^*}^{-1}\Sigma_0\Sigma_{h^*h^*}^{-1},$$

where Σ_0 is the positive semi-infinite matrix

$$\Sigma_0 = \Sigma_{h^*h^*} - \Sigma_{h^*z}\Sigma_{zz}^{-1}\Sigma_{zh^*}. \tag{7.34}$$

Therefore the relative asymptotic efficiency of the two-step estimators with respect to the IV estimators depends on the 'sign' of $\sigma_{ee} - \sigma_{uu} = a_1^2\sigma_{vv} - 2a_1\sigma_{uv}$. When $\sigma_{uv} = 0$, it is clear that $\sigma_{ee} - \sigma_{uu} = a_1^2\sigma_{vv} > 0$, and $V(\sqrt{n}\hat{\mathbf{a}}_{IV}) \geqslant V(\sqrt{n}\hat{\mathbf{a}}_{2S})$.

7.2.5 The Equivalence of the Likelihood Functions under the Errors-in-variables and Substitution Methods

Consider now the problem of full-information ML estimation of $\mathbf{a}$ based on the errors-in-variables (EV) representation given by equations (7.28) and (7.29). Let $\boldsymbol{\eta} = (\mathbf{e}', \mathbf{v}')$, then the log-likelihood function associated with the EV method will be

$$l_{EV}(\boldsymbol{\theta}) \propto -\tfrac{1}{2}\log|V(\boldsymbol{\eta})| - \tfrac{1}{2}\boldsymbol{\eta}'[V(\boldsymbol{\eta})]^{-1}\boldsymbol{\eta}, \tag{7.35}$$

where $V(\boldsymbol{\eta})$ is the variance matrix of $\boldsymbol{\eta}$. In view of (7.30) we can write

$$\boldsymbol{\eta} = \begin{bmatrix} \mathbf{e} \\ \mathbf{v} \end{bmatrix} = \begin{bmatrix} 1 & -a_1 \\ 0 & 1 \end{bmatrix} \begin{bmatrix} \mathbf{u} \\ \mathbf{v} \end{bmatrix},$$

or

$$\boldsymbol{\eta} = R\boldsymbol{\xi}, \tag{7.36}$$

where

$$R = \begin{bmatrix} 1 & -a_1 \\ 0 & 1 \end{bmatrix}.$$

Using (7.36) it follows that[3] $V(\boldsymbol{\eta}) = (R\Sigma R') \otimes I_n$, and $|V(\boldsymbol{\eta})| = |R\Sigma R'|^n = |\Sigma|^n$. Substituting these results into (7.35) now yields

$$l_{EV}(\boldsymbol{\theta}) \propto -\frac{n}{2}\log|\Sigma| - \tfrac{1}{2}\boldsymbol{\upsilon}'(\Sigma^{-1} \otimes I_n)\boldsymbol{\upsilon}, \tag{7.37}$$

where $\boldsymbol{\upsilon} = (R^{-1} \otimes I_n)\boldsymbol{\eta}$. It is easily seen that

$$\boldsymbol{\upsilon} = \begin{bmatrix} I_n & a_1 I_n \\ 0 & I_n \end{bmatrix} \begin{bmatrix} \mathbf{e} \\ \mathbf{v} \end{bmatrix} = \begin{bmatrix} \mathbf{e} + a_1\mathbf{v} \\ \mathbf{v} \end{bmatrix},$$

which in view of (7.30) establishes that $\boldsymbol{\upsilon} = \boldsymbol{\xi}$. Substituting this result into (7.37), it now follows that $l_{EV}(\boldsymbol{\theta})$ given by (7.35) is algebraically equivalent to the log-likelihood function associated with the substitution method given by (7.14).

The above equivalence result is important not only because it clarifies the relationship that exists between estimators based on the substitution and errors-in-variables methods, but also because it establishes the asymptotic efficiency of the three-stage least squares method applied to the errors-in-variables representation of the RE model given by (7.28) and (7.29).

7.3 RE Models with Current Unanticipated Effects

One important extension of the basic model which has figured prominently in the literature is

$$y_t = a_1 x_t^* + \mathbf{a}_2'\mathbf{w}_t + c(x_t - x_t^*) + ut, \tag{7.38}$$

which includes $x_t - x_t^*$, the 'unanticipated' component of x_t, as a separate variable. This model has been utilized extensively in the empirical analysis of the efficient market hypothesis and the natural rate-rational expectations hypothesis. Notice that the above specification is quite general and allows for

[3] Note that $|R| = 1$.

the inclusion of lagged values of y_t or x_t as components of $\mathbf{w}_t$. The problem of identification of this type of models has already been discussed in example 6.2 in the previous chapter. Without some *a priori* restriction on σ_{uv}, (7.38) and the basic model (7.1) will be observationally equivalent. To see this, note that under the REH, $x_t - x_t^* = v_t$ and the errors-in-variables version of (7.38), in matrix notation, will still be given by (7.28), though the disturbances $\mathbf{e}$ will now be given by

$$\mathbf{e} = \mathbf{u} - (a_1 - c)\mathbf{v}, \tag{7.39}$$

instead of by (7.30). Hence, in general when σ_{uv} is unrestricted, the extended model (7.38) and the basic model (7.1) will be observationally equivalent and it will not be possible to identify c. Notice, however, that in (7.38), the parameters a_1 *and* $\mathbf{a}_2$ will be identified irrespective of whether σ_{uv} is *a priori* restricted or not.

Under the restriction $\sigma_{uv} = 0$, using (7.39) we have

$$\sigma_{ev} = -(a_1 - c)\,\sigma_{vv}. \tag{7.40}$$

The parameters a_1, $\mathbf{a}_2$, $\mathbf{b}$, σ_{ev}, σ_{vv} are all identifiable and can be estimated by the IV method applied to equations (7.28) and (7.29). The IV estimator of c can then be obtained using (7.40), namely

$$\hat{c}_{\text{IV}} = \hat{\sigma}_{vv}^{-1}\hat{\sigma}_{ve} + \hat{a}_{1,\text{IV}}, \tag{7.41}$$

where

$$\hat{\sigma}_{vv} = n^{-1}(\mathbf{x}'M_z\mathbf{x}), \quad \hat{\sigma}_{ve} = n^{-1}\mathbf{x}'M_z(\mathbf{y} - H\hat{\mathbf{a}}_{\text{IV}}),$$

and $\hat{\mathbf{a}}_{\text{IV}}$ has already been defined in section 7.2.3. Using these estimates in (7.41) now yields

$$\hat{c}_{\text{IV}} = (\mathbf{x}'M_z\mathbf{x})^{-1}\mathbf{x}'M_z(\mathbf{y} - \mathbf{W}\hat{\mathbf{a}}_{2,\text{IV}}). \tag{7.42}$$

When W is contained in Z, the above result further simplifies to

$$\hat{c}_{\text{IV}} = (\mathbf{x}'M_z\mathbf{x})^{-1}\mathbf{x}'M_z\mathbf{y}$$

which is the scalar coefficient in the regression of $\mathbf{y}$ on $M_z\mathbf{x} = (\mathbf{x} - \hat{\mathbf{x}}^*)$. In this case the IV and the two-step estimators of c are the same numerically.

The asymptotic variance matrix of $\sqrt{n}(\hat{\mathbf{a}}_{\text{IV}} - \mathbf{a})$ is still given by (7.31) with the difference that σ_{ee} is now defined by

$$\sigma_{ee} = \sigma_{uu} + (\text{a}_1 - c)^2\,\sigma_{vv}. \tag{7.43}$$

To obtain the asymptotic variance of $\sqrt{n}(\hat{c}_{\text{IV}} - c)$, we first note, using (7.42), that

$$\hat{c}_{\text{IV}} - c = (\mathbf{v}'M_z\mathbf{v})^{-1}\mathbf{v}'M_z\mathbf{u} - (\mathbf{v}'M_z\mathbf{v})^{-1}(\mathbf{v}'M_z W)(\hat{\mathbf{a}}_{2,\text{IV}} - \mathbf{a}_2).$$

But under assumptions 7.1 and 7.2 and the *a priori* restriction $\sigma_{uv} = 0$, we have

$$n^{-1}(\mathbf{v}'M_z\mathbf{v}) \xrightarrow{p} \sigma_{vv},$$
$$n^{-1}(\mathbf{v}'M_z\mathbf{u}) \xrightarrow{p} 0,$$
$$n^{-1}(\mathbf{v}'M_z W) \xrightarrow{p} 0.$$

Therefore[4]

$$\sqrt{n}(\hat{c}_{IV}-c)\overset{a}{\sim}\sigma_{vv}^{-1}\sqrt{n}\mathbf{u}'\mathbf{v},$$

and, since by assumption u_t and v_t are independently distributed, it is then easily seen that

$$\sqrt{n}(\hat{c}_{IV}-c)\overset{a}{\sim}N(0,\sigma_{uu}/\sigma_{vv}). \tag{7.44}$$

From the above results it also follows that $\hat{\mathbf{a}}_{IV}$ and $\hat{c}_{IV}$ are independently distributed asymptotically, which is hardly surprising once it is recognized that under the REH, the unanticipated variable $v_t = x_t - x_t^*$ in (7.38) is distributed independently of the other explanatory variables in the model.

Under the identifying restriction $\sigma_{uv}=0$, the parameters of (7.38) can also be estimated by the two-step or the full-information ML methods as set out in the previous section. The asymptotic variance matrices of these estimators can also be obtained along similar lines. For the ML estimators we have

$$V(\sqrt{n}\hat{\mathbf{a}}_{ML})=\{\sigma_{ee}^{-1}\Sigma_{h^*h^*}+(\sigma_{uu}^{-1}-\sigma_{ee}^{-1})\Sigma_0\}^{-1}, \tag{7.45}$$

and

$$V(\sqrt{n}\hat{c}_{ML})=\sigma_{uu}/\sigma_{vv}, \tag{7.46}$$

where $\Sigma_{h^*h^*}$ and Σ_0 are given as before by (7.7) and (7.34), respectively, and σ_{ee} is defined above by (7.43). From these results it follows that the IV estimator of c given by (7.42) is asymptotically efficient irrespective of whether W is contained in Z or not. The asymptotic efficiency of $\hat{\mathbf{a}}_{IV}$, however, depends on whether $W \subset Z$. The same is also true of the two-step estimators. Nothing can be gained by the ML estimation of c asymptotically. As far as the estimators of $\mathbf{a}$ are concerned, under the identifying restriction $\sigma_{uv}=0$, asymptotically we have

$$V(\sqrt{n}\hat{\mathbf{a}}_{IV}) \geqslant V(\sqrt{n}\hat{\mathbf{a}}_{2S}) \geqslant V(\sqrt{n}\hat{\mathbf{a}}_{ML}),$$

which suggests that, in large samples, the two-step estimator of $\mathbf{a}$ is preferable to the corresponding IV estimator, assuming that $\sigma_{uv}=0$. This result, however, critically depends on the maintained assumption that the process generating x_t is correctly specified. When important variables influencing x_t are incorrectly omitted from equation (7.2), two-step estimators of $\mathbf{a}$ and c, and the IV estimator of c, will no longer be consistent. However, this type of misspecification does not affect the consistency property of the IV estimator of $\mathbf{a}$.

7.4 RE Models with Current and Lagged Unanticipated Effects

The results obtained so far are relatively simple and can be easily applied in practice. Unfortunately, they do not survive the inclusion of lagged values of x_t^* or $x_t - x_t^*$ in the model. Consider the following general distributed lag

[4] The notation $\overset{a}{\sim}$ stands for 'distributed asymptotically as'.

version of (7.38)

$$y_t = \sum_{i=0}^{s} a_i x^*_{t-i} + \mathbf{a}'_{s+1}\mathbf{w}_t + \sum_{i=0}^{s} c_i(x_{t-i} - x^*_{t-i}) + u_t, \tag{7.47}$$

where $x^*_{t-i} = E(x_{t-i}|\Omega_{t-i-1})$. This model has been extensively analysed in the literature, notably by Abel and Mishkin (1983), Leiderman (1980), and Attfield et al. (1981). (Also see the discussion in example 6.2.) The presence of lagged values of the unanticipated variables amongst the regressors has important implications for the asymptotic distribution of ML estimators and the efficiency of two-step estimators. This is primarily due to the fact that, although under the REH, $v_t = x_t - x^*_t$ is uncorrelated with x^*_t, $\mathbf{w}_t$ and their lagged values, the same is not necessarily true of v_t and the future values of x^*_t and $\mathbf{w}_t$. In consequence, the asymptotic distribution of estimators of $\mathbf{c} = (c_0, c_1, \ldots, c_s)'$ will not be independent of the asymptotic distribution of the estimators of $\mathbf{a} = (a_0, a_1, \ldots, a_s, \mathbf{a}'_{s+1})'$, and the two-step estimator of $\mathbf{c}$ will no longer be asymptotically efficient. For the two-step estimator of $\mathbf{c}$ to be asymptotically efficient we need to impose the more restrictive assumptions

$$n^{-1} \sum_{t=1}^{n} \mathbf{f}_{t+i} v_t \xrightarrow{p} 0, \quad \text{for } i = 1, 2, \ldots$$

which are not warranted under the REH.

7.4.1 IV Estimators

In principle all the three estimation methods discussed above can be aplied to the present model. To obtain the IV or the errors- in-variables estimators, we first rewrite the model as

$$y_t = \sum_{i=0}^{s} a_i x_{t-i} + \mathbf{a}'_{s+1}\mathbf{w}_t + e_t, \tag{7.48}$$

where e_t is now given by the composite disturbance term

$$e_t = u_t - \sum_{i=0}^{s} (a_i - c_i) v_{t-i}. \tag{7.49}$$

Notice that these disturbances are now autocorrelated and need no longer be orthogonal to the predetermined variables $\mathbf{f}_t$ or their lagged values $\mathbf{f}_{t-1}, \ldots, \mathbf{f}_{t-s+1}$. The estimation problems arising from the nature of disturbances in (7.48) have been discussed in the literature, primarily in the context of models with future expectations, by Flood and Garber (1980), McDonald (1983), Cumby et al. (1983), Hayashi and Sims (1983), and others (see also the second part of this chapter). To demonstrate these problems in the case of the present model, take the simple case where $s = 1$. Then

$$e_t = u_t - \delta_0 v_t - \delta_1 v_{t-1},$$

in which $\delta_i = a_i - c_i$, $i=0, 1$. Under the identifying restriction $\sigma_{uv}=0$, and assuming as before that the disturbances u_t and v_t are conditionally homoscedastic with respect to the information set Ω_{t-1} (see assumption 7.1), we have

$$E(e_t^2) = \sigma_{uu} + (\delta_0^2 + \delta_1^2)\sigma_{vv}, \tag{7.50a}$$

$$E(e_t e_{t-1}) = \delta_1 \delta_0 \sigma_{vv} \neq 0, \tag{7.50b}$$

$$E(e_t e_{t-i}) = 0, \quad \text{for } i=2, 3, \ldots \tag{7.50c}$$

From these results it follows that the composite disturbance term e_t is serially correlated and has a first-order moving-average representation (see, for example, Anderson, 1971, pp. 224–5). This serial correlation problem on its own is not serious, and could be handled in the usual manner, except for the fact that, under the REH, e_t need no longer be orthogonal to the information set Ω_{t-1}. In particular, since $E(e_t|\mathbf{f}_t) = -\delta_1 E(v_{t-1}|\mathbf{f}_t) \neq 0$, then the use of $\mathbf{f}_t$ as instruments may not be valid. Moreover, as is already pointed out by Flood and Garber (1980), and others, the use of Fair's (1970) instrumental variables technique which exploits the serial correlation pattern of e_t can result in inconsistent parameter estimates. Consistent parameter estimates that do not exploit the serial correlation properties of the disturbances e_t can, however, be obtained using lagged values of $\mathbf{f}_t$ as instruments. In the general case where $s \geqslant 1$, the composite disturbance term e_t will follow an MA(s) process, and the appropriate set of instruments for obtaining consistent (but inefficient) estimates of $\mathbf{a} = (a_0, a_1, \ldots, a_s, \mathbf{a}'_{s+1})'$ in (7.48) would include[5] $\mathbf{f}_{t-s}$, $\mathbf{f}_{t-s-1}$, ... and x_{t-s-1}, x_{t-s-2}, ... To obtain the IV (or the moment) estimators of c_i, the following moment conditions can be utilized

$$E(e_t v_{t-i}) = (c_i - a_i)\sigma_{vv}, \quad \text{for } i=0, 1, 2, \ldots, s.$$

An asymptotically efficient estimate of σ_{vv} can still be obtained from the OLS regression of $\mathbf{x}$ on Z, and the moments $E(e_t v_{t-i})$ can be consistently estimated by $n^{-1}\Sigma_{t=i+1}^{n} \hat{v}_{t-i}\hat{e}_t$, where $\hat{v}_t$ are the OLS residuals of the regression of $\mathbf{x}$ on Z, and $\hat{e}_t$ represents the IV estimates of e_t defined by (7.48). In computing the asymptotic variance matrix of the IV estimators of $\mathbf{a}$ and $\mathbf{c}$, special care should be taken of the fact that the composite disturbance term e_t has the MA(s) representation. This considerably complicates the use of IV estimators for models such as (7.47) in the general case where $s \geqslant 1$.

7.4.2 Two-step Estimators

The two-step estimation of the general model (7.47) does not, however, pose any special problems. Rewriting the general model in terms of the first step estimators $\hat{\mathbf{x}}^*(-i) = Z(-i)(Z'Z)^{-1}Z'\mathbf{x} = P_i\mathbf{x}$, for $i=0, 1, 2, \ldots, s$, we have

$$\mathbf{y} = \hat{H}_* \mathbf{a} + \hat{V}\mathbf{c} + \boldsymbol{\varepsilon} = \hat{G}\mathbf{d} + \boldsymbol{\varepsilon} \tag{7.51}$$

---

[5] Notice that in the case $s \geqslant 1$, even the predetermined variables $\mathbf{w}_t$ are not orthogonal to e_t. This is already implicit in the condition that only lagged values of $\mathbf{f}_t = (\mathbf{w}_t, z_t)'$ of order s and higher are valid instruments for estimation of (7.48).

where

$$\hat{H}_* = (\hat{\mathbf{x}}_*, \hat{\mathbf{x}}_*(-1), \ldots, \hat{\mathbf{x}}_*(-s), W),$$
$$\hat{V} = (\hat{\mathbf{v}}, \hat{\mathbf{v}}(-1), \ldots, \hat{\mathbf{v}}(-s)),$$
$$\boldsymbol{\varepsilon} = \mathbf{u} - \sum_{i=0}^{s} (a_i - c_i) Z(-i)(\hat{\mathbf{b}} - \mathbf{b}), \tag{7.52}$$

where $\hat{\mathbf{y}}(-i) = \mathbf{x}(-i) - P_i\mathbf{x}$, $\mathbf{x}(0) = \mathbf{x}$, $Z(0) = Z$, and so on. Then the two-step estimator of $\mathbf{d} = (\mathbf{a}', \mathbf{c}')'$ will be

$$\hat{\mathbf{d}}_{2S} = (\hat{G}'\hat{G})^{-1}\hat{G}'\mathbf{y}. \tag{7.53}$$

The asymptotic variance matrices of two step estimators in the general case are, however, much more complicated to compute. Substituting for $\mathbf{y}$ from (7.51) into (7.53), we have

$$\hat{\mathbf{d}}_{2S} - \mathbf{d} = (\hat{G}'\hat{G})^{-1}\hat{G}'\boldsymbol{\varepsilon}. \tag{7.54}$$

When the x_t process in (7.2) is correctly specified, the disturbance vector $\boldsymbol{\varepsilon}$ in (7.52) can also be written as

$$\boldsymbol{\varepsilon} = \mathbf{u} - \left(\sum_{i=0}^{s} \delta_i P_i\right)\mathbf{v} \tag{7.55}$$

in which $\delta_i = a_i - c_i$ and $P_i = Z(-i)(Z'Z)^{-1}Z'$ defined previously. To prove the consistency of $\hat{\mathbf{d}}_{2S}$ and to derive its asymptotic variance matrix, we need the following extensions of assumptions 7.2 to 7.4.

Assumption 7.2' As $n \to \infty$, the matrices $W'Z(-i)/n$ and $Z'(-i)Z(-j)/n$, for $i, j = 0, 1, 2, \ldots, s$, converge to the finite probability limits Σ_{wi} and Σ_{ij}, respectively.

Assumption 7.3' As $n \to \infty$, the matrix $\hat{G}'\hat{G}/n$ converges to the non-singular matrix Σ_{gg} defined by

$$\Sigma_{gg} = \operatorname*{plim}_{n\to\infty} (\hat{G}'\hat{G}/n) = \begin{bmatrix} \Sigma_{h^*h^*} & \Sigma_{h^*v} \\ \Sigma_{vh^*} & \Sigma_{vv} \end{bmatrix}, \tag{7.56}$$

$$\Sigma_{h^*h^*} = \begin{bmatrix} \mathbf{b}'\Sigma_{00}\mathbf{b} & \mathbf{b}'\Sigma_{01}\mathbf{b} & \ldots & \mathbf{b}'\Sigma_{0s}\mathbf{b} & \mathbf{b}'\Sigma_{0w} \\ \mathbf{b}'\Sigma_{10}\mathbf{b} & \mathbf{b}'\Sigma_{11}\mathbf{b} & \ldots & \mathbf{b}'\Sigma_{1s}\mathbf{b} & \mathbf{b}'\Sigma_{1w} \\ \vdots & \vdots & & \vdots & \vdots \\ \mathbf{b}'\Sigma_{s0}\mathbf{b} & \mathbf{b}'\Sigma_{s1}\mathbf{b} & \ldots & \mathbf{b}'\Sigma_{ss}\mathbf{b} & \mathbf{b}'\Sigma_{sw} \\ \Sigma_{w0}\mathbf{b} & \Sigma_{w1}\mathbf{b} & \ldots & \Sigma_{ws}\mathbf{b} & \Sigma_{ww} \end{bmatrix}, \tag{7.57}$$

which is a direct generalization[6] of the expression given in (7.7) for the case

[6] Notice that, in terms of our previous notation, $\Sigma_{00} = \Sigma_{zz}$, and $\Sigma_{0w} = \Sigma_{zw}$.

$s=0$. Explicit expressions for

$$\Sigma_{h^*v}=\operatorname*{plim}_{n\to\infty}(\hat{H}'_*\hat{V}/n) \quad \text{and} \quad \Sigma_{vv}=\operatorname*{plim}_{n\to\infty}(\hat{V}'\hat{V}/n)$$

can also be derived but, in general, they will be rather complicated functions of the covariances between v_t and future values of $\mathbf{w}_t$ and z_t.

Under the above more general assumptions, using (7.55) we first note that

$$\operatorname*{plim}_{n\to\infty}(\hat{\mathbf{d}}_{2S}-\mathbf{d})=\Sigma_{gg}^{-1}\operatorname*{plim}_{n\to\infty}(\hat{G}'\boldsymbol{\varepsilon}/n).$$

In view of (7.55), it is now easily established that $W'\boldsymbol{\varepsilon}/n$, $Z'(-i)\boldsymbol{\varepsilon}/n$, and $\mathbf{v}'(-i)\boldsymbol{\varepsilon}/n$, and hence $\hat{G}'\boldsymbol{\varepsilon}/n$, converge to a zero vector in probability as the sample size increases. Therefore,

$$\operatorname*{plim}_{n\to\infty}(\hat{\mathbf{d}}_{2S})=\mathbf{d},$$

which establishes that $\hat{\mathbf{d}}_{2S}$ is a consistent estimator of $\mathbf{d}$ under fairly general conditions.

Derivation of the asymptotic distribution of $\hat{\mathbf{d}}_{2S}$ can also be carried out in the usual manner using (7.54). Asymptotically, we have

$$\begin{aligned}\sqrt{n}(\hat{\mathbf{d}}_{2S}-\mathbf{d}) &\overset{a}{\sim}\Sigma_{gg}^{-1}\left(\frac{1}{\sqrt{n}}\hat{G}'\boldsymbol{\varepsilon}\right)\\ &\overset{a}{\sim}\Sigma_{gg}^{-1}\left(\frac{1}{\sqrt{n}}G'\boldsymbol{\varepsilon}\right),\end{aligned}$$

where G is the $n\times(2s+p+2)$ matrix

$$G=(Z\mathbf{b}, Z(-1)\mathbf{b}, \ldots, Z(-s)\mathbf{b}, W, \boldsymbol{v}, \boldsymbol{v}(-1), \ldots, \boldsymbol{v}(-s)). \tag{7.58}$$

Therefore

$$\sqrt{n}(\hat{\mathbf{d}}_{2S}-\mathbf{d})\overset{a}{\sim}N(0, V(\sqrt{n}\hat{\mathbf{d}}_{2S})),$$

where

$$V(\sqrt{n}\hat{\mathbf{d}}_{2S})=\Sigma_{gg}^{-1}\Omega\Sigma_{gg}^{-1}, \tag{7.59}$$

in which $\Omega=\lim_{n\to\infty}\{n^{-1}E(G'\boldsymbol{\varepsilon}\boldsymbol{\varepsilon}'G)\}$. But

$$E(G'\boldsymbol{\varepsilon}\boldsymbol{\varepsilon}'G)=E\{G'E(\boldsymbol{\varepsilon}\boldsymbol{\varepsilon}'|Z,Z(-1),\ldots,)\,G\}, \tag{7.60}$$

and using (7.55) it is easily seen that, under the identifying restriction $\sigma_{uv}=0$,

$$E(\boldsymbol{\varepsilon}\boldsymbol{\varepsilon}'|Z,Z(-1),\ldots)=\sigma_{uu}I_n+\sigma_{vv}\sum_{i=0}^{s}\sum_{j=0}^{s}\delta_i\delta_j\Delta_{ij}, \tag{7.61}$$

where

$$\Delta_{ij}=P_iP_j'=Z(-i)(Z'Z)^{-1}Z'(-j), \quad i,j=0,1,2,\ldots,s. \tag{7.62}$$

Using (7.61) in (7.60), we have

$$\Omega = \lim_{n\to\infty}\left\{\sigma_{uu}\mathrm{E}(G'G/n) + \sigma_{vv}\sum_{i=0}^{s}\sum_{j=0}^{s}\delta_i\delta_j E(G'\Delta_{ij}G)\right\}.$$

Finally, substituting this result into (7.59) and noting that

$$\lim_{n\to\infty} E(G'G/n) = \Sigma_{gg}$$

and

$$\lim_{n\to\infty} E(G'\Delta_{ij}G) = \Sigma_{gi}\Sigma_{zz}^{-1}\Sigma_{jg},$$

where

$$\Sigma_{gi} = \Sigma'_{ig} = \operatorname*{plim}_{n\to\infty}\{G'Z(-i)/n\}, \tag{7.63}$$

the following expression for the asymptotic variance matrix of $\hat{\mathbf{d}}_{2S}$ results

$$V(\sqrt{n}\hat{\mathbf{d}}_{2S}) = \sigma_{uu}\Sigma_{gg}^{-1} + \sigma_{vv}\Sigma_{gg}^{-1}\left(\sum_{i=0}^{s}\sum_{j=0}^{s}\delta_i\delta_j\Sigma_{gi}\Sigma_{zz}^{-1}\Sigma_{jg}\right)\Sigma_{gg}^{-1}. \tag{7.64}$$

A consistent estimate of this variance matrix is given by

$$\hat{V}(\hat{\mathbf{d}}_{2S}) = \hat{\sigma}_{uu}(\hat{G}'\hat{G})^{-1} + \hat{\sigma}_{vv}(\hat{G}'\hat{G})^{-1}\,\hat{G}'\hat{Q}\hat{G}(\hat{G}'\hat{G})^{-1}, \tag{7.65}$$

where

$$\hat{Q} = \sum_{i=0}^{s}\sum_{j=0}^{s}\delta_i\delta_j Z(-i)(Z'Z)^{-1}Z'(-j). \tag{7.66}$$

Here, two-step estimators are denoted by the circumflex. This result clearly shows that the OLS variance matrix routinely computed at the second step in the computation of two-step estimators, namely $\hat{\sigma}_{uu}(\hat{G}'\hat{G})^{-1}$, gives an inconsistent estimate of the true variance matrix of these estimators. The OLS estimates generally underestimate the true variances of the two-step estimators. This follows immediately from (7.65) by noting that $\hat{G}'\hat{Q}\hat{G}$ is a semi-positive definite matrix.[7] (See also theorem 8 in Pagan, 1984).

7.4.3 ML and Two-step Asymptotically Efficient Estimators

Apart from the substantial computations involved in obtaining a consistent estimate of the variance matrix of two-step estimators, these estimators will not be asymptotically efficient even if W is contained in Z. For these reasons, estimation and hypothesis testing in RE models with lagged anticipated or lagged unanticipated variables are best carried out in the full-information maximum-likelihood framework set out in sections 7.2.1 and 7.2.5. Under the

[7] Let $\hat{R} = \Sigma_{i=0}^{s}\delta_i Z(Z'Z)^{-1}Z'(-i)$, then it is easily seen that $\hat{G}'\hat{Q}\hat{G} = \hat{G}'\hat{R}'\hat{R}\hat{G} \geqslant 0$, which establishes that $\hat{V}(\hat{\mathbf{d}}_{2S}) \geqslant \hat{\sigma}_{uu}(\hat{G}'\hat{G})^{-1}$.

identifying restriction $\sigma_{uv}=0$, the joint log-likelihood function of the model in the general case may be written as

$$l(\boldsymbol{\theta}) \propto -\frac{n}{2}\log\sigma_{uu} - \frac{1}{2\sigma_{uu}}\mathbf{u}'\mathbf{u} - \frac{n}{2}\log\sigma_{vv} - \frac{1}{2\sigma_{vv}}\boldsymbol{v}'\boldsymbol{v} \tag{7.67}$$

where $\boldsymbol{\theta}=(\mathbf{a}', \mathbf{c}', \mathbf{b}', \sigma_{uu}, \sigma_{vv})'$ and, as before, $\mathbf{v}=\mathbf{x}-Z\mathbf{b}$,

$$\mathbf{u}=\mathbf{y}-\sum_{i=0}^{s} a_i Z(-i)\mathbf{b} - W\mathbf{a}_{s+1} - \sum_{i=0}^{s} c_i\{\mathbf{x}(-i)-Z(-i)\mathbf{b}\}$$

$$=\mathbf{y}-G\mathbf{d},$$

which can also be written equivalently as

$$\mathbf{u}=\mathbf{y}-S\mathbf{b}-W\mathbf{a}_{s+1}-\sum_{i=0}^{s} c_i\mathbf{x}(-i),$$

in which

$$S=\sum_{i=0}^{s}(a_i-c_i)Z(-i). \tag{7.68}$$

Matrix G is already defined by (7.58).

Computation of ML estimators can be carried out by means of the scoring algorithm, iterating from some initial consistent estimates. The ML procedure requires the iterative process to converge, but as is shown, for example, by Pagan (1986, theorem 7), that the estimators obtained even after one iteration of the scoring algorithm will be asymptotically efficient, assuming that the iterations commence from a consistent estimate of $\boldsymbol{\theta}$. This result also underlies the two-step asymptotically efficient estimator proposed by Pagan (1986) for the efficient estimation of a variety of RE models. In the case of the present model, the two-step asymptotically efficient estimator of $\boldsymbol{\gamma}=(\mathbf{d}', \hat{\mathbf{b}}')$, denoted by $\hat{\boldsymbol{\gamma}}_{2SML}$, is given by

$$\hat{\boldsymbol{\gamma}}_{2SML}=\hat{\boldsymbol{\gamma}}_{2S}+\Delta\boldsymbol{\gamma}, \tag{7.69}$$

where $\Delta\boldsymbol{\gamma}$ are the coefficient estimates in the double-length regression of

$$\begin{bmatrix}\hat{\sigma}_{uu}^{-1/2}\hat{\mathbf{u}}\\ \hat{\sigma}_{vv}^{-1/2}\hat{\mathbf{v}}\end{bmatrix} \quad \text{on} \quad \begin{bmatrix}\hat{\sigma}_{uu}^{-1/2}\hat{G} & \hat{\sigma}_{uu}^{-1/2}\hat{S}\\ 0 & \hat{\sigma}_{vv}^{-1/2}Z\end{bmatrix}.$$

All the unknown parameters in this regression are replaced by the two-step estimators, namely $\hat{\boldsymbol{\gamma}}_{2S}=(\hat{\mathbf{d}}'_{2S}, \hat{\mathbf{b}}')'$. The above double-length regression also provides a consistent estimate of the asymptotic variance matrix of $\hat{\boldsymbol{\gamma}}_{2SML}$. The expression for the estimate of the asymptotic variance matrix of $\hat{\mathbf{d}}_{2SML}$ (the parameters of the RE equation (7.47)) is given by

$$\hat{V}(\hat{\mathbf{d}}_{2SML}) = \hat{\sigma}_{uu}[\hat{G}'\hat{G} - \hat{G}'\hat{S}(\hat{S}'\hat{S} + \lambda Z'Z)^{-1}\hat{S}'\hat{G}]^{-1}, \tag{7.70}$$

where $\hat{\lambda} = \hat{\sigma}_{uu}/\hat{\sigma}_{vv}$.

7.4.4 *Multivariate RE Models*

The results obtained so far in this chapter can be easily extended to multivariate RE models where the model may contain more than one expectational variable and/or more than one equation with unobserved expectations. A general form of such a model can be written as

$$\mathbf{y}_t = \sum_{i=0}^{s} A_i'\mathbf{x}_{t-i}^* + A_{s+1}'\mathbf{w}_t + \sum_{i=0}^{s} C_i'(\mathbf{x}_{t-i} - \mathbf{x}_{t-i}^*) + \mathbf{u}_t, \tag{7.71}$$

$$\mathbf{x}_t = B'\mathbf{z}_t + \mathbf{v}_t, \tag{7.72}$$

$$\mathbf{x}_{t-i}^* = E(\mathbf{x}_{t-i}|\Omega_{t-i-1}) = B'\mathbf{z}_{t-i}, \tag{7.73}$$

where $\mathbf{y}_t$ and $\mathbf{x}_t$ are now column vectors of orders m and k, respectively, and A_i, C_i, B are unknown parameter matrices of dimensions conformable with the vectors of the endogenous and predetermined variables of the model. The variance matrix of the $(k+m)\times 1$ joint disturbance vector $\boldsymbol{\xi}_t = (\mathbf{u}_t', \boldsymbol{v}_t')'$ is now given by

$$\Sigma = \begin{pmatrix} \Sigma_{uu} & \Sigma_{uv} \\ \Sigma_{vu} & \Sigma_{vv} \end{pmatrix},$$

which is a multi-equation generalization of (7.4). As in the univariate case, the identification of the above multivariate models requires *a priori* restrictions on the elements of C_0 or Σ_{uv}, one important example being $C_0 = 0$ or $\Sigma_{uv} = 0$. In addition, it is also necessary that $h \geqslant k$. This order condition is clearly satisfied in the case of the univariate model, but should be imposed *a priori* when the RE model contains more than one expectational variable (see example 6.2). The details of alternative methods of estimating the parameters of the model (7.71)–(7.73) and its various specializations can be found in Pesaran (1986), where it is shown how the results for single-equation rational expectations models can be extended to the multivariate case.

7.5 Cross-equation Tests of Rationality and Policy Neutrality

From an hypothesis testing view-point, the REH is best characterized as a particular type of cross-equation restriction, relating the reduced form parameters of the RE equation(s) to the parameters of the equation(s) that generate the forcing variables (i.e. x's in our notation). This characterization underlies most *indirect* tests of the REH and suggests that one possible method of testing the REH is to see whether the cross-equation restrictions implied by the hypothesis are valid.

The idea behind cross-equation tests can be easily demonstrated in the context of the basic model (7.12)–(7.13). Sustituting $\mathbf{x}^* = Z\mathbf{b}$ in (7.12), the RE model can be written equivalently as

$$\mathbf{y} = Z\boldsymbol{\beta} + W\mathbf{a}_2 + \mathbf{u},$$

$$\mathbf{x} = Z\mathbf{b} + \mathbf{v},$$

subject to the cross-equation (parameter) restrictions

$$\boldsymbol{\beta} = a_1\mathbf{b}.$$

In practice, however, not all these restrictions need be binding. This can happen when some or all columns of W (or their linear combinations) are contained in Z. To allow for this possibility let $Z = (Z_1, Z_2)$ be partitioned into h_1 and h_2 columns, where $h_1 + h_2 = h$, and suppose that $W = (Z_2, \bar{W})$, where $\bar{W}$ represents the $n \times (p - h_2)$ columns of W that are not contained in Z. In this more general set-up, the basic RE model will be equivalent to the equation system

$$\mathbf{y} = Z_1\boldsymbol{\delta}_1 + Z_2\boldsymbol{\delta}_2 + \bar{W}\mathbf{a}_{22} + \mathbf{u}, \tag{7.74}$$

$$\mathbf{x} = Z_1\mathbf{b}_1 + Z_2\mathbf{b}_2 + \mathbf{v}, \tag{7.75}$$

subject to the cross-equation restrictions

$$\boldsymbol{\delta}_1 = a_1\mathbf{b}_1, \tag{7.76}$$

and

$$\boldsymbol{\delta}_2 = a_1\mathbf{b}_2 + \mathbf{a}_{21}. \tag{7.77}$$

The relations in (7.77) uniquely determine $\mathbf{a}_{21}$ and therefore do not impose any cross-equation restrictions. Only the restrictions in (7.76) are binding and, in the context of the simultaneous equation model (7.74) and (7.75), provide us with $h_1 - 1$ over-identifying restrictions. Seen from this perspective, the cross-equation restrictions $\boldsymbol{\delta}_1 = a_1\mathbf{b}_1$ can be viewed as over-identifying restrictions, and cross-equation tests as tests of over-identification in a standard simultaneous equation framework.

A suitable procedure for testing the cross-equation restrictions $H_0: \boldsymbol{\delta}_1 = a_1\mathbf{b}_1$ is the likelihood ratio (LR) test. Denoting the maximized values of the log-likelihood functions for the unrestricted model (7.74)–(7.75) and the restricted model (7.12)–(7.13) by LL_u and LL_r, respectively, the LR statistic for testing the cross-equation restrictions is given by

$$\mathrm{LR} = 2(\mathrm{LL}_u - \mathrm{LL}_r),$$

or using standard results on concentrating the log-likelihood function by

$$\mathrm{LR} = n \log\{|\hat{\Sigma}_r|/|\hat{\Sigma}_u|\}, \tag{7.78}$$

where $\hat{\Sigma}_u$ and $\hat{\Sigma}_r$ are, respectively, the unrestricted and the restricted estimates of Σ. Under assumptions 7.1–7.4, it is now easily seen that, when $H_0: \boldsymbol{\delta}_1 = a_1\mathbf{b}_1$ holds, the above LR statistic is asymptotically distributed as a χ^2

variate with $h_1 - 1$ degrees of freedom. A test based on the LR principle leads to rejection of H_0 when the computed value of LR in (7.78) exceeds the critical value from the $\chi^2_{h_1-1}$ distribution.

As far as computation of the LR statistic is concerned, it is worth noting that when W is contained in Z (i.e. $\bar{W} \equiv 0$ in (7.74)), then Σ_u can be estimated by two separate OLS regressions of **y** and **x** on Z. But in the general case where W is not contained in Z, the ML estimation of Σ in the unrestricted model necessitates the application of Zellner's (1962) method of seemingly unrelated regression equations (SURE).

It is important to bear in mind that the validity of cross-equation tests as tests of the REH crucially depends on the validity of the unrestricted model within which the REH is embodied. In general, the rejection of the cross-equation restrictions does not necessarily lead to the rejection of the REH. It can always be argued that cross-equation restrictions have been rejected not because the REH is false, but due to mis-specification in the underlying economic model. This considerably weakens the relevance of cross-equation tests as tests of the REH, since it is unlikely that, in practice, the unrestricted model can be maintained without any reservation.[8]

The extension of the above cross-equation tests to models with current and lagged unanticipated effects is straightforward. The LR statistic given in (7.78) is still the appropriate statistic to use, although it is now necessary to impose the *a priori* identifying restriction $\sigma_{uv} = 0$. Other hypotheses of interest, such as the neutrality hypothesis of the new classical macroeconomics, can also be tested separately, or jointly with the cross-equation restrictions implicit in the rationality hypothesis, using the Wald or LR procedures.

Consider the general distributed lag model (7.47), and let y_t be the rate of unemployment, x_t the money supply growth, and $\mathbf{w}_t$ a $p \times 1$ vector containing lagged values of y_t and other determinants of the 'natural' rate of unemployment or output. Maintaining the rationality hypothesis, the neutrality hypothesis that anticipated changes in monetary policy will have no effect on unemployment or output can now be tested by testing the hypothesis $H_N: a_0 = a_1 = \ldots = a_s = 0$, in (7.47). Such a test can be carried out by the Wald procedure using, for example, the large sample variance matrix given in (7.70). Alternatively, one can employ the LR principle. A joint test of the rationality and the neutrality hypotheses can also be carried out in the context of the following unrestricted model

$$\mathbf{y} = \sum_{i=0}^{s} Z(-i)\boldsymbol{\delta}_i + W\mathbf{a}_{s+1} + \sum_{i=0}^{s} c_i\mathbf{x}(-i) + \mathbf{u}, \tag{7.79a}$$

$$\mathbf{x} = Z\mathbf{b} + \mathbf{v}. \tag{7.79b}$$

The rationality hypothesis imposes the following cross-equation restrictions

$$H_R: \boldsymbol{\delta}_i = (a_i - c_i)\mathbf{b}, \quad \text{for } i = 0, 1, 2, \ldots, s,$$

[8] Cross-equation tests are often referred to as *indirect* tests of the REH to distinguish them from the *direct* tests of the rationality hypothesis based on the observed expectations data. Direct tests of the REH will be covered in detail in the next chapter.

while the neutrality hypothesis imposes

$$H_N : a_i = 0, \quad \text{for } i = 0, 1, 2, \ldots, s.$$

Both of these hypotheses can be tested separately or jointly by means of the LR statisic such as the one given in (7.78). Assuming for simplicity that none of the columns of W (or their linear combinations) are contained in $[Z, Z(-1), \ldots, Z(-s)]$, the hypotheses H_R and H_N, respectively, impose $(h-1)(s+1)$ and $s+1$ over-identifying restrictions on the parameters of the unrestricted simultaneous equation model (7.79). The number of restrictions implied by the joint hypotheses H_{RN}, namely $\boldsymbol{\delta}_i = -c_i\mathbf{b}$, is equal to $h(s+1)$. The validity of the LR tests of these hypotheses, however, crucially depends on the assumption that the maintained model (7.79) generating $\mathbf{y}$ and $\mathbf{x}$ is correctly specified. For a study of the effects of mis-specification of the x_t process on the LR tests of the H_R and H_N, see Frydman and Rappoport (1984).

In general, the hypotheses H_R and H_N are testable only under the identifying restriction $\sigma_{uv} = 0$. But, as already pointed out in example 6.2, when the model under consideration does not contain lagged unanticipated effects it is possible to carry out a *joint* test of the rationality and the neutrality hypothesis even if $\sigma_{uv} \neq 0$. To see this, consider the unrestricted model

$$\mathbf{y} = a_1\mathbf{x}^* + W\mathbf{a}_2 + c(\mathbf{x} - \mathbf{x}^*) + \mathbf{u},$$

$$\mathbf{x} = Z\mathbf{b} + \mathbf{v},$$

$$\mathbf{x}^* = Z\bar{\mathbf{b}}.$$

The two hypotheses of interest can then be specified as:

Neutrality hypothesis, $\quad H_N$: $a_1 = 0$,

Rationality hypothesis, $\quad H_R$: $\mathbf{b} = \bar{\mathbf{b}}$.

Substituting for $\mathbf{x}$ and $\mathbf{x}^*$, and assuming for simplicity of exposition that none of the columns of W can be written as linear functions of the columns of Z, we have

$$\mathbf{y} = Z\boldsymbol{\delta} + W\mathbf{a}_2 + \boldsymbol{\varepsilon}, \tag{7.80}$$

where

$$\boldsymbol{\varepsilon} = \mathbf{u} + c\mathbf{v},$$

$$\boldsymbol{\delta} = a_1\bar{\mathbf{b}} + c(\mathbf{b} - \bar{\mathbf{b}}).$$

Therefore, a valid test of the joint hypothesis H_{RN}, namely $a_1 = 0$ and $\mathbf{b} = \bar{\mathbf{b}}$, can be carried out by the usual F-test of $\boldsymbol{\delta} = 0$ in (7.80), irrespective of whether $\mathbf{u}$ and $\mathbf{v}$ are correlated or not. This result also demonstrates the equivalence of the Granger (1969) non-causality test and the test of the neutrality–rationality hypothesis in the case where $\mathbf{w}_t$ is specified to contain only lagged values of y_t and/or deterministic components, such as time trends.

Unfortunately, none of these results extend to models with lagged unanticipated components and/or with serially correlated errors.

B: Models with Future Expectations

A variety of methods for estimation of RE models with future expectations have been proposed in the literature, notably by McCallum (1976), Hansen and Hodrick (1980), Hansen and Sargent (1980, 1982), Chow (1980), Cumby et al. (1983), Hayashi and Sims (1983), Watson (1986), and Wickens (1986). This part reviews some of these methods, first in the context of models of exchange rate determination and then more generally in the case of RE models with lagged dependent variables and future expectations of arbitrary orders. In the general case we develop appropriate methods for dealing with regular and irregular RE models and show the importance of distinguishing between these cases in practice. In particular, we demonstrate the pitfalls in an indiscriminate application of the IV estimation method to RE models with future expectations of the endogenous variables.

7.6 Models of Exchange Rate Determination

Rational expectations models of exchange rate determination are generally based on the application of the efficient market hypothesis to the foreign exchange market.[9] Denoting the logarithms of the spot exchange rate and the m-period forward exchange rate determined at time t by y_t and x_t, respectively, then an approximate measure of the expected rate of return to speculation is given by $E(y_{t+m}-x_t|\Omega_t)$, where Ω_t is the information set containing *at least* the observations on y_t, x_t and their past values. Under the efficient market hypothesis the expected rate of return to speculation in the forward exchange market is zero and we have

$$E(y_{t+m}|\Omega_t)=x_t. \tag{7.81}$$

This is, however, a highly simplistic version of the efficient market hypothesis and holds only under a number of very restrictive assumptions; including risk neutrality, time-separable utility functions, perfect capital markets, information homogeneity, zero transaction costs, and a non-distortionary tax system. A more general exchange rate model which nests (7.81) as a special case may be written as

$$E(y_{t+m}|\Omega_t)=a_1x_t+\mathbf{a}_2'\mathbf{w}_t+u_t, \tag{7.82}$$

[9] For an account of the efficient market hypothesis and the assumptions that underlie it, see example 6.3.

where u_t is a white-noise disturbance term with variance σ_{uu}, and $\mathbf{w}_t$ is a $p \times 1$ vector of predetermined variables in Ω_t, representing observable factors responsible for possible deviations from the ideal conditions that underlie (7.81). The disturbance term u_t summarizes the effect of unobservable factors operating on the relationship between x_t and $E(y_{t+m}|\Omega_t)$. In this more general framework, a test of the efficiency of the foreign exchange market, conditional on the REH, can be carried out by testing the hypothesis that $a_1 = 1$, $\mathbf{a}_2 = 0$, and $\sigma_{uu} = 0$. Equations such as (7.82) also arise in tests of the REH using directly observed expectations data (see chapter 8).

Consistent estimation of (7.82) does not pose any difficulties. This is because, under the REH, the m-period ahead expectations errors,

$$\varepsilon_{t,m} = y_{t+m} - E(y_{t+m}|\Omega_t), \qquad (7.83)$$

are orthogonal to the information set Ω_t. Substituting (7.83) into (7.82), we can write

$$y_{t+m} = \mathbf{a}'\mathbf{h}_t + \xi_{t,m}, \quad t = 1, 2, \ldots, n, \qquad (7.84)$$

in which $\mathbf{a} = (a_1, \mathbf{a}_2')'$, $\mathbf{h}_t = (x_t, \mathbf{w}_t')'$, and

$$\xi_{t,m} = u_t + \varepsilon_{t,m}. \qquad (7.85)$$

It is now easily seen that, under the REH, $E(\xi_{t,m}|\Omega_t) = 0$ and the OLS regression of y_{t+m} on x_t and $\mathbf{w}_t$ results in consistent estimates. However, the conventional formula for the variance matrix of the OLS estimators of $\mathbf{a}$ will not be valid even asymptotically if the forecast horizon exceeds the sampling interval, that is, if $m > 1$. The conventional formula for the computation of the OLS standard errors is based on the assumption that the disturbances $\xi_{t,m}$ are serially uncorrelated, but as will be shown below, under the REH $\{\xi_{t,m}\}$ need not be serially uncorrelated and can in fact follow an MA($m-1$) process. This situation also arises in the case of direct tests of the REH when expectations are observed at intervals finer than the forecast interval (see, for example, Brown and Maital (1981)). Only in the case of non-overlapping samples (i.e. for $m = 1$) is it possible to avoid the problem of serial correlation in $\xi_{t,m}$.

The reason for the possible serial correlation in $\xi_{t,m}$ lies in the fact that the expectations errors $\varepsilon_{t,m}$ are not realized until period $t+m$. A general proof can be given along the following lines: for $s \geqslant m$, since $\varepsilon_{t,m}$ is in Ω_{t+m}, we can write

$$E(\varepsilon_{t+s,m}\varepsilon_{t,m}|\Omega_{t+m}) = \varepsilon_{t,m}E(\varepsilon_{t+s,m}|\Omega_{t+m}),$$

and using (7.83)[10]

$$\begin{aligned} E(\varepsilon_{t+s,m}|\Omega_{t+m}) &= E[\{y_{t+s+m} - E(y_{t+s+m}|\Omega_{t+s})\}|\Omega_{t+m}], \\ &= E(y_{t+s+m}|\Omega_{t+m}) - E(y_{t+s+m}|\Omega_{t+m}), \\ &= 0. \end{aligned}$$

[10] See property P4 in appendix A.

Consequently,

$$E(\varepsilon_{t+s,m}\varepsilon_{t,,m}|\Omega_{t+m})=0, \quad \text{for } s \geqslant m,$$

or, unconditionally,

$$E(\varepsilon_{t+s,m}\varepsilon_{t,m})=0, \quad \text{for } s \geqslant m.$$

But for $s<m$, $E(\varepsilon_{t+s,m}, \varepsilon_{t,m})$ need not be equal zero since expectations errors $\varepsilon_{t,m}$ are not in the information set Ω_{t+s} $(s<m)$. Therefore under the REH, $\varepsilon_{t,m}$ and hence the composite disturbance term $\xi_{t,m}$, can at most have a moving-average representation of order $m-1$. This result also shows that when $m=1$, $\xi_{t,m}$ will be serially uncorrelated and the standard OLS results are applicable to (7.84).

The condition under which $\xi_{t,m}$ *will not* be an MA$(m-1)$, are rather restrictive and, for this reason, the possibility of an MA$(m-1)$ structure for $\xi_{t,m}$ needs to be taken into account. There are two possibilities. One option is to be content with the OLS estimates of **a**, but allow for the serial correlation of $\xi_{t,m}$ in the computation of standard errors. This procedure, followed in Hansen and Hodrick (1980), yields consistent estimates of **a** and their standard errors but will not be asymptotically efficient. An alternative procedure would be to employ estimators proposed by Hansen (1982), Hayashi and Sims (1983), and Cumby et al. (1983), which correct for serial correlation and are asymptotically more efficient than the OLS estimators.

7.6.1 The Hansen–Hodrick Procedure

In the case of the first option, a consistent estimate of the standard errors can be obtained in the following manner. Writing (7.84) in matrix notation.

$$\mathbf{y}_m = H\mathbf{a}+\boldsymbol{\xi}, \tag{7.86}$$

and assuming that the y_t and $\mathbf{h}_t$ processes are jointly stationary and ergodic, then the correct expression for the asymptotic variance matrix of $\hat{\mathbf{a}}_{\text{OLS}}=(H'H)^{-1}H'\mathbf{y}_m$ is easily seen to be

$$V(\sqrt{n}\hat{\mathbf{a}}_{\text{OLS}})=\Sigma_{hh}^{-1}\Phi\Sigma_{hh}^{-1}, \tag{7.87}$$

where, as before, $\Sigma_{hh}=E(H'H/n)$ and

$$\Phi=\lim_{n\to\infty}\{n^{-1}E(H'\boldsymbol{\xi}\boldsymbol{\xi}'H)\}.$$

Cumby et al. (1983, pp. 343–4), for example, show that Φ may be computed from

$$\Phi=\sum_{s=-m+1}^{m-1} E(\mathbf{h}_t'\xi_{t,,}\xi_{t-s,m}\mathbf{h}_{t-s}). \tag{7.88}$$

Under the conditional homoscedasticity assumption for serially correlated residuals,[11]

$$E(\xi_{t,m}\xi_{t-s,m}|\mathbf{h}_t, \mathbf{h}_{t-1}, \dots, \mathbf{h}_{t-s})$$
$$= E(\xi_{t,m}\xi_{t-s,m}) = \gamma_\xi(s), \quad \text{for } s < m, \tag{7.89}$$

and matrix Φ simplifies to

$$\Phi = \sum_{s=-m+1}^{m-1} \gamma_\xi(s)\Sigma_{hs}, \tag{7.90}$$

where[12]:

$$\Sigma_{hs} = \Sigma'_{sh} = E(\mathbf{h}_t\mathbf{h}'_{t-s}). \tag{7.91}$$

A consistent estimate of $V(\sqrt{n}\hat{\mathbf{a}}_{\text{OLS}})$ can now be obtained by replacing the population moments appearing in (7.87) by their corresponding sample estimates. As shown in Hansen and Hodrick (1980) this estimate can be written as

$$\hat{V}(\hat{\mathbf{a}}_{\text{OLS}}) = (H'H)^{-1}(H'\hat{\psi}H)(H'H)^{-1}, \tag{7.92}$$

where the lower-triangular part of the $n \times n$ matrix $\hat{\psi}$ is given by

$$\hat{\psi} = \begin{bmatrix} \hat{\gamma}_\xi(0) & & & & & \\ \hat{\gamma}_\xi(1) & \hat{\gamma}_\xi(0) & & & & \\ \vdots & & \ddots & & & \\ \hat{\gamma}_\xi(m-1) & \vdots & & \ddots & & \\ 0 & & & & & \\ \vdots & \ddots & & & \ddots & \\ 0 & 0 & \dots & \hat{\gamma}_\xi(m-1) & \dots & \hat{\gamma}_\xi(1) & \hat{\gamma}_\xi(0) \end{bmatrix}, \tag{7.93}$$

in which

$$\hat{\gamma}_\xi(s) = n^{-1}\sum_{t=s+1}^{n} \hat{\xi}_{t,m}\hat{\xi}_{t-s,m},$$

and $\hat{\xi}_{t,m} = y_{t+m} - \mathbf{h}'_t\hat{\mathbf{a}}_{\text{OLS}}$ are the OLS residuals.

Consistent estimators of Φ that do not depend on the conditional homoscedasticity assumption (7.89) are proposed by Hansen (1982) and others. Although the estimator suggested by Hansen (1982), namely

$$\hat{\Phi}_H = \sum_{s=-m+1}^{m-1}\left\{n^{-1}\sum_{t=1}^{n} \mathbf{h}'_t\hat{\xi}_{t,m}\hat{\xi}_{t-s,m}\mathbf{h}_{t-s}\right\}, \tag{7.94}$$

is relatively simple to compute, it is not guaranteed to be positive-definite. To

---

[11] When $\xi_{t,m}$ is normally distributed, condition (7.89) is implied by $E(\xi_{t,m}|\Omega_t) = 0$ (see Hayashi and Sims, 1983, p. 788).

[12] Note that $\Sigma_{h0} = \Sigma_{0h} = \Sigma_{hh}$.

ensure positive-definiteness of the estimator of Φ, both frequency domain and time domain techniques have been proposed in the literature (see Hansen, 1982; Cumby et al., 1983; Eichenbaum et al., 1984; and Newey and West, 1985).

7.6.2 *The Hayashi–Sims Procedure*

In order to improve on the OLS estimates of **a**, appropriate allowance has to be made for the particular pattern of serial correlation that is present in $\xi_{t,m}$. But the application of the generalized least squares (GLS) method to (7.84) in order to take account of the serial correlation in $\xi_{t,m}$ is not appropriate in the present context, and can lead to inconsistent coefficient estimates. This is because the 'backward' transformations involved in the GLS method generate non-zero correlations between the transformed disturbances and the transformed regressors, even if no such correlations had existed between the untransformed variables. As an illustration, consider the simple example where $m=2$. In this case the $\xi_{t,2}$ process has the MA(1) representation

$$\xi_{t,2}=\varepsilon_t+\phi\varepsilon_{t-1}, \quad |\phi|<1,$$

where ε_t is a serially uncorrelated process. The GLS method for the estimation of **a** in (7.84) is based on the transformed regression

$$\bar{y}_{t+m}=\mathbf{a}'\bar{\mathbf{h}}_t+\varepsilon_t,$$

where

$$\begin{aligned}\bar{y}_{t+m}&=(1+\phi L)^{-1}y_{t+m},\\ \bar{\mathbf{h}}_t&=(1+\phi L)^{-1}\mathbf{h}_t,\\ \varepsilon_t&=(1+\phi L)^{-1}\xi_{t,2},\end{aligned} \tag{7.95}$$

and L stands for the one-period lag operator. It is now clear that $E(\varepsilon_t|\bar{\mathbf{h}}_t)\neq 0$, even though $E(\xi_{t,2}|\bar{\mathbf{h}}_t)=0$. Notice that the transformed disturbances ε_t defined by (7.95) depend on past values of $\xi_{t,2}$, which are not realized at time t, and therefore need not be orthogonal to $\mathbf{h}_t$. More specifically, we have

$$\begin{aligned}E(\varepsilon_t|\bar{\mathbf{h}}_t)&=\sum_{i=0}^{\infty}\phi^i E(\xi_{t-i,2}|\bar{\mathbf{h}}_t),\\ &=\sum_{i=1}^{\infty}\phi^i E(\xi_{t-i,2}|\bar{\mathbf{h}}_t)\neq 0.\end{aligned}$$

To circumvent the serial correlation problem in the above context, Hayashi and Sims (1983) suggest a 'forward filtering' of the observations followed by an IV regression. In the case of the above example, the Hayashi–Sims forward transformations can be written as

$$\tilde{y}_{t+m} = -\phi(1-\phi L^{-1})^{-1} y_{t+m},$$
$$\tilde{\mathbf{h}}_t = -\phi(1-\phi L^{-1})^{-1} \mathbf{h}_t,$$
$$v_t = -\phi(1-\phi L^{-1})^{-1} \xi_{t,2}, \tag{7.96}$$

where $\xi_{t,2} = v_{t+1} - \phi^{-1} v_t$, is the forward first-order MA representation of $\xi_{t,2}$. Unlike ε_t in (7.95), the serially uncorrelated disturbances v_t in (7.96) are orthogonal to $\mathbf{h}_t$ as well as to all their past values. This suggests estimating **a** by the IV regression of $\tilde{y}_{t+m}$ on $\tilde{\mathbf{h}}_t$, using $\mathbf{h}_t$ and possibly their past values as instruments. The Hayashi–Sims procedure can be easily generalized to higher-order MA error processes. Note, however, that their procedure is based on the premise that the conditional homoscedasticity assumption for serially correlated residuals in (7.89) holds.

To obtain the Hayashi–Sims estimators in the general case, let $E(\boldsymbol{\xi}\boldsymbol{\xi}') = \psi$. Then there always exists an upper-triangular matrix T such that $\psi^{-1} = T'T$, with T non-singular. Application of the transformation matrix T to both sides of (7.86) yields

$$T\mathbf{y}_m = TH\mathbf{a} + T\boldsymbol{\xi}. \tag{7.97}$$

Apart from being serially uncorrelated, the transformed residuals $T\boldsymbol{\xi}$ are also orthogonal to H.[13] The IV estimation of (7.97) with H (and possibly lagged values of H) as instruments yields the Hayashi–Sims estimator. The computation of this 'forward filtered' estimator, however, requires a consistent estimate of T. In the case of the present problem, such an estimate is provided through the relation $\hat{\psi}^{-1} = \hat{T}'\hat{T}$, noting that $\hat{\psi}$ is already defined by (7.93).

7.6.3 ML and Other Procedures

Compared with the Hansen–Hodrick procedure, the Hayashi–Sims forward filtered estimator may or may not be asymptotically more efficient. This is because the forward filter estimator utilizes only *some* of the restrictions implied by the efficient market hypothesis.

An alternative approach would be to develop ML estimators of **a**, and then to employ classical procedures to test the efficiency hypothesis. For this purpose the joint distribution of $(y_t, \mathbf{h}_t, u_t)$ needs to be specified more fully. For expositional convenience, assume $u_t \equiv 0$ and that $(y_t, \mathbf{h}_t)$ has a multivariate covariance–stationary normal distribution. Then, by Wold's decomposition theorem, we can write

$$y_t = \sum_{i=0}^{\infty} \boldsymbol{\phi}_i' \boldsymbol{\varepsilon}_{t-i}, \tag{7.98}$$

---

[13] We have $E(T\boldsymbol{\xi}\boldsymbol{\xi}'T') = TE(\boldsymbol{\xi}\boldsymbol{\xi}')T' = T\psi T'$. But since $\psi = (T'T)^{-1}$, then it follows that $E(T\boldsymbol{\xi}\boldsymbol{\xi}'T') = I_n$. The orthogonality of $T\boldsymbol{\xi}$ to H follows from the fact that, because of the upper-triangular form of T, the transformed residuals depend only on the current and future values of $\xi_{t,m}$.

$$\mathbf{h}_t = \sum_{i=0}^{\infty} \Phi_i' \boldsymbol{\varepsilon}_{t-i}, \tag{7.99}$$

where $\boldsymbol{\varepsilon}_t$ is the $(p+2)\times 1$ vector of innovations in y_t and $\mathbf{h}_t$ or, more specifically,

$$\boldsymbol{\varepsilon}_t = \begin{bmatrix} y_t - E(y_t|\Omega_{t-1}) \\ \mathbf{h}_t - E(\mathbf{h}_t|\Omega_{t-1}) \end{bmatrix} = \begin{bmatrix} \varepsilon_{ty} \\ \boldsymbol{\varepsilon}_{th} \end{bmatrix}, \tag{7.100}$$

and $\boldsymbol{\phi}_i = (\phi_{iy}, \boldsymbol{\phi}_{ih}')'$, $\Phi_i = (\Phi_{iy}', \Phi_{ih}')'$ are fixed coefficient matrices of orders $(p+2)\times 1$ and $(p+2)\times(p+1)$, respectively. These coefficient matrices are subject to the restrictions $\phi_{0y} = 1$, $\boldsymbol{\phi}_{0h} = 0$, $\Phi_{0y} = 0$, and $\Phi_{0h} = I_{p+1}$.

Under the REH, from (7.98) we have

$$E(y_{t+m}|\Omega_t) = \sum_{i=m}^{\infty} \boldsymbol{\phi}_i' \boldsymbol{\varepsilon}_{t+m-i}, \tag{7.101a}$$

which may also be written as

$$E(y_{t+m}|\Omega_t) = y_{t+m} - \sum_{i=0}^{m-1} \boldsymbol{\phi}_i' \boldsymbol{\varepsilon}_{t+m-i}. \tag{7.101b}$$

Using (7.101a) together with (7.82) now yields[14]

$$\sum_{i=0}^{\infty} \boldsymbol{\phi}_i' \boldsymbol{\varepsilon}_{t+m-i} = \sum_{i=0}^{\infty} \mathbf{a}' \Phi_i' \boldsymbol{\varepsilon}_{t-i},$$

which implies the following cross-equation restrictions on the parameters of (7.98) and (7.99):

$$\Phi_i \mathbf{a} = \Phi_{i+m}, \quad i = 0, 1, 2, \ldots \tag{7.102}$$

Clearly, further cross-equation restrictions result if $\mathbf{h}_t$ includes y_t or any of its lagged values. The computation of ML estimators now entails the ML estimation of the multivariate system (7.98)–(7.99) (or a suitably truncated version of it) subject to the cross-equation restrictions (7.102). This procedure is computationally very demanding, especially when $p+1$, the dimension of $\mathbf{h}_t$, is relatively high. The main advantage of the ML approach, however, lies in the fact that it provides an appropriate framework for testing jointly and separately the REH (via the cross-equation restrictions), and the 'risk neutrality' hypothesis (via the restrictions, $a_1 = 1$, $\mathbf{a}_2 = 0$). The details are similar to those already described in section 7.5 for testing the REH and the policy neutrality hypothesis.

Baillie et al. (1983) adopt a truncated autoregressive representation of (7.98)–(7.99) in the simple case where $\mathbf{h}_t = x_t$ (the logarithm of the forward rate). They perform Wald tests of the joint hypothesis of rationality and risk

[14] Notice that, by assumption, $u_t \equiv 0$.

neutrality using weekly data on six currencies traded on the New York foreign exchange market over the period June 1973 to April 1980. They reject this joint hypothesis conclusively for all six currencies they consider. They do not, however, attempt to test the REH and the risk neutrality hypothesis separately.

The above likelihood framework can also be employed to develop two-step estimators of the type already discussed in detail for models with current expectations. Substituting (7.101b) into (7.82), we obtain

$$y_{t+m} = \mathbf{a}'\mathbf{h}_t + \sum_{i=0}^{m-1} \boldsymbol{\phi}_i' \boldsymbol{\varepsilon}_{t+m-i} + u_t, \tag{7.103}$$

or, noting that $\boldsymbol{\phi}_0' = (1, 0)$,

$$y_t = \mathbf{a}'\mathbf{h}_{t-m} + \sum_{i=1}^{m-1} \boldsymbol{\phi}_i' \boldsymbol{\varepsilon}_{t-i} + \varepsilon_{ty} + u_{t-m}. \tag{7.104}$$

Equation (7.103) is the counterpart of (7.84) with the difference that $\xi_{t,m}$ is now explicitly linked to the innovations in the $(y_t, \mathbf{h}_t)$ processes. A two-step estimator of $\mathbf{a}$ exploits this relationship and in the second step (using (7.104)) computes $\hat{\mathbf{a}}_{2S}$ by an OLS regression of y_t on $\mathbf{h}_{t-m}$ and $\hat{\boldsymbol{\varepsilon}}_{t-1}, \ldots, \hat{\boldsymbol{\varepsilon}}_{t-m+1}$, where $\hat{\boldsymbol{\varepsilon}}_t$ is a consistent estimate of $\boldsymbol{\varepsilon}_t$ obtained in the first step. Such a two-step estimator has recently been proposed by Gregory (1986), who refers to it as a 'generated regressor estimator' in order to highlight its origin in the work of Pagan (1984).

It is, however, worth bearing in mind that in practice estimation of $\boldsymbol{\varepsilon}_t$ requires approximating (7.98) and (7.99) by finite-order vector ARMA processes. This approximation may lead to an inconsistent estimate of $\boldsymbol{\varepsilon}_t$ if, because of inadequate degrees of freedom, low-order AR or ARMA processes are adopted incorrectly. The use of an inconsistent estimate of $\boldsymbol{\varepsilon}_t$ will then destroy the consistency property of the two-step estimator of $\mathbf{a}$. This problem does not, however, afflict the estimation procedures advanced by Hansen and Hodrick, or Hayashi and Sims. The derivation of the asymptotic variance matrix of $\hat{\mathbf{a}}_{2S}$, and other computational details for the case $m=4$ and $\mathbf{h}_t = (x_t, 1)'$, can be found in Gregory (1986).

7.7 Models with Future Expectations of the Endogenous Variable

Consider now the following general autoregressive RE model

$$y_t = \sum_{i=1}^{m} \lambda_i y_{t-i} + \sum_{i=1}^{q} \alpha_i E(y_{t+i} \mid \Omega_t) + \sum_{i=0}^{s} \boldsymbol{\gamma}_i' \mathbf{x}_{t-i} + u_t, \tag{7.105}$$

supplemented by

$$\mathbf{x}_t = \sum_{i=1}^{r} R_i \mathbf{x}_{t-i} + \boldsymbol{v}_t, \tag{7.106}$$

where, as before, u_t and $\boldsymbol{v}_t$ are independently distributed white-noise processes, and $\alpha_q \neq 0$. The $k \times 1$ vector $\mathbf{x}_t$ contains all the predetermined variables of the model except for lagged y's that are specified explicitly. The set Ω_t represent agents' information at time t and contains observations at least on y_t, $\mathbf{x}_t$ and u_t, as well as on their past values. Notice that, in this specification, it is assumed that at time t only agents (and not the observing econometrician) have direct information on the true values of u_t. The econometrician can at best obtain estimates of u_t indirectly from observations on y_t and $\mathbf{x}_t$.

Alternative methods of solving the above RE model have already been covered in detail in section 5.3. For estimation purposes the martingale difference method due to Broze et al. (1985), which is closely related to the errors-in-variables approach, is most convenient and will be adopted here. Denoting the revision in expectations of y_{t+i} between periods t and $t-1$ by

$$\varepsilon_t^i = E(y_{t+i} \mid \Omega_t) - E(y_{t+i} \mid \Omega_{t-1}), \quad i = 0, 1, 2, \ldots$$

we have (cf. Broze et al., 1985, pp. 343–4)

$$E(y_{t+i} \mid \Omega_t) = y_{t+i} - \sum_{j=0}^{i-1} \varepsilon_{t+i+j}^i, \quad i = 1, 2, \ldots, q, \tag{7.107}$$

where $E(\varepsilon_t^i \mid \Omega_t) = 0$, for $i = 0, 1, 2, \ldots, q-1$. The revision processes $\{\varepsilon_t^i, i = 0, 1, \ldots, q-1\}$ are q arbitrary martingale difference processes (see section 5.3 for further details). Substituting (7.107) into (7.105) yields

$$y_t = \sum_{i=1}^{m} \lambda_i y_{t-i} + \sum_{i=1}^{q} \alpha_i y_{t+i} + \sum_{i=0}^{s} \boldsymbol{\gamma}_i' \mathbf{x}_{t-i} + \xi_t, \tag{7.108}$$

where the new disturbance term ξ_t is given by a linear combination of the revision processes plus the original disturbances u_t in (7.105), namely

$$\xi_t = u_t - \sum_{i=1}^{q} \sum_{j=0}^{i-1} \alpha_i \varepsilon_{t+i-j}^j. \tag{7.109}$$

As far as consistent estimation of the parameters is concerned, this composite disturbance term has two important properties: as will be shown below, it has an MA(q) representation, and it is orthogonal to $\mathbf{x}_t$ and all lagged y's and lagged x's. The latter property follows from the assumption of the independence of u_t and $\mathbf{y}_t$ and the fact that $E(\varepsilon_{t+j}^i \mid \Omega_t) = 0$, for $i = 0, 1, \ldots, q-1$, and $j = 1, 2, \ldots, q$. More specifically, using (7.109) we first note that

$$E(\xi_t \mid \Omega_t) = E(u_t \mid \Omega_t),$$

and since $E(u_t \mid v_t) = E(u_t \mid \mathbf{x}_t) = 0$ by assumption, it then follows that

$$E(\xi_t \mid \mathbf{x}_t, \mathbf{x}_{t-1}, \ldots; y_{t-1}, y_{t-2}, \ldots) = 0. \tag{7.110}$$

7.7.1 *IV, 2S2SLS and Forward Filter Estimators*

The orthogonality condition (7.110) suggests that a consistent estimate of the parameters λ_i, α_i and γ_i (but not σ_{uu}) can, in principle, be obtained by applying the IV method to (7.108) using $\mathbf{x}_t, \mathbf{x}_{t-1}, \ldots; y_{t-1}, y_{t-2}, \ldots$ as instruments.[15] The condition (7.110), though necessary, is by no means sufficient to ensure the consistency of IV estimators. Denoting the vector of instruments by $\mathbf{z}_t = (y_{t-1}, y_{t-2}, \ldots; \mathbf{x}_t, \mathbf{x}_{t-1}, \ldots)'$ and the vector of regressors of (7.108) by $\mathbf{h}_t = (y_{t-1}, \ldots, y_{t-m}, y_{t+1}, y_{t+2}, \ldots, y_{t+q}, \mathbf{x}_t, \mathbf{x}_{t-1}, \ldots, \mathbf{x}_{t-s})'$, it is also required that $n^{-1}\Sigma_{t=1}^{n}\mathbf{z}_t\mathbf{z}_t'$ converges in probability to the constant non-singular matrix Σ_{zz}, and that $n^{-1}\Sigma_{t=1}^{n}\mathbf{z}_t\mathbf{h}_t'$ converges in probability to the constant matrix Σ_{zh} of full rank $m+q+(s+1)k$. Whether this latter condition is satisfied is bound up with the problem of identification of RE models, which was covered in detail in section 6.4. In circumstances where some or all of the parameters λ_i, α_i and γ_i are unidentifiable, the rank condition needed for the validity of the IV estimators will not be satisfied.

Example 7.1

As an example, consider the following simple specialization of (7.105) and (7.106):

$$y_t = \alpha E(y_{t+1} \mid \Omega_t) + \gamma x_t + u_t,$$
$$x_t = \rho x_{t-1} + v_t, \quad |\rho| < 1, \tag{7.111}$$

where x_t is a scalar exogenous variable. Equation (7.108) now simplifies to

$$y_t = \alpha y_{t+1} + \gamma x_t + \xi_t, \tag{7.112}$$

where

$$\xi_t = u_t - \alpha \varepsilon_{t+1}^0.$$

Suppose now that $\mathbf{z}_t = (x_{t-1}, x_t)'$ is chosen as the vector of instrumental variables. Clearly the components of this vector satisfy the orthogonality condition (7.110). Furthermore, using (7.111) and noting that $E(x_t x_{t-j}) = \sigma_{xx}\rho^j$, for $|\rho| < 1$, where $\sigma_{xx} = V(x_t) = \sigma_{vv}/(1-\rho^2)$, it follows that the matrix

$$\Sigma_{zz} = \sigma_{xx}\begin{pmatrix} 1 & \rho \\ \rho & 1 \end{pmatrix},$$

is non-singular as required. To compute the rank of Σ_{zh}, an explicit solution of y_t in terms of x_t and possibly its lagged values is required. But as we have already seen (section 5.3.1), the solution of y_t depends on whether or not $|\alpha| < 1$.

---

[15] The use of the IV method for consistent estimation of RE models with future expectations was first suggested by McCallum (1976).

First, suppose that $|\alpha|<1$, then the unique stationary solution for y_t is given by (see (6.31′), p. 136)

$$y_t=\theta x_t+u_t,$$

where $\theta=\gamma/(1-\alpha\rho)$. This result, together with (7.111), now yields

$$\Sigma_{zh}=E(\mathbf{z}_t\mathbf{h}_t')=\begin{bmatrix}E(x_{t-1}y_{t+1}) & E(x_{t-1}x_t)\\ E(x_ty_{t+1}) & E(x_t^2)\end{bmatrix},$$

$$=\sigma_{xx}\begin{bmatrix}\theta\rho^2 & \rho\\ \theta\rho & 1\end{bmatrix},$$

which establishes that rank$(\Sigma_{zh})=1$. Therefore, when $|\alpha|<1$, the matrix Σ_{zh} is not of full rank and the application of the IV method to (7.112) fails to yield consistent estimates of α and γ. This is hardly surprising since from proposition 6.2, (p. 137), we already know that α and γ are unidentifiable.[16] The above result continues to hold no matter which variable, or group of variables, is employed as instrument(s) for y_{t+1}.

Consider now the case $|\alpha|>1$, where (7.110) has an infinite number of solutions indexed by the arbitrary martingale difference process ε_t^0. These solutions can be written as (see (6.42), p. 141)

$$y_t=\alpha^{-1}y_{t-1}-\alpha^{-1}\gamma x_{t-1}-\alpha^{-1}\xi_{t-1}$$

or, in the 'backward' form,

$$y_{t+1}=-\alpha^{-1}\gamma\sum_{i=0}^{\infty}\alpha^{-i}x_{t-i}-\alpha^{-1}\sum_{i=0}^{\infty}\alpha^{-i}\xi_{t-i},$$

where $\xi_t=u_t-\alpha\varepsilon_{t+1}^0$. Hence, for $s=0, 1, 2, \ldots$, it follows that

$$E(x_{t-s}y_{t+1})=\frac{\gamma\rho^s\sigma_{xx}}{\rho-\alpha}-\alpha^{-1}\sum_{i=s+1}^{\infty}\alpha^{-i}E(x_{t-s}\xi_{t-i}). \tag{7.113}$$

Given the arbitrary nature of the martingale difference process ε_t^0, the computation of the second term in the above expression in general is not possible. The issue of whether α and γ can be estimated consistently using x_t, $x_{t-1}, x_{t-2}, \ldots$ as instruments will therefore be subject to some ambiguity when $|\alpha|>1$. In the case where x_{t-1} and x_t are used as instruments, the necessary and sufficient condition for Σ_{zh} to have full rank is given by

$$E\{(x_{t-1}-\rho x_t)y_{t+1}\}\neq 0,$$

which, upon using (7.113), can be written equivalently as

---

[16] Since $s=0$ and $r=1$ in this example, it follows that the necessary condition for identification, namely $r>s+1$, is not satisfied.

$$(\rho/\alpha)E(x_t\xi_{t-1})+\sum_{i=2}^{\infty}\alpha^{-i}E\{(\rho x_t-x_{t-1})\xi_{t-i}\}\neq 0. \tag{7.114}$$

It is clear that this condition is not satisfied when x_t is strictly exogenous, or under perfect foresight where future as well as current and past values of x_t are included in the information set at time t. When x_t is non-stochastic, or is strictly exogenous, then $E(x_{t-s}\xi_{t-i})=0$ for all i and s, and the necessary condition for the matrix Σ_{zh} to have full rank will not be met. For most x_t processes, however, it is reasonable to assume that the identification condition will be satisfied and, as a rule, in cases where $|\alpha|>1$, the application of the IV method to (7.112) will be valid.

The above example clearly demonstrates the danger of indiscriminate application of the IV method to the RE models, a problem which is often ignored in the literature. Prior to applying the IV method the conditions necessary for identification of the underlying RE model should be checked. For this purpose, as argued in the previous chapter, a distinction should be made between the case where the RE model has a unique stationary solution and the case where it has an infinite number of stationary solutions or, to use Sargan's (1984) terminology, the 'regular' and the 'irregular' cases, respectively.

Another important issue in the application of the IV method to RE models with future expectations arises in connection with the computation of asymptotically valid standard errors for the parameter estimates. Since ξ_t can be serially correlated under the REH, the standard formula for the computation of standard errors of IV estimators will not be valid. The problem is similar to that discussed in connection with the Hansen–Hodrick procedure (see section 7.6.1). Writing (7.108) in matrix notation and denoting the matrix of instruments by Z, the IV estimator of $\mathbf{a}=(\lambda_1, \lambda_2, \ldots, \lambda_m, \alpha_1, \alpha_2, \ldots, \alpha_q, \gamma_0', \gamma_1', \ldots, \gamma_s')'$ is given by

$$\hat{\mathbf{a}}_{IV}=(H'P_zH)^{-1}H'P_z\mathbf{y}, \tag{7.115}$$

where $H=(\mathbf{y}(-1), \ldots, \mathbf{y}(-m), \mathbf{y}(+1), \ldots, \mathbf{y}(+q), \mathbf{x}, \mathbf{x}(-1), \ldots, \mathbf{x}(-s))$, and $P_z=Z(Z'Z)^{-1}Z'$. As has already been pointed out, for $\hat{\mathbf{a}}_{IV}$ to be a consistent estimator of $\mathbf{a}$, it is necessary that the matrix $E(H'Z/n)$ is of full rank as $n\to\infty$. Throughout, we assume that this condition is satisfied and that

$$\lim_{n\to\infty} E(Z'Z/n)=\Sigma_{zz},$$

is non-singular. (Notice that our analysis is confined to stationary processes.) The correct expression for the asymptotic variance matrix of $\hat{\mathbf{a}}_{IV}$ can now be obtained following the Hansen–Hodrick procedure. We have

$$\hat{V}(\hat{\mathbf{a}}_{IV})=n(H'P_zH)^{-1}H'Z(Z'Z)^{-1}\hat{\Phi}(Z'Z)^{-1}Z'H(H'P_zH)^{-1},$$

where $\hat{\Phi}$ represents a consistent estimator of[17]

[17] Alternative procedures for obtaining $\hat{\Phi}$ were discussed in section 7.6.1. Notice, however, that in the present case the IV estimator of ξ, namely $\hat{\xi}=\mathbf{y}-H\hat{\mathbf{a}}_{IV}$, should be used in the computation of $\hat{\Phi}$.

$$\Phi = \sum_{j=-q}^{q} E(\mathbf{z}_t'\xi_t\xi_{t-j}\mathbf{z}_{t-j}). \qquad (7.116)$$

When the conditional homoscedasticity assumption (7.89) is satisfied for ξ_t, the expression for $\hat{V}(\hat{\mathbf{a}}_{\mathrm{IV}})$ simplifies to[18]

$$\hat{V}(\hat{\mathbf{a}}_{\mathrm{IV}}) = (\tilde{H}'\tilde{H})^{-1}(\tilde{H}'\hat{\psi}\tilde{H})(\tilde{H}'\tilde{H})^{-1},$$

where $\tilde{H} = P_z H$, and $\hat{\psi}$ is a consistent estimate of the variance matrix of $\boldsymbol{\xi}$.[19] This result is the IV generalization of (7.92).

Like the exchange rate model of the previous section, it is possible to improve upon the IV estimators in (7.115) by allowing for the MA(q) nature of the disturbances. Such estimators have been proposed by Hansen (1982), Cumby et al. (1983), and Hayashi and Sims (1983). Hansen's generalized method of moments estimator and Cumby et al.'s two-step two-stage least squares (2S2SLS) estimator are efficient in the class of IV estimators based on a finite number of instrumental variables, $\mathbf{z}_t$. The 2S2SLS estimator of $\mathbf{a}$ is

$$\hat{\mathbf{a}}_{\mathrm{2S2SLS}} = (H'Z\hat{\Phi}^{-1}Z'H)^{-1}H'Z\hat{\Phi}^{-1}Z'\mathbf{y},$$

and its asymptotic variance matrix is estimated consistently by

$$\hat{V}(\hat{\mathbf{a}}_{\mathrm{2S2SLS}}) = n^{-1}(H'Z\hat{\Phi}^{-1}Z'H)^{-1}.$$

The 'forward filter' estimator of Hayashi and Sims for the present problem is given by

$$\hat{\mathbf{a}}_{\mathrm{FF}} = (\bar{H}'P_z\bar{H})^{-1}\bar{H}'P_z\bar{\mathbf{y}},$$

where $\bar{H} = \hat{T}H$, $\bar{\mathbf{y}} = \hat{T}\mathbf{y}$, and $\hat{T}$ is the upper-triangular matrix defined by $\hat{\psi}^{-1} = \hat{T}'\hat{T}$.[20] This is the IV version of the Hayashi–Sims procedure already discussed in section 7.6.2. As compared to the 2S2SLS estimator, for a fixed set of instruments the forward filter estimator may be more or less efficient. But as is shown by Hayashi and Sims (1983), when the conditional homoscedasticity assumption holds the forward filter and 2S2SLS estimators approach the same limiting distribution as the sample size and the instrument list increase without bounds. Neither of these estimators is, however, fully efficient.

7.7.2 *ML Estimators*

One possible method of obtaining fully efficient estimators would be to use the ML procedure. Computation of ML estimators in the general case is, however, rather complicated, and in particular depends on whether the RE

[18] The condition (7.89) in the present IV context can be written as $E(\xi_t\xi_{t-j}|\mathbf{z}_t, \mathbf{z}_{t-1}, \ldots, \mathbf{z}_{t-j}) = E(\xi_t\xi_{t-j}) = \gamma_\xi(j)$, for $j \leqslant q$.

[19] The expression for $\hat{\psi}$ is the same as that given in (7.93), with $m-1=q$ and $\hat{\xi}_{t,m} = \hat{\xi}_t = \mathbf{y} - \mathbf{h}_t'\mathbf{a}_{\mathrm{IV}}$.

[20] Note that when there are no surplus instruments and $H'Z$ is a square non-singular matrix, then the 2S2SLS estimator reduces to $\hat{\mathbf{a}}_{\mathrm{IV}}$. The same is not true, however, of the forward filter estimator, $\hat{\mathbf{a}}_{\mathrm{FF}}$.

model under consideration has a unique stationary solution or not. The ML method also requires a complete specification of the processes generating $\mathbf{x}_t$ and the relationships that may exist between the martingale difference processes ε_t^i and the innovations in $\mathbf{x}_t$, u_t and $\mathbf{b}_t$. The $\mathbf{b}_t$ represents a vector of 'extraneous' variables that are included in Ω_t but do not appear explicitly in the model. The idea behind introducing $\mathbf{b}_t$ into the econometric analysis is to allow for the 'bubbles' or 'boot-strap' effects on y_t, a phenomenon already discussed in section 5.3.2.

Suppose now that $(y_t, \mathbf{x}_t, u_t, \mathbf{b}_t)$ has a covariance stationary multivariate normal distribution, or is transformed to such a distribution by means of first differencing or by transformations of the type suggested by Box and Cox (1964).[21] Let $\boldsymbol{\varepsilon}_t$ be the vector of innovations in $(v_t, \mathbf{x}_t, u_t, \mathbf{b}_t)$. Then using the Wold representation of y_t in (7.98), we have

$$\begin{aligned}\varepsilon_t^i &= E(y_{t+i}|\Omega_t) - E(y_{t+i}|\Omega_{t-1}),\\ &= \boldsymbol{\phi}_i'\boldsymbol{\varepsilon}_t,\end{aligned}$$

where, in partitioned form, $\boldsymbol{\varepsilon}_t = (\varepsilon_{ty}, \boldsymbol{\varepsilon}_{tx}', \varepsilon_{tu}, \boldsymbol{\varepsilon}_{tb}')'$, $\boldsymbol{\phi}_i = (\phi_{iy}, \boldsymbol{\phi}_{ix}', \phi_{iu}, \boldsymbol{\phi}_{ib}')'$. Substituting this result into (7.109) now yields

$$\xi_t = u_t - \sum_{i=1}^{q} \boldsymbol{\beta}_i'\boldsymbol{\varepsilon}_{t+i}, \tag{7.117}$$

where

$$\boldsymbol{\beta}_i = \sum_{j=i}^{q} \alpha_j \boldsymbol{\phi}_{j-i}, \quad i = 1, 2, \ldots, q. \tag{7.118}$$

This result shows how the composite disturbance term ξ_t is related to all the innovations in the variable observed by agents (but not necessarily by the econometrician), and also demonstrates that ξ_t does, in fact, have a qth-order moving-average representation.

To exploit the relationship that exists between ξ_t and the innovations $\boldsymbol{\varepsilon}_t$ in the estimation process, we first need to eliminate $\varepsilon_{t+i,y}$ from (7.117). Lagging equation (7.108) q periods and taking conditional expectations with respect to Ω_{t-1}, it is easily seen that

$$\varepsilon_{ty} = -\alpha_q^{-1}\{\xi_{t-q} - E(\xi_{t-q}|\Omega_{t-1})\},$$

which, with the help of (7.117) and assuming $\alpha_q \neq \beta_{qy}$, yields

$$\varepsilon_{ty} = (\alpha_q - \beta_{qy})^{-1}(\boldsymbol{\beta}_{qx}'\boldsymbol{\varepsilon}_{tx} + \beta_{qu}\varepsilon_{tu} + \boldsymbol{\beta}_{qb}'\boldsymbol{\varepsilon}_{tb}). \tag{7.119}$$

This result is of interest in its own right and shows that, in the case of stationary linear models, unexpected changes in endogenous variables can

[21] Note that this assumption rules out certain bubbles effects that arise in non-stationary environments that do not lend themselves to stationary characterizations through first differencing or other data transformations.

always be written as linear functions of *current* unexpected changes in the forcing variables (including speculative bubbles), irrespective of the orders of leads and lags, namely q, m and s, of the variables in the structural model.

Substituting (7.119) into (7.117) and rearranging terms now gives

$$\xi_t = u_t + \sum_{i=1}^{q} d_{iu}\varepsilon_{t+i,u} + \sum_{i=1}^{q} \mathbf{d}'_{ix}\boldsymbol{\varepsilon}_{t+i,x} + \sum_{i=1}^{q} \mathbf{d}'_{ib}\boldsymbol{\varepsilon}_{t+i,b}, \tag{7.120}$$

where

$$d_{iu} = -\{\beta_{iu} + \beta_{iy}(\alpha_q - \beta_{qy})^{-1}\beta_{qu}\},$$
$$\mathbf{d}_{ix} = -\{\boldsymbol{\beta}_{ix} + \beta_{iy}(\alpha_q - \beta_{qy})^{-1}\boldsymbol{\beta}_{qx}\},$$
$$\mathbf{d}_{ib} = -\{\boldsymbol{\beta}_{ib} + \beta_{iy}(\alpha_q - \beta_{qy})^{-1}\boldsymbol{\beta}_{qb}\},$$

for $i = 1, 2, \ldots, q$. The 'auxiliary' parameters d_{iu}, $\mathbf{d}_{ix}$ and $\mathbf{d}_{ib}$ can be obtained uniquely in terms of the structural parameters λ_i, α_i, and $\boldsymbol{\gamma}_i$ only in the regular case where the RE model has a unique stationary solution. This situation comes about when the characteristic equation

$$\sum_{i=1}^{m} \lambda_i z^{-i} + \sum_{i=1}^{q} \alpha_i z^{i} = 1 \tag{7.121}$$

has exactly q roots outside the unit circle, with the remaining m roots falling strictly inside the unit circle (see section 5.3.4). The elimination of the q unstable roots allows a unique determination of the auxiliary parameters in terms of the structural parameters (see section 6.4.2 for specific examples). Computation of the ML eliminators, therefore, depends on whether or not the RE model has a unique stationary solution. The dependence of ξ_t on innovations in $\mathbf{x}_t$ also reiterates the fact that ML estimation of RE models requires a complete specification of the processes generating $\mathbf{x}_t$. In what follows we discuss the problem of ML estimation of (7.105) separately for the regular and irregular cases, under the assumption that u_t is serially uncorrelated and that $\mathbf{x}_t$ is generated by (7.106).[22] With these assumptions, it follows that

$$\varepsilon_{tu} = u_t,$$

$$\boldsymbol{\varepsilon}_{tx} = \boldsymbol{v}_t = \mathbf{x}_t - \mathbf{x}_t^* = \mathbf{x}_t - \sum_{i=1}^{r} R_i \mathbf{x}_{t-i}.$$

Hence, using (7.120),

$$\xi_t = \sum_{i=1}^{q} \mathbf{d}'_{ix}(\mathbf{x}_{t+i} - \mathbf{x}^*_{t+i}) + \eta_t, \tag{7.122}$$

[22] The approach followed in this section can be readily extended to cases where u_t is serially correlated and/or $\mathbf{x}_t$ is generated according to feedback rules, where lagged values of y_t are also included among the regressors in (7.106).

where η_t now represents the unobserved (that is, to the econometrician) combined effects of disturbances and 'bubbles' on y_t, namely

$$\eta_t = u_t + \sum_{i=1}^{q} d_{iu} u_{t+i} + \sum_{i=1}^{q} \mathbf{d}'_{ib} \boldsymbol{\varepsilon}_{t+i,b}.$$

Substituting (7.122) in (7.108) and allowing for the fact that under (7.106)

$$\mathbf{x}_t^* = \sum_{i=1}^{r} R_i \mathbf{x}_{t-i},$$

we now have

$$A_{m+q}(L) y_t = C_l(L) \mathbf{x}_t + D_q(L) u_t + B_{q-1}(L) \boldsymbol{\varepsilon}_{tb}, \tag{7.123}$$

where $A_{m+q}(L)$, $C_l(L)$, $D_q(L)$, $B_{q-1}(L)$ are lag polynomials of orders $m+q, l = \max(s+q, r+q-1), q$, and $q-1$, respectively, defined by

$$A_{m+q}(L) = L^q \left(1 - \sum_{i=1}^{m} \lambda_i L^i - \sum_{i=1}^{q} \alpha_i L^{-i}\right), \tag{7.124a}$$

$$C_l(L) = \sum_{i=0}^{s} \boldsymbol{\gamma}'_i L^{i+q} + \sum_{i=1}^{q} \mathbf{d}'_{ix} \left(I_k - \sum_{j=1}^{r} R_j L^j\right) L^{q-i}, \tag{7.124b}$$

$$D_q(L) = L^q \left(1 + \sum_{i=1}^{q} d_{iu} L^{-i}\right), \tag{7.124c}$$

$$B_{q-1}(L) = \sum_{i=1}^{q} \mathbf{d}'_{ib} L^{q-i}. \tag{7.124d}$$

ML Estimation in the Regular Case

In this case the characteristic equation of (7.123), namely $A_{m+q}(z^{-1}) = 0$, which is also given by (7.121), has exactly q unstable roots. The unique stationary solution is obtained by factorizing out all the q unstable roots from both sides of (7.123). Consider the factorization

$$A_{m+q}(L) = A_m(L) \bar{A}_q(L), \tag{7.125}$$

where all the m roots of $A_m(z^{-1}) = 0$, and all the q roots of $\bar{A}_q(z^{-1}) = 0$, fall inside and outside the unit circle, respectively. Then, up to a scale factor, the necessary and sufficient conditions for (7.123) to be the unique stationary solution of the RE model are

$$C_l(L) = C_{l-q}(L) \bar{A}_q(L), \tag{7.126a}$$

$$D_q(L) = \bar{A}_q(L), \tag{7.126b}$$

$$B_{q-1}(L) = 0, \tag{7.126c}$$

where $C_{l-q}(L)$ is a lag polynomial function of order $l-q$. Condition (7.126c) ensures that the solution does not contain bubbles effects, and conditions (7.126a) and (7.126b) allow unique determination of the auxiliary parameters $\mathbf{d}_{ix}$ and d_{iu}, by imposing restrictions on the lag polynomials $C_l(L)$ and $D_q(L)$. An example of the determination of these parameters in terms of the structural parameters λ_i, α_i, γ_i, and R_i for the case $q=1$ was given in section 6.4.2. More generally, starting with the polynomial factorization (7.125), the coefficients of $C_{l-q}(L)$ can then be obtained in a recursive manner using (7.126a) and (7.126b).

In the regular case, therefore, the solution (7.123) reduces to

$$A_m(L)y_t = C_{l-q}(L)\mathbf{x}_t + u_t, \tag{7.127}$$

which is a standard autoregressive-distributed lag model with serially uncorrelated disturbances. The new lag polynomials $A_m(L)$ and $C_{l-q}(L)$ depend on λ_i, α_i, and γ_i as well as on R_i (the parameters of the $\mathbf{x}_t$ process), but do not depend on the auxiliary parameters $\mathbf{d}_{ix}$, d_{iu} and $\mathbf{d}_{ib}$. The *joint* estimation of (7.127) and (7.106) by the ML method now enables us to compute the ML estimators of the structural parameters assuming, of course, that the model is identified. The necessary condition for identification in this general case is given by

$$m+(l-q+1)k \geqslant q+m+(s+1)k,$$

or

$$(l-q)k \geqslant q+sk, \tag{7.128}$$

which is clearly not satisfied if $s+q \geqslant r+q-1$ since in this case, $l=\max(s+q, r+q-1)=s+q$. It is therefore necessary that $r>s+1$ (see also proposition 6.2). When this condition is met, $l=r+q-1$ and the order condition (7.128) becomes

$$(r-s-1)k \geqslant q.$$

This above result also shows that when the order condition $r>s+1$ is satisfied, the RE solution (7.127) will be subject to $(r-s-1)k-q$ cross-equation (or over-identifying) restrictions. A test of the REH can therefore be carried out in the regular case by testing these cross-equation restrictions using the likelihood framework. The details of cross-equation restrictions and the steps involved in the computation of ML estimators are best demonstrated in terms of a specific example.

Example 7.2 A Target-seeking Decision Problem under Adjustment Costs

An important example of RE models with future expectations that admit a unique stationary solution arises in target-seeking decision problems subject to adjustment costs and uncertainty. Consider an economic agent who faces the problem of deciding on $y_{t+\tau}$ (which, for example, could represent the number of workers to be employed or the level of stocks to be held by a firm) in order to achieve stochastic targets $\bar{y}_{t+\tau}$, $\tau = 1, 2, \ldots$, determined by the relations

$$\bar{y}_{t+\tau} = \bar{\gamma} x_{t+\tau} + \bar{u}_{t+\tau}, \quad \tau = 1, 2, \ldots, \tag{7.129}$$

where x_t follows a stationary rth-order autoregressive process with parameters $\rho_1, \rho_2, \ldots, \rho_r$, and $\bar{u}_t$ is a white-noise process. Suppose the information set of the agent at time t is $\Omega_t = (y_t, y_{t-1}, \ldots; x_t, x_{t-1}, \ldots; \bar{u}_t, \bar{u}_{t-1}, \ldots)$ and $y_{t+\tau}$ is determined by solving the following optimization problem

$$\min_{y_t, y_{t+1} \ldots} E\left(\sum_{\tau=0}^{\infty} \beta^{\tau} \{ \delta (y_{t+\tau} - \bar{y}_{t+\tau})^2 + (y_{t+\tau} - y_{t+\tau-1})^2 \} \mid \Omega_t \right),$$

where $0 \leqslant \beta < 1$ is the discount factor, and $\delta > 0$ measures the cost of deviating from the target relative to the adjustment cost. The first-order condition for this minimization problem is given by (see, for example, Sargent, 1978; Kennan, 1979):

$$E\{ \delta (y_{t+\tau} - \bar{y}_{t+\tau}) + (y_{t+\tau} - y_{t+\tau-1}) - \beta (y_{t+\tau+1} - y_{t+\tau}) \mid \Omega_t \} = 0,$$

for $\tau = 0, 1, 2, \ldots$ In particular, the decision rule for the current period ($\tau = 0$) may be written as the following generalized partial adjustment equation

$$y_t - y_{t-1} = \left(\frac{\delta}{\delta + \beta + 1} \right) (\bar{y}_t - y_{t-1}) + \left(\frac{\beta}{\delta + \beta + 1} \right) (E(y_{t+1} \mid \Omega_t) - y_{t-1}).$$

The standard partial adjustment model can be obtained from this result by assuming that the agent in question is either myopic or has an infinitely large subjective rate of discount (i.e. $\beta = 0$). Using (7.129), the above partial adjustment model can be written as a special case of (7.105) with $m = k = 1$ and $s = 0$, namely

$$y_t = \lambda y_{t-1} + \alpha E(y_{t+1} \mid \Omega_t) + \gamma x_t + u_t, \tag{7.130}$$

where

$$\lambda = (\delta + \beta + 1)^{-1}, \qquad \alpha = \beta (\delta + \beta + 1)^{-1},$$
$$\gamma = \delta (\delta + \beta + 1)^{-1} \bar{\gamma}, \quad u_t = \delta (\delta + \beta + 1)^{-1} \bar{u}_t.$$

As in the general case, it will be assumed that the agent (but not the econometrician) has completely solved the learning problem involved and knows the parameters $\rho_1, \rho_2, \ldots, \rho_r$, as well as λ, α, and γ, and also observes $\bar{u}_t$.[23] The econometrician's task here is to solve the 'reverse' problem and obtain efficient estimates of λ, α, γ and σ_{uu} (and hence δ, β, $\bar{\gamma}$ and $\sigma_{\bar{u}\bar{u}}$), given direct observations on y_t and x_t, for $t = 1, 2, \ldots, n$.

The characteristic equation of (7.130), using (7.124a), is given by

$$A_2(z^{-1}) = z^{-1}(1 - \lambda z^{-1} - \alpha z) = 0,$$

[23] For a discussion of the learning problem in the context of RE models, see chapters 3 and 9.

with roots μ and μ'. Since $\mu\mu' = \lambda/\alpha = \beta^{-1} > 1$, then at least one of the two roots (say μ) should fall outside the unit circle. But since

$$\begin{aligned}(\mu-1)(\mu'-1) &= \mu\mu' - (\mu+\mu') + 1,\\ &= \beta^{-1} - \beta^{-1}(\delta+\beta+1) + 1,\\ &= -\delta\beta^{-1} < 0,\end{aligned}$$

the other root (μ') should fall inside the unit circle. This establishes that (7.130) has a unique stationary solution. The factorization (7.125) in this case can be written as

$$A_2(L) = -\alpha(1-\mu' L)(1-\mu L),$$

where $(1-\mu L)$ is the unstable factor and, for a unique stationary solution, must be eliminated from both sides of

$$A_2(L)y_t = C_r(L)x_t + D_1(L)u_t, \tag{7.131}$$

where

$$C_r(L) = \gamma L + d_x\left(1 - \sum_{i=1}^{r} \rho_i L^i\right), \tag{7.132}$$

$$D_1(L) = L + d_u. \tag{7.133}$$

We therefore need to impose the restrictions

$$C_r(\mu^{-1}) = D_1(\mu^{-1}) = 0,$$

which, in view of (7.132) and (7.133), give the following results

$$d_u = -\mu^{-1},$$

$$d_x = -\left(1 - \sum_{i=1}^{r} \rho_i \mu^{-i}\right)(\gamma/\mu),$$

thereby linking the auxiliary parameters to the structural parameters of the model. Substituting these results into (7.131)–(7.133) and eliminating the unstable factor $(1-\mu L)$, we arrive at the following unique stationary solution

$$y_t = \mu' y_{t-1} - \alpha^{-1} C_{r-1}(L)x_t + (\alpha\mu)^{-1} u_t,$$

where the lag polynomial $C_{r-1}(L)$ is determined by

$$(1-\mu L)C_{r-1}(L) = C_r(L).$$

Hence[24]

$$y_t = \mu' y_{t-1} + \sum_{i=0}^{r-1} \theta_i x_{t-i} + (\alpha\mu)^{-1} u_t, \tag{7.134}$$

where (assuming $r > 2$)[25]

---

[24] This solution can also be obtained directly using result (5.76) in chapter 5, p. 110.

[25] Compare this with the result (6.57) obtained in the previous chapter, p. 146.

$$\theta_0 = -\alpha^{-1} d_x = (\alpha\mu)^{-1}\left(1 - \sum_{i=1}^{r} \rho_i \mu^{-i}\right)^{-1} \gamma, \tag{7.135a}$$

$$\theta_1 = (\mu - \rho_1)\theta_0 - \alpha^{-1}\gamma, \tag{7.135b}$$

$$\theta_i = \mu\theta_{i-1} - \rho_i\theta_0, \quad i = 2, 3, \ldots, r-1. \tag{7.135c}$$

The ML estimators can now be obtained by jointly estimating (7.134) and the process generating x_t, namely

$$x_t = \sum_{i=1}^{r} \rho_i x_{t-i} + v_t,$$

subject to the non-linear cross-equation restrictions in (7.135). On the whole, there are $r-3$ (cross-equation) over-identifying restrictions which can be written as

$$H_R\colon \quad \frac{\rho_2\theta_0 + \theta_2}{\theta_1} = \frac{\rho_3\theta_0 + \theta_3}{\theta_2} = \ldots = \frac{\rho_{r-1}\theta_0 + \theta_{r-1}}{\theta_{r-2}}.$$

An indirect test of the REH can be carried out by testing the validity of these cross-equation restrictions.

ML Estimation in the Irregular Case

The general solution for this case is given by (7.123), where it is now assumed that the characteristic equation (7.121) has $\bar{q} < q$ unstable roots.[26] The polynomial factorizations in (7.125) and (7.126) may now be written more generally for $\bar{q} = 0, 1, 2, \ldots, q-1$ as

$$A_{m+q}(L) = A_{m+q-\bar{q}}(L)\bar{A}_{\bar{q}}(L), \tag{7.125'}$$

$$C_l(L) = C_{l-\bar{q}}(L)\bar{A}_{\bar{q}}(L), \tag{7.126a'}$$

$$D_q(L) = D_{q-\bar{q}}(L)\bar{A}_{\bar{q}}(L), \tag{7.126b'}$$

$$B_{q-1}(L) = B_{q-\bar{q}-1}(L)\bar{A}_{\bar{q}}(L), \tag{7.126c'}$$

where all the $\bar{q}$ roots of $\bar{A}_{\bar{q}}(z^{-1}) = 0$ fall outside the unit circle, $\bar{A}_0(L) \equiv D_0(L) \equiv B_0(L) \equiv 1$, and $B_{-1}(L) \equiv 0$. The regular case discussed above is nested within the irregular case and can be obtained from it by setting $\bar{q} = q$. The restrictions implicit in (7.125′) and (7.126′) enable us to determine $(\mathbf{d}_{ix}, d_{iu}, \mathbf{d}_{ib})$, for $i = 1, 2, \ldots, \bar{q} < q$, in terms of the structural parameters. As a result, the general solution (7.123) will only be a function of the remaining auxiliary parameters $\mathbf{d}_{ix}$, d_{iu}, and $\mathbf{d}_{ib}$, for $i = \bar{q}+1, \bar{q}+2, \ldots, q$. Accordingly, the reduced-form equation in this case will be

$$A_{m+q-\bar{q}}(L) y_t = C_{l-\bar{q}}(L)\mathbf{x}_t + \zeta_t, \tag{7.136}$$

---

26 Recall that if (7.121) has $\bar{q} > q$ unstable roots, then it is not possible for the RE model to have a stationary solution.

where

$$\zeta_t = D_{q-\bar{q}}(L)u_t + B_{q-\bar{q}-1}(L)\boldsymbol{\varepsilon}_{tb}. \quad (7.137)$$

There are a number of points that are worth emphasizing with respect to this solution. Firstly, it is clear that in the absence of direct observations on $\boldsymbol{\varepsilon}_{tb}$, in general, it will not be possible to identify $D_{q-\bar{q}}(L)$ and $B_{q-\bar{q}-1}(L)$. In particular, the coefficients of boot-strap effects $\boldsymbol{\varepsilon}_{tb}$ are not identifiable and cannot be distinguished from the coefficients of the disturbances u_t. (On this point, also see section 6.4.2 and the recent paper by Hamilton and Whiteman (1985).) Secondly, the new composite disturbance term ζ_t follows an unrestricted moving average process of order $q-\bar{q}$, the order of the moving average process generally being less than q. Only in the extreme case where $\bar{q}=0$ is the order of the moving average process equal to q. At first this result appears to contradict the one obtained in the case of 2S2SLS and forward filter estimators discussed in section 7.7.1. The difference, however, is due to the fact that, by not exploiting the dependence of ξ_t on the innovations in $\mathbf{x}_t$ (see (7.120)), the two-step estimators treat the innovations in $\mathbf{x}_t$ as part of the unobserved disturbances, thereby maintaining the assumption that ξ_t has a moving average process of order q, irrespective of whether $\bar{q}$, the number of unstable roots of the model, is equal to or less than q.

Notice, however, that for the computation of ML estimators we need to know how many of the roots of (7.123) fall outside the unit circle *a priori*. This information is needed not only for the derivation of the cross-equation restrictions (7.126′), but also for the determination of the order of the moving average process of ζ_t defined in (7.137).[27] Computation of the ML estimators in this general case involves the joint estimation of (7.136) and (7.106) subject to the cross-equation restrictions (7.126′), bearing in mind that the disturbances of (7.136) follow an unrestricted moving average process of order $q-\bar{q}$. This poses a rather formidable computational problem, and will not be pursued further here.

7.8 Concluding Remarks

This chapter, together with the two preceding ones on solution and identification, completes the econometric analysis of linear RE models. Identification, estimation and hypothesis testing in RE models often present difficult econometric problems, some of which are only beginning to be fully understood. This is particularly true of models with future expectations. Identification of these models requires *a priori* information regarding both the type of solution these models have (i.e. whether they have a unique stationary solution or a multiplicity of stationary solutions), and the lag lengths of the forcing variables

[27] Although this type of information is not needed in the computation of two-step estimators, they are nevertheless of crucial importance in the process of checking the consistency of two-step estimators. Recall from example 7.1 how the conditions for the consistency of IV estimators depend on whether $|\alpha|<1$ or not.

that they contain. The difficulty in establishing the identifiability of RE models also has important implications for a consistent estimation of the parameters. Although it is true that RE models can be consistently estimated by the IV method, apparently with a minimum amount of *a priori* information, in reality, as example 7.1 shows, the consistency of IV estimators depends crucially on knowing beforehand that the model under consideration is identified; and this, as we know, entails *a priori* knowledge of the solution form and the processes generating the forcing variables. What is often overlooked, or is at least not emphasized enough, in the literature is the fact that the orthogonality property of the REH which underlies the IV estimation of RE models, though necessary, is by no means sufficient for the consistency of IV estimators. Therefore, before employing these estimators it is important to check that the conditions necessary for the identification of the RE model under consideration are met. Considerable *a priori* information is also needed for fully efficient estimation of RE models. We need to know beforehand the exact specification of the processes generating the forcing variables ($\mathbf{x}_t$ and u_t), as well as the exact number of unstable roots of the model if it happens to contain future expectations of the endogenous variable.

On a technical level, despite the significant contributions in the past decade, a great deal remains to be done. Work on the small sample properties of the various estimators and test procedures for RE models has barely started, and important research needs to be carried out on non-linear and multivariate RE models, especially those with future expectations.

In addition to the above technical and informational considerations, the identification and estimation methods discussed in this and in the previous chapter presume that the 'representative' agent whose behaviour is under consideration knows, or has already learned perfectly, all the structural and auxiliary parameters of the model, while it is only the observing econometrician who is supposed to be left in the dark! Clearly, this is not a satisfactory analytical framework and, for the sake of greater realism, the implications of the problems of incomplete learning and information heterogeneity, discussed in chapters 3 and 4, should be investigated for the econometric analysis of RE models.

Another important consideration which emerges from the discussion concerns the problem of hypothesis testing in RE models. While it is possible to test the REH via tests of cross-equation restrictions, the outcome of such tests will generally be ambiguous. For this reason it is important to supplement the indirect cross-equation tests of the REH with direct tests based on observed expectations whenever possible, and this is the subject to which we shall now turn.

Part III

Use of Direct Observations on Expectations

8 Measurement of Expectations and Direct Tests of the REH

8.1 Introduction

The importance of direct measures of expectations for the analysis of the effect of expectations on economic behaviour, as well as for the study of the expectations formation process, has long been recognized in the literature. For early contributions see Klein (1954), Modigliani and Sauerlender (1955), Haavelmo (1958, pp. 356–7), and Katona (1958). In the absence of direct observations on expectations, empirical analysis of the expectations formation process can be carried out only indirectly, and conditional on the behavioural model which embodies the expectational variables. This means that conclusions concerning the expectations formation process will not be invariant to the choice of the underlying behavioural model. Although tests of cross-equation parameter restrictions discussed in the previous chapter in the context of rational expectations models are useful as tests of the consistency of the expectations formation process and the underlying behavioural model, they are of little help as tests of theories of expectations formation. Only when direct observations on expectations are available is it possible to satisfactorily compare and contrast alternative models of expectations formation. For a better understanding of the expectations formation process it is therefore important to consider carefully the problems associated with the measurement of expectations, and to study the econometric problems that arise in the analysis of directly observed expectations data.

This chapter deals with the quantification of qualitative expectations data, and discusses the alternative procedures which can be used for this purpose. In particular, it critically reviews the probability method proposed by Theil (1952), and Carlson and Parkin (1975), and contrasts it with the regression method discussed in Pesaran (1984b). These methods are also demonstrated by applying them to the surveys of businessmen's expectations of price changes of their products carried out by the Confederation of British Industries over the period 1958–85. In the analysis particular attention is paid to the problem of measurement errors in expectations data, and the econometric issues involved in testing the REH from aggregate data on expectations are discussed in some detail. Bearing these theoretical considerations in mind 'rationality' of the inflation expectations series is then tested by examining the orthogonality of the expectations errors to the costless and publicly available information. The chapter ends, with some concluding remarks.

8.2 Measurement of Expectations

One important source of direct measurement of expectations is the public and professional opinion survey data which are now available for a wide range of variables in most industrialized countries. These surveys can be broadly classified into 'quantitative' and 'qualitative', depending on whether the respondents are required to give precise quantitative answers or not. One basic form of qualitative survey, also known as 'tendency surveys', arises when the respondents are questioned only about the expected direction of change: whether a variable is expected to 'go up', to 'stay the same', or to 'go down'. Qualitative surveys with more than three but a finite number of response categories are also sometimes known as 'polychotomous' surveys. All three types of survey are encountered in the literature.

One of the important examples of tendency surveys are the monthly surveys of the IFO-Institute of Munich which started in the beginning of 1950 and cover both the actual and expected directions of change of a number of key microvariables relevant to the analysis of entrepreneurial behaviour; such as selling prices, production, orders, and stocks of finished goods and raw materials. All the IFO-Institute survey results are qualitative in nature and do not contain any information on the exact magnitude of the quantities involved. As Theil (1955, p. 184) explains, the organizers of the survey did not feel that questions which needed exact quantitative response would be answered by the leaders of the enterprises concerned. The results of the IFO-Institute surveys, also referred to as 'Munich Business Test' data, have been extensively studied, notably by Anderson (1952) and Theil (1952, 1955, 1966). In the case of the USA, surveys of expectations include the Livingston half-yearly survey of inflation expectations, the Michigan and Conference Board consumer surveys, the McGraw-Hill and Commerce/SEC investment surveys and a host of other surveys concerning wages and interest rate expectations. Livingston's inflation expectations series are quantitative and record specific point forecasts of a small and variable sample of professional economists, and have proved to be by far the most popular measure of inflation expectations in the USA.[1] Turnovsky (1970), Turnovsky and Wachter (1972), Pesando (1975), McGuire (1976), Carlson (1977), Mullineaux (1978, 1980), Jacobs and Jones (1980), Brown and Maital (1981), Figlewski and Wachtel (1981) and others have used the Livingston series to study the formation of

[1] The Livingston surveys are published in the *Philadelphia Bulletin* and are based on a sample of about 50 professional and business economists. For further details see, for example, Chan-Lee (1980).

inflationary expectations, and Pyle (1972), Gibson (1972), Lahiri (1976) and Cargil (1976) have used it to study the 'Fisher effect' on nominal interest rates. Survey expectations data on other variables in the USA have been employed by Friedman (1980) in the case of interest rates, by De Leeuw and McKelvey (1981) in the case of price expectations of business firms, and by Leonard (1982) in the case of wage expectations.

The main sources of survey data on expectations in the UK are the monthly Gallup Polls and the CBI's Industrial Trends surveys, both of which yield qualitative responses. The Gallup Poll survey results have been used by Carlson and Parkin (1975), Holden and Peel (1977), Smith (1982), Severn (1983), and Evans and Gulamani (1984) to study the general public's inflation expectations. The method employed by Carlson and Parkin to convert the qualitative survey results to quantitative measures of inflation expectations is basically the same as the method first proposed by Theil in 1952 in his study of Munich Business Test data and will be described below. Knöbl (1974), De Menil and Bhalla (1975), and Danes (1975) have used similar methods to derive expected inflation rate series from qualitative surveys in West Germany, the USA and Australia respectively.[2] Batchelor (1982, 1984) has used a modification of the Carlson and Parkin technique to quantify businessmen's expectations of inflation and output for Belgium, France, Germany and Italy, using monthly surveys of manufacturing enterprises co-ordinated by the Directorate General for Economic and Social Affairs of the Commission of the European Communities. The use of survey data in the case of Japan, Austria, Norway, Finland and the OECD countries as a whole, has also been reported by Aiginger (1981). Detailed reviews of the literature on measurement of inflation expectations can be found in Chan-Lee (1980), and Visco (1984b, 1986).

Clearly this resurgence of interest in direct measures of expectations has not come about by accident, and can be traced to the advent of the rational expectations hypothesis and the ambiguities that surround the indirect tests of this hypothesis proposed in the literature. The need to embed the REH within a particular economic theory, such as the natural rate hypothesis or the efficient market hypothesis, creates numerous difficulties, and in the final analysis can only allow a joint test of the validity of the REH and the underlying economic theory. Survey data on expectations are not, however, without their shortcomings: the results of sample surveys can be quite sensitive to sampling errors and the phrasing of questions. Respondents may express opinions that are different from the ones they actually choose to act upon. Quantitative measurement of expectations from qualitative survey results are generally based on rather restrictive and often untestable assumptions. These problems are real enough and have led some researchers to doubt the usefulness of survey-based expectations in econometric analysis. Others have sought to derive measures of expectations as they are manifested in market

---

[2] It has been pointed out to me by Ignazio Visco that besides Carlson and Parkin, and Knöbl, Theil's method was also independently suggested by Shuford (1970), Juster (1974), and De Menil (1974).

prices on the assumption that a particular economic theory is valid. Assuming financial markets are efficient and the real rate of interest is fixed, Fama (1975), for example, has suggested the nominal interest rate minus a fixed constant (representing the value of the assumed constant real rate of interest) as a proxy for the measurement of the expected rate of inflation. In the same vein, by relaxing the hypothesis that the real rate of interest is fixed in the short run but maintaining the assumption that it is constant in the long run, Frenkel (1982) has also proposed an 'implicit' method of measuring the long-term expectations of the rate of inflation (up to a constant term) from the observed term structure of interest rates.[3] Such 'implicit' methods of the measurement of inflation expectations are, however, only as good as the theory and the auxiliary assumptions that underlie them. They are of little use in empirical testing of the theories that help to generate them, and should not be regarded as substitutes for direct survey measurements of expectations. What is needed are better and more robust techniques of measuring expectations from opinion survey data rather than the abandonment of direct methods of measurement of expectations in favour of theory-loaded implicit methods.

The above-mentioned objections to the measurement of expectations on the basis of survey data are not, however, applicable with the same force to all surveys. Surveys that require respondents to give point forecasts for the variables in question are more likely to be susceptible to sampling and measurement errors than tendency surveys that only question the respondents about the expected direction of change (on this also see Visco, 1984b, pp. 28–9). As is pointed out by Katona (1958, p. 70), quantitative questions about prospects of, say, prices or profits may suggest that 'business managers ought to have that information, and the information may therefore be given even though substantial uncertainty exists'. Moreover, cardinal measures of individual expectations are useful as a basis of computing an aggregate measure of expectations, if they are also accompanied by probability statements indicating the degree of confidence that individual respondents attach to their answers. This type of information, however, is not available, and even if it were available it is most likely that it would be subject to large margins of error. An alternative approach would be to start with ordinal responses and then convert these responses into quantitative measures under certain assumptions.[4] The conversion of ordinal responses into quantitative measures of expectations is needed not only for studying the expectations formation process but, more importantly, for incorporating direct measurement

---

[3] In order to derive his inflation expectations series Frenkel (1982) is also forced to make a number of further assumptions involving the adjustment mechanism of the short-term real rate of interest to its long-run value, and the relationship between maturity and the liquidity premium. Elsewhere Frenkel (1977) has also proposed the measurement of inflation expectations based on data from forward foreign exchange markets.

[4] At a microeconometric level it is also possible to use ordinal responses (both for expectations and realizations) in log-linear probability models or probit models of the type considered, for example, by Nerlove and his associates (Koenig et al., 1981; Nerlove, 1983), Kawasaki et al. (1982, 1983), and McIntosh et al. (1986a, b).

of expectations in macroeconomic models. The use of ordinal measures of expectations in conventional aggregative time-series econometric models is extremely cumbersome, if not impossible, and will not be pursued here. Instead the next section will consider the various methods proposed in the literature for converting qualitative expectations data to quantitative measurements.

8.3 Methods of Quantification of Ordinal Responses

It is important to recognize from the outset that in so far as expectations are 'attitudes' or 'states of mind', any attempt at their quantitative measurement is, to some extent, bound to be arbitrary. At the individual level the best that can be hoped for is an ordinal measurement in the form of categorical data. But at the aggregate level, assuming certain assumptions hold, it is possible to obtain quantitative measures of expectations (up to a scalar factor) averaged over individual respondents. Such a possibility was first demonstrated by Theil (1952) and later independently by Knöbl (1974), and Carlson and Parkin (1975). The conversion method proposed by these authors (which we refer to as the 'probability method') is based on the assumption that, except for a finite number of parameters, the form of the subjective probability distribution of the respondents over future changes in the variable in question is the same, and further assumes that an expected change will be reported only when respondents expect the variable in question to change by more than a certain threshold value. This method has been employed extensively in the literature, see, for example, De Menil and Bhalla (1975), Danes (1975) and Batchelor (1982). An alternative method of computing 'average' expectations from individuals' categorical responses which does not require making assumptions concerning the subjective probability distribution of respondents, has been proposed in Pesaran (1984b). This alternative method (which may be called the 'regression method') can be applied whenever surveys report on past perceptions as well as on future expectations of the respondents. The method exploits the relationship between the actual changes in the variable in question, as measured by official statistics, and the realizations perceived by the respondents as reported in the tendency surveys in order to convert the categorical expectations data into quantitative measures. Unlike the subjective probability approach, the choice of the conversion formula in the regression approach depends on the data set under investigation. The formula for the conversion of categorical responses to an average quantitative measure can be obtained statistically by a time-series regression (possibly a non-linear one) of the actual rate of change of the variable, say prices, on the proportion of the respondents that report a 'rise' or a 'fall' in the past prices of their own product. A regression of this kind is not a causal explanation of price changes, but simply identifies the relationship between two different sources of information (namely official statistics and survey results) and serves as a 'yardstick' by means of which categorical responses concerning the direction of future changes in prices can be converted into quantitative measures.

Before going into the details of the alternative methods of quantification of qualitative expectations data, it is important to note that there are no limits to the types of expectations data that can be collected. Individuals or firms may be asked about their expectations of the variables over which they have some control (such as the type and amount of durable goods that households intend or expect to purchase, or the prices at which firms plan or expect to sell their product), or they may be asked about their expectations of economy-wide measures such as interest rates, inflation, output and unemployment. In the case of individual specific variables, expectations data can also be interpreted as plans and intentions of the respondent, and it is not clear how one could distinguish between expectations, intentions and plans of individuals from the survey results alone. It is also possible to ask firms about their expectations of output and pricing decisions of other firms in the industry. Such expectations data will be particularly relevant to the study of behaviour of firms in oligopolistic market conditions. In addition there are a large number of possibilities regarding the time horizon over which expectations are surveyed and the frequency with which they are observed. In the face of such a variety of expectations data it is unlikely that one method of measurement and quantification of expectations could be viewed as superior to all other methods.

8.3.1 *The Probability Method*

This method was first employed by Theil (1952) in order to provide an alternative theoretical justification for Anderson's (1951, 1952) use of 'balance' statistics (defined as the difference between the percentage of respondents who report an increase of, say, prices or production and the percentage of respondents who report a decrease) to quantify the IFO-Munich Survey results. Suppose that we are interested in quantification of expected changes of prices reported by firms in a sample of size N. Let ${}_tR^e_{t+1}$ be the proportion of firms (appropriately weighted to account for their size differences in the sample) that at time t expect a rise in their prices over the period t to $t+1$, and ${}_tF^e_{t+1}$ the proportion of firms that at time t expect a fall in their prices. Then, apart from a scaling factor, the balance statistic defined by

$${}_tB^e_{t+1} = {}_tR^e_{t+1} - {}_tF^e_{t+1} \tag{8.1}$$

provides an accurate measure of 'average' expected changes in prices if the percentage change in prices of firms reporting a price increase and the percentage change of firms reporting a price decrease are constant over time (Anderson, 1952). Theil considered this requirement to be unduly restrictive, and set out to provide an alternative justification in terms of subjective probability distributions of individual respondents. Theil's solution is based on the following assumptions:

Assumption 8.1 Each firm i bases its survey response on a subjective probability distribution $h_i(\Pi_{i,t+1} \mid \Phi_{it})$ defined over the future change in its selling price, conditional on the information set Φ_{it} available to it at time t, such that

$$ {}_t\Pi^e_{i,t+1} = E(\Pi_{i,t+1} \mid \Phi_{it}). \tag{8.2} $$

Here the mathematical expectations are taken with respect to the subjective probability distribution of the firm, and there is no presumption that $h_i(\Pi_{i,t+1} \mid \Phi_{it})$ should necessarily coincide with the objective probability distribution of $\Pi_{i,t+1}$.

Assumption 8.2 There exists an interval $(-a_{it}, b_{it})$, called the 'indifference interval' by Theil, a_{it} and b_{it} being positive, such that a firm reports an increase in its price if

$$ {}_t\Pi^e_{i,t+1} \geqslant b_{it}, $$

and reports a decrease in its price if

$$ {}_t\Pi^e_{i,t+1} \leqslant -a_{it}. $$

Otherwise it reports 'no change' in its price.[5]

Assumption 8.3 The subjective distributions $h_i(\Pi_{i,t+1} \mid \Phi_{it})$ are such that they can be employed to derive an 'aggregate' probability distribution $h(\Pi_{t+1} \mid \Omega_t)$ with finite first- and second-order moments, where

$$ \Omega_t = \bigcup_{i=1}^{N} \Phi_{it} $$

is the union of individual firms' information sets and

$$ \Pi_t = \sum_{i=1}^{N} w_i \Pi_{it}, \tag{8.3} $$

in which Π_t denotes the actual percentage change in 'average' selling prices of firms in the industry, Π_{it} is the actual percentage change in the selling price of the ith firm and w_i is the weight of this firm in the industry.

The above assumptions provide the necessary framework for the subjective probability approach, but by themselves are not sufficient to yield estimates of ${}_t\Pi^e_{t+1}$, the 'average' expected rate of price changes, from the knowledge of the signs of ${}_t\Pi^e_{i,t+1}$. The following additional assumptions are also needed:

Assumption 8.4 The response threshold a_{it} and b_{it} are symmetric and remain fixed both across firms and over time. That is $a_{it} = b_{it} = c$, for all i and t.

---

[5] Here, it is implicitly assumed that there are no 'do not know' responses in the sample, or that if such responses are present, their numbers have been appropriately allocated (say, proportionately) to the other three response categories.

Assumption 8.5 The subjective probability distributions $h_i(\Pi_{i,t+1} | \Phi_{it})$ are independent and have the same known form across firms.

Under assumptions 8.3 and 8.5, ${}_t\Pi^e_{i,t+1}$ can be regarded as independent drawings from the 'aggregate' distribution $h(\Pi_{t+1} | \Omega_t)$, while assumptions 8.2 and 8.4 specify the form of the 'response function' of firms, relating their qualitative responses to the underlying quantitative changes in their expectations. On the basis of these assumptions we now can write

$$\text{prob}\{\Pi_{t+1} \leqslant -c | \Omega_t\} = H_t(-c) = {}_tF^e_{t+1}, \tag{8.4}$$

$$\text{prob}\{\Pi_{t+1} \geqslant c | \Omega_t\} = 1 - H_t(c) = {}_tR^e_{t+1}, \tag{8.5}$$

where $H_t(\cdot)$ denotes the cumulative density function of $h(\Pi_{t+1} | \Omega_t)$. An estimate of ${}_t\Pi^e_{t+1} = E(\Pi_{t+1} | \Omega_t)$ can now be obtained from (8.4) and (8.5), assuming that the response threshold c is known (or can be estimated independently of (8.4) and (8.5)), and that, except for its mean and/or variance the form of the aggregate density function $h(\Pi_{t+1} | \Omega_t)$, is known completely. It is clear that even under assumptions 8.1–8.5, the quantification of qualitative responses, summarized by the statistics ${}_tF^e_{t+1}$ and ${}_tR^e_{t+1}$ still crucially depends on the particular value chosen for the response thresholds and the specific form adopted for the aggregate density function $h(\Pi_{t+1} | \Omega_t)$.

Important examples of $h(\Pi_{t+1} | \Omega_t)$ considered in the literature are the uniform distribution, the normal distribution, and the logistic distribution.

Example 8.1: the Uniform Distribution

Suppose $\Pi_{t+1,i}$ are random drawings from a uniform distribution with mean ${}_t\Pi^e_{t+1} = E(\Omega_{t+1} | \Omega_t)$ and a constant range equal to $2q$. In this case

$$h(\Pi_{t+1} | \Omega_t) = \frac{1}{2q}, \quad \text{for } {}_t\Pi^e_{t+1} - q \leqslant \Pi_{t+1} \leqslant {}_t\Pi^e_{t+1} + q, \tag{8.6}$$

$$= 0, \text{ otherwise.}$$

A graphical exposition is provided in figure 8.1. Now using (8.4) and (8.5) we have

$${}_tF^e_{t+1} = \frac{-{}_t\Pi^e_{t+1} + q - c}{2q}, \tag{8.7}$$

$${}_tR^e_{t+1} = \frac{{}_t\Pi^e_{t+1} + q - c}{2q}, \tag{8.8}$$

which yield the following estimate of ${}_t\Pi^e_{t+1}$

$${}_t\Pi^e_{t+1} = q({}_tR^e_{t+1} - {}_tF^e_{t+1}), \tag{8.9}$$

$$= q\,{}_tB^e_{t+1}.$$

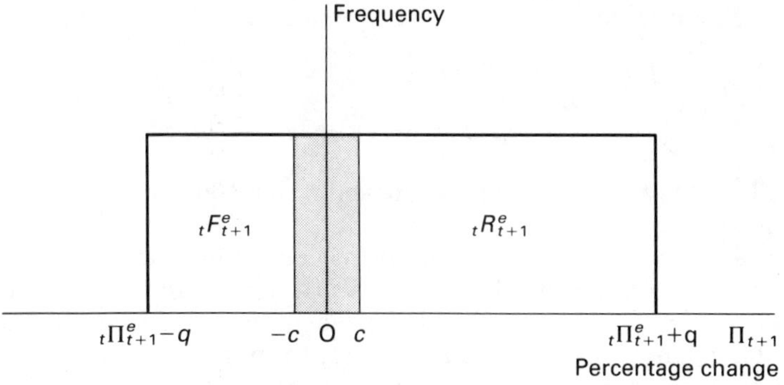

Figure 8.1 Quantification of ordinal responses (uniform distribution)

As in Anderson's approach this result provides an estimate of the average expected change in prices in terms of the balance statistic, $_tB^e_{t+1}$. An alternative justification for Anderson's use of balance statistics will be given below.

A straightforward generalization of (8.9) can also be obtained by relaxing the assumption that the indifference interval $(-a,b)$ is symmetrical with respect to the origin. In this more general case equations (8.7) and (8.8) become

$$_tF^e_{t+1} = \frac{-\,_t\Pi^e_{t+1} + q - a}{2q},$$

$$_tR^e_{t+1} = \frac{_t\Pi^e_{t+1} + q - b}{2q},$$

and give the following solution for $_t\Pi^e_{t+1}$

$$_t\Pi^e_{t+1} = \alpha\,_tR^e_{t+1} - \beta\,_tF^e_{t+1}, \tag{8.10}$$

where

$$\alpha = \frac{2q(q-a)}{2q-a-b}, \quad \beta = \frac{2q(q-b)}{2q-a-b}. \tag{8.11}$$

It is clear that if the indifference interval is symmetric around the origin, i.e. $a=b=c$, (8.10) reduces to (8.9). Notice, however, that irrespective of whether (8.9) or (8.10) is used to quantify expectations, some *a priori* estimates of the scaling parameters q or α and β will be needed. Some authors, such as Carlson and Parkin (1975), have suggested estimating the scaling parameters assuming that expectations are, on average, unbiased. This procedure, apart from being based on a rather restrictive assumption, is only applicable to (8.9) where the conversion formula depends on a *single* unknown scaling parameter. The imposition of the unbiasedness condition on (8.9) yields the following estimate for q

$$\hat{q} = \sum_{t=1}^{n} \Pi_t \Big/ \sum_{t=1}^{n} {}_{t-1}B^e_t,$$

where Π_t is the actual rate of inflation, and n is the number of time periods in the sample.[6]

The above probability approach can also be used to compute higher-order moments of the 'aggregate' distribution, $h(\Pi_{t+1} | \Phi_t)$. On the assumption that individual expectations represent independent drawings from this aggregate distribution, the dispersion of $h(\Pi_{t+1} | \Phi_t)$ also provides us with a direct measure of dispersion of expectations across firms. Such a measure is particularly of interest in empirical studies that attempt to capture the effect of inflation or output uncertainty on pricing or output policy of firms (cf. Demetriades, 1987). Most measures of inflation uncertainty used in the literature are obtained indirectly and estimate inflation uncertainty, for example, by the standard error of the actual inflation rate (Loque and Willet, 1976), the absolute changes in the actual inflation rate (Foster, 1978), or by the variance of expectations errors as in Fischer (1981) and Pagan et al. (1983). In the case of the uniform distribution (8.6), the dispersion is determined solely by the range of the distribution and is therefore fixed over time. Explicitly we have:[7]

$${}_t\sigma^e_{t+1} = \frac{1}{\sqrt{3}}\, q.$$

The time invariance of ${}_t\sigma^e_{t+1}$ is clearly an undesirable feature and casts doubt on the validity of the uniform distribution with a fixed range, as the basis for the conversion of qualitative responses to quantitative measures.

But as shown in Visco (1984b, pp. 69–71), the assumption of a fixed range is not necessary for quantification of qualitative responses and is made by Theil (1952) in order to provide a justification for the use of balance statistics. In the case where the range of the uniform distribution (i.e. $2q_t$) varies with

---

[6] It has been pointed out to me by Roy Batchelor that this scaling method does not make expectations unbiased in the statistical sense, and that to obtain an unbiased estimate of the scaling parameter, q should be estimated as the coefficient in the regression through the origin of the rate of inflation on unscaled expectations. Notice, however, that this procedure may still fail to result in an unbiased estimate of q, if the unscaled expectations are themselves measured with errors.

[7] Notice, however, that in the case of the uniform distribution the use of the variance of expectations errors, namely

$$(\Pi_{t+1} - {}_t\Pi^e_{t+1})^2 = (\Pi_{t+1} - q\ {}_tB^e_{t+1})^2,$$

as a proxy for inflation uncertainty, leads to a measure which varies over time and differs from ${}_t\sigma^e_{t+1}$, which is time-invariant.

time, and a symmetric indifference interval $(-c, c)$ is assumed, then using (8.9) and noting that $c/q_t = 1 - {}_tR^e_{t+1} - {}_tF^e_{t+1}$, we have

$$ {}_t\Pi^e_{t+1} = c({}_tB^e_{t+1}/{}_tS^e_{t+1}) = c_t d^e_{t+1}, \tag{8.9'} $$

where ${}_tS^e_{t+1} = 1 - {}_tF^e_{t+1} - {}_tR^e_{t+1}$ represents the proportion of firms that at time t do not expect any change in their prices over the period t to $t+1$. Under an asymmetric indifference interval $(-a, b)$, the relevant conversion formula is still given by (8.10), but the parameter q should now be replaced with $q_t = \frac{1}{2}(a+b)/{}_tS^e_{t+1}$. In this case we obtain

$$ {}_t\Pi^e_{t+1} = aX^e_{1,t+1} - bX^e_{2,t+1}, \tag{8.10'} $$

where

$$ X^e_{1,t+1} = \frac{(1 - 2{}_tS^e_{t+1}){}_tR^e_{t+1} - {}_tF^e_{t+1}}{2{}_tS^e_{t+1}(1 - {}_tS^e_{t+1})}, $$

and

$$ X^e_{2,t+1} = \frac{(1 - 2{}_tS^e_{t+1}){}_tF^e_{t+1} - {}_tR^e_{t+1}}{2{}_tS^e_{t+1}(1 - {}_tS^e_{t+1})}. $$

The corresponding formulae for ${}_t\sigma^e_{t+1}$ under the symmetric and the asymmetric indifference intervals are given by $c/(\sqrt{3}{}_tS^e_{t+1})$, and $(a+b)/(2\sqrt{3}{}_tS^e_{t+1})$, respectively.

Example 8.2: The Normal Distribution

In this case it is assumed that $\Pi_{t+1,i}$ are random drawings from a normal distribution. Using (8.4) and (8.5) we have

$$ \Phi\left(\frac{-c - {}_t\Pi^e_{t+1}}{{}_t\sigma^e_{t+1}}\right) = {}_tF^e_{t+1}, \tag{8.12} $$

$$ \Phi\left(\frac{c - {}_t\Pi^e_{t+1}}{{}_t\sigma^e_{t+1}}\right) = 1 - {}_tR^e_{t+1}, \tag{8.13} $$

where $\Phi(\cdot)$ stands for the cumulative distribution function of a standard normal variate (see figure 8.2 for a graphical representation). The above equations can now be solved for ${}_t\Pi^e_{t+1}$ and ${}_t\sigma^e_{t+1}$ in terms of ${}_tR^e_{t+1}$, ${}_tF^e_{t+1}$, and the value of the response threshold c. Using (8.12) and (8.13) we first note that

$$ {}_tf^e_{t+1} = \Phi^{-1}(F^e_{t+1}) = \frac{-c - {}_t\Pi^e_{t+1}}{{}_t\sigma^e_{t+1}}, \tag{8.14} $$

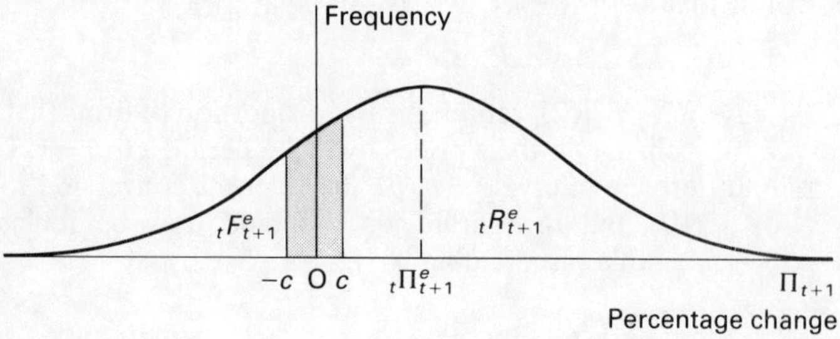

Figure 8.2 Quantification of ordinal responses (normal distribution)

and

$$ {}_tr^e_{t+1} = \Phi^{-1}(1 - {}_tR^e_{t+1}) = \frac{c - {}_t\Pi^e_{t+1}}{{}_t\sigma^e_{t+1}}, \tag{8.15}$$

where ${}_tf^e_{t+1}$ and ${}_tr^e_{t+1}$ are the abscissa of the frequencies ${}_tF^e_{t+1}$ and $1 - {}_tR^e_{t+1}$ of the cumulative normal distribution. More explicitly,

$$\Phi({}_tf^e_{t+1}) = {}_tF^e_{t+1}, \tag{8.16}$$

$$\Phi({}_tr^e_{t+1}) = 1 - {}_tR^e_{t+1}. \tag{8.17}$$

From (8.14) and (8.15) it now follows that

$$ {}_t\Pi^e_{t+1} = c\ {}_td^e_{t+1}, \tag{8.18}$$

and

$$ {}_t\sigma^e_{t+1} = \frac{2c}{{}_tr^e_{t+1} - {}_tf^e_{t+1}}, \tag{8.19}$$

where

$$ {}_td^e_{t+1} = \frac{{}_tf^e_{t+1} + {}_tr^e_{t+1}}{{}_tf^e_{t+1} - {}_tr^e_{t+1}}. \tag{8.20}$$

For most empirical applications involving ${}_t\Pi^e_{t+1}$ and ${}_t\sigma^e_{t+1}$, the value of the response threshold c also needs to be estimated. Under the unbiasedness condition we obtain

$$\hat{c} = \sum_{t=1}^{n} \Pi_t \Big/ \sum_{t=1}^{n} {}_{t-1}d^e_t. \tag{8.21}$$

Other methods of estimating c will be discussed below.

Example 8.3: The Logistic Distribution

This distribution has been used in the literature as an alternative to the normal distribution and, except for its tails, is very similar to the normal distribution. Like the normal it is symmetric but is more highly peaked. (This distribution has been used, for example, by Fishe and Lahiri (1981), Batchelor (1984), and Wren-Lewis (1986).) The cumulative function $H_t(\cdot)$ in this example has the logistic form

$$H(\Pi_{t+1} \mid \Omega_t) = \frac{1}{1 + \exp(-(\Pi_{t+1} - {}_t\Pi^e_{t+1})/\beta_t\}},$$

where ${}_t\sigma^e_{t+1} = (\pi/\sqrt{3})\beta_t$.[8] Again, using (8.4) and (8.5), we arrive at (8.18) except that for the logistic distribution ${}_tf^e_{t+1}$ and ${}_tr^e_{t+1}$ are given by

$$_tf^e_{t+1} = \log\left(\frac{1 - {}_tF^e_{t+1}}{{}_tF^e_{t+1}}\right), \tag{8.22}$$

$$_tr^e_{t+1} = \log\left(\frac{{}_tR^e_{t+1}}{1 - {}_tR^e_{t+1}}\right). \tag{8.23}$$

Similarly, for ${}_t\sigma^e_{t+1}$ we have

$$_t\sigma^e_{t+1} = \frac{2\pi c}{\sqrt{3}({}_tf^e_{t+1} - {}_tr^e_{t+1})}. \tag{8.24}$$

As our exposition shows, the probability approach is based on a number of rather restrictive assumptions, and its use in practice can be subject to a number of important drawbacks:

1. The form of the aggregate probability distribution of respondents is usually unknown and, as is pointed out by Batchelor (1981), it may diverge significantly from normality whenever the subjective probability distributions of respondents do not have finite first- and second-order moments.[9]
2. There is no reason why the response thresholds should be symmetric.
3. The assumption that the response thresholds are constant over time can give rise to peculiar results in the case of normal or logistic distributions. If, for example, more than half of the respondents say prices will 'go up', a shift in responses from the 'stay the same' to the 'down'

---

[8] Note that π here represents the number $\pi = 3.14$ ...

[9] The possibility of non-normality of respondents' subjective probabilities has been emphasized by Carlson (1975) in relation to Livingston's price expectation.

category will cause the expected inflation measured by the probability approach to increase! This is because the variance of the aggregate distribution must increase to allow for the smaller percentage of respondents who say prices will stay the same. This can be readily demonstrated in the case of the logistic distribution. Differentiating (8.18) with respect to ${}_tF^e_{t+1}$, noting that in the case of the logistic distribution ${}_tf^e_{t+1}$ and ${}_tr^e_{t+1}$ are defined by (8.22) and (8.23) respectively, we have

$$\frac{\partial \Pi}{\partial F} = \frac{2rc}{(f-r)^2 F(1-F)},$$

where for the sake of simplicity of notations we have suppressed the time subscripts and the expectations superscript *e*. Therefore, the sign of $\partial\Pi/\partial F > 0$ is the same as that of *rc*, and for a fixed response threshold value *c*, the sign of $\partial\Pi/\partial F$ changes depending on whether $R > 1/2$ or not. For example, in inflationary periods when $c > 0$, $\partial\Pi/\partial F > 0$, whenever, $R > 1/2$ (or $r = \log(R/(1-R)) > 0$), which is the opposite of what one would expect on *a priori* grounds. A similar result also follows when $c < 0$, and $R < 1/2$ (or $r < 0$).[10]

4 Another difficulty with the probability approach, initially pointed out by Theil (1952, p. 111), is that the approach breaks down whenever the percentage of respondents reporting a rise (or a fall) in prices is equal to zero. For example, when ${}_tF^e_{t+1} = 0$, from (8.4) we should have $H_t(-c) = 0$, and for continuous probability distributions this is not possible.

5 Finally, the Carlson and Parkin method of estimating the response threshold parameter which assumes expectations are unbiased is not clearly satisfactory, especially if the expectations data are to be used in tests of the REH. The modification of the Carlson and Parkin method of estimating response threshold parameters by Batchelor (1982) is also subject to a similar criticism and involves assuming that the mean square errors of expectations is minimum.[11]

These limitations, some of which are inherent in the probability approach to the quantification of qualitative data, are not easily overcome. However, when

---

[10] Recent empirical analysis carried out by Batchelor (1986a) also casts serious doubts on the assumption of constant thresholds, at least in the case of inflation expectations.

[11] Batchelor (1982, p. 5) estimates parameters c_0 and c_1 (see his relation (12)) by the method of ordinary least squares, which is based on the assumption that the disturbances u_t have zero means and are distributed independently of p^e_t. But his relations (12) and (13) together also imply that

$$P_t = p^e_t + u_t,$$

and the assumption that u_t have zero means is equivalent to *assuming* price expectations are unbiased predictors of actual price changes. The problem of estimation of the response threshold can, however, be dealt with more satisfactorily if respondents are also asked about their perception of past changes as well as about their expectations (see below, section 8.4.1).

surveys question respondents about their perception of the past as well as their expectations of the future, the conversion problem can be solved under assumptions that are testable, as well as being less restrictive than the probability approach of Theil, and Carlson and Parkin.

8.3.2 The Regression Method

The basic idea behind this approach is to use the relationship between realizations (measured by official statistics) and respondents' perception of the past (reported in tendency surveys) as a *yardstick* for the quantification of respondents' expectations about the future.

The relationship between actual changes in, say, prices of manufactured goods and respondents' qualitative perception of the past can be formalized along the lines suggested by Anderson (1952). Consider equation (8.3) which gives the actual percentage change in average selling prices of firms in the industry, and suppose the same relationship holds for the sample of firms in the survey. If we now categorize the firms in the sample according to whether, at time t, they experienced a 'rise', a 'fall', or 'no change' in their prices, (8.3) can also be written as:

$$\Pi_t = \Sigma w_i^+ \Pi_{it}^+ + \Sigma w_i^- \Pi_{it}^-, \tag{8.25}$$

where the superscripts + and − denote the firms showing an increase and a decrease in their prices respectively. Clearly, firms with no change in their prices will not appear in (8.25). Since tendency surveys of firms' perception of past price changes do not give exact quantitative information on Π_{it}^+ (or Π_{it}^-), some assumption concerning the variations of Π_{it} across firms and over time is needed. Anderson implicitly assumed that $\Pi_{it}^+ = \alpha$ and $\Pi_{it}^- = -\beta$ and therefore obtained:

$$\Pi_t = \alpha \Sigma w_i^+ - \beta \Sigma w_i^-,$$

where α and β are both positive unknown parameters. In this relation the sums, Σw_i^+ and Σw_i^-, are the percentages of firms (appropriately weighted) that experience and report respectively a 'rise' and a 'fall' in their prices. Under Anderson's assumptions the relationship between actual price changes and the survey responses will be

$$\Pi_t = \alpha R_t - \beta F_t, \tag{8.26}$$

where R_t and F_t stand for the percentages of firms reporting a price rise and price fall respectively. The observations on R_t and F_t represent realizations corresponding to the expectations data ${}_{t-1}R_t^e$ and ${}_{t-1}F_t^e$ respectively. If it is now further assumed that relation (8.26) holds for expectations as well as for realizations we arrive at the following conversion formula

$${}_{t-1}\Pi_t^e = \alpha\, {}_{t-1}R_t^e - \beta\, {}_{t-1}F_t^e. \tag{8.27}$$

This result is the same as (8.10) obtained by the probability method, assuming a uniform distribution with a constant range and asymmetric response thresholds. It is, however, important to note that the parameters α and β in the above conversion formula have a very different interpretation from those in (8.10). Here α and β represent the average rates of change of prices (in absolute values) of firms experiencing a rise and a fall in their prices respectively, while α and β in (8.10) are defined in terms of response thresholds (a, b), and the range of the uniform distribution, q. Anderson's method of deriving (8.27) has the advantage that it allows an empirically observable interpretation for the unknown parameters α and β. These parameters could in principle be obtained directly from observations on individual firms' price changes. Micro-information of this type is not, however, generally available. Neither tendency surveys nor official statistics provide information on individual firms or households. This does not, of course, mean that such information cannot be collected. Even in the case of qualitative surveys of expectations, firms (or households) could be asked for quantitative information about the past (i.e. realizations) and for qualitative information about the future (i.e. plans or expectations). In the absence of quantitative information on Π_{it}, an alternative approach would be to estimate α and β *indirectly* by the regression of Π_t on R_t and F_t.

Although Anderson (1952) and Theil (1952) both found strong empirical support for (8.26) in their analysis of Munich Business Test data, in periods of rising and variable inflation Anderson's assumption of fixed Π_{it}^{+} and Π_{it}^{-} may not be appropriate. During periods of generally rising prices it is more reasonable to expect an asymmetrical relationship to exist between the rate of change of individual firms' prices and the average rate of inflation, depending on whether the firm reports a price fall or a price rise. Here we adopt the following hypothesis:

For Π_{it}^{+} we postulate that

$$\Pi_{it}^{+} = \alpha + \lambda \Pi_t + \varepsilon_{it}^{+},\ \alpha \geqslant 0,\ 0 \leqslant \lambda < 1,\ \Pi_t \geqslant 0, \tag{8.28a}$$

where ε_{it}^{+} represents the overall effect of firm-specific factors assumed to be distributed randomly with zero means and a constant variance σ_{+}^{2}. But for Π_{it}^{-}, except for a disturbance term, we retain Anderson's assumption and write

$$\Pi_{it}^{-} = -\beta + \varepsilon_{it}^{-},\ \beta \geqslant 0, \tag{8.28b}$$

where ε_{it}^{-} are assumed to have zero means and a constant variance σ_{-}^{2}, distributed independently of ε_{it}^{+}.

Relation (8.28a) is intended to capture the general effect of rising money wages on manufacturing prices and should be regarded as a first approximation to the complicated relationship that underlies changes in prices of individual firms and the overall rate of inflation as well as firm-specific factors.[12] Using relations (8.28) in (8.25) now yields

[12] Note that unlike the assumptions underlying the probability approach the assumptions concerning the relationship between Π_{it}^{+} and Π_{it}^{-}, and the overall rate of inflation can, in principle, be tested directly.

$$(1-\lambda R_t)\Pi_t = \alpha R_t - \beta F_t + v_t, \tag{8.29}$$

where

$$v_t = \Sigma \omega_i^+ \varepsilon_{it}^+ + \Sigma w_i^- \varepsilon_{it}^- . \tag{8.30}$$

Alternatively, we can write

$$\Pi_t = \frac{\alpha R_t - \beta F_t}{1-\lambda R_t} + u_t, \tag{8.31}$$

where

$$u_t = v_t/(1-\lambda R_t). \tag{8.32}$$

Given observations on R_t and F_t, disturbances v_t or u_t will have zero means but need not be homoscedastic or serially uncorrelated. From (8.30), the variance of v_t is easily seen to be

$$V(v_t) = \sigma_+^2 \Sigma (w_i^+)^2 + \sigma_-^2 \Sigma (w_i^-)^2,$$

which, in general, is unlikely to remain fixed over time. Expressions for $\Sigma(w_i^-)^2$ can be computed from the survey results, but are not usually made available by the survey organizers. As a first approximation, $V(v_t)$ can be modelled in terms of R_t and F_t. (Recall the $\Sigma w_i^+ = R_t$, and $\Sigma w_i^- = F_t$.) Residual autocorrelation in v_t can also arise if ε_{it}^+ and ε_{it}^- are serially correlated.

Like (8.26), the non-linear formulation (8.29) or (8.31) can be used for the conversion of the qualitative test variates, ${}_tR_{t+1}^e$ and ${}_tF_{t+1}^e$ to a quantitative measure, ${}_t\Pi_{t+1}^e$. Assuming that (8.29) or (8.31) holds for realizations as well as for expectations, as a first approximation the following conversion formula can be used[13]

$${}_t\Pi_{t+1}^e = \frac{\alpha\, {}_tR_{t+1}^e - \beta\, {}_tF_{t+1}^e}{1-\lambda\, {}_tR_{t+1}^e}. \tag{8.33}$$

Further adjustments to the above formula are needed whenever the disturbances, v_t are autocorrelated. For example if v_t follows a first-order autoregressive scheme with parameter ρ, then the correct expression for ${}_t\Pi_{t+1}^e$ becomes

$${}_t\Pi_{t+1}^e = \frac{\alpha\, {}_tR_{t+1}^e - \beta\, {}_tF_{t+1}^e + \rho[(1-\lambda R_t)\Pi_t - \alpha R_t + \beta F_t]}{1-\lambda\, {}_tR_{t+1}^e} \tag{8.34}$$

The unknown parameters α, β, λ and ρ in the above conversion formula can be estimated by means of non-linear regression of actual price changes

[13] Given the non-linearities involved, derivation of an exact conversion formula based on (8.29) or (8.31) will be rather complicated, and requires knowledge of the variances as well as the means of the test variates. The latter are not usually made available in the survey results.

against the realized qualitative test variates R_t and F_t. Depending on their empirical performance, relations (8.26), (8.29) or (8.31) can then be chosen as the basis of the formula for the conversion of qualitative survey responses to quantitative measures.

The above regression approach to quantification of expectations has a number of advantages over the probability method. The procedure does not break down if one of the percentages R_t, F_t, ${}_tR^e_{t+1}$, ${}_tF^e_{t+1}$ vanishes. A shift from the 'same' category to the 'fall' category does not result in an increase in price expectations. The estimation of the unknown scaling parameters (i.e. α, β, λ and ρ) can be carried out independently of whether expectations are unbiased or not. The procedure can be easily extended to surveys with more than three response categories. The underlying assumptions of the approach are, in principle, testable.

8.4 Alternative Measures of Inflation Expectations in British Manufacturing

This section demonstrates the methods of quantification of expectations discussed above by applying them to the results of the CBI Industrial Trends Surveys in the case of average selling prices of British firms in the manufacturing sector. The CBI surveys were first introduced in 1958 and cover a significant proportion of firms in the manufacturing sector. They ask each firm about past actual trends, as well as future expected trends in a number of variables including the average selling prices of their product, their export prices, costs, output, and capacity.[14] The CBI surveys differ in a very important way from the Gallup Poll or other surveys that ask respondents to forecast the trend in the wide-economy averages such as the general level of prices, interest rates or output. Because the CBI asks each firm individually about the output it intends to produce, or the average price at which it expects or plans to sell its own product, the results are less likely to be subject to the influence of newspaper headlines, and the announcement of inflation forecasts by government and private agencies. Of course, had firms been asked about their expectations of the general level of manufacturing prices, the survey results might have been more subject to the influence of public announcements of inflation forecasts.

The CBI surveys were initially conducted three times each year, but since 1972 they have been carried out every quarter. Despite this change in their frequency all the CBI surveys relate to the same time horizon, and question the respondents about their expectations (or plans) over a 4-month period. The surveys are weighted according to the size of the firms in the industries.

---

[14] A useful description of the CBI surveys in the period prior to 1969 can be found in Glynn (1969). More recent discussions are given in Smith (1978), and Klein and Moore (1981). At present the CBI surveys cover around 1650 firms accounting for about 3 million employees and nearly half of the UK's manufacturing exports. The number of respondents to the surveys has varied significantly from a low of 550 in 1958 to a high of 2100 in 1978.

In the case of price expectations the weights used are based on the firms' employment and net output, and closely match the weights used in the construction of the indices of the Wholesale Prices of Manufactured Goods published monthly by the Central Statistical Office (CSO).

The questions regarding selling prices were asked in the following manner:

> Excluding seasonal variations, what has been the trend over the PAST FOUR MONTHS and what are the expected trends for the NEXT FOUR MONTHS ...

The survey results are in the form of qualitative responses giving the expected direction of changes classified into four categories: 'up', 'stay the same', 'down', and 'N/A'. The percentages of firms falling in these categories (for realizations and expectations) over the period 1958–85 are given in table A.1 in the data appendix. In the computations that follow, the 'N/A' category is ignored, and the other three categories are adjusted to sum to 100. This is equivalent to assuming 'N/A' responses are distributed independently of the other responses.[15] The data on the actual rate of change of manufacturing prices Π_t are given in table A.2. In computing Π_t, especial care has been taken to ensure that the rates of change of prices measured by official statistics correspond to the respondents' time span of their own price changes (see the data appendix for more details).

8.4.1 Measurements Based on the Probability Approach

In this approach the exact formula for converting qualitative expectations data to quantitative measurements depends on the choice of the 'aggregate' distribution $h(\Pi_{t+1} | \Omega_t)$. We computed the unscaled measures, ${}_td^e_{t+1}$, for the uniform, normal and logistic distributions, using the conversion formulae already derived in examples 8.1 to 8.3 respectively.[16] To scale these measures two different approaches have been suggested in the literature. One by Carlson and Parkin (1975), involves scaling ${}_tB^e_{t+1}$ or ${}_td^e_{t+1}$ by imposing the unbiasedness condition on the expectations series. This leads to the estimate $\hat{c}$ given in (8.21). However, as was pointed out earlier, this is not satisfactory. The other procedure (which is available in the case of the CBI data, but not in the case of surveys such as the Gallup Poll where respondents are asked only about their expectations) estimates the value of the response threshold by relating the official statistics (in our example, inflation in the manufacturing sector as measured by Π_t) to the test variates, R_t and F_t that are based on realizations reported in the survey. This procedure initially proposed by Bennett (1984), and used recently by Wren-Lewis (1986), is based on the

[15] There are, of course, other possible ways of dealing with the answers in the 'N/A' category. For example, see Carlson and Parkin (1975, p. 125). A critical analysis of Carlson and Parkin's treatment of the 'N/A' category can be found in Visco (1984b, pp. 30–2).

[16] The computations reported below refer to the uniform distribution with a variable range. The results for the uniform distribution with a fixed range were, as to be expected, not satisfactory and will not be reported.

assumption that the same aggregate distribution function, $h_t(\cdot)$, and the indifference interval, $(-c, c)$, can be used for conversion of qualitative responses irrespective of whether they refer to expectations or realizations. These are admittedly rather strong assumptions, but allow us to estimate c without having to impose unbiasedness, or other restrictions that presuppose a degree of rationality in expectations. Under these assumptions we have

$$\Pi_t = cd_t, \tag{8.34}$$

where d_t is now computed from realizations and is given by

$$d_t = (R_t - F_t)/(1 - R_t - F_t), \tag{8.35a}$$

for the case of the uniform distribution (with variable range), and by

$$d_t = \frac{f_t + r_t}{f_t - r_t}, \tag{8.35b}$$

for the normal and logistic distributions. In the case of the normal distribution f_t and r_t are determined by $\Phi(f_t) = F_t$, and $\Phi(r_t) = 1 - R_t$; and for the logistic distribution they are given by $f_t = \log(F_t^{-1} - 1)$, and $r_t = -\log(R_t^{-1} - 1)$. There are three possible ways of estimating c:

1 regression of Π_t on d_t;
2 the reverse regression of d_t on Π_t;
3 the ratio of means, namely $\bar{\Pi}/\bar{d}$.[17]

Since d_t is more likely to be subject to measurement errors than Π_t, procedures (2) and (3) are preferable to (1). Alternative estimates of the scaling parameters, c, for the CBI inflation expectations data computed over the period 1959(1)–1985(2) are given in table 8.1. The results indicate a certain degree of downward bias in the estimates obtained by the Carlson and Parkin method which imposes the unbiasedness condition on the expectations. Given the measurement error problem, a consistent estimate of c is likely to fall between the estimates obtained from the regression of Π on d and the reverse regression of d on Π. The Carlson and Parkin method of estimating c yields estimates inside the consistent range only in the case of the uniform distribution. For the normal and logistic distributions it is the estimates of c based on the ratio of means that fall inside the consistent range. In view of this it was decided to use the estimates based on the ratio of means (see the third row of table 8.1) for scaling the inflation expectations series. The results are summarized in table A.2. Graphical displays of these expectations series in relation to the actual rate of inflation are given in figures 8.3 to 8.5. A detailed comparison of these measures will be attempted below.

8.4.2 Measurements Based on the Regression Method

This method has already been demonstrated in Pesaran (1984b), using the CBI data over the period 1959(1)–1981(4). Here the procedure will be

[17] $\bar{\Pi}$ and $\bar{d}$ represent the time-averages of Π_t and d_t respectively.

Table 8.1 Alternative estimates of the scaling parameter used in the quantification of inflation expectations, 1959(1)–1985(2)

Estimation procedure	Choice of the probability distribution		
	Uniform	Normal	Logistic
Regression of Π on d	2.78	0.0371	0.0386
Regression of d on Π	3.13	0.0413	0.0435
Ratio of means $(\bar{\Pi}/\bar{d})$	3.39	0.0395	0.0405
Carlson and Parkin method[a]	2.95	0.0352	0.0362

[a] The estimates in this row are computed assuming that expectations are unbiased.
Source: tables A.1 and A.2, data appendix.

reviewed in the light of additional data which have since become available. Starting with Anderson's specification we first estimated (8.26) by the ordinary least squares (OLS) method over the extended period 1959(1)–1985(2). We obtained the following results:[18]

$$\Pi_t = \underset{(23.77)}{8.61} R_t - \underset{(-2.87)}{4.47} F_t + \hat{v}_t, \tag{8.36}$$

$$LL = -155.70, \quad \bar{R}^2 = 0.7225, \quad DW = 0.8083, \quad \hat{\sigma} = 1.30, \quad n = 93,$$
$$\chi^2_{SC}(1) = 32.74, \quad \chi^2_{FF}(2) = 38.19, \quad \chi^2_N(2) = 40.98, \quad \chi^2_H(1) = 15.72.$$

The figures in parentheses are ratios of estimated parameters to their (asymptotic) standard errors. LL is the maximized log-likelihood value, $\bar{R}$ is the adjusted multiple correlation coefficient, DW is the Durbin-Watson statistic, $\hat{\sigma}$ is the estimated standard error of the disturbances, v_t, n is the total number of observations, and χ^2_{SC}, χ^2_{FF}, χ^2_N, χ^2_H are diagnostic statistics asymptotically distributed as chi-squared variables (degrees of freedom in parentheses) for testing mis-specifications arising from residual serial correlation, functional form, non-normal errors, and heteroscedasticity, respectively.[19] This is not, clearly, a satisfactory result. Although the parameter estimates ($\hat{\alpha} = 8.61$, and $\hat{\beta} = -4.47$) have the correct signs and are statistically significant, the estimated equation is nevertheless rejected on the basis of all the four mis-specification tests. Moreover, the maximum (4-monthly) rate of inflation that can be predicted using (8.36) is equal to 8.61 per cent, which

[18] The parameter estimates reported in this section, are computed measuring R_t and F_t in fractions and Π_t in percentages. Notice also that the CBI data are available only three times a year over the period 1959–71.

[19] The regressions and test statistics are computed on the Data-FIT package. For details of relevant computer algorithms see Pesaran and Pesaran (1987).

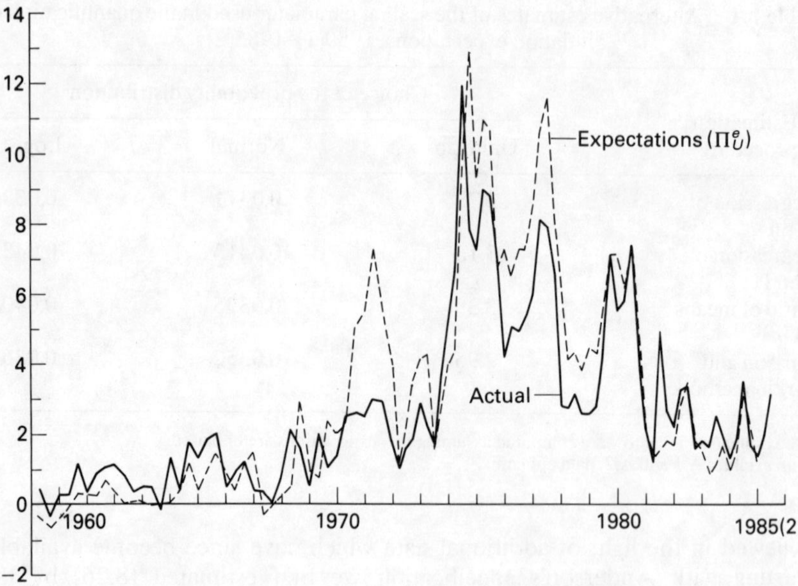

Figure 8.3 Actual and expected rates of inflation in British manufacturing (expectations quantified using a uniform distribution)

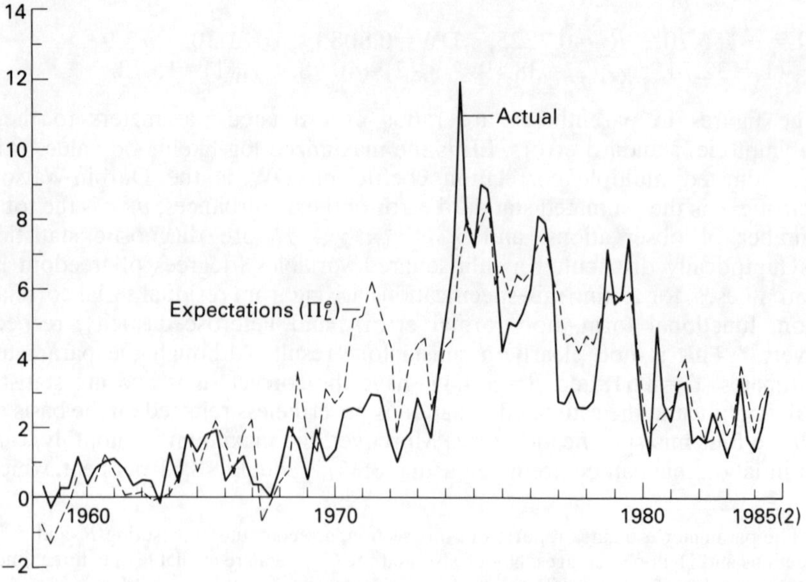

Figure 8.4 Actual and expected rates of inflation in British manufacturing (expectations quantified using a logistic distribution)

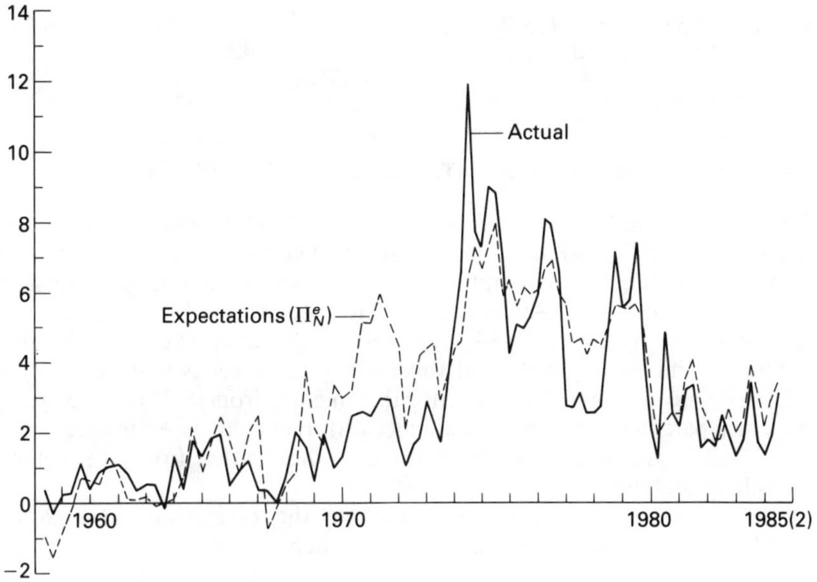

Figure 8.5 Actual and expected rates of inflation in British manufacturing (expectations quantified using a normal distribution)

is substantially below the maximum rate of 11.94 per cent observed over the sample period. These results confirm the earlier findings in Pesaran (1984b), obtained for the period 1959(1)–1981(4), and show that the addition of 14 new observations (i.e. from 1982(1) to 1985(2)) to the original data set has made little difference to the results. A linear specification such as (8.36) does not appear to be capable of capturing the asymmetry which seems to exist in the response of prices of individual firms showing a price rise and a price fall, to the overall rate of inflation. The non-linear specifications (8.29) and (8.31) that allow for such an asymmetrical response are more suitable. Estimation of these relations by the ML method over the whole sample period 1959(1)–1985(2) yielded the following results:[20]

$$\Pi_t = \frac{\underset{(23.16)}{4.12}R_t}{1 - \underset{(5.01)}{0.82}R_t} + \hat{u}_t, \tag{8.37a}$$

$$\hat{u}_t = \underset{(4.41)}{0.416}\hat{u}_{t-1} + \hat{\varepsilon}_t, \tag{8.37b}$$

LL $= -123.42$, $\bar{R}^2 = 0.8632$, DW $= 2.13$, $\hat{\sigma} = 0.9162$, $n = 93$,

[20] The parameter β in (8.29) and (8.31) turned out to be statistically insignificant.

and

$$(1-0.85R_t)\Pi_t = 3.915R_t + \hat{v}_t, \qquad (8.38a)$$
$$\quad (7.16) \qquad (14.99)$$

$$\hat{v}_t = 0.32\hat{v}_{t-1} + 0.25\hat{v}_{t-2} + \hat{\eta}_t, \qquad (8.38b)$$
$$\quad (3.21) \qquad (2.50)$$

$$\mathrm{LL} = -109.30, \quad \bar{R}^2 = 0.8990; \quad \mathrm{DW} = 2.11, \quad \hat{\sigma} = 0.7872, \quad n = 93.$$

The values reported for LL, $\bar{R}^2$, and $\hat{\sigma}$, in the case of both regressions refer to the inflation rate Π_t, and not to the transformed variable $(1-0.85R_t)\Pi_t$. As a result they are directly comparable. Both of the above non-linear regressions are clearly preferable to Anderson's simple specification (8.36). As far as a choice between (8.37) and (8.38) is concerned, the latter gives a much better fit. The maximized log likelihood value for (8.38) exceeds that of (8.37) by 14.12, which is substantial, considering that in going from (8.37) to (8.38) only one extra parameter has been estimated. Moreover, it is easily seen that, unlike (8.37), the specification (8.38) does not suffer from the heteroscedasticity problem.[21]

Using (8.38) as our 'preferred' relation, the conversion formula for quantification of survey results can now be written as

$${}_t\Pi^e_{t+1} = \frac{3.92\,{}_tR^e_{t+1} + 0.32\hat{v}_t + 0.25\hat{v}_{t-1}}{1-0.85\,{}_tR^e_{t+1}}, \qquad (8.39)$$

where

$$\hat{v}_{t-i} = (1-0.85R_{t-i})\Pi_{t-i} - 3.92R_{t-i}, \quad i = 0, 1.$$

We shall refer to the above measure of inflation expectations as the regression measure, and denote it by ${}_t\Pi^e_{t+1,R}$, to distinguish it from the other inflation expectations measures ${}_t\Pi^e_{t+1,U}$, ${}_t\Pi^e_{t+1,N}$ and ${}_t\Pi^e_{t+1,L}$ based on the uniform, normal, and logistic distributions, respectively. All these four measures, computed over the period 1959(1)–1985(2), are given in table A.2 in the data appendix. Correlation coefficients and other summary statistics for these measures are given in table 8.2.

It is clear that all the four measures are closely related to one another, and all have a high degree of correlation with the actual rate of inflation. Nevertheless they all tend to over-estimate the inflation rate, and show less variability than the actual rate of inflation. Of the four measures, the regression-based measure Π^e_{tR} follows the actual rate of inflation most closely, while the measure based on the logistic distribution, Π^e_{tL}, has the lowest correlation with Π_t (see table 8.2 and figures 8.3–8.6). There is little to choose between the expectations measures based on the normal and the logistic distributions, although in periods of high inflation Π^e_{tN} tends to be more sensitive to changes

[21] Both non-linear specifications yield maximum rates of inflation that are well above the actual rate of inflation observed in the sample.

Table 8.2 Correlation coefficients and other summary statistics for alternative measures of inflation expectations

	Π^e_{tU}	Π^e_{tN}	Π^e_{tL}	Π^e_{tR}	Π_t
Π^e_{tU}	1.00				
Π^e_{tN}	0.9628	1.00			
Π^e_{tL}	0.9403	0.9971	1.00		
Π^e_{tR}	0.9746	0.9571	0.9401	1.00	
Π_t	0.8986	0.8558	0.8338	0.9044	1.00
Means	3.27	3.19	3.18	3.11	2.85
Standard deviations	3.22	2.41	2.26	2.45	2.48

Source: table A.2, data appendix.

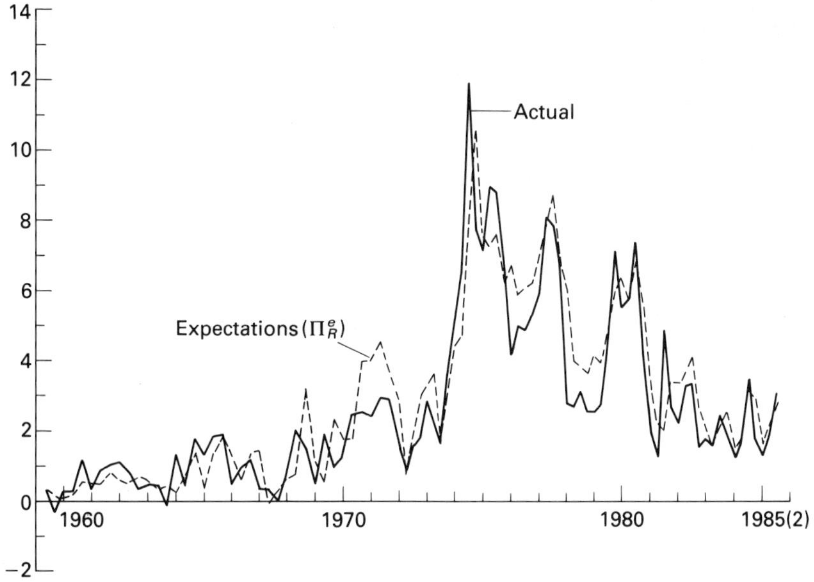

Figure 8.6 Actual and expected rates of inflation in British manufacturing (expectations quantified by the regression method)

in the test variates ${}_tR^e_{t+1}$ and ${}_tF^e_{t+1}$, and is therefore preferable to Π^e_{tL} (see figure 8.7). It is, however, difficult to choose between Π^e_{tU}, Π^e_{tN}, and Π^e_{tR}. In the remainder of this chapter attention is focused on Π^e_{tN} and Π^e_{tR} as alternative measures of inflation expectations in the British manufacturing industries.

Despite the differences that exist in the method of constructing Π^e_{tN} and Π^e_{tR}, these two series have a number of features in common, and for the most

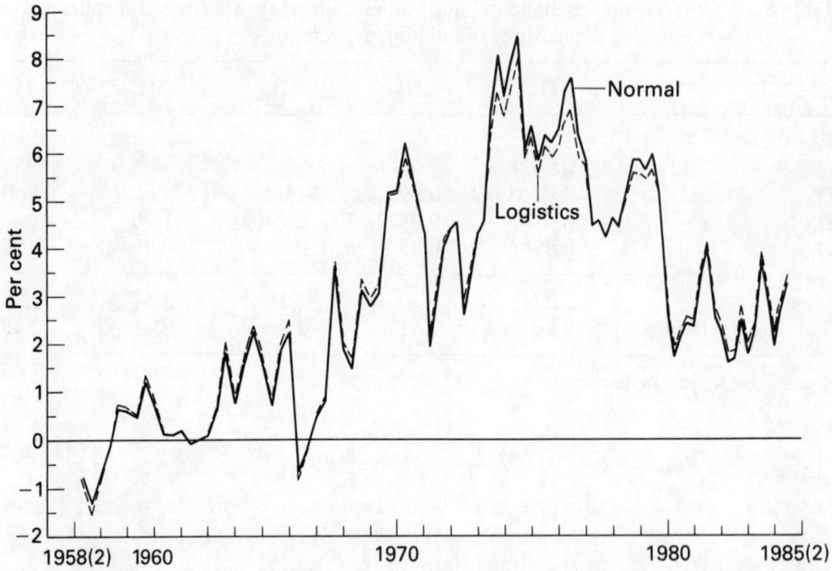

Figure 8.7 Inflation expectations based on normal and logistic distributions

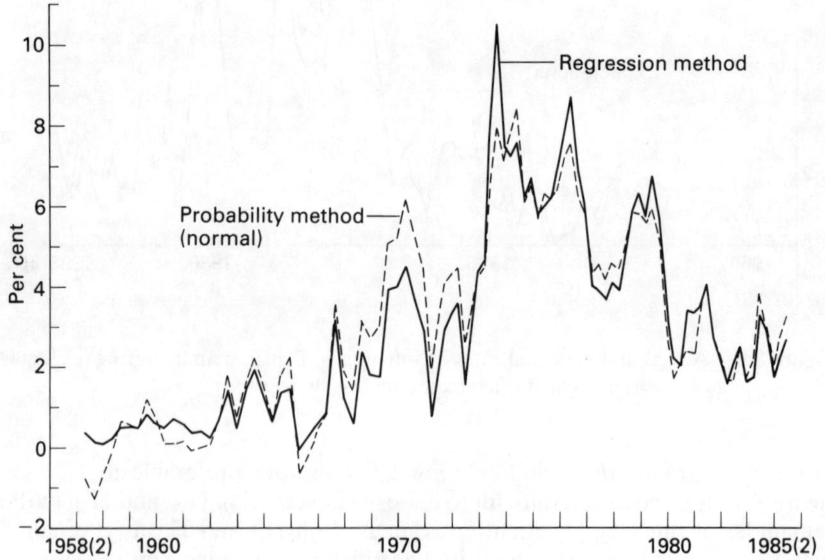

Figure 8.8 Alternative measures of inflation expectations based on the probability and the regression approaches

part of the period follow one another quite closely (see figure 8.8). They both show greater variations over the high-inflation period 1971–81, and hence provide some support for the hypothesis of a close positive relationship between the variability and the level of inflation expectations. They both tend to over-predict the inflation rate when it is falling. However, the two series exhibit different patterns of serial correlation. The inflation expectations measure based on the regression method provides a much better forecast of the actual rate of inflation than the measure based on the probability method. The root-mean-squared forecast error of the Π^e_{tR} series is equal to 1.105 as compared to a figure of 1.352 for the Π^e_{tN} series. In fact the Π^e_{tR} series also conclusively outperform univariate Box-Jenkins forecasts of Π_t. Over the period 1959(1)–1985(2) the best fitting univariate model for the actual rate of inflation turned out to be

$$\underset{}{\hat{\Pi}_t = \underset{(2.33)}{0.4923} + \underset{(14.85)}{0.8363}\Pi_{t-1},}$$

$$\bar{R}^2 = 0.7047, \quad \text{DW} = 2.04, \quad \hat{\sigma} = 1.346, \quad n = 93.$$

Using the naive inflation forecast $\hat{\Pi}_t$ in combination with the expectations series Π^e_{tR} it is now easy to show that the latter is 'conditionally efficient' with respect to the former in the sense defined by Granger and Newbold (1973). Following the procedure proposed by Nelson (1972), we obtained

$$\Pi_t = \underset{(0.05)}{0.009} + \underset{(7.37)}{0.931}\Pi^e_{tR} - \underset{(-0.147)}{0.022}\hat{\Pi}_t + \text{Error},$$

$$\bar{R}^2 = 0.8139, \quad \text{DW} = 1.75, \quad \hat{\sigma} = 1.069, \quad n = 93, \quad 1959(1)\text{–}1985(2),$$

which supports the conditional efficiency of Π^e_{tR} with respect to univariate Box–Jenkins forecasts. The same is not, however, true of the expectations series Π^e_{tN}. These results continue to hold even if necessary allowance is made for the loss in the degree of freedom involved in the process of quantification of the survey data. The superior one-step-ahead forecasting performance of the Π^e_{tR} series should not, however, be taken to mean that it is necessarily a more accurate measure of inflation expectations. In our empirical investigations we employ both measures. This enables us to see how robust (or sensitive) the results are to the particular method chosen for the conversion of the qualitative survey data into quantitative measures.[22]

8.5 Measurement Errors in Expectations

Before the inflation expectations series Π^e_{tR} or Π^e_{tN} can be employed in direct tests of the REH, or in other empirical studies involving expectations, special attention should be paid to the fact that these series are not perfect measures

---

[22] The above results also provide further support for the findings in Pesaran (1985), and establish that the results arrived at on the basis of data from period 1959–81 remain valid for the extended period, 1959–85.

of the 'true' inflation expectations, Π_t^*, and are likely to be subject to errors of measurement. These errors can arise out of incorrect scaling of the qualitative data, or can be due to the general uncertainty attached to quantitative measurement of expectations, not to mention errors of sampling and aggregation. Furthermore, since Π_{tR}^e and Π_{tN}^e are partly obtained by means of regressions involving past observations on the actual rate of inflation, their use as regressands and regressors in expectations formation models will be subject to the 'generator regressor' problem highlighted by Pagan (1984). In order to deal with some of these problems we treat the inflation expectation series Π_{tR}^e and Π_{tN}^e as given data, but explicitly recognize that they may be subject to errors of measurement. Although this approach does not satisfactorily deal with the errors of sampling associated with the generation of Π_{tR}^e and Π_N^e from first-stage regressions, it does nevertheless focus on other important sources of errors in the measurement of inflation expectations from survey data.

The existence of measurement errors in directly observed expectations series has been acknowledged in the literature (see, for example, Carlson and Parkin, 1975, p. 133; Lahiri, 1981; and Visco, 1984b, pp. 212–14).[23] Lahiri (1981) considers the problem of measurement errors when directly observed expectations are used as *exogenous* regressors in a simultaneous equation model. But so far no serious attempt has been made to explore the econometric consequences of the measurement errors in directly observed expectations series for the estimation and testing of expectations formation models. Consider the following linear 'measurement' models

$$\Pi_{tj}^e = \alpha_j + \beta_j \Pi_t^* + \varepsilon_{tj}, \quad j = N, R, \quad t = 1, 2, \ldots, n, \tag{8.40}$$

where ε_{tj} are the random components of the measurement errors in Π_{tj}^e. The parameters α_j and β_j are intended to capture the systematic components. When errors due to scaling are negligible we should have $\alpha_j = 0$, and $\beta_j = 1$. It will be assumed that the random components, ε_{tj}, are distributed independently of Π_t^* with zero means and constant variances τ_j^2, but unlike the classical errors-in-variables model (EVM) we do not rule out the possibility of serial correlation in ε_{tj}. However, we assume that by comparison to the proxy measures of Π_t^*, observations on the past realizations of variables such as the inflation rate, the rate of change of raw material prices, the rate of change of manufacturing output, and exchange rates are all free from serious errors of measurement. This does not seem to be an unduly restrictive assumption and will be needed at the estimation stage. The implications of measurement errors in Π_{tN}^e and Π_{tR}^e, for testing the REH, and for the estimation of expectations formation models, will be discussed later in this and the next chapter.

---

[23] The errors involved in the measurement of expectations from qualitative responses also have been investigated by Defris and Williams (1981), Batchelor (1986b), and Batchelor and Dua (1987) in the case of surveys that report comparative data on quantitative and qualitative expectations. These studies are, however, based on the strong assumption that quantitative responses measure expectations accurately (see section 8.2).

Table 8.3[a] Least Squares and Instrumental Variable estimates of the direct and the reverse regressions of Π^e_{tN} on Π^e_{tR}, 1959(1)–1985(2)

	OLS estimates		IV estimates[b]	
Regressors	Π^e_{tN}	Π^e_{tR}	Π^e_{tN}	Π^e_{tR}
Intercept	0.2701	−0.0022	0.3931	−0.3742
	[0.1178]	[0.1235]	[0.1212]	[0.1423]
Π^e_{tN}	—	0.9751	—	1.0862
		[0.0309]		[0.0368]
Π^e_{tR}	0.9395	—	0.9052	—
	[0.0298]		[0.0310]	
DW	0.46	0.48	0.46	0.47
$\hat{\sigma}$	0.701	0.714	0.692	0.748
$\bar{R}^2$	0.915	0.915	0.916	0.907
$\chi^2_{SC}(1)$	51.99	52.02	48.89	45.02
$\chi^2_{FF}(2)$	32.84	27.24	22.05	20.50
$\chi^2_{N}(2)$	0.98	11.29	0.28	0.57
$\chi^2_{H}(1)$	6.54	12.93	3.27	5.80

[a] The figures in square brackets are asymptotic standard errors. DW is the Durbin-Watson statistic, $\hat{\sigma}$ is the estimated standard error of the regression and $\bar{R}$ is the adjusted multiple correlation coefficient. $\chi^2_{SC}(1)$, $\chi^2_{FF}(2)$, $\chi^2_{N}(2)$ and $\chi^2_{H}(1)$, are diagnostic statistics distributed as chi-squared variates (with degrees of freedom in parentheses) for tests of residual serial correlation, functional form misspecification, non-normal errors, and heteroscedasticity, respectively. The details of the computations and algorithms can be found in Pesaran and Pesaran (1987).

[b] The IV estimates are computed using $(1, \Pi_{t-1}, \Pi_{t-2}, \Pi_{t-3}, f_{t-1}, f_{t-2}, f_{t-3}, q_{t-1} q_{t-2}, q_{t-3}, e_{t-1}, e_{t-2},$ and $e_{t-3})$ as instruments.

Source: table A.2, data appendix.

Here we utilize the two measures of Π^*_t, namely Π^e_{tN} and Π^e_{tR} to shed some light on the nature of the measurement errors involved.

Eliminating the unobservable Π^*_t from the two relations in (8.40) yields

$$\beta_R \Pi^e_{tN} - \beta_N \Pi^e_{tR} = (\beta_R \alpha_N - \beta_N \alpha_R) + \beta_R \varepsilon_{tN} - \beta_N \varepsilon_{tR}. \qquad (8.41)$$

An estimate of β_N/β_R can now be obtained either from the direct regression of Π^e_{tN} on Π^e_{tR}, or from the reverse regression of Π^e_{tR} on Π^e_{tN}. Although because of the correlation that exists between Π^e_{tj} and ε_{tj}, neither of these estimates will be consistent, they together place a 'consistent bound' on the unknown ratio β_N/β_R.[24] The OLS estimates of the direct and the reverse regressions of Π^e_{tN} on Π^e_{tR} are summarized in table 8.3. These results firstly show that the consistent bound for β_N/β_R is given by the interval 0.940–1.026. This interval just covers $\beta_N/\beta_R=1$. From the OLS results it is not, however, possible to say definitely whether the two series differ in the way they are scaled. The results

[24] This result was originally demonstrated by Frisch (1934), and has been recently extended to the case of general multivariate linear regressions by Klepper and Leamer (1984).

in table 8.3 also indicate that the measurement errors in one or both of the inflation expectations series are serially correlated. To check the validity of these inferences we also estimated the two regressions by the generalized instrumental variable (IV) method due to Sargan (1958). As the set of instruments, in addition to past rates of change of manufacturing prices, we used the quarterly changes in raw material and fuel prices (f_t), manufacturing output (q_t), and Sterling's effective exchange rate (e_t).[25] More specifically we obtained the estimates given in the last two columns of table 8.2, using $\mathbf{z}_t = (1, \Pi_{t-1}, \Pi_{t-2}, \Pi_{t-3}, f_{t-1}, f_{t-2}, f_{t-3}, q_{t-1}, q_{t-2}, q_{t-3}, e_{t-1}, e_{t-2}, e_{t-3})'$, as the instrumental variables. These instruments were chosen in the belief that they are important determinants of Π_t^*, and are unlikely to be correlated with the random errors in the measurement of inflation expectations. The IV results clearly confirm our earlier findings. The ratio β_N/β_R is now estimated to be 0.905, if we consider the regression of Π_{tN} on Π_{tR}, and it turns out to be equal to 0.921 ($=1/1.086$), if the reverse regression is employed. The two estimates are very close to one another and are both significantly different from unity. This suggests that the two series differ in the way they are scaled, but only marginally. The IV results also confirm that the residuals from both regressions are subject to a high degree of serial correlation. This last result is particularly important in testing the REH and for the efficient estimation of models that use the expectations series Π_{tN}^e or Π_{tR}^e.

8.6 Direct Tests of the Rationality of Inflation Expectations

We are now in a position to examine the Muth-rationality of the observed inflation expectations series. Although the aggregate nature of the expectations series Π_{tN}^e and Π_{tR}^e may, as stressed by Nerlove (1983), preclude a satisfactory test of the rationality hypothesis; nevertheless, given the interest shown in this area by other investigators, tests of the 'rationality' hypothesis carried out on the series Π_{tN}^e and Π_{tR}^e may still be of some interest.

When direct observations on expectations exist, the various testable implications of the rational expectations hypothesis are usually classified under four broad headings and are referred to as tests of **unbiasedness, lack of serial correlation, efficiency**, and **orthogonality** (see chapter 2 for proofs and further details). The first two of these tests can be carried out unambiguously only if expectations are measured without systematic and/or random errors. In view of the results discussed in the previous section there seems to be little point in testing the expectations series Π_{tN}^e and Π_{tR}^e for bias or serial correlation, considering that they will most likely suffer from the measurement error problem. The efficiency test is concerned with the efficient use of the information contained only in the history of past price changes, and is a special case of the orthogonality test that requires the expectations errors to be orthogonal to

[25] For the definition of variables and sources of data see data appendix.

the costless information available at the time expectations are formed.[26] Here we confine our attention to the orthogonality test which seems to us to be the most comprehensive test of the rationality hypothesis.

A major consideration in the application of the orthogonality test to direct observations on expectations is the *a priori* identification of the information set which is available to economic agents (firms in our example) at the time they are forming their expectations. In the case of individual agents this is not, at least in principle, a serious problem. However, when expectations data refer to the 'average' of expectations across firms or households, special care should be taken in the choice of variables to be used in the orthogonality tests. While past information on individual-specific factors (such as individuals' past expectations) can be utilized legitimately in testing the rationality hypothesis at the individual level, the use of such private information (or their aggregates) in testing the rationality hypothesis at the aggregate level is not justifiable.

The above point, which has direct bearing on most tests of the rationality hypothesis carried out in the literature, can be readily demonstrated in the case of the CBI inflation expectations data. Consider the following equation

$$\Pi_{it} - \Pi_{it}^{*} = c_i + \boldsymbol{\theta}_i'\mathbf{h}_{t-1} + \boldsymbol{\delta}_i'\mathbf{x}_{i,t-1} + \xi_{it}, \tag{8.42}$$

where as before Π_{it} represents the actual rate of price changes of the ith firm, and Π_{it}^{*} the 'true', but unobserved, expectations of Π_{it} formed at time $t-1$ by the ith firm. The vector $\mathbf{x}_{i,t-1}$ stands for the information on firm specific variables (e.g. Π_{it}^{*}) known only to firm i at time $t-1$, and $\mathbf{h}_{t-1}$ the commonly available information. Under the REH, applied to the ith firm, we have

$$H_R^i\colon \quad c_i = 0, \quad \boldsymbol{\theta}_i = 0, \quad \boldsymbol{\delta}_i = 0, \tag{8.43}$$

with the disturbances ξ_{it} being orthogonal to the information available to the firm i (but not to the private information of other firms) at time $t-1$. In situations where observations on Π_{it}^{*} are not made at intervals that are finer than the expectations' horizon, the disturbances ξ_{it} will also be serially uncorrelated if the REH holds.[27]

In the absence of direct quantitative observations for Π_{it}^{*} (or for $\mathbf{x}_{i,t-1}$), one possibility would be to test the implications of the rationality hypothesis, H_R^i, $i = 1, 2, \ldots, N$, at the aggregate level. Applying the aggregation rule (8.3) to (8.42) we obtain

$$\Pi_t - \Pi_t^{*} = c + \boldsymbol{\theta}'\mathbf{h}_{t-1} + X_{t-1} + \xi_t, \tag{8.44}$$

---

[26] Strictly speaking, according to the REH, agents would utilize all available information to the point where the marginal cost and the expected marginal benefit of information are equalized. In this sense the orthogonality test involving costlessly available information is a relatively weak test, as it ignores the use of costly, but beneficial information.

[27] The possibility of serial correlation in errors of rationally formed expectations in the case of overlapping forecast horizons was first pointed out by Brown and Maital (1981). The same kind of problem arises in testing the efficiency of forward exchange markets already discussed in detail in section 7.6. In the case of the CBI data the problem arises only for the post-1971 period where expectations are sampled every quarter, and as a result the expectations horizon exceeds the observations interval by 1 month. This, in principle, can introduce some serial correlation in ξ_{it} even if the REH is valid.

where Π_t^* stands for the 'average' inflation expectations, and

$$c = \sum_{i=1}^{N} w_i c_i, \quad \boldsymbol{\theta} = \sum_{i=1}^{N} w_i \boldsymbol{\theta}_i,$$

$$X_{t-1} = \sum_{i=1}^{N} w_i \delta_i' \mathbf{x}_{i,t-1}, \quad \xi_t = \sum_{i=1}^{N} w_i \xi_{it}.$$

The rationality of expectations at the firm level (that is under H_R^i) now has the following implications for the aggregate equation (8.44):

(i) $\bar{H}_R$: $c=0, \boldsymbol{\theta}=0$,

(ii) $E(\xi_t|\mathbf{h}_{t-1}) = \sum_{i=1}^{N} w_i E(\xi_{it}|\mathbf{h}_{t-1}) = 0.$

But ξ_t need not be orthogonal to X_{t-1}:[28]

(iii) $E(\xi_t|X_{t-1}) = \sum_{i=1}^{N} w_i E(\xi_{it}|X_{t-1}) \neq 0.$

In addition, the aggregate disturbances will also be serially uncorrelated if the expectations horizon does not exceed the observations interval. It is then clear that the aggregate equation (8.44) satisfies all the properties predicted by the REH at the firm level except when the information involved refers to private or firm specific variables, such as $\mathbf{x}_{i,t-1}$. The REH can nevertheless be tested using the aggregate equation (8.44), if it is assumed that the processes generating the private information $\mathbf{x}_{it}$, and the public information $\mathbf{h}_t$ are independently distributed, and that $\mathbf{x}_{it}$ have constant means, $\boldsymbol{\mu}_{ix}$. Under these assumptions (8.44) can be written as

$$\Pi_t - \Pi_t^* = \mu + \boldsymbol{\theta}'\mathbf{h}_{t-1} + v_t, \tag{8.45}$$

where

$$\mu = c + \sum_{i=1}^{N} w_i \boldsymbol{\delta}_i' \boldsymbol{\mu}_{ix},$$

and

$$v_t = \xi_t + \sum_{i=1}^{N} w_i \boldsymbol{\delta}_i'(\mathbf{x}_{i,t-1} - \boldsymbol{\mu}_{ix}).$$

Under the REH and the above assumptions concerning the private and the public information of agents, these new disturbances satisfy the orthogonality

[28] Notice that since $x_{j,t-1}$ is not in the information set of the ith firm $(i \neq j)$, then $E(\xi_{it}|X_{t-1})$ need not be equal to zero even if the REH holds at the level of individual firms.

property

$$E(v_t|\mathbf{h}_{t-1})=0.$$

A test of the REH can now be carried out by testing $\bar{H}_R$: $\mu=0$, $\boldsymbol{\theta}=0$, in the aggregate equation (8.45).[29] Notice also that under the REH, v_t in (8.45) will be serially uncorrelated if the expectations horizon does not exceed the observations interval. In short, if the processes generating the private and the public information are distributed independently, it would be possible, in principle, to test some of the implications of the rationality hypothesis at the individual level by means of the aggregative data. The validity of such an aggregative approach, however, crucially depends on the appropriate choice of the variables $\mathbf{h}_t$ representing the public information, and the reliability of the available direct observations on expectations as measures of Π_t^*.

In the context of the manufacturing sector as a whole, it seems reasonable to assume that when forming their expectations, firms at least know the past rates of price changes and output in the manufacturing sector, and can readily obtain information on economy-wide aggregates such as the money supply growth, the effective exchange rate, and the rate of unemployment.[30] In the orthogonality tests to be reported below we chose $\mathbf{h}_t=(\Pi_t, f_t, q_t, e_t, \text{RU}_{t-1}, m_{t-1})$, where the rate of growth of money supply (m_t), and the unemployment rate (RU_t) are included in the information set with a one-quarter lag to allow for the delay in the publication of the official statistics.

Another important consideration in carrying out the orthogonality test concerns the computation of the test statistic. Although a consistent estimate of $\boldsymbol{\gamma}=(\mu, \boldsymbol{\theta}')$ in (8.45) can be readily obtained by the OLS regression of $\Pi_t-\Pi_t^*$ on $\mathbf{g}_t=(1, \mathbf{h}_{t-1}')'$, the computation of the standard errors of the OLS estimators of μ and $\boldsymbol{\theta}$ by the standard OLS formula will not be valid, and can result in incorrect inferences. This is because, even under the REH, the disturbances ξ_t can still exhibit heteroscedasticity, and in general need not be independent of $\mathbf{h}_{t'-1}$, for $t'<t$. Denoting the OLS estimates of $\boldsymbol{\gamma}$ by $\hat{\boldsymbol{\gamma}}_{\text{OLS}}$, then under the REH we have:[31]

$$\sqrt{n}\hat{\boldsymbol{\gamma}}_{\text{OLS}}=\left(\sum_{t=1}^{n}\mathbf{g}_t\mathbf{g}_t'/n\right)^{-1}\left(\sum_{t=1}^{n}\mathbf{g}_t\xi_t/\sqrt{n}\right)\overset{a}{\sim}\Sigma_{gg}^{-1}\left(\sum_{t=1}^{n}\mathbf{g}_t\xi_t/\sqrt{n}\right),$$

where $\Sigma_{gg}=E(\Sigma_{t=1}^{n}\mathbf{g}_t\mathbf{g}_t'/n)$. It is now easily seen that under the usual regularity conditions on $\mathbf{g}_t$ and ξ_t,

$$\sqrt{n}\hat{\boldsymbol{\gamma}}_{\text{OLS}}\overset{a}{\sim}N(0, \Sigma_{gg}^{-1}\Phi\Sigma_{gg}^{-1}), \tag{8.46}$$

---

[29] Recall that under (8.43), $\mu=0$.

[30] Contrary to what is often practised in the literature, the inclusion of Π_t^* in (8.45), as an element of $\mathbf{h}_{t-1}$, is not legitimate when testing the orthogonality hypothesis at the aggregate level. This is because, even if the REH holds at the disaggregate level, Π_t^* being the weighted average of expectations of individual firms, need not be orthogonal to ξ_t (or v_t). Only when the orthogonality hypothesis is tested at the disaggregate level is it valid to include Π_{it}^* in the available information set of the agent at time $t-1$.

[31] Notice that under the REH at the disaggregate level (as defined in (8.43)), we have $v_t=\xi_t$.

where

$$\Phi = \lim_{n\to\infty} E\left(\sum_{t=1}^{n}\sum_{t'=1}^{n} \mathbf{g}_t \xi_t \xi_{t'} \mathbf{g}'_{t'}/n\right). \tag{8.47}$$

In general, it is clear that Φ need not be proportional to Σ_{gg}, and therefore the standard OLS formula for the covariance matrix of $\sqrt{n}\hat{\gamma}_{\text{OLS}}$ will not be valid. It is, however, possible to simplify (8.47) considerably by assuming that the fourth-order cumulants between elements of $\mathbf{g}_t$, $\mathbf{g}_{t'}$, ξ_t and $\xi_{t'}$ are zero. This condition is, for example, satisfied if, apart from deterministic components, $(\xi_t, \mathbf{g}_t)$ are jointly normally distributed. Under this assumption we have:[32]

$$E(\mathbf{g}_t \xi_t \xi_{t'} \mathbf{g}'_{t'}) = E(\mathbf{g}_t \xi_t) E(\xi_{t'} \mathbf{g}'_{t'}) + E(\mathbf{g}_t \xi_{t'}) E(\xi_t \mathbf{g}'_{t'}) + E(\xi_t \xi_{t'}) E(\mathbf{g}_t \mathbf{g}'_{t'}).$$

But under the REH,

$$E(\mathbf{g}_t \xi_t) = E(\xi_{t'} \mathbf{g}'_{t'}) = 0, \quad \text{for all } t \text{ and } t',$$
$$E(g_t \xi_{t'}) = 0, \quad \text{for } t \leqslant t',$$
$$E(\xi_t \mathbf{g}'_{t'}) = 0, \quad \text{for } t \geqslant t',$$

and assuming that the expectations horizon does not exceed the observations interval

$$E(\xi_t \xi_{t'}) = \begin{cases} 0, & \text{for } t \neq t', \\ \sigma_{tt}, & \text{for } t = t'. \end{cases}$$

Using these results in (8.47) now yields

$$\Phi = \sum_{t=1}^{n} \sigma_{tt} E(\mathbf{g}_t \mathbf{g}'_t/n),$$

which if substituted back in (8.46) gives the variance matrix that underlies White's (1980) heteroscedasticity-consistent covariance estimator. This result would, of course, have also followed under the much stronger assumption requiring the elements of $\mathbf{g}_t$ to be strongly exogenous with respect to ξ_t.

A valid test of the REH can now be based on the statistic

$$d = \hat{\gamma}_{\text{OLS}}(G'G)\hat{V}^{-1}(G'G)\hat{\gamma}_{\text{OLS}}, \tag{8.48}$$

where G denotes the $n \times (s+1)$ matrix of observations on $(1, \mathbf{h}_{t-1})$, and

$$\hat{V} = n^{-1} \sum_{t=1}^{n} \hat{\xi}_t^2 (\mathbf{g}_t \mathbf{g}'_t), \tag{8.49}$$

in which $\hat{\xi}_t = \Pi_t - \Pi_t^* - \hat{\mu}_{\text{OLS}} - \hat{\boldsymbol{\theta}}'_{\text{OLS}} \mathbf{h}_{t-1}$. Under the REH, and assuming that the expectations horizon does not exceed the observations interval, and that

[32] This result follows from the definition of the fourth-order cumulants. See, for example, Bartlett (1978, p. 302).

the fourth-order cumulants of $(\mathbf{g}_t, \mathbf{g}_{t'}, \xi_t, \xi_{t'})$ are zero, the statistic d in (8.48) will be asymptotically distributed as a chi-squared variate with $s+1$ degrees of freedom, where s stands for the number of elements in $\mathbf{h}_{t-1}$.

In applying the above test to directly observed expectations data, allowance should also be made for possible errors in the measurement of expectations. In the case of the CBI data, Π_t^* in (8.45) can be replaced by the expectations series Π_{tN}^e or Π_{tR}^e. For example, using Π_{tR}^e we have

$$\Pi_t - \beta_R^{-1}\Pi_{tR}^e = c_R + \boldsymbol{\theta}'\mathbf{h}_{t-1} + \eta_{tR}, \tag{8.50}$$

where

$$c_R = \mu - (\alpha_R/\beta_R),$$
$$\eta_{tR} = v_t - (\varepsilon_{tR}/\beta_R).$$

A similar result can also be obtained for Π_{tN}^e. Therefore, so long as the series Π_{tR}^e and Π_{tN}^e are not perfect measures of Π_t^*, the scope for testing the implications of the REH by means of the aggregate (observable) equation (8.50) may be rather limited. For example, when $\alpha_R \neq 0$, and the random measurement errors, ε_{tR}, are serially correlated, a non-zero value for c_R and the existence of serial correlation in the disturbances, η_{tR}, do not necessarily constitute a refutation of the REH. A test of $\boldsymbol{\theta} = 0$ based on (8.50) should therefore allow for an intercept term, and should also take account of the possible autocorrelation of the disturbances.[33] But before $\boldsymbol{\theta} = 0$ can be tested an estimate of β_R is needed. However, since both Π_{tR}^e and Π_t are correlated with η_{tR}, the OLS estimation of (8.50), whether by means of a regression of Π_t on Π_{tR}^e and $\mathbf{h}_{t-1}$ or by a regression of Π_{tR}^e on Π_t and $\mathbf{h}_{t-1}$, will not be valid.[34] The IV method cannot be applied either, because all the variables that are deemed to be suitable as instruments for Π_t or Π_{tR}^e are also likely candidates for inclusion in the information set $\mathbf{h}_{t-1}$. Future values of $\mathbf{h}_t$ cannot be used as instruments either, since under the REH, ξ_t and hence v_t need not be orthogonal to the future values of $\mathbf{h}_t$. Therefore, consistent estimation of the scaling parameters β_R or β_N does not seem to be possible, and a test of $\boldsymbol{\theta} = 0$ can be carried out only under *a priori* assumed values for β_R or β_N.

In the case of CBI inflation expectations data we carried out the orthogonality test under three alternative values of β_N and β_R, namely 0.9, 1.0 and 1.1. These are compatible with the values of 0.905 and 0.921 estimated for the ratio β_N/β_R in section 8.5. Below we only report the results for $\beta_R = 1.0$ and $\beta_N = 0.9$. In the case of the expectations series Π_{tR}^e, using the whole data set we obtained

$$\begin{aligned}\Pi_t - \Pi_{tR}^e = \underset{\{0.1600\}}{0.0079} - \underset{\{0.0527\}}{0.1682}\Pi_{t-1} + \underset{\{0.0311\}}{0.1750}f_{t-1} \\ + \underset{\{0.0403\}}{0.0803}e_{t-1} - \underset{\{0.0490\}}{0.0522}q_{t-1} - \underset{\{0.0224\}}{0.0272}\mathrm{RU}_{t-2},\end{aligned}$$

[33] Of course, as pointed out above, η_{tR} could be serially correlated even in the absence of serially correlated measurement errors.

[34] Notice that Π_t will be correlated with v_t, and Π_{tR}^e with ε_{tR}.

$\bar{R}^2 = 0.2902$, DW $= 1.67$, $\hat{\sigma} = 0.9081$, $n = 93$, 1959(1)–1985(2),
$\chi^2_{SC}(1) = 2.72$, $\chi^2_{FF}(2) = 1.95$, $\chi^2_N(2) = 1.23$, $\chi^2_H(1) = 0.24$,

where the figures in braces are White's (1980) heteroscedasticity consistent estimates of the standard errors of the OLS parameter estimates, adjusted for the degrees of freedom. It is clear from the above results that the coefficients of Π_{t-1}, f_{t-1} and e_{t-1} are all highly significant, and therefore do not support the rationality hypothesis. The value of the statistic d defined by (8.48) for the above regression is equal to 61.27 which is well above the one percent critical value of the χ^2 distribution with 6 degrees of freedom.

Similarly, for the expectations series Π^e_{tN} we obtained,

$$\Pi_t - 0.9\Pi^e_{tN} = \underset{\{0.2373\}}{-0.3136} + \underset{\{0.0498\}}{0.0079\Pi_{t-1}} + \underset{\{0.0483\}}{0.1817 f_{t-1}}$$

$$+ \underset{\{0.0472\}}{0.0932 e_{t-1}} - \underset{\{0.0560\}}{0.0268 q_{t-1}} - \underset{\{0.0254\}}{0.0171 \mathrm{RU}_{t-2}},$$

$\bar{R}^2 = 0.1976$, DW $= 1.07$, $\hat{\sigma} = 1.1488$, $n = 93$, 1959(1)–1985(2),
$\chi^2_{SC}(1) = 20.38$, $\chi^2_{FF}(2) = 8.84$, $\chi^2_N(2) = 3.36$, $\chi^2_H(1) = 1.38$.

This result again suggests rejection of the REH: the coefficients of f_{t-1} and e_{t-1} are highly significant, and the regression residuals exhibit a substantial degree of serial correlation. Whether the presence of residual autocorrelation should be taken as evidence against the REH depends on the nature of the errors involved in the measurement of Π^*_t by Π^e_{tN}. But even if residual autocorrelation in the above result is taken to be due entirely to measurement errors, the remaining evidence against the REH is still substantial.

In short, our results reject the REH and show that businessmen could have significantly improved the accuracy of their inflation expectations by a better understanding of the processes generating price changes and by a more 'efficient' use of the available information, especially with respect to past movements in fuel and raw material prices, and changes in the effective exchange rate.[35]

8.7 Concluding Remarks

This chapter has emphasized the importance of direct measurement of expectations for the study of the expectations formation process. The crucial issue here is the accuracy with which expectations can be measured. The approach advocated in this chapter is to start with qualitative data on individual expectations, which are relatively error-free, and then to convert these qualitative data into quantitative measures of 'aggregate' or 'average' expectations. The advantage of this approach lies in the fact that it provides

---

[35] We also obtained similar results for other periods. In the estimates for the period 1964(1)–1985(2) the rate of change of money supply (lagged two quarters) was also included, but was not found to be significant.

direct measurement of expectations that can be used as 'data' in empirical studies of the expectations formation process, as well as in the development of macroeconometric models. It is, however, important to recognize that the quantification of qualitative data, no matter whether it is carried out by the probability or the regression methods, will most likely be subject to the measurement error problem, and this should be taken into account in the econometric analysis. This chapter has suggested methods that can be used to shed light on the nature of the measurement errors involved and to allow for such errors when testing the REH. The next chapter will examine the implications of the measurement error problem for the modelling of expectations. In practice it is possible to reduce the possibility of errors in the measurement of expectations if surveys ask the respondents to provide *quantitative* information about the *past* (or realizations) and *qualitative* information about the *future* (or plans or expectations).[36] In this way the regression method for quantification of expectations can be based on concrete information at the level of individual firms or households, thus avoiding the need to rely on doubtful assumptions concerning the relationship between past changes in micro and macro variables under consideration.

Another important issue surrounding the use of quantitative expectations data in empirical analysis of expectations relates to the 'aggregative' nature of the expectations series. This is particularly important in testing the REH, where individual agents, and not some fictitious 'representative' agent, are the subject of the analysis.

This chapter has considered some of the problems involved in testing the REH and has set out the conditions under which the rationality hypothesis can be tested from aggregate data. One important consideration in this analysis is the identification of the relevant private and public information. At the aggregate level only publicly available information can be used in testing the orthogonality property of the expectations errors under the REH. This, for example, precludes the use of current or past information on 'average' expectations in the orthogonality test at the aggregate level, a consideration which is generally ignored in the vast literature that exists on testing the REH using aggregate data. The analysis also shows that the validity of the tests of the REH at the aggregate level crucially depends on whether the processes generating the private information and the public information are independently distributed. When this condition is not met the tests of the REH based on aggregate data can give misleading results. Finally, since under the REH the expectations errors need not be homoscedastic, and could also be correlated with the future values of the variables in the information set, the standard statistics used in testing the orthogonality property may not be valid. A test statistic which allows for these complications can be derived along the lines of the work by Hansen and Hordrick (1980), which has already been reviewed in the previous chapter. The resultant test statistic is rather

---

[36] The Dun and Bradstreet Survey of Plant and Product Performance, organized by Marc Nerlove, is an example of such a survey. I am grateful to Fabio Schiantarelli for drawing my attention to this survey.

complicated to compute, but can be considerably simplified under certain assumptions concerning the fourth-order cumulants of the expectations errors and the variables in the information set. Whether the application of this new test to the previously analysed expectations data is likely to lead to substantially different conclusions is difficult to say. In the case of the CBI inflation expectations series the results are robust to the choice of the test statistics, and indicate strong rejection of the REH. This is not an isolated finding, and is in line with the general conclusion that so far has emerged from the analysis of survey results on expectations.

The direct observations on expectations do not support the REH.[37] It is therefore important to consider other models of expectations formation.

[37] For recent reviews of the empirical literature on testing the REH using survey-based expectations data, see Holden et al. (1985), and Lovell (1986).

9 Models of Expectations Formation under Bounded Rationality

9.1 Introduction

The thrust of the analysis in this volume has so far been that the REH, in the strong sense advocated by Muth (1961), is based on untenable informational and methodological foundations, and represents a rather extreme view of how individuals actually form expectations. Here we consider other, informationally less demanding, models of expectations formation. Within this class of models those such as the extrapolative or the adaptive models, which precede the REH, stand at the other extreme to the REH and assume that expectations are influenced *only* by the past history of the variable in question. These models have been used extensively in the past, but being based on a rather limited information set they can be woefully inadequate in practice. While the REH attributes to agents information which they may not possess, the adaptive/extrapolative hypothesis assumes agents form their expectations on the basis of an information set far more restricted than the one which they may actually have. What is needed is an expectations formation mechanism which lies somewhere between the two extremes of the purely adaptive and the fully rational expectations formation models. This is the problem which will be addressed in this chapter.

Section 9.2 briefly reviews the various adaptive/extrapolative models that have been proposed in the literature and studies their suitability as models of expectations formation using the error-learning framework first introduced by Meiselman (1962), and later developed by Mincer (1969). Section 9.3 considers a more general framework than the one adopted by Mincer, and assumes that agents form their expectations on the basis of a reduced-form model. It derives an augmented error-learning model of expectations formation which yields all the other expectations formation models proposed in the literature as special cases. This approach to modelling expectations has the advantage of explicitly allowing variables other than the past history of the variable under consideration to influence expectations without invoking the extreme information assumptions that underlie the REH. It is also closely related to the approach employed in the recent literature on the learning problem under bounded rationality reviewed in chapter 3, and could be seen as a first step towards an integrated approach to the learning and the expectations formation problems in applied econometric research. In section 9.4 the CBI inflation expectations data, quantified in the previous chapter, will be used to estimate a number of expectations formation models including an augmented adaptive-learning model. In carrying out this analysis special attention is paid to the measurement error problem discussed in section 8.5. The results provide strong empirical support for the augmented models of inflation expectations in general, and for the augmented adaptive-learning model in particular. The chapter ends with some general conclusions.

9.2 Extrapolative/Adaptive Models of Expectations Formation

The simplest form of an extrapolative expectations formation model is given by

$$ {}_ty^*_{t+1} = y_t, $$

where as before ${}_ty^*_{t+1}$ stands for expectations of y_{t+1} formed at time t. This model is known as the 'naive' expectations formation model, and has been used frequently in the past to interpret the inclusion of lagged values in economic models as 'proxy' measures for expectations. A more realistic extrapolative model is

$$ {}_ty^*_{t+1} = y_t + \lambda(y_t - y_{t-1}), \tag{9.1} $$

where the naive expectations are modified in view of past changes in y_t. The expectations coefficient, λ, could take both positive and negative values. When $\lambda < 0$, (9.1) is also known as the regressive expectations model, and has been employed in studies of inflation expectations with some success, for example, by Turnovsky (1970).[1] A more general variant of (9.1) is the 'return-to-normality' model

$$ {}_ty^*_{t+1} = y_t + \mu(y_t - y^n_t), \quad \mu < 0, \tag{9.2} $$

where y^n_t stands for the 'normal' or the 'average' level of y_t. The value of y^n_t is usually defined by a moving-average of y_t. However, more general specifications relating y^n_t to the long-term determinants of y_t are also possible. The models (9.1) and (9.2) are observationally equivalent under

$$ y^n_t = (1-\omega)y_t + \omega y_{t-1}, \quad \omega > 0. $$

But, in general, (9.2) nests (9.1) as a special case, so long as y_{t-1} is included amongst the determinants of y^n_t.

Other extrapolative/adaptive models can also be derived from (9.2). For example, setting

$$ y^n_t = (1-\omega)y_t + \omega\, {}_{t-1}y^*_t, \quad \omega > 0, $$

[1] For more details and references to the literature, see, for example, Visco (1984b, section 6.1.1).

yields the familiar first-order adaptive scheme (with $\theta = 1 + \mu\omega$)

$$ {}_t y^*_{t+1} - {}_{t-1} y^*_t = \theta (y_t - {}_{t-1} y^*_t), \tag{9.3} $$

already discussed in some detail in chapter 2. This model has been generalized in the literature in a number of ways. One possibility is to include second- or higher-order error terms in (9.3) (see relation (2.2) in chapter 2). An alternative procedure, proposed by Frenkel (1975), is to combine the adaptive and the regressive expectations models. The main feature of Frenkel's formulation lies in the distinction that it draws between the determination of the short-term and the long-term expectations. For the determination of long-term expectations, using arguments due to Keynes (1936), Frenkel assumes that these expectations adjust slowly according to the simple adaptive mechanism

$$ y^n_{t+1} - y^n_t = \gamma (y_t - y^n_t), \quad 0 < \gamma < 2. \tag{9.4} $$

As far as the short-term expectations, ${}_t y^*_{t+1}$, are concerned, Frenkel postulates the following adjustment rule

$$ {}_t y^*_{t+1} - {}_{t-1} y^*_t = \mu_1 (y_t - {}_{t-1} y^*_t) + \mu_2 (y_t - y^n_t), \quad \mu_1 > 0, \quad \mu_2 < 0, \tag{9.5} $$

relating changes in the short-term expectations to the deviations of the actual values from the short-term and the long-term expectations. Using (9.4) we have

$$ y^n_{t+1} = \left\{ \frac{\gamma}{1 - (1-\gamma)L} \right\} y_t, $$

where L is the lag-operator ($L^j y_t = y_{t-j}$). Substituting this result in (9.5) now yields the following short-term expectations formation model

$$ {}_t y^*_{t+1} - {}_{t-1} y^*_t = \mu_1 (y_t - {}_{t-1} y^*_t) + \left\{ \frac{\mu_2 (1-L)}{1 - (1-\gamma)L} \right\} y_t, $$

which, after some algebra, can also be written as

$$ \begin{aligned} {}_t y^*_{t+1} - {}_{t-1} y^*_t = {} & (1 - \gamma - \mu_1)({}_{t-1} y^*_t - {}_{t-2} y^*_{t-1}) + \gamma\mu_1 (y_{t-1} - {}_{t-2} y^*_{t-1}) \\ & + (\mu_1 + \mu_2)(y_t - y_{t-1}). \end{aligned} \tag{9.6} $$

The above expectations formation models can all be derived as special cases of the general distributed lag specification

$$ {}_t y^*_{t+1} = \sum_{i=0}^{\infty} \omega_i y_{t-i}, \tag{9.7} $$

$$ = \left(\sum_{i=0}^{\infty} \omega_i L^i \right) y_t = W(L) y_t. \tag{9.7'} $$

by the imposition of suitable restrictions on the shape of the lag operator function $W(L)$. For example the $W(L)$ function for the first-order adaptive model (9.3) is given by

$$W(L)=\frac{\theta}{1-(1-\theta)L},$$

while in the case of Frenkel's adaptive-regressive model we have

$$W(L)=\frac{(\mu_1+\mu_2)-(\mu_1+\mu_2-\gamma\mu_1)L}{\{1-(1-\gamma)L\}\{1-(1-\mu_1)L\}}.$$

9.2.1 *Optimality of Extrapolative Models*

The question of the optimality of the first-order adaptive model was addressed in section 2.3.2. There it was shown that the first-order adaptive model is optimal, in the minimum mean squared error sense, if the process generating y_t follows the ARIMA(0,1,1) process. Following Mincer (1969) we now consider the optimality of the extrapolative models in the general case. Suppose y_t has the infinite moving-average representation

$$y_t=\sum_{i=0}^{\infty}\beta_i\varepsilon_{t-i}=\beta(L)\varepsilon_t,\quad \beta_0\equiv 1, \tag{9.8}$$

where $\{\varepsilon_t\}$ is a white-noise process. Notice, however, that y_t need not be stationary. Then the statistically optimal one-step-ahead forecast of y_{t+1} is given by

$$_t\tilde{y}_{t+1}=\sum_{i=1}^{\infty}\beta_i\varepsilon_{t+1-i},$$

$$=\left(\sum_{i=1}^{\infty}\beta_i L^{i-1}\right)\varepsilon_t.$$

When (9.8) holds, expectations $_ty^*_{t+1}$ formed according to the general distributed lag specification (9.7), may also be written as

$$_ty^*_{t+1}=W(L)\beta(L)\varepsilon_t.$$

For these expectations to be statistically optimal we should have

$$_ty^*_{t+1}={}_t\tilde{y}_{t+1},\quad \text{for all } t,$$

or

$$W(L)\beta(L)=\sum_{i=1}^{\infty}\beta_i L^{i-1}.$$

The above optimality conditions can also be written more explicitly as

$$\sum_{j=0}^{i} \omega_i \beta_{i-j} = \beta_{i+1}, \quad i=0, 1, 2, \ldots \tag{9.9}$$

with $\beta_0 = 1$. Given a sequence of β_i, optimal values for the weights ω_i can be readily obtained using the above recursive relations. For example, in the case where $\beta_i = \theta$, $i = 1, 2, \ldots$, the optimal values of ω_i are given by

$$\omega_i = \theta(1-\theta)^i, \quad i=0, 1, 2, \ldots$$

which are the weights implied by the first-order adaptive model, (9.3). Notice that when $\beta_i = \theta$, $i = 1, 2, \ldots$, the data generating process (9.8) becomes

$$y_t = \varepsilon_t + \theta \sum_{i=1}^{\infty} \varepsilon_{t-i},$$

which can be written equivalently as the ARIMA(0,1,1) process[2]

$$y_t - y_{t-1} = \varepsilon_t - (1-\theta)\varepsilon_{t-1}.$$

One important implication of the above optimality result, first emphasized by Mincer (1969), is that so long as y_t are generated according to (9.8), then it is always possible to write the optimal forecasts ${}_t\tilde{y}_{t+1}$ in the form of an adaptive error-learning model. Consider optimal forecasts formed at dates t and $t-1$ in the past for the same date $t+p$ in the future,

$${}_t\tilde{y}_{t+p} = \sum_{i=p}^{\infty} \beta_i \varepsilon_{t+p-i}, \qquad p=1, 2, \ldots$$

$${}_{t-1}\tilde{y}_{t+p} = \sum_{i=p+1}^{\infty} \beta_i \varepsilon_{t+p-i}. \quad p=1, 2, \ldots$$

Subtracting these results from each other the following revision functions for the p-span forecasts can be obtained,

$$\begin{aligned} {}_t\tilde{y}_{t+p} - {}_{t-1}\tilde{y}_{t+p} &= \beta_p \varepsilon_t, \\ &= \beta_p(y_t - {}_{t-1}\tilde{y}_t). \end{aligned} \tag{9.10}$$

That is, forecasts are revised adaptively in response to the past forecast error. A similar result also obtains for expectations ${}_t\tilde{y}_{t+1}$, formed according to the general distributed lag model (9.7). We have

$${}_t y^*_{t+p} - {}_{t-1}y^*_{t+p} = \gamma_p(y_t - {}_{t-1}y^*_t), \tag{9.11}$$

[2] This provides an alternative proof to that already given in section 2.4 concerning the (statistical) optimality of the first-order adaptive hypothesis when the underlying data generating mechanism is the ARIMA(0,1,1) process.

where

$$\gamma_p = \sum_{j=0}^{p-1} \omega_j \gamma_{p-1-j}, \quad \gamma_0 \equiv 1. \tag{9.12}$$

In cases where ω_i's are obtained optimally in terms of β_i, since ${}_t\tilde{y}_{t+1} = {}_ty^*_{t+1}$, it then immediately follows from a comparison of (9.10) and (9.11) that $\gamma_p = \beta_p$.

The error-learning model (9.11) was first introduced by Meiselman (1962) in an empirical study of the term structure of interest rates and is particularly suitable in situations where observations on expectations formed at different dates for the *same* future date are available. The error-learning model also provides a useful alternative representation of the general extrapolative model (9.7). The revision coefficients γ_p characterize the pattern of revisions of future expectations in response to the current error of expectations. There is a one-to-one relationship between revision coefficients γ_p and the weights ω_i. Different expectations formation models can be formulated under different assumptions about the pattern of the revision coefficients. Mincer distinguishes between expectations formation models depending on whether the γ_p coefficients are declining, fixed or increasing with span, p. He shows that revision coefficients will be falling when the weights ω_i decline more than exponentially. Only in the first-order adaptive case, where the weights ω_i decline at an exponential rate, will the revision coefficients γ_p remain fixed for all spans. The two cases of falling and rising revision coefficients are referred to by Mincer as *convex* and *concave* expectations hypotheses, respectively.

The simple adaptive expectations hypothesis, apart from having fixed revision coefficients, is also the *only* expectations hypothesis (in the context of the general distributed lag model (9.7)) which yields 'stable' or 'unchanging' expectations in the sense that expectations formed at the same date for different future dates are the same. That is:

$${}_ty^*_{t+p} = {}_ty^*_{t+1}, \quad \text{for all } p \geqslant 1. \tag{9.13}$$

We first show that this property is implied by the first-order adaptive hypothesis. Writing (9.3) for the date $t+p\,(p \geqslant 2)$,

$${}_{t+p-1}y^*_{t+p} - {}_{t+p-2}y^*_{t+p-1} = \theta(y_{t+p-1} - {}_{t+p-2}y^*_{t+p-1}),$$

and assuming that expectations are formed consistently at time t, we have:[3]

$${}_ty^*_{t+1} - {}_ty^*_{t+p-1} = \theta({}_ty^*_{t+p-1} - {}_ty^*_{t+p-1}) = 0.$$

Hence

$${}_ty^*_{t+p} = {}_ty^*_{t+p-1} = {}_ty^*_{t+1}, \quad p = 2, 3, \ldots$$

which establishes that the first-order adaptive model does in fact satisfy the conditions (9.13). We now show that the first-order adaptive hypothesis is the

[3] Expectations ${}_{t+j}y^*_{t+p}$ are said to be formed consistently if expectations of ${}_{t+j}y^*_{t+p}$ formed at time t are equal to ${}_ty^*_{t+p}$, for all j.

only member of the general extrapolative model (9.7) that satisfies the expectations stability conditions (9.13). Since

$$ {}_t y^*_{t+2} = \omega_0 \, {}_t y^*_{t+1} + \omega_1 y_t + \omega_2 y_{t-1} + \ldots, $$

then imposing ${}_t y^*_{t+2} = {}_t y^*_{t+1}$ gives

$$ {}_t y^*_{t+2} = \sum_{i=1}^{\infty} \left(\frac{\omega_i}{1-\omega_0} \right) y_{t+1-i}, $$

$$ {}_t y^*_{t+1} = \sum_{i=0}^{\infty} \omega_i y_{t-i}. $$

Therefore, for expectations to be stable over horizons $t+1$ and $t+2$, the weights ω_i should satisfy the difference equation

$$ \omega_i = (1-\omega_0)\,\omega_{i-1}, \quad i = 0, 1, 2, \ldots $$

Solving for $\omega_i = \omega_0(1-\omega_0)^i$, $i = 0, 1, 2, \ldots$ and substituting the results in (9.7) gives the first-order adaptive model (9.3) with $\theta = \omega_0$.

9.2.2 *The Time-series Approach to Modelling Expectations*

This approach assumes that expectations of y_t are formed *optimally* on the basis of an ARIMA model fitted to past observations on y_t, using a suitable time-series modelling strategy, such as the one suggested by Box and Jenkins (1970).[4] It is similar to the REH, although it employs a univariate time-series model rather than a structural model of the economy. Suppose the process generating y_t can be approximated by the ARIMA (p,d,q) model

$$ \mu(L)(1-L)^d y_t = \phi(L)\,\varepsilon_t, \tag{9.14} $$

where $\mu(L)$ and $\phi(L)$ are polynomial lag operators

$$ \mu(L) = 1 - \mu_1 L - \mu_2 L^2 \ldots - \mu_p L^p, $$
$$ \phi(L) = 1 - \phi_1 L - \phi_2 L^2 - \ldots - \phi_q L^q, $$

assumed to satisfy the usual stationarity and invertibility conditions.[5] The optimal forecast of y_{t+1} based on information available at time t can now be obtained easily by first writing (9.14) in the pure autoregressive form

$$ \phi^{-1}(L)\,\mu(L)(1-L)^d y_{t+1} = \varepsilon_{t+1}, $$

or equivalently as

$$ y_{t+1} = W(L)\,y_t + \varepsilon_{t+1}, \tag{9.15} $$

---

[4] See, for example, Rose (1972, 1976), Trivedi (1973), Feige and Pearce (1976), and Nerlove et al. (1979).

[5] These conditions are satisfied when all the roots of the polynomial equations $\mu(z) = 0$, and $\phi(z) = 0$ fall outside the unit circle.

where

$$W(L)=\sum_{i=0}^{\infty}\omega_i L^i=\frac{\phi(L)-\mu(L)(1-L)^d}{L\phi(L)}. \tag{9.16}$$

From (9.15) we now have

$${}_t y^*_{t+1}={}_t\tilde{y}_{t+1}=W(L)y_t,$$

which is the same as the general distributed lag specification (9.7).[6] The difference between the time-series and the extrapolative/adaptive approaches lies in the way $W(L)$ is arrived at. Under the time-series approach $W(L)$ is estimated directly via (9.16) by first fitting the ARIMA model (9.14) to past observations on y_t. Under the extrapolative hypothesis the choice of the $W(L)$ function is often made *a priori*, or is derived empirically when direct observations on expectations are available.

9.3 Augmented Error-learning Models of Expectations Formation

The purely extrapolative expectations formation models set out above are suitable for modelling expectations of exogenously determined variables. In general, however, these models are rather limited in scope, as they ignore the possible independent effect of variables, other than the past history of y_t, on expectations. It is therefore important to consider expectations formation models that augment the purely extrapolative model (9.7), by past information on variables other than past values of y_t which are believed to have an independent influence on expectations. The nature of the additional information to be incorporated in the expectations formation process, and the precise manner in which this additional information is used by agents in forming their expectations, are, however, far from clear. One possible answer to this problem is provided by the REH. But as already argued in chapters 2 and 3, this is rather an extreme hypothesis which pre-assumes that the process of learning is completed, and that agents already know the structural model of the economy (including its parameter values!). An informationally less demanding approach would be to consider augmentation of the purely

---

[6] Notice that the weights ω_i in (9.16) sum up to unity so long as $d\neq 0$. This result is the same as that already proved in note 11 on page 20. When $d=0$, we have

$$\sum_{i=0}^{\infty}\omega_i=W(1)=\left(\sum_{i=1}^{p}\mu_i-\sum_{i=1}^{q}\phi_i\right)\Big/\left(1-\sum_{i=1}^{q}\phi_i\right),$$

and assuming that $\mu(L)$ and $\phi(L)$ satisfy the usual conditions (see note 5) then it is easily seen that

$$\sum_{i=0}^{\infty}\omega_i<1.$$

extrapolative mechanism with the variables that are likely to enter the reduced form model of y_t. In following this approach it is important to distinguish between two cases, depending on whether agents know the parameters of the reduced form model or not. Such a distinction is also helpful in establishing a link between the learning problem reviewed in chapter 3 and the problem of formation and revision of expectations which concerns us here.

9.3.1 *Modelling Expectations when the Reduced-form Parameters are Known*

When agents already know the parameters of the reduced-form model, expectations can be modelled by means of the following general augmented-extrapolative specification

$$ {}_t y^*_{t+1} = \sum_{i=0}^{\infty} \omega_i y_{t-i} + \sum_{i=0}^{\infty} \boldsymbol{\alpha}'_i \mathbf{x}_{t-i} + v_t, \tag{9.17} $$

where $\mathbf{x}_t$ represents a $k \times l$ vector of exogenous variables, and v_t an unobservable component. The introduction of v_t into the model is intended to capture the unobserved individual effects on expectations. The above expectations formation model can also be rationalized as the conditional linear forecast of y_{t+1}, derived with respect to the information available at time t. This model captures the most appealing feature of the REH by recognizing that variables other than the past values of y_t can influence expectations, but falls short of adhering to the extreme orthogonality properties of the REH. When direct observations on expectations ${}_t y^*_{t+1}$ are available the coefficients ω_i, and $\boldsymbol{\alpha}_i$ can be estimated freely, and the extent to which variables other than past values of y_t have a direct *independent* influence on expectations can be ascertained. (As a demonstration of this procedure see section 9.4.2 below.)

The augmented expectations formation model (9.17) can also be used to derive an augmented error-learning model of the type analysed by Mincer (1969) (see section 9.2.1). Assuming expectations are formed consistently over different spans using (9.17) we also have

$$ {}_{t-1} y^*_{t+1} = \omega_0 \, {}_{t-1} y^*_t + \sum_{i=1}^{\infty} \omega_i y_{t-i} + \boldsymbol{\alpha}'_0 \, {}_{t-1}\mathbf{x}^*_t + \sum_{i=1}^{\infty} \boldsymbol{\alpha}'_i \mathbf{x}_{t-i} + {}_{t-i} v^*_t. \tag{9.18} $$

Subtracting this result from (9.17) now yields the following augmented error-learning model

$$ {}_t y^*_{t+1} - {}_{t-1} y^*_{t+1} = \omega_0 (y_t - {}_{t-1} y^*_t) + \boldsymbol{\alpha}'_0 (\mathbf{x}_t - {}_{t-1}\mathbf{x}^*_t) + \xi_t, \tag{9.19} $$

where $\xi_t = v_t - {}_{t-1} v^*_t$. This model simply states that revision in expectations of y_{t+1} between the period $t-1$ to t is a linear function of errors of expectations in the endogenous and exogenous variables, y_t and x_t. The term ξ_t represents the unobservable influence of individual effects on expectations. Notice that (9.19) is not necessarily incompatible with the REH. When expectations are formed rationally the revision in expectations ${}_t y^*_{t+1} - {}_{t-1} y^*_{t+1}$, and the expectations errors $y_t - {}_{t-1} y^*_t$, $\mathbf{x}_t - {}_{t-1}\mathbf{x}^*_t$ all will be martingale difference processes (see chapter 5), and the error-learning model (9.19) can be specified without contradicting the REH, so long as ξ_t is also a martingale difference process. The reverse is not, of course, true. The error-learning model can provide a satisfactory characterization of how expectations are actually formed even when the REH does not hold.

Despite its apparently simple form, the use of (9.19) in empirical analysis is rather limited, since it involves direct observations on expectations of y_{t+1} formed at time $t-1$ as well as at time t, and survey data on expectations formed at different dates in the past for the same future date are not generally available. This means that in practice the error-learning model needs to be simplified before it can be employed in empirical analysis. A useful method of achieving this is to write the unobserved expectations ${}_{t-1}y^*_{t+1}$ in terms of ${}_{t-1}y^*_t$. Consider the multiplicative decomposition

$$ {}_{t-1}y^*_{t+1} = \lambda_t\, {}_{t-1}y^*_t . $$

The variable λ_t captures the extent to which expectations formed at time $t-1$ are revised when the expectations horizon is increased from t to $t+1$. Simplified versions of the error-learning model (9.19) (or equivalently that of (9.17)) can now be obtained by imposition of *a priori* plausible restrictions on the variable λ_t. For example by setting $\lambda_t = 1$, which has the same effect as imposing the restriction ${}_{t-1}y^*_{t+1} = {}_{t-1}y^*_t$ on (9.19), we obtain the first-order augmented-adaptive model

$$ {}_t y^*_{t+1} - {}_{t-1}y^*_t = \omega_0(y_t - {}_{t-1}y^*_t) + \boldsymbol{\alpha}'_0(\mathbf{x}_t - {}_{t-1}\mathbf{x}^*_t) + \xi_t. \tag{9.20} $$

Placing restrictions on λ_t can also be viewed as a very effective method of imposing restrictions on the coefficients ω_i and $\boldsymbol{\alpha}_i$. To see this suppose ${}_{t-1}\mathbf{x}^*_t$ are formed according to the general multivariate distributed lag model

$$ {}_{t-1}\mathbf{x}^*_t = \sum_{i=1}^{\infty} R_i \mathbf{x}_{t-i}, $$

where R_i are $k \times k$ parameter matrices. Now using (9.17) and (9.18) it is easily seen that

$$ \lambda_t - \omega_0 = \frac{\sum_{i=1}^{\infty} \omega_i y_{t-i} + \sum_{i=1}^{\infty} \{\boldsymbol{\alpha}'_0 R_i + \boldsymbol{\alpha}'_i\}\mathbf{x}_{t-i} + {}_{t-1}v^*_t}{\sum_{i=1}^{\infty} \omega_{i-1}\, y_{t-i} + \sum_{i=1}^{\infty} \boldsymbol{\alpha}'_{i-1}\mathbf{x}_{t-i} + v_{t-1}}, \quad \text{for all } t. $$

For example, in the case of the first-order augmented-adaptive model (9.20), where $\lambda_t = 1$ the above conditions imply the following restrictions on ω_i, $\boldsymbol{\alpha}_i$, and v_t.

$$ \omega_i = (1-\omega_0)\,\omega_{i-1}, \qquad i = 0, 1, 2, \ldots $$
$$ \boldsymbol{\alpha}_i = (1-\omega_0)\,\boldsymbol{\alpha}_{i-1} - R'_i \boldsymbol{\alpha}_0, \quad i = 1, 2, \ldots $$
$$ {}_{t-1}v^*_t = (1-\omega_0) v_{t-1}. $$

This last restriction will be satisfied when v_t follows an AR(1) process with parameter $1 - \omega_0$.

Less restricted versions of the first-order augmented-adaptive model can also be specified. One obvious example is when λ_t is set equal to the constant parameter λ, not necessarily equal to unity. For this choice of λ_t we have the following augmented expectations formation model

$$ {}_ty^*_{t+1} = \lambda\, {}_{t-1}y^*_t + \omega_0(y_t - {}_{t-1}y^*_t) + \boldsymbol{\alpha}'_0(\mathbf{x}_t - {}_{t-1}\mathbf{x}^*_t) + \xi_t. \tag{9.21} $$

When λ_t is treated as a free time-varying parameter we obtain

$$ {}_ty^*_{t+1} = \lambda_t\, {}_{t-1}y^*_t + \omega_0(y_t - {}_{t-1}y^*_t) + \boldsymbol{\alpha}'_0(\mathbf{x}_t - {}_{t-1}\mathbf{x}^*_t) + \xi_t, \tag{9.22} $$

where the model can be estimated by continuous updating procedures such as the Kalman filter approach (Harvey, 1981).

In estimating the above augmented error-learning models, direct observations on expectations of the exogenous variables $\mathbf{x}_t$ are also required. In the absence of such data, one possibility would be to replace expectations of $\mathbf{x}_t$ by their ARIMA forecasts. Alternatively, the general model (9.17) can be estimated directly under plausible restrictions on the weights ω_i and $\boldsymbol{\alpha}_i$.

9.3.2. *Modelling Expectations under Incomplete Learning*

The reduced-form approach to modelling expectations set out above is informationally less demanding than the structural-form approach that underlies the REH. But it still requires that when forming their expectations, individuals should already know the reduced-form coefficients ω_i and $\boldsymbol{\alpha}_i$. This is clearly unrealistic and ignores the learning process that is generally involved in the formation and revision of expectations. Under incomplete learning there are likely to be feedbacks from expectations to outcomes, and the reduced-form coefficients need no longer be time-invariant (see chapter 3 for further details).[7]

Assuming that learning is taking place according to the boundedly rational model discussed in section 3.3 the expectations formation model under incomplete learning can be written as

$$ {}_ty^*_{t+1} = \mathbf{z}'_t\boldsymbol{\gamma}_t + v_t, \tag{9.23} $$

where $\mathbf{z}_t$ is an $h \times l$ vector containing current and lagged values of y_t and $\mathbf{x}_t$, and $\boldsymbol{\gamma}_t$ is the agent's estimate of the unknown reduced-form parameters based on the information available at time t. The term v_t represents the unobserved individual-specific component of expectations. In the context of incomplete learning we also need to specify how the estimates $\boldsymbol{\gamma}_t$ are updated in the face of new information. This problem has already been addressed extensively in the literature, using both Bayesian and classical procedures (for relevant references see section 3.4). Here we employ the general method due to Albert and Gardner (1967), which is discussed in some detail in chapter 3. As was

[7] Expectations formation models with time-varying coefficients have been considered in the literature, for example, by Turnovsky (1969), Friedman (1979) and Visco (1984b, ch. 4).

pointed out earlier, the basic idea behind the Albert–Gardner updating formula is very simple, and in the notations of this chapter can be written as

$$\gamma_t - \gamma_{t-1} = \mathbf{g}_t(y_t - {}_{t-1}y_t^*), \tag{9.24}$$

where $\mathbf{g}_t$, known as the 'gain sequence', is an $h \times l$ vector which represents the weights that individuals place on observed errors of expectations when updating their estimates of γ. When the updating is carried out by the OLS method the gain sequence, $\mathbf{g}_t$ will be the same across agents and will be given by (see section 3.4):[8]

$$\mathbf{g}_t = \left(\sum_{j=1}^{t} \mathbf{z}_j\mathbf{z}_j'\right)^{-1} \mathbf{z}_t, \quad \text{for } t \geqq h. \tag{9.25}$$

We are now in a position to develop a generalized adaptive-learning model by combining the expectations formation model (9.23) with the updating formula (9.24). Writing (9.23) in a first-difference form we have

$${}_ty_{t+1}^* - {}_{t-1}y_t^* = \mathbf{z}_t'(\gamma_t - \gamma_{t-1}) + (\Delta\mathbf{z}_t)'\gamma_{t-1} + \Delta v_t,$$

which upon using (9.24) and (9.25) yields the adaptive-learning model (for $t-1 > h$).

$${}_ty_{t+1}^* - {}_{t-1}y_t^* = \mu_t(y_t - {}_{t-1}y_t^*) + (\Delta\mathbf{z}_t)'\gamma_{t-1} + \Delta v_t, \tag{9.26}$$

where

$$\mu_t = \mathbf{z}_t'\left(\sum_{j=1}^{t} \mathbf{z}_j\mathbf{z}_j'\right)^{-1} \mathbf{z}_t, \tag{9.27}$$

and

$$\gamma_{t-1} = \left(\sum_{j=1}^{t-1} \mathbf{z}_j\mathbf{z}_j'\right)^{-1}\left(\sum_{j=1}^{t-1} \mathbf{z}_jy_j\right). \tag{9.28}$$

In this model the adaptive parameter μ_t changes with time and is updated in the light of new information on $\mathbf{z}_t$. The behaviour of μ_t over time depends on the process generating $\mathbf{z}_t$. But for most time-series encountered in economics it is reasonable to expect μ_t to tend to zero as $t \to \infty$.[9] The tendency for μ_t to

---

[8] The condition $t \geqslant h$ ensures that there are enough data available to compute the OLS gain sequence $\mathbf{g}_t$. When $t < h$, or more generally, when matrix $(\Sigma_{j=1}^{t} \mathbf{z}_j\mathbf{z}_j')$ is not of full rank, the OLS gain sequence is not defined and γ_t needs to be updated by some other procedure.

[9] Here we are assuming that h, the dimension of $\mathbf{z}_t$, is fixed. In the case where the process $\mathbf{z}_t$ is stationary and ergodic we have

$$\Sigma_t = t^{-1}\sum_{j=1}^{t} \mathbf{z}_j\mathbf{z}_j' \overset{\text{a.s.}}{\to} E(\mathbf{z}_t\mathbf{z}_t') = \Sigma,$$

and hence

$$\mu_t = \text{Tr}\{t^{-1}\Sigma_t(\mathbf{z}_t\mathbf{z}_t')\} \approx \text{Tr}(\Sigma\Sigma^{-1}/t) = h/t,$$

which tends to zero as $t \to \infty$.

converge to zero is also in accordance with the available evidence from experimental psychology on the learning process (see, for example, Rotter, 1954, pp. 165–83). In situations where the learning process converges, the expectations formation model simplifies to

$$ {}_{t}y^{*}_{t+1} - {}_{t-1}y^{*}_{t} = (\Delta \mathbf{z}_t)'\bar{\gamma} + \Delta v_t, \tag{9.29}$$

where $\bar{\gamma}$ represents the probability limit of γ_{t-1} as $t \leftarrow \infty$. This specification can also be derived from (9.17), by first truncating the lag-distributions on y_t and $\mathbf{x}_t$ and then first-differencing the results. The difference between the formulations (9.17) and (9.29) lies in the different emphases these specifications place on the formation and revision of expectations. Model (9.17) specifies how expectations are formed, while (9.29) explains how agents change their previously held expectations. In situations where individual or group expectations are subject to often non-quantifiable sociological factors, by concentrating on changes in expectations of the same individuals over time the importance of explicitly modelling non-quantitative influences on expectations will be greatly reduced, as norms, conventions and habits of thought tend to change only sluggishly. This suggests that from an empirical viewpoint model (9.29) may be preferable to (9.17) (similarly (9.26) may be preferable to (9.23)). Whether this is in fact the case depends on the nature and the significance of the effects of non-quantifiable factors on expectations.

9.4 Models of Inflation Expectations in British Manufacturing

This section estimates some of the key expectations formation models described above, using the inflations expectations series Π^{e}_{tN} and Π^{e}_{tR} which were derived in chapter 8 from the CBI qualitative data on inflation expectations of firms in British manufacturing. In particular we consider the following expectations formation models:

First-order adaptive model

$$M_1\colon \Pi^*_t - \Pi^*_{t-1} = \theta(\Pi_{t-1} - \Pi^*_{t-1}) + v_t, \quad \theta > 0$$

where Π^*_{t+i} represents the 'true' expectations of Π_{t+i}, the rate of inflation at time $t+i$, formed one period earlier at time $t+i-1$.

Frenkel's adaptive-regressive model

$$M_2\colon \Pi^*_t - \Pi^*_{t-1} = \delta_1(\Pi^*_{t-1} - \Pi^*_{t-2}) + \delta_2(\Pi_{t-2} - \Pi^*_{t-2}) + \delta_3(\Pi_{t-1} - \Pi_{t-2}) + v_t,$$

where $\delta_2 > 0$, with δ_1 and δ_3 taking positive or negative values.

Augmented-extrapolative model

$$M_3\colon \Pi^*_t = \mathbf{z}'_{t-1}\gamma + v_t,$$

where $\mathbf{z}_{t-1}$ contains information on past values of Π_t and $\mathbf{x}_t$, where $\mathbf{x}_t$ represents the vector of variables that in addition to past price changes enter the reduced-form equation for determination of Π_t. (See below for details of the likely components of $\mathbf{x}_t$.)

Augmented adaptive-learning model

$$M_4: \Pi_t^* - \Pi_{t-1}^* = \mu_{t-1}(\Pi_{t-1} - \Pi_{t-1}^*) + (\Delta \mathbf{z}_{t-1})' \boldsymbol{\gamma}_{t-2} + v_t,$$

where μ_{t-1} and $\boldsymbol{\gamma}_{t-2}$ are the time-varying parameters already defined by (9.27) and (9.28), with Π_j replacing y_j in (9.28).

Specifications M_1 and M_2 fall in the class of purely extrapolative models and attempt to explain inflation expectations only in terms of the past history of the actual rate of inflation, while specifications M_3 and M_4 augment the extrapolative model with information on other variables, $\mathbf{x}_t$, that are expected to influence price changes in the manufacturing sector. In identifying the possible elements of $\mathbf{x}_t$ it is useful to distinguish between three types of variables influencing Π_t, and hence inflation expectations.

First, the cost and output variables that are specific to the manufacturing sector. These include the rate of change of raw material and fuel prices (f_t), the rate of change of basic weekly wage rates (w_t), and the rate of change of the effective exchange rate (e_t), as indicators of cost changes, and the rate of change of manufacturing output (q_t) as an indicator of demand changes in the manufacturing sector.

Second, the policy variables that influence expectations either directly or indirectly through their effect on general economic outlooks. Amongst the various policy changes experienced over our sample period, 1959–85, we concentrate on the 1967 sterling devaluation, the adoption of the floating exchange rate regime in 1971–72, and the various prices policies implemented over the period 1965–78. For the 1967 devaluation and the change in the exchange rate regime we use simple dummy variables. These we denote by DEV_t and DER_t respectively. The DEV_t variable, which is intended to capture the once-and-for-all announcement effect of the devaluation, is defined to take the value of unity in the last quarter of 1967 and zero elsewhere. The DER_t variable, on the other hand, is defined to take the value of zero in the pre-1971 period and the value of unity afterwards, thus representing a permanent change in the exchange rate regime. As a measure of prices policies we shall use an updated Fels–Hopkin index of the strength of the prices policies used by Coutts et al. (1978) in their study of the normal cost pricing in the UK manufacturing sector. This index, which is specifically designed to measure the relative strengths of the various prices policies, is clearly superior to a simple zero-one dummy variable (see Coutts et al., 1978, pp. 103–4). We denote this index by FHI_t. (See the data appendix for more details.)

Third, the economy-wide variables that influence inflation expectations by altering the general economic conditions. As a proxy for general economic conditions we use the overall rate of unemployment (RU_t), and the lagged rate of change of money supply (m_{t-1}, the M_3 definition).

9.4.1 *Econometric Implications of the Presence of Measurement Errors in Inflation Expectations*

In estimating the expectations formation models M_1 to M_4, special attention should be paid to the measurement error problem already discussed in section 8.5, pp. 233–6. Assuming that the measurement equations (8.40) hold, we can write

$$\Pi_t^* = \beta_j^{-1}(\Pi_{tj}^e - \alpha_j - \varepsilon_{tj}), \quad j = N, R, \tag{9.30}$$

where Π_{tN}^e and Π_{tR}^e are the expectations series obtained by converting the CBI's qualitative survey data on inflation expectations to quantitative measures using the probability and the regression methods respectively (see section 8.3). Substituting (9.30) in M_1, we obtain the following reduced form equation in terms of the observed expectations series, Π_t^e. (To keep the notations simple, what follows will omit the subscript j which identifies the method of quantification of expectations.)

$$R_1: \quad \Pi_t^e - \Pi_{t-1}^e = \alpha\theta - (1-\beta)\theta\Pi_{t-1} + \theta(\Pi_{t-1} - \Pi_{t-1}^e) + u_t, \tag{9.31}$$

where

$$u_t = \varepsilon_t - (1-\theta)\varepsilon_{t-1} + \beta v_t. \tag{9.32}$$

Now before this result can be used in estimation there are a number of econometric considerations that should be borne in mind.

First, the disturbances in (9.31) will be generally serially correlated even when v_t and ε_t are serially independent. This arises because of the autoregressive form of the adaptive model. The pattern and the significance of the autocorrelation in u_t will be governed by the order of the autoregression in Π_t^*, and the variance of the measurement errors. In the case of model M_1, where Π_t^* has a first-order autoregressive representation, the composite disturbance term u_t in (9.32) will follow an MA(1) process, assuming that v_t and ε_t are both serially uncorrelated. Similarly, it is easily seen that the composite disturbances in the reduced-form equation of M_2 will follow an MA(2) process. However, in situations where the measurement errors, ε_t, are themselves positively serially correlated very little can be said *a priori* about the serial correlation pattern of u_t.

The second more serious difficulty, associated with the estimation of (9.31), arises because of the statistical dependence that generally exists between the disturbances u_t and the lagged expectations series, Π_{t-1}^e. The extent of the correlation between Π_{t-1}^e and u_t depends on the serial correlation pattern of the measurement errors. For example, suppose $\{\varepsilon_t\}$ follows an AR(1) process with parameter ρ. Then, under the assumption that v_t is a white-noise process distributed independently of ε_t, using (9.30) and (9.32) we have

$$E(u_t\Pi_{t-1}^e) = \{\rho - (1-\theta)\}\tau^2, \quad \tau^2 \neq 0,$$

where τ^2 is the variance of the measurement errors, ε_t. Therefore, only in the extreme case where $\rho = (1-\theta)$, Π_{t-1}^e and u_t will be uncorrelated. In general the presence of measurement errors in expectations, by introducing correlation between lagged expectations and the disturbances, invalidates the estimation of adaptive models by ordinary least squares (OLS) method. Consistent estimates of adaptive models can, in principle, be obtained by the instrumental variable (IV) method, assuming there exists a set of instruments that are uncorrelated with the composite disturbances u_t, but which have a reasonably high degree of correlation with Π^e_{t-1}. The existence of suitable instruments for the consistent estimation of adaptive models is, however, more problematic than it may appear at first. This is because an instrument which has a reasonable degree of correlation with lagged expectations is itself a potential candidate for inclusion amongst the regressors of the expectations formation model. But as soon as it is included in the expectations formation model, that variable can no longer be used as an instrument for past observed expectations, Π^e_{t-1}.

Finally, the existence of errors of scaling in the measurement of expectations can also result in an identification problem. To see this consider the following generalization of the first-order adaptive model[10]

$$\Pi^*_t = \phi_0 + \phi_1 \Pi^*_{t-1} + \phi_2 \Pi_{t-1} + v_t. \tag{9.33}$$

Using (9.30), the reduced-form equation of this model will be

$$\Pi^e_t = \phi_0 \beta + \alpha(1-\phi_1) + \beta\phi_2 \Pi_{t-1} + \phi_1 \Pi^e_{t-1} + u_t, \tag{9.34}$$

$$u_t = \varepsilon_t - \phi_1 \varepsilon_{t-1} + \beta v_t, \tag{9.35}$$

which is observationally equivalent to the reduced-form equation of the first-order adaptive model given by (9.31)–(9.32).[11] A test of M_1 against the more general specification (9.33) is possible only when some *a priori* information about the scaling parameters α and β is available. In the absence of such information the model M_1 and its generalization given by (9.33) will be empirically indistinguishable from one another.[12] It should be noted that the identification problem encountered here differs from that generally associated with the classical errors-in-variables model. In the context of the latter, identification will be a problem even if there are no systematic measurement errors (i.e. $\alpha = 0$, $\beta = 1$). But in the case of the expectations models, where the problem of the measurement errors is confined to direct observations on expectations, lack of identification is primarily due to possible errors in scaling of the expectations series.

Similar econometric issues also arise in empirical analysis of models M_2 and M_4, where lagged expectations are included amongst the regressors. The reduced-form equations of these models, which we denote by R_2, and R_4 respectively, are given by

---

[10] Model M_1 can be obtained from (9.33) by imposing the restrictions $\phi_0 = 0$, and $\phi_1 + \phi_2 = 1$.

[11] In situations where $\alpha \neq 0$ and $\beta \neq 1$, equations (9.34)–(9.35) can not be used to test the first-order adaptive restrictions $\phi_0 = 0$ and $\phi_1 + \phi_2 = 1$.

[12] Notice, however, that if the first-order adaptive model M_1 can be maintained *a priori*, then it will be possible to identify the scaling parameters α and β using the reduced-form equation (9.31).

$$R_2:\quad \Pi_t^e - \Pi_{t-1}^e = \alpha\delta_2 - (1-\beta)\delta_2\Pi_{t-2} + \delta_1(\Pi_{t-1}^e - \Pi_{t-2}^e) + \delta_2(\Pi_{t-2} - \Pi_{t-2}^e) + \beta\delta_3(\Pi_{t-1} - \Pi_{t-2}) + u_t,$$

in which $u_t = \varepsilon_t - (1-\delta_1)\varepsilon_{t-1} + (\delta_1 + \delta_2)\varepsilon_{t-2} + \beta v_t$, and

$$R_4:\quad \Pi_t^e - \Pi_{t-1}^e = \alpha\mu_{t-1} - (1-\beta)\mu_{t-1}\Pi_{t-1} + \mu_{t-1}(\Pi_{t-1} - \Pi_{t-1}^e) + \beta(\Delta \mathbf{z}_{t-1})'\boldsymbol{\gamma}_{t-2} + u_t,$$

in which $u_t = \varepsilon_t - (1-\mu_{t-1})\varepsilon_{t-1} + \beta v_t$. Notice, however, that the existence of measurement errors in expectations does not have the same serious implications for empirical analysis of models such as M_3 which do not contain an adaptive or an autoregressive component. In the case of model M_3, the reduced-form equation is given by

$$R_3:\quad \Pi_t^e = \alpha + \beta \mathbf{z}_{t-1}'\boldsymbol{\gamma} + u_t,$$

where $u_t = \varepsilon_t + \beta v_t$. Apart from the scaling parameters α and β, the coefficients of this reduced form model can be estimated consistently by the OLS method.[13] In situations where the measurement errors ε_t, or the unobserved component of expectations v_t, are serially correlated, the parameters of the reduced-form equation R_3, can be estimated efficiently by the Cochrane–Orcutt iterative procedure, or other estimation methods that appropriately allow for the presence of autocorrelation in the composite disturbances, u_t. Moreover, the fact that the scaling parameter β is now known, does not pose any difficulty for testing zero restrictions on the elements of $\boldsymbol{\gamma}$. (Notice that it can be safely assumed that $\beta \neq 0$.)

9.4.2 *Empirical results*

Purely Extrapolative Expectations Formations Models

The results for the first-order adaptive model, M_1, obtained by estimating the reduced-form equation R_1 are summarized in table 9.1. As we have already seen, the inclusion of the intercept term and the lagged inflation term Π_{t-1} in the specification of the first-order adaptive model allows for the possible errors of scaling in the measurement of Π_t^* by Π_{tN}^e or Π_{tR}^e. The first two columns of table 9.1 give the OLS estimates of R_1 using the expectations series Π_{tN}^e and Π_{tR}^e computed over the period 1959(2)–1985(2). The OLS results provide strong empirical support in favour of the first-order adaptive model. The estimates show a reasonable fit and pass, with a comfortable margin, the diagnostic tests for residual autocorrelation (χ_{SC}^2), functional form misspecification (χ_{FF}^2), non-normal errors (χ_{N}^2), and heteroscedasticity (χ_{H}^2). Moreover, on the assumption that M_1 is the true data-generating process, the results suggest significant errors of scaling in measurement of Π_t^* by Π_{tN}^e (or Π_{tR}^e) only so far as the intercept term α_N (or α_R) is concerned. The only disturbing feature of the OLS results seems to be the marked difference that

---

[13] Parameter α can be identified only when model M_3 does not contain an intercept term.

Table 9.1[a] Estimates of the first-order adaptive expectations formation model, M_1, 1959(2)–1985(2)

	OLS estimates		IV estimates[b]	
Regressors	$\Delta\Pi^e_{tN}$	$\Delta\Pi^e_{tR}$	$\Delta\Pi^e_{tN}$	$\Delta\Pi^e_{tR}$
Intercept	0.3693	0.3529	0.6179	0.4614
	(2.28)	(2.53)	(3.06)	(3.08)
Π_{t-1}	−0.0714	−0.0502	−0.1329	−0.0701
	(−1.72)	(−1.40)	(−2.52)	(−1.86)
$\Pi_{t-1}-\Pi^e_{t-1}$	0.3492	0.6761	0.7137	0.8659
	(4.46)	(8.18)	(4.09)	(7.72)
$\hat{\sigma}$	0.9339	0.8277	1.0416	0.8518
$\bar{R}^2$	0.8463	0.8856	0.8088	0.8789
$\chi^2_{SC}(1)$	0.38	3.55	4.62	5.98
	{3.84}	{3.84}	{3.84}	{3.84}
$\chi^2_{FF}(2)$	0.28	0.57	7.04	3.26
	{5.99}	{5.99}	{5.99}	{5.99}
$\chi^2_{N}(2)$	0.87	0.37	1.52	0.99
	{5.99}	{5.99}	{5.99}	{5.99}
$\chi^2_{H}(1)$	0.23	0.48	5.92	0.88
	{3.84}	{3.84}	{3.84}	{3.84}
n	92	92	92	92

[a] The figures in parentheses are t-ratios and those in braces are the relevant 5 per cent critical values of the chi-squared tests. $\hat{\sigma}$ is the estimated standard error of the regression, $\bar{R}$ is the adjusted multiple correlation coefficient computed taking Π^e_{tN} (or Π^e_{tR}) as the dependent variable, and n is the number of observations. $\chi^2_{SC}(1)$, $\chi^2_{FF}(2)$, $\chi^2_{N}(2)$ and $\chi^2_{H}(1)$, are diagnostic statistics distributed as chi-squared variates (with degrees of freedom in parentheses), for tests of residual serial correlation, functional form misspecification, non-normal errors, and heteroscedasticity, respectively. The details of the computations and the algorithms can be found in Pesaran and Pesaran (1987).

[b] The IV estimates are computed using $(1, \Pi_{t-1}, \Pi_{t-2}, f_{t-2}, q_{t-2})$ as instruments.

exists between the estimates of the adaptive parameter θ, namely 0.349 and 0.676, obtained using the expectations series Π^e_{tN} and Π^e_{tR}, respectively.

The results based on the OLS estimates can, however, be highly misleading as they ignore the presence of the random errors ε_{tN} (or ε_{tR}) in the measurement of Π^*_t by Π^e_{tN} (or Π^e_{tR}).[14] In the presence of random errors of measurement the OLS estimates will be inconsistent and the diagnostic tests based on the OLS residuals can no longer be relied upon to provide evidence on residual autocorrelation, functional form misspecification, etc. One possible method of dealing with the measurement error problem is to estimate R_1 by the IV method. For this purpose the instruments should be chosen in such a way that they are orthogonal to the reduced-form disturbances u_t, and at the

[14] As examples of studies that ignore the measurement error problem in estimation of expectations formation models, see Turnovsky (1970), Carlson and Parkin (1975), Danes (1975), Holden and Peel (1977), Mills (1981), and De Leeuw and McKelvey (1981).

same time have a non-zero correlation with $\Pi^e_{t-1,j}$, $j = N, R$. With this in mind we estimated the reduced-form model R_1 by the IV method using $\mathbf{h}_t = (1, \Pi_{t-1}, \Pi_{t-2}, f_{t-2}, q_{t-2})'$ as instruments. The first two elements of $\mathbf{h}_t$ serve as instruments for the intercept and the lagged inflation terms, and the variables Π_{t-2}, f_{t-2}, and q_{t-2} are intended as instruments for lagged inflation expectations $\Pi^e_{t-1,N}$ (or $\Pi^e_{t-1,R}$). The variables Π_{t-2}, f_{t-2} and q_{t-2} were chosen in the belief that they are measured relatively accurately (especially as compared with the inflation expectations series Π^e_{tN} or Π^e_{tR}), and also because, as will be shown later, they are important determinants of Π^*_{t-1}.[15] The IV estimates of R_1, for the two expectations series Π^e_{tN} and Π^e_{tR} are summarized in the last two columns of table 9.1. These estimates provide further empirical support for the first-order adaptive scheme, and give more plausible estimates of θ. As compared with the OLS estimates, the IV estimates of the adaptive parameter, θ based on the two expectations series are now much closer to one another. In fact the IV estimate of θ based on Π^e_{tR} is now only 21 per cent higher than the corresponding estimate based on Π^e_{tN}, as compared with the figure of 94 per cent in the case of the OLS estimates. However, the IV results now give a very different picture as far as the diagnostic tests are concerned. In contrast to the OLS estimates, the diagnostic test statistics computed on the basis of the IV residuals provide significant evidence of residual serial correlation, and in the case of the expectations series Π^e_{tN}, also show a significant degree of functional form mis-specification, and heteroscedasticity.

Similar considerations also apply to the estimation of Frenkel's adaptive-regressive model, M_2. The OLS and the IV estimates of the reduced-form equation of this model, namely R_2, are given in table 9.2. On the basis of the OLS estimates, Frenkel's model is highly significant, and fits the expectations series better than the simple adaptive model. But a totally different result emerges when the IV estimates are considered. These estimates no longer support the adaptive-regressive model. With the exception of lagged changes in the rate of inflation, $\Delta\Pi_{t-1}$, all the other regressors in R_2 lose their significance. The IV results suggest that in the class of purely extrapolative models the expectations formation model supported by the available data takes the form of a simple acceleration mechanism (i.e. $\Delta\Pi^*_t = \phi\Delta\Pi_{t-1} + v_t$).[16]

Augmented Expectations Formation Models

We shall now turn our attention to the estimation of the augmented expectations formation models M_3 and M_4. The failure of the purely autoregressive

---

[15] Notice that on the assumption that the instruments satisfy the orthogonality conditions $\text{cov}(\varepsilon_{t-i}, \mathbf{h}_t) = 0$, $i = 0, 1$, it readily follows from (8.40) that $\text{cov}(\Pi^e_{t-1}, \mathbf{h}_t) = \beta\,\text{cov}(\Pi^*_{t-1}, \mathbf{h}_t)$. Therefore, in general, if $\mathbf{h}_t$ are important determinants of Π^*_{t-1}, they will also be correlated with expectations series $\Pi^e_{t-1,N}$ or $\Pi^e_{t-1,R}$.

[16] A similar result is also reported in Pesaran (1985) for the period 1959(2)–1981(4). Notice, however, that the result in Pesaran (1985) was obtained by a direct estimation of the distributed lag representation

$$\Pi^e_t = c_0 + \sum_{i=1}^{m} \omega_i \Pi_{t-i} + v_t.$$

Table 9.2[a] Estimates of Frenkel's adaptive-regressive expectations formation model, M_2, 1959(3)–1985(2)

	OLS estimates		IV estimates[b]	
Regressors	$\Delta\Pi^e_{tN}$	$\Delta\Pi^e_{tR}$	$\Delta\Pi^e_{tN}$	$\Delta\Pi^e_{tR}$
Intercept	0.3617	0.2852	0.2775	0.2983
	(2.31)	(2.06)	(1.09)	(1·78)
Π_{t-2}	−0.0820	−0.0556	−0.0671	−0.0554
	(−2.04)	(−1.57)	(−1.29)	(−1.53)
$\Delta\Pi^e_{t-1}$	−0.3996	−0.5079	−0.3428	−0.5699
	(−3.41)	(−3.96)	(−1.10)	(−1.85)
$\Pi_{t-2}-\Pi^e_{t-2}$	0.1998	0.3623	0.0833	0.4096
	(2.27)	(2.93)	(0.27)	(1.35)
$\Delta\Pi_{t-1}$	0.4244	0.6429	0.3914	0.6665
	(5.22)	(8.15)	(2.59)	(4.85)
$\hat{\sigma}$	0.8768	0.7895	0.8860	0.7906
$\bar{R}^2$	0.8603	0.8953	0.8574	0.8950
$\chi^2_{SC}(1)$	0.08	0.01	0.00	0.06
	{3.84}	{3.84}	{3.84}	{3.84}
$\chi^2_{FF}(2)$	7.19	0.38	4.97	0.34
	{5.99}	{5.99}	{5.99}	{5.99}
$\chi^2_{N}(2)$	1.84	0.30	2.71	0.30
	{5.99}	{5.99}	{5.99}	{5.99}
$\chi^2_{N}(1)$	0.07	0.00	0.12	0.01
	{3.84}	{3.84}	{3.84}	{3.84}
n	91	91	91	91

[a] See footnote [a] to Table 9.1.
[b] The IV estimates are computed using $(1, \Pi_{t-1}, \Pi_{t-2}, \Pi_{t-3}, f_{t-1}, f_{t-2}, q_{t-1}, q_{t-2}, \Delta\text{FHI}_{t-1}, \Delta\text{FHI}_{t-2})$ as instruments. For the definition of the variables and sources of data see the data appendix.

schemes to provide a satisfactory explanation of inflation expectations clearly points out the need for the incorporation of other relevant information into the expectations formation model. With this in mind we first estimated the following unrestricted distributed lag form of model M_3, using the expectations series Π^e_{tN} and Π^e_{tR},

$$\Pi^e_{tj} = a_{0j} + \sum_{i=1}^{5} a_{ij}\Pi_{t-i} + \sum_{i=1}^{3} \mathbf{b}'_{ij}\mathbf{x}_{t-i} + u_{tj}, \quad j = N, R, \tag{9.36}$$

where $u_{tj} = \varepsilon_{tj} + \beta v_t$. As elements of $\mathbf{x}_t$ we chose the various components of costs and demand changes, as well as general economic variables such as the unemployment rate, the money supply growth, and variables representing changes in policy regimes.[17] In particular, initially we experimented with

[17] A more detailed rationale behind the choice of $\mathbf{x}_t$ is given above, p. 258.

$\mathbf{x}_t = (f_t, w_t, e_t, q_t, RU_t, m_{t-1}, \text{FHI}_t)$. Since lagged expectations are not included in the above specification, consistent estimates of the parameters can be obtained by the OLS method. But because of the possible serial correlation in ε_{tj} and/or v_t we estimated (9.36) under different autocorrelated error specifications. For a valid inference it is important that the serial correlation in u_{tj} is taken into account. The results suggest that, apart from past values of Π_t, the only other variables significantly influencing inflation expectations are the lagged changes in the price of raw material and fuels, (f_{t-1}), the rate of change of manufacturing output (q_{t-1}), and the prices policy variable, FHI_{t-1}. We could not find any significant effects either for the 1967 devaluation, or for the change in the exchange rate regime on the inflation expectations. The unemployment variable turned out to be marginally significant only in the case of the Π^e_{tN} expectations series. In the case of Model M_3 our preferred specification (in the case of Π^e_{tN}) estimated over the period 1959(2)–1985(2) turned out to be:[18]

$$\begin{aligned} \Pi^e_{tN} = {} & \underset{(1.61)}{3.14} + \underset{(6.14)}{0.3773}\Pi_{t-1} - \underset{(-0.4022)}{0.0242}\Pi_{t-2} + \underset{(2.60)}{0.1582}\Pi_{t-3} + \underset{(3.65)}{0.0866} f_{t-1} \\ & + \underset{(3.15)}{0.0985} q_{t-1} - \underset{(-1.62)}{0.3029}\text{RU}_{t-1} - \underset{(-4.40)}{0.0344}\text{FHI}_{t-1} + \hat{u}_{tN}, \end{aligned} \tag{9.37}$$

$$\hat{u}_{tN} = \underset{(7.40)}{0.7552}\hat{u}_{t-1,N} + \underset{(2.01)}{0.2054}\hat{u}_{t-2,N} + \hat{\eta}_{tN}$$

$$\bar{R}^2 = 0.8732, \quad \hat{\sigma} = 0.8483, \quad \text{DW} = 1.73, \quad n = 92.$$

The above result allows for an AR(2) error specification, and is computed by the exact maximum likelihood method described in Pesaran and Slater (1980). As already pointed out, the residual autocorrelation in this regression can be traced to the serial correlation in measurement errors, ε_{tN}, and does not necessarily imply that the expectations formation model is misspecified. All the estimated coefficients have the correct signs except for the coefficient of Π_{t-2}, which is small and statistically insignificant. Not surprisingly inflation expectations are positively affected by past increases in manufacturing prices, raw material and fuel prices, and in output, and are negatively influenced by a rise in the rate of unemployment and a strengthening of prices policy. However, we could not detect any significant effect for changes in money wages and exchange rates on expectations. The absence of a significant independent exchange rate effect can be readily explained in terms of a mark-up pricing model. To the extent that variations in exchange rates are already reflected in raw material and fuel prices, there seems to be no reason for an independent exchange rate effect on inflation expectations. The ineffectiveness of past changes in money wages on inflation expectations is, however, more difficult to explain. The fact that money wages and prices in the manufacturing sector tend to move together may be one reason for not observing an *independent* money-wage effect on inflation expectations.

[18] A similar result was also obtained for the expectations series, Π^e_{tR}.

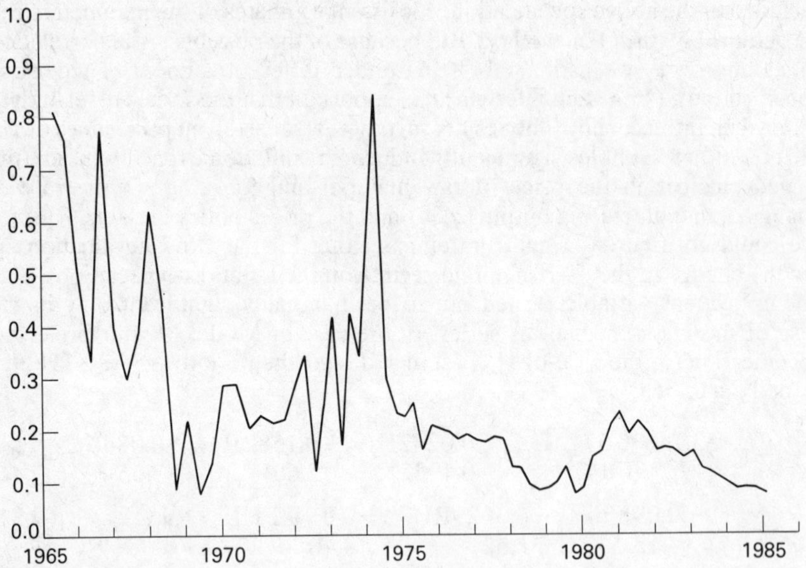

Figure 9.1 Values of the adaptive coefficient $(\mu_t)-1965(2)-1985(1)$

Overall, the augmented expectations formation model, M_3 provides a more plausible explanation of inflation expectations than either of the purely extrapolative models M_1 and M_2. Nevertheless, it is based on unrealistic assumptions concerning the knowledge that firms are supposed to have about the parameters of the final form model, $\Pi_t = \mathbf{z}_{t-1}\boldsymbol{\gamma} + \text{error}$.

Amongst the various expectations formation models discussed in this chapter, the least informationally demanding specification is the augmented adaptive-learning model, M_4. In the case of this model the adaptive coefficients μ_t, and the final-form parameters $\boldsymbol{\gamma}_t$ need to be updated every period according to the formula (9.27) and (9.28), respectively. (Note that in (9.28) y_j should be replaced by Π_j.) The computations involved in estimating model M_4 are heavy but straightforward.[19] Assuming $\mathbf{z}_t$ includes information on Π_t, f_t, q_t, RU_t and FHI_t we first computed μ_t using (9.27). The results are shown in figure 9.1. The adaptive coefficient, μ_t varies considerably over the period 1965(2)–1985(1), and reaches its peak in mid-1974 when the inflation

[19] The amount of computations required can be substantially reduced by using the following recursive equations. Denoting $\Sigma_{j=1}^{t}\mathbf{z}_j\mathbf{z}_j'$, by A_t and $\Sigma_{j=1}^{t}\mathbf{z}_j\Pi_j$, by $\mathbf{d}_t$, we have $A_t^{-1} = A_{t-1}^{-1} - (1+\mathbf{z}_t'A_{t-1}^{-1}\mathbf{z}_t)^{-1}(A_{t-1}^{-1}\mathbf{z}_t\mathbf{z}_t'A_{t-1}^{-1})$, and $\mathbf{d}_t = \mathbf{d}_{t-1} + \Pi_t\mathbf{z}_t$, for $t = h+1, h+2, \ldots, n$. Recall that h stands for the dimension of $\mathbf{z}_t$. To start the recursions one needs only to compute the inverse of $A_h = \Sigma_{j=1}^{h}\mathbf{z}_j\mathbf{z}_j'$. The initial value for $\mathbf{d}_t$ is given by $\mathbf{d}_h = \Sigma_{j=1}^{h}\mathbf{z}_j\Pi_j$. For proofs and further details see, for example, Brown et al. (1975). I am grateful to Bahram Pesaran for writing the relevant computer programs for carrying out the computations. These computations are now incorporated in Data — FIT (see Pesaran and Pesaran (1987)).

rate was at its highest level. There is a clear tendency for the adaptive coefficient to rise sharply with inflation, but when inflation begins to fall the adaptive coefficient tends to fall only gradually. This suggests that the rate at which learning is taking place is rather slow. The significant variations observed in μ_t provide further evidence against both the REH and the simple adaptive expectations hypothesis.

The empirical validity of model M_4 can now be investigated by estimating R_4 (the reduced-form of M_4), using either of the expectations series Π^e_{tN} or Π^e_{tR}. In order to reduce the impact of initializing the learning process on the results we discarded the pre-1972 observations and estimated R_4 over the 1972(1)–1985(2) period. We obtained the following OLS estimates:

$$\begin{aligned} R_4:\quad \Pi^e_{tN} - \Pi^e_{t-1,N} = {} & \underset{(0.25)}{0.0623} + \underset{(1.96)}{3.5655}\mu_{t-1} - \underset{(-2.86)}{0.8446}\mu_{t-1}\Pi_{t-1} \\ & + \underset{(3.67)}{1.6850}\mu_{t-1}(\Pi_{t-1} - \Pi^e_{t-1,N}) \\ & + \underset{(2.85)}{0.2830}(\Delta\mathbf{z}_{t-1})'\boldsymbol{\gamma}_{t-2} + \hat{u}_t, \end{aligned}$$

$$\bar{R}^2 = 0.8168, \quad \hat{\sigma} = 0.8231, \quad \mathrm{DW} = 1.95, \quad n = 54\,(1972(1)\text{–}1985(2)),$$

$$\chi^2_{\mathrm{SC}}(1) = 0.06, \quad \chi^2_{\mathrm{FF}}(2) = 1.50, \quad \chi^2_{\mathrm{N}}(2) = 4.10, \quad \chi^2_{\mathrm{H}}(1) = 0.01.$$

Except for the intercept term, all the coefficients are significant and have the expected signs. However, the estimate obtained for β (namely, $0.1554 = 1 - 0.8446$) is not plausible. The same is also true of the estimate obtained for the coefficient of the adaptive variable, $\mu_{t-1}(\Pi_{t-1} - \Pi^e_{t-1,N})$. On the assumption that R_4 is valid we would expect a coefficient of unity for the adaptive variable, and a coefficient equal to β for $(\Delta\mathbf{z}_{t-1})'\boldsymbol{\gamma}_{t-2}$.

The OLS estimates of R_4 can, however, be misleading, as they do not allow for the presence of random errors in the measurement of expectations. To deal with the measurement error problem we re-estimated R_4 by the IV method using $\{1, \mu_{t-1}, \mu_{t-1}\Pi_{t-1}, \Pi_{t-1}, \Pi_{t-2}, \Pi_{t-3}, f_{t-1}, f_{t-2}, q_{t-1}, q_{t-2}, \Delta\mathrm{FHI}_{t-1}, \Delta\mathrm{FHI}_{t-2}, (\Delta\mathbf{z}_{t-1})'\boldsymbol{\gamma}_{t-2}\}$ as instruments.[20] We obtained the following results

$$\begin{aligned} R_4:\quad \Pi^e_{tN} - \Pi^e_{t-1,N} = {} & \underset{(0.06)}{0.0140} + \underset{(1.54)}{2.9599}\mu_{t-1} - \underset{(-1.92)}{0.6636}\mu_{t-1}\Pi_{t-1} \\ & + \underset{(2.42)}{1.3593}\mu_{t-1}(\Pi_{t-1} - \Pi^e_{t-1,N}) \\ & + \underset{(2.97)}{0.2993}(\Delta\mathbf{z}_{t-1})'\boldsymbol{\gamma}_{t-2} + u_t, \end{aligned}$$

$$\bar{R}^2 = 0.8157, \quad \hat{\sigma} = 0.8273, \quad n = 54\,(1972(1)\text{–}1985(2)),$$

$$\chi^2_{\mathrm{SC}}(1) = 0.55, \quad \chi^2_{\mathrm{FF}}(2) = 0.34, \quad \chi^2_{\mathrm{N}}(2) = 4.57, \quad \chi^2_{\mathrm{H}}(1) = 0.04.$$

---

[20] The results proved to be fairly robust to the choice of instruments.

The IV estimates are more plausible, and provide further empirical support for the adaptive-learning model. The coefficient of the adaptive variable, namely $\mu_{t-1}(\Pi_{t-1}-\Pi^e_{t-1,N})$, is not significantly different from unity,[21] and the estimate of β given by the coefficient of $(\Delta\mathbf{z}_{t-1})'\boldsymbol{\gamma}_{t-2}$ is now only marginally different from the estimate of β obtained using the coefficient of the $\mu_{t-1}\Pi_{t-1}$ variable.[22] Finally, the diagnostic test statistics computed for the IV estimates do not provide any evidence of residual autocorrelation, functional form misspecification, or heteroscedasticity. The value of the diagnostic statistic for the normality test, $\chi^2_{\mathrm{N}}(2)$, in comparison with the other diagnostic statistics is high, but it is still insignificant at the 5 per cent significance level.

Before accepting the adaptive-learning model as our preferred explanation of the inflation expectations we also need to compare its performance against other models such as the simple-adaptive model, M_1, or the Frenkel model, M_2. Therefore we re-estimated these models by the IV method over the shorter period 1972(1)–1985(2), using the same instruments as before. The following results were obtained:

$$\mathrm{R}_1:\quad \underset{}{\Pi^e_{tN}-\Pi^e_{t-1N}}=\underset{(3.09)}{1.4715}-\underset{(-3.06)}{0.2881}\Pi_{t-1}+\underset{(3.71)}{0.7969}(\Pi_{t-1}-\Pi^e_{t-1,N}),$$

$$\bar{R}^2=0.7454,\quad \hat{\sigma}=0.9724,\quad n=54\,(1972(1)\text{–}1985(2)),$$

$$\chi^2_{\mathrm{SC}}(1)=4.33,\quad \chi^2_{\mathrm{FF}}(2)=5.70,\quad \chi^2_{\mathrm{N}}(2)=3.78,\quad \chi^2_{\mathrm{H}}(1)=3.90.$$

$$\mathrm{R}_2:\quad \Pi^e_{tN}-\Pi^e_{t-1,N}=-\underset{(-0.30)}{0.1815}+\underset{(0.15)}{0.0167}\Pi_{t-2}-\underset{(-0.37)}{0.1287}(\Pi^e_{t-1,N}-\Pi^e_{t-2,N})$$

$$-\underset{(-0.64)}{0.2130}(\Pi_{t-2}-\Pi^e_{t-2,N})+\underset{(1.86)}{0.2767}(\Pi_{t-1}-\Pi_{t-2}),$$

$$\bar{R}^2=0.7546,\quad \hat{\sigma}=0.9547,\quad n=54\,(1972(1)\text{–}1985(2)),$$

$$\chi^2_{\mathrm{SC}}(1)=0.22,\quad \chi^2_{\mathrm{FF}}(2)=4.24,\quad \chi^2_{\mathrm{N}}(2)=2.50,\quad \chi^2_{\mathrm{H}}(1)=0.27.$$

These results are similar in character to those already reported in tables 9.1 and 9.2 for the period 1959(2)–1985(2). Comparing these results with the IV estimates obtained for model M_4 now shows that the adaptive-learning model is clearly superior to the purely extrapolative models M_1 and M_2. The degree of explanation achieved using the adaptive-learning model also compares favourably with the augmented extrapolative model, M_3.

The above findings turned out to be quite robust to the choice of the expectations series, which is remarkable considering the important quantitative differences that exist between the two expectations series Π^e_{tN} and Π^e_{tR}.

[21] The t-ratio for the test of the hypothesis that the coefficient of $\mu_{t-1}(\Pi_{t-1}-\Pi^e_{t-1,N})$ is unity is equal to 0.64.

[22] The two possible estimates of β obtained from the coefficients of $\mu_{t-1}\Pi_{t-1}$ and $(\Delta\mathbf{z}_{t-1})'\boldsymbol{\gamma}_{t-2}$ are respectively equal to 0.3364 and 0.2993.

9.5 Concluding Remarks

This chapter has emphasized the importance of learning in the process of expectations formation. The expectations formation models proposed in the econometric literature ignore the learning problem, either by assuming that complete learning is achieved (as is the case with the REH), or that no further learning is possible. In reality neither of these extremes is tenable. We need to consider models that explicitly allow for the learning process. The augmented adaptive-learning model proposed in this chapter is intended to go some way towards meeting this need. The empirical results obtained using this model are encouraging, and it would be interesting to see how the model performs in other applications.

10 Conclusions

The preceding chapters have attempted a critical examination of a number of issues that surround the Muth version of the REH, in the belief that only by a critical evaluation of the scope and the limits of this influential hypothesis is it possible to fully ascertain its relevance to the study of economic decision-making under uncertainty.

The REH, in the strong sense advanced by Muth (1961), is based on two important premises:

1. subjective beliefs are capable of being formalized in terms of probability distributions;
2. subjective beliefs and the 'objective reality' coincide in the sense that the probability distribution of events held subjectively by economic agents will be the same as the corresponding objective probability distribution.

Whether it is plausible to assume that the above premises hold in practice is a highly controversial matter and, as argued in chapter 2, depends on the nature and sources of uncertainty. In the analysis we distinguish between 'behavioural' and 'exogenous' uncertainties. By behavioural (or endogenous) uncertainty is meant the uncertainty that arises because agents are incapable of perfectly anticipating the behaviour and actions of others in the market place, and it is contrasted with the more readily understood type which, for all practical purposes, is exogenous to the agent's decision-making process. In making this distinction the concern has not been with the primarily philosophical controversy that surrounds (1), i.e. whether probability is measurable, but whether the subjective probability distribution attached to uncertain events by individuals remains invariant with respect to their own actions or the perception they have of the actions of others. It is argued that in the case of behavioural uncertainty, because of the feedback from subjective beliefs to the data generating process, an objective basis for the characterization of uncertainty need not exist. The situation is, however, more favourable to the REH when uncertainty is exogenous. This view is also based on the belief that the 'Law of Uniformity of Nature' needed for the validity of induction is more likely to be satisfied in the case of exogenous rather than endogenous uncertainty.

The most important issue underlying the REH is the problem of learning. The question is whether or not it is possible or worthwhile for individuals to learn the 'true' model of the economy from their own experience, or perhaps from the experience of others. The answer to this question is rather mixed and depends on a large number of considerations, including the nature of uncertainty that individuals face, the extent of their *a priori* knowledge, and the costs involved in the acquisition and processing of information. In the case of rational learning models, where information is costless and individuals are assumed to know the correct specifications of the equilibrium relationships between market prices and private signals, it can be shown that learning with respect to a finite number of parameters of the model does in fact take place. Such an approach is, however, at least as demanding in terms of what it assumes about the *a priori* knowledge and analytic ability of agents as the idea of the REH itself. A less informationally demanding, and in many respects more relevant, approach to the problem of learning is provided by the boundedly rational learning models. But even in the case of the simplest examples of this approach considered in the literature, the 'common knowledge' assumptions needed for the convergence of the learning process are highly restrictive, and in effect rule out the possibility of individuals having different beliefs or information either about the way the economy functions or about the probability distributions of the exogenous variables.

The relaxation of the information homogeneity assumption presents a number of conceptual as well as technical difficulties for the analysis of rational expectations models. The decision-making process will become subject to behavioural uncertainty, and necessitates that each individual adopt rules, not only for revision of unknown parameters of the processes generating the exogenous variables influencing the economy, but also for learning about the private information and the behaviour of other individuals in the economy. It will no longer be possible to justify the derivation of the REH as a solution to the problem of economic optimization in the case of a 'representative' agent. The existence of information heterogeneity across agents presents an additional type of aggregation problem, and delivers a further blow to the relevance of the concept of 'representative' agent in economic analysis. There is clearly a need for a comprehensive study of the problem of information heterogeneity and the implications that it has for the REH and the underlying learning process.

The problem of learning becomes even more complicated when the cost of acquisition and processing of information is explicitly allowed for in the analysis. Under costly information, first, it may not be advantageous to identify all the profitable opportunities, and there will therefore be no reason for all systematic errors of expectations to be eliminated through trade, even if it were possible to learn the true model of the economy. Secondly, the learning process may fail to converge to the 'true' model simply because individuals wrongly believe that it is not worth collecting and processing the necessary information. In such circumstances individuals may become trapped in what may be called a 'vicious circle of ignorance'.

Despite recent important contributions, the literature on learning is rather fragmentary and, except for a few isolated examples, discusses the learning problem only when the acquisition and processing of information is costless.

There is clearly a great deal of scope for further research in this area. What is needed is an integrated approach to the dual problems of learning and expectations formation. Both the REH and the adaptive expectations hypothesis that preceded it are based on untenable informational and methodological foundations. The REH presupposes that complete learning is achieved, while the adaptive/extrapolative hypothesis assumes that no further learning is possible. In reality neither of these extremes is tenable, and expectations formation models that explicitly allow for the learning process should be considered. This volume has made some attempts towards this end, and has developed an augmented adaptive-learning model which explains how individuals change their expectations under incomplete learning. The application of the model to the inflation expectations in British manufacturing industries has produced encouraging results. It would now be interesting to see how the adaptive-learning model performs in other applications.

Notwithstanding the learning problem, the REH is ofen employed in the literature as a model-consistent method of expectations formation. This view admits the methodological and informational difficulties associated with the REH, but adopts it in econometric analysis as a method of imposing restrictions on parameters of the econometric model. Seen from this perspective the REH is not viewed as an embodiment of 'rationality' but rather simply as another way of imposing parameter restrictions, similar in spirit to the exclusion restrictions or the common factor restrictions often utilized in applied econometrics research to obtain more parsimonious econometric specifications. Whether the parameter restrictions implied by the REH are more plausible than other types of parameter restrictions becomes a matter of empirical expediency.

The formulation of the REH in terms of a set of parameter restrictions imposed on an otherwise standard econometric model has been an important factor in the rapid acceptance of the REH in the econometrics literature. The past decade has witnessed significant technical advances in the econometric analysis of rational expectations models. (Some of these developments are reviewed in part II of this book.) Despite this there are still important gaps that remain: these include the problem of solution, identification and estimation of dynamic multivariant models with future expectations, and the econometric issues involved in the analysis of non-linear rational expectations models and models with heterogeneous information. Research also needs to be carried out on the small sample properties of the various asymptotic estimation and test procedures that are available in the case of rational expectations models.

There is no doubt that the REH has already had a major impact on the way macroeconomics is practised, and it seems unlikely that the account of its limitations set out in this volume will significantly alter this situation. It is, however, hoped that the present volume will make a contribution to a better understanding of the methodological and technical issues that underlie the application of the REH in econometric analysis, and generate further interest in the use of direct measures of expectations in empirical analyses of learning and expectations formation in economics.

Appendix A

Conditional Expectations and Martingales: General Properties

This appendix briefly reviews some of the properties of conditional (mathematical) expectations needed for the analysis of rational expectations models and their solutions. Those readers interested in a rigorous and formal exposition should consult advanced textbooks on probability and stochastic processes, such as Doob (1953, chapters 1 and 7), and Billingsley (1979, sections 34 and 35).

A.1 Conditional Expectations

Consider first the simple case of two continuous random variables and suppose that X and Y have the joint probability density function $f(x, y)$ and marginal probability density functions $f(x)$ and $f(y)$ respectively. Assume, further, that $f(x)>0$. Then the conditional expectations of Y given $X=x$ is denoted by $E(Y|X=x)$, or simply $E(Y|x)$, and is given by

$$E(Y|x)=\int_R \{yf(x, y)/f(x)\}\,\mathrm{d}y=\psi(x), \tag{A.1}$$

where R stands for the range of Y. For the more general case of interest in this volume we adopt the following definition:

Definition A1 Let Y_t be a random variable at time t whose expectations exist (i.e. $E|y_t|<\infty$), and let $\mathbf{X}_t$ be a vector of random variables jointly distributed with Y_s for all t and s. Consider now the information set $\Omega_t=(y_t, y_{t-1}, \ldots; \mathbf{x}_t, \mathbf{x}_{t-1}, \ldots)$ containing all the realizations of Y and $\mathbf{X}$ up to and including time t. Then the *conditional expectations of Y_t given Ω_{t-1}* is defined as

$$E(Y_t|\Omega_{t-1})=E(Y_t|Y_{t-1}=y_{t-1}, Y_{t-2}=y_{t-2}, \ldots;$$
$$\mathbf{X}_{t-1}=\mathbf{x}_{t-1}, \mathbf{X}_{t-2}=\mathbf{x}_{t-2}, \ldots).$$

The expression for $E(Y_t|\Omega_{t-1})$ in terms of the realizations $y_{t-1}, y_{t-2}, \ldots; \mathbf{x}_{t-1}, \mathbf{x}_{t-2}, \ldots$ can be obtained by the integration or summation of relevant conditional probability distributions similar to the one given by A.1 for the two-variable case.

A.2 Properties of Conditional Expectations

Assuming that $\mathrm{E}(\mathrm{Y}_t|\Omega_{t-1})$ is measurable with respect to Ω_{t-1}, and noting that $\Omega_t \supset \Omega_{t-1} \supset \Omega_{t-2} \ldots$, we have

Property P1 The conditional expectations $\mathrm{E}(\mathrm{Y}_t|\Omega_{t-1})$ can be expressed as a function of the realizations, $y_{t-1}, y_{t-2}, \ldots; \mathbf{x}_{t-1}, \mathbf{x}_{t-2}, \ldots$ (see Doob, 1953, p. 603).

Property P2 If $Y_t = a$ with probability 1, then $\mathrm{E}(\mathrm{Y}_t|\Omega_{t-1}) = a$.

Property P3 For a constant scalar a and a constant vector $\mathbf{b}$ comformable to $\mathbf{x}_t$, then $E(aY_t + \mathbf{b}\mathbf{X}_t|\Omega_{t-1}) = aE(Y_t|\Omega_{t-1}) + \mathbf{b}E(\mathbf{X}_t|\Omega_{t-1})$.

Property P4 (the law of iterated conditional expectations) For non-negative integers i and j such that $j \geqslant i$, then

$$E\{\mathrm{E}(\mathrm{Y}_t|\Omega_{t-i})|\Omega_{t-j}\} = \mathrm{E}(\mathrm{Y}_t|\Omega_{t-i}).$$

Similarly, if S_t is a subset of Ω_t, then

$$E\{E(Y_t|\Omega_{t-1})|S_{t-1}\} = \mathrm{E}(\mathrm{Y}_t|S_{t-1}).$$

Property P5 (unconditional expectations) For a non-negative integer i, we have

$$E\{E(Y_t|\Omega_{t-i})\} = E(Y_t).$$

Property P6 $|\mathrm{E}(\mathrm{Y}_t|\Omega_{t-1})| \leqslant E(|Y_t|\,|\Omega_{t-1})$.

The validity of properties P2–P6 follow directly from theorems 34.1–34.4 in Billingsley (1979).

The relationship between conditional expectations and optimal predictors is given by the following theorem.

Theorem A1 (least squares approximation theorem) Suppose the random variables $Y, X_1, X_2, \ldots, X_k$ have a multivariate normal distribution with zero expectations. Then the function $f(X_1, X_2, \ldots, X_k)$ which uniquely minimizes the mean squares forecast error criterion function $E\{Y - f(X_1, X_2, \ldots, X_k)\}^2$ is given by the conditional mathematical expectations $E(Y|\mathrm{X}_1, X_2, \ldots, X_k)$.

Proof Since $Y, X_1, X_2, \ldots, X_k$ are normally distributed it follows that the conditional distribution of Y given $X_1, X_2, \ldots, X_k$ is normal with $E(Y|\mathbf{X}) = \mathbf{a}'\mathbf{X}$ where $\mathbf{X}' = (\mathrm{X}_1, X_2, \ldots, X_k)$, and $\mathbf{a} = \Sigma_{xx}^{-1}\Sigma_{xy}$. The matrices Σ_{xx} and Σ_{xy} stand for the $k \times k$ covariance matrix of $\mathbf{X}$, and the $k \times 1$ covariance vector of $\mathbf{X}$ and Y respectively. Therefore, $Y - E(Y|\mathbf{X}) = Y - \mathbf{a}'\mathbf{X}$ is normally distributed with mean zero and is uncorrelated and hence independent of $\mathrm{X}_1, X_2, \ldots, X_k$. The independence of $Y - \mathbf{a}'\mathbf{X}$ from $\mathbf{X}$ also means that

$Y-E(Y|\mathbf{X})$ is independent and therefore orthogonal to every function $f(\mathbf{X})$. Hence

$$E[\{Y-E(Y|\mathbf{X})\}\{E(Y|\mathbf{X})-f(\mathbf{X})\}]=0,$$

and

$$E\{Y-f(\mathbf{X})\}^2=E\{Y-E(Y|\mathbf{X})\}^2+\{E(Y|\mathbf{X})-f(\mathbf{X})\}^2.$$

Consequently, the mean squares criterion function $E\{Y-f(\mathbf{X})\}^2$ will be minimized uniquely by setting $f(\mathbf{X})$ equal to $E(Y|\mathbf{X})$. QED

Remark The normality assumption in the above theorem ensures that $E(Y|\mathbf{X})=\mathbf{a}'\mathbf{X}$ is the 'optimal' conditional predictor of Y with respect to *any* function $f(\mathbf{X})$ measurable on the sample space of $X_1, X_2, \ldots, X_k$. If we now relax the normality assumption but assume only that $E(X_i^2)<\infty$, and $E(Y^2)<\infty$, it can be shown that $\mathbf{a}'\mathbf{X}$ will still minimize $E\{Y-f(\mathbf{X})\}^2$ but for all *linear* combinations f of the X_i's. This latter solution is referred to as the *linear least squares approximation*. Therefore, the optimality of $E(Y|\mathbf{X})$ as a predictor of Y conditional on $\mathbf{X}$ can be established either under the joint normality of $(Y, \mathbf{X})$, or under the linearity of the forecast function.

A.3 Martingales

Definition A2 Let $\mathcal{M}_1, \mathcal{M}_2, \ldots$ be a sequence of random variables, and let $\Omega_1, \Omega_2, \Omega_3, \ldots$ be an increasing sequence of information sets (i.e. $\Omega_1 \subset \Omega_2 \subset \Omega_3 \ldots$), then $\{\mathcal{M}_t\}$ is said to be a *martingale* with respect to $\{\Omega_t\}$, if the following conditions are met:

1 $\mathcal{M}_t$ is measurable with respect to Ω_t,
2 Expectations of $\mathcal{M}_t$ exists [i.e. $E|\mathcal{M}_t|<\infty$],
3 $E(\mathcal{M}_t|\Omega_{t-1})=\mathcal{M}_{t-1}$, with probability 1.

Properties of martingales

Property P7 $E(\mathcal{M}_t)=\mu$, for all t.

Property P8 $E|\mathcal{M}_t| \leqslant E|\mathcal{M}_{t+1}| \leqslant E|\mathcal{M}_{t+2}| \leqslant \ldots$

To prove P7 note that by definition $E(\mathcal{M}_{t+1}|\Omega_t)=\mathcal{M}_t$ or $E\{E(\mathcal{M}_{t+1}|\Omega_t)\}=E(\mathcal{M}_t)$. But using property P5, $E\{E(\mathcal{M}_{t+1}|\Omega_t)\}=E(\mathcal{M}_{t+1})$. Hence $E(\mathcal{M}_t)=E(\mathcal{M}_{t+1})$ for all t. The validity of P8 can be established along similar lines using P6. That is $E\{|\mathcal{M}_{t+1}||\Omega_t\} \geqslant |E(\mathcal{M}_{t+1}|\Omega_t)|=|\mathcal{M}_t|$. Taking expectations of both sides of this inequality now yields $E|\mathcal{M}_{t+1}| \geqslant E|\mathcal{M}_t|$. (See property P5.)

Theorem A2 (Martingale convergence theorem) Let $\mathcal{M}_1, \mathcal{M}_2, \ldots$ be a martingale sequence with respect to the information sets $\Omega_1 \subset \Omega_2 \subset \Omega_3 \ldots$. If $E\{|\mathcal{M}_t|\} \leqslant K < \infty$ for all t, then $\mathcal{M}_t \to M$ with probability 1, where M is a random variable satisfying $E\{|M|\} \leqslant K$.

Proof Doob, 1953, theorem 4.1.

Appendix B

Solution of Linear Rational Expectations Models under Heterogeneous Information

B.1 Introduction

Consider an economy (or an industry) composed of N individuals (or firms), and suppose that each individual i decides on the value of y_{it} according to the following rule

$$y_{it} = \lambda_i E(y_t \mid \Omega_{it}) + w_{it}, \quad i = 1, 2, \ldots, N, \tag{B.1}$$

where

$$y_t = \sum_{i=1}^{N} y_{it}, \tag{B.2}$$

and Ω_{it} is the information available to the ith individual at time t. The variable w_{it} represents the effect of exogenous or predetermined variables on y_{it} and in general can be decomposed into the individual-specific component x_{it}, and the macro-component $\beta_i z_t$:

$$w_{it} = x_{it} + \beta_i z_t. \tag{B.3}$$

The structure of information sets Ω_{it} across individuals is given by

$$\Omega_{it} = \Phi_{it} \cup \psi_{t-1}, \quad i = 1, 2, \ldots, N,$$

where Φ_{it} represents the individual-specific or the private information set, and ψ_{t-1} the commonly known or the public information set. More specifically it will be assumed that

$$\Phi_{it} = (y_{it}, y_{i,t-1}, \ldots; x_{it}, x_{i,t-1}, \ldots),$$

$$\psi_{t-1} = (y_{t-1}, y_{t-2}, \ldots; x_{t-1}, x_{t-2}, \ldots; z_{t-1}, z_{t-2}, \ldots),$$

where $x_t = \Sigma_{i=1}^{N} x_{it}$. We also assume that $N > 2$, which rules out the possibility of an individual extracting the private information of other individuals from the publicly available information.

The above model is a simple example of a linear RE model with heterogeneous information and arises, for example, in studies of pricing or output policies of firms in a decentralized market with private information. For instance, combining the output decision rules give below and discussed in chapter 4

$$q_{it} = \alpha_i\{\mathrm{E}(P_t|\Omega_{it}) - \eta_{it}\}, \quad i = 1, 2, \ldots, N,$$

with the demand function

$$P_t = \mathrm{a} - bq_t + \varepsilon_t,$$

yields[1]:

$$q_{it} = -b\alpha_i E(q_t|\Omega_{it}) + \alpha_i(\mathrm{a} - \eta_{it}), \tag{B.4}$$

which has the same form as the general specification (B.1), with $y_{it} = q_{it}$, $\lambda_i = -b\alpha_i$, and $w_{it} = \alpha_i(\mathrm{a} - \eta_{it})$.

Keynes's famous example of a beauty contest can also be formalized in the context of the above heterogeneous information model (Keynes, 1936, p. 156). Suppose N individuals taking part in a beauty contest are asked to choose the most beautiful picture out of the two possible pictures A and B. The winner of the contest is selected according to all the N answers, the winner being the one whose answer is nearest to the average of all the answers. This is a simplified version of Keynes's original example. The decision-rule of the participants in this context can be formalized in the following manner: Let the choice of the ith individual be represented by the random variable y_i, and suppose that y_i is set equal to unity if picture A is chosen, otherwise it is set equal to zero. The problem facing the ith individual is to choose the value of y in such a way that it is nearest to the average $\bar{y} = N^{-1}\Sigma_{i=1}^{N} y_i = y/N$. The choice of y_i clearly depends on what individual i expects $\bar{y}$ to be. Denoting this (subjective) expectations by $E(\bar{y}\,|\,\Omega_i)$ we have

$$\begin{aligned} y_i &= E(\bar{y}|\Omega_i), \\ &= N^{-1}E(y|\Omega_i), \quad \text{for } i = 1, 2, \ldots, N. \end{aligned}$$

Therefore, Keynes's beauty contest can be viewed as a special case of model (B.1) with $\lambda_i = 1/N$, and $w_{it} = 0$.

B.2 Solution by the Method of Infinite Regress

Here we adopt the method of infinite regress already discussed in chapter 4 to obtain a general solution for (B.1). The procedure involves first aggregating (B.1) over all individual. That is

$$y_t = \lambda F^1(y_t) + w_t, \tag{B.5}$$

[1] Notice that since by assumption $\{\varepsilon_t\}$ is a white-noise process, then $E(\varepsilon_t|\Omega_{it}) = 0$.

where

$$w_t = \sum_{i=1}^{N} w_{it}, \quad \lambda = \sum_{i=1}^{N} \lambda_i,$$

and $F^1(y_t)$ is the first-order average expectations of y_t defined by

$$F^1(y_t) = \lambda^{-1} \sum_{i=1}^{N} \lambda_i E(y_t | \Omega_{it}). \tag{B.6}$$

Taking conditional expectations of (B.5) with respect to the information set Ω_{it} and substituting the results in (B.1) we have

$$y_{it} = \lambda_i \lambda E\{F^1(y_t) | \Omega_{it}\} + \lambda_i \mathrm{E}(\mathrm{w_t} | \Omega_{it}) + w_{it}, \quad i = 1, 2, ..., N.$$

Aggregating over all individuals now gives

$$y_t = \lambda^2 F^2(y_t) + \lambda F^1(w_t) + w_t,$$

where $F^2(y_t)$ stands for the second-order average expectations of y_t defined by

$$F^2(\mathrm{y_t}) = \lambda^{-1} \sum_{i=1}^{N} \lambda_i E\{F^1(y_t) | \Omega_{it}\},$$

and $F^1(w_t)$ is the first-order average expectations of w_t defined similarly by

$$F^1(w_t) = \lambda^{-1} \sum_{i=1}^{N} \lambda_i E(w_t | \Omega_{it}).$$

In Keynes's terminology $F^2(y_t)$ is what the average opinion expects the average opinion (i.e. $F^1(y_t)$) to be.

The above procedure whereby expectations $E(y_t | \Omega_{it})$ are determined in terms of average expectations and average of average expectations and so on, can be repeated to arrive at

$$y_t = \lambda^r F^r(y_t) + \sum_{j=1}^{\mathrm{r}-1} \lambda^j F^j(w_t) + w_t, \tag{B.7}$$

where $F^j(y_t)$ and $F^j(w_t)$ are defined by the recursive relations

$$F^j(y_t) = \lambda^{-1} \sum_{i=1}^{N} \lambda_i E\{F^{j-1}(y_t) | \Omega_{it}\}, \quad j = 2, 3, ...$$

$$F^j(x_t) = \lambda^{-1} \sum_{i=1}^{N} \lambda_i E\{F^{j-1}(w_t) | \Omega_{it}\}, \quad j = 2, 3, ...$$

In the case of the beauty contest example $w_t = F^j(w_t) = 0$, for all j. But since $\lambda_i = N^{-1}$, then the term $F^r(y_t)$ in (B.7) does not disappear, even if r is allowed to increase without bound. Therefore, not surprisingly, the beauty contest problem does not admit a determinate solution. For the equations (B.1) to have a determinate solution, it is necessary that

$$\lim_{r\to\infty} \lambda^r F^r(y_t) = 0. \tag{B.8}$$

This condition ensures that in the limit the arbitrary component $F^r(y)$ is eliminated from (B.7). In situations where y_t is expected to remain bounded and this is common knowledge, we have $|F^r(y_t)| < \infty$ for all r, and the condition (B.8) will be satisfied if $|\lambda| = |\Sigma_{i=1}^{N} \lambda_i| < 1$. Under these assumptions (B.7) becomes

$$y_t = w_t + \sum_{j=1}^{\infty} \lambda^j F^j(w_t), \tag{B.9}$$

which we refer to as the 'infinite regress' solution of (B.1). Unfortunately, this solution still depends on the unobservable average expectations $F^1(w_t)$, $F^2(w_t), \ldots$, and in general will not be determinate. In order to arrive at a determinate solution severe restrictions on the processes generating w_{it} should also be imposed. Here we consider a few examples where a determinate solution to the infinite-regress problem can be found.

Example B.1

Suppose that only macro-effects, z_t operate on y_{it}. That is

$$w_{it} = \beta_i z_t, \quad i = 1, 2, \ldots, N.$$

Further assume that z_t is generated according to the following linear process

$$z_t = \sum_{j=1}^{\infty} \alpha_j z_{t-j} + \sum_{j=1}^{\infty} b_j y_{t-j} + v_t,$$

where $E(v_t|\Omega_{it}) = 0$. In this case, using (B.3), $w_t = \beta z_t$ and

$$E(w_t|\Omega_{it}) = \beta z_t^*,$$

where

$$\beta = \sum_{i=1}^{N} \beta_i, \quad \text{and } z_t^* = \sum_{j=1}^{\infty} a_j z_{t-j} + \sum_{j=1}^{\infty} b_j y_{t-j}.$$

It is also easily seen that

$$F^r(w_t) = \beta z_t^*, \quad r = 1, 2, \ldots$$

Substituting these results in (B.9) now yields the following determinate form for the infinite-regress solution:

$$y_t = \beta z_t + \left(\frac{\lambda}{1-\lambda}\right) \beta z_t^*.$$

It also follows from this solution that despite the heterogeneity of information expectations are homogeneous across individuals, namely

$$E(y_t|\Omega_{it})=\left(\frac{\beta}{1-\lambda}\right)z_t^*, \quad i=1, 2, \ldots, N.$$

This is a general result and holds whenever w_{it} do not depend on individual-specific components.

Example B.2

Consider now the case where (B.1) contains individual specific components, but suppose that expectations of the ith individual about other individual-specific components, x_{jt}, $j \neq i$, can be written as

$$E(x_{jt}|\Omega_{it})=\theta_j x_t^*, \quad \text{for all } j\neq i, \tag{B.10a}$$

where $x_t^*=E(x_t|\psi_{t-1})$. Notice also that since x_{it} is in Ω_{it} then

$$E(x_{it}|\Omega_{it})=x_{it}, \quad \text{for all } i. \tag{B.10b}$$

The assumption (B.10a) is rather restrictive and states that in the absence of public information on x_{jt}, individual $i(i\neq j)$ takes $E(x_{jt}|\Omega_{it})$ to be a fixed fraction of the commonly known expectations of the macro-variable $x_t=\Sigma_{i=1}^N x_{it}$. In this example we shall also assume that x_t^* are given. But under the REH, x_t^* can be obtained from the knowledge of the process generating x_t in the usual manner.

Under the above assumptions and assuming that θ_i, x_t^* and z_t^* are common knowledge we first note that[2]:

$$E(w_t|\Omega_{it})=\theta x_t^*+\beta z_t^*+(x_{it}-\theta_i x_t^*), \tag{B.11}$$

where $\theta=\Sigma_{i=1}^N\theta_i$. Notice that in this result $(x_{it}-\theta_i x_t^*)$ represents the information advantage of the ith individual over the others as far as the value of x_{it} is concerned. Substituting (B.11) in the expression for the average expectations of w_t now yields

$$F^1(\mathrm{w}_t)=\theta x_t^*+\beta z_t^*+\lambda^{-1}\sum_{i=1}^N \lambda_i(x_{it}-\theta_i x_t^*).$$

Similarly,

$$E\{(F^1(w_t)|\Omega_{it}\}=\theta x_t^*+\beta z_t^*+\lambda^{-1}\lambda_i(x_{it}-\theta_i x_t^*),$$

and

$$F^2(w_t)=\theta x_t^*+\beta z_t^*+\lambda^{-2}\sum_{i=1}^N \lambda_i^2(x_{it}-\theta_i x_t^*).$$

[2] In the present example $w_t=x_t+\beta z_t$.

More generally,

$$F^r(w_t) = \theta x_t^* + \beta z_t^* + \lambda^{-r} \sum_{i=1}^{N} \lambda_i^r (x_{it} - \theta_i x_t^*), \quad r = 1, 2, \ldots \tag{B.12}$$

Substituting these results in (B.9) gives the following determinate infinite-regress solution of (B.1)

$$y_t = x_t + \left(\frac{\theta\lambda}{1-\lambda}\right) x_t^* + \beta \left\{ z_t + \frac{\lambda}{1-\lambda} z_t^* \right\} + \sum_{i=1}^{N} \left(\frac{\lambda_i}{1-\lambda_i}\right) (x_{it} - \theta_i x_t^*), \tag{B.13}$$

from which it is easily seen that[3]:

$$E(y_t | \Omega_{it}) = (1-\lambda_i)^{-1} (x_{it} - \theta_i x_t^*) + (1-\lambda)^{-1} (\theta x_t^* + \beta z_t^*). \tag{B.14}$$

Using this result in (B.1) now gives

$$y_{it} = \left(\frac{1}{1-\lambda_i}\right) x_{it} + \lambda_i \left(\frac{\theta}{1-\lambda} - \frac{\theta_i}{1-\lambda_i}\right) x_t^* + \beta_i z_t + \left(\frac{\beta\lambda_i}{1-\lambda}\right) z_t^*. \tag{B.15}$$

This solution can be readily applied to the output decision rules (B.4). In terms of the above notations we have:

$$x_{it} = -\alpha_i \eta_{it},\ z_t = \mathrm{a},\ \beta_i = \alpha_i,\ \lambda_i = -ba_i,\ \lambda = -b \sum_{i=1}^{N} \alpha_i = -b\alpha.$$

Now assuming $|\alpha b| < 1$, and that η_{it} are serially uncorrelated (i.e. $\theta_i = 0$) then using (B.15) we have

$$q_{it} = \alpha_i \left\{ \frac{\mathrm{a}}{1+\alpha b} - \frac{\eta_{it}}{1+\alpha_i b} \right\},$$

which is the same as the solution given in section 4.2.2, for the case of serially independent supply shocks. In the situation where the supply shocks are correlated, under the assumption that

$$E(\eta_{jt} | \Omega_{it}) = \theta_j \eta_t^*, \quad \text{for all } j \neq i$$

the solution (B.15) is still applicable and yields

$$q_{it} = \alpha_i \left\{ \frac{\mathrm{a}}{1+\alpha b} - \frac{\eta_{it}}{1+\alpha_i b} \right\} - b\alpha_i \left\{ \frac{\theta}{1+\alpha b} - \frac{\theta_i}{1+\alpha_i b} \right\} \eta_t^*.$$

However, in so far as this solution depends on η_t^* it will be indeterminate, and this indeterminacy cannot be resolved by replacing η_t^* in terms of past values of $\eta_t = \Sigma_{i=1}^{N} \eta_{it}$. This is because lagged values of η_t are not usually observed in decentralized markets. (See section 4.2, pp. 61–63 for a more detailed discussion.)

---

[3] Notice that $E(x_t | \Omega_{it}) = \theta x_t^* + (x_{it} - \theta_i x_t^*)$.

Appendix C

Solution of Rational Expectations Models with Future Expectations by the Martingale Method

C.1 The Univariate Case[1]

Consider the following univariate first-order linear rational expectations (LRE) equation:

$$y_t = \alpha E(y_{t+1} \mid \Omega_t) + \omega_t, \tag{C.1}$$

where $\Omega_t = \{y_t, y_{t-1}, \ldots; \omega_t, \omega_{t-1}, \ldots\}$ and α is a non-zero scalar constant.

The martingale solution method involves transforming (C.1) into a martingale process by means of the auxiliary variables Y_t, X_t, and Z_t, defined as

$$Y_t = \alpha^t (y_t - \omega_t), \tag{C.2}$$

$$X_t = -\alpha^t \omega_t, \tag{C.3}$$

$$\left.\begin{aligned} Z_t &= E\left(\sum_{j=1}^{t} X_j \mid \Omega_t\right), && \text{for } t \geqslant 1, \\ &= 0, && \text{for } t = 0, \\ &= E\left(-\sum_{j=t+1}^{0} X_j \mid \Omega_t\right), && \text{for } t \leqslant -1. \end{aligned}\right\} \tag{C.4}$$

Using (C.2) and (C.3) in (C.1), it is now easily established that

$$Y_t = E(Y_{t+1} - X_{t+1} \mid \Omega_t). \tag{C.5}$$

---

[1] This part of appendix C first appeared in Pesaran (1981).

Turning to Z_t, for $t \geqslant 1$, we have

$$Z_t = E\left\{\left(\sum_{j=1}^{t+1} X_j - X_{t+1}\right) \mid \Omega_t\right\},$$

$$= E\left\{\left[E\left(\sum_{j=1}^{t+1} X_j \mid \Omega_{t+1}\right) - X_{t+1}\right] \mid \Omega_t\right\},$$

or

$$Z_t = E\{(Z_{t+1} - X_{t+1}) \mid \Omega_t\}.$$

Also for $t = 0$,

$$\begin{aligned} Z_0 &= E(X_1 - X_1 \mid \Omega_0), \\ &= E\{E(X_1 \mid \Omega_1) - X_1 \mid \Omega_0\}, \\ &= E(Z_1 - X_1 \mid \Omega_0), \end{aligned}$$

and similarly, for $t \leqslant -1$, we have

$$Z_t = E\left(-\sum_{i=t+2}^{0} X_i - X_{t+1} \mid \Omega_t\right),$$

$$= E\left\{E\left(-\sum_{i=t+2}^{0} X_i \mid \Omega_{t+1}\right) - X_{t+1} \mid \Omega_t\right\},$$

$$= E(Z_{t+1} - X_{t+1} \mid \Omega_t).$$

Thus, for all t, we can write:[2]

$$Z_t = E(Z_{t+1} - X_{t+1} \mid \Omega_t). \tag{C.6}$$

If we now subtract (C.6) from (C.5) and set $\mathscr{M}_t = Y_t - Z_t$, we get $E(\mathscr{M}_{t+1} \mid \Omega_t) = \mathscr{M}_t$, which means that $\mathscr{M}_t$ is a martingale process,[3] and using (C.2) the general solution of (C.1) can be obtained as

$$y_t = \alpha^{-t} Y_t + \omega_t = \alpha^{-t}(\mathscr{M}_t + Z_t) + \omega_t.$$

Now for $t \geqslant 1$, using the definition of Z_t, given above in (C.4), the general solution of (C.1) becomes

$$y_t = \alpha^{-t}\mathscr{M}_t - \alpha^{-t}\sum_{j=1}^{t-1} \alpha^j E(\omega_j \mid \Omega_t),$$

---

[2] Note that since only finite sums are involved, the expression given on the right-hand side of (C.6) exists if expectations $E(X_i \mid \Omega_t)$ exist for all i.

[3] A brief account of martingales and their properties can be found in appendix A.

and since for $i \leqslant t$, $E(\omega_i | \Omega_t) = \omega_i$, the above solution simplifies to

$$y_t = \alpha^{-t}\mathscr{M}_t - \sum_{j=1}^{t-1} \alpha^{-j}\omega_{t-j}, \quad t \geqslant 1.$$

If the information set Ω_t in (C.1) is replaced by Ω_{t-1}, the relevant solution for y_t can be shown to be

$$y_t = \alpha^{-t}\mathscr{M}_{t-1} + \{\omega_t - E(\omega_t | \Omega_{t-1})\} - \sum_{j=1}^{t-1} \alpha^{-j}\omega_{t-j}. \tag{C.7}$$

In the first instance these solutions appear to be very different from the other solutions obtained in the literature. This is due solely to the martingale $\mathscr{M}_t$ that is present in the solution. As there are an infinite number of stochastic processes that have a martingale representation, the solution of (C.1) is not unique and, as a result, a large number of apparently different but basically equivalent solutions of y_t can be encountered.

C.2 The Multivariate Case

The above solution method can be readily extended to multivariate linear RE equations, such as

$$\mathbf{z}_t = \mathrm{A}E(\mathbf{z}_{t+1} | \Omega_t) + \boldsymbol{\omega}_t, \tag{C.8}$$

where $\mathbf{z}_t$ and $\boldsymbol{\omega}_t$ are n-dimensional vectors, and A is the $n \times n$ coefficient matrix of the expectational variables. The solution of this equation crucially depends on whether A is invertible or not.

C.2.1 A General Martingale Solution when A *is Invertible*

When A is non-singular the general martingale solution of (C.8) can be written as

$$\mathbf{z}_t = A^{-t}\mathscr{M}_t - \sum_{j=1}^{t-1} A^{-j}\boldsymbol{\omega}_{t-j}, \tag{C.9}$$

where $\mathscr{M}_t$ now represents a multivariate martingale vector process comprising *n distinct* martingale processes with respect to the information set Ω_t. In the 'regular' case where all the eigenvalues of A fall within the unit circle, and $\{\boldsymbol{\omega}_t\}$ follows a multivariate stationary process, the unique stationary solution of (C.8) is given by the forward solution, i.e.

$$\mathbf{z}_t = \sum_{i=0}^{\infty} A^i E(\boldsymbol{\omega}_{t+i} | \Omega_t). \tag{C.10}$$

Solutions (C.9) and (C.10) can also be used to obtain the martingale solution of higher order univariate LRE models. Consider first the sth order equation ($\alpha_s \neq 0$)

$$y_t = \sum_{j=1}^{s} \alpha_i E(y_{t+i} | \Omega_t) + \omega_t. \tag{C.11}$$

Introduce

$$\mathbf{z}_t = \begin{bmatrix} z_{t1} \\ z_{t2} \\ \vdots \\ z_{ts} \end{bmatrix} = \begin{bmatrix} y_t \\ E(y_{t+1} | \Omega_t) \\ \vdots \\ E(y_{t+s-1} | \Omega_t) \end{bmatrix}, \ E(\mathbf{z}_{t+1} | \Omega_t) = \begin{bmatrix} E(y_{t+1} | \Omega_t) \\ E(y_{t+2} | \Omega_t) \\ \vdots \\ E(y_{t+s} | \Omega_t) \end{bmatrix}, \ \boldsymbol{\omega}_t = \begin{bmatrix} \omega_t \\ 0 \\ \vdots \\ 0 \end{bmatrix}.$$

Then the sth-order equation (C.11) reduces to the multivariate first-order equation (C.8), whose general solution is given by (C.9).

Consider now the autoregressive-rational expectations model of order (m, s), ($\lambda_m \neq 0$, $\alpha_s \neq 0$)

$$y_t = \sum_{i=1}^{m} \lambda_i y_{t-i} + \sum_{i=1}^{s} \alpha_i E(y_{t+i} | \Omega_t) + \omega_t. \tag{C.12}$$

Introduce

$$\mathbf{z}_t = \begin{bmatrix} z_{t1} \\ z_{t2} \\ \vdots \\ z_{ts} \\ z_{t,s+1} \\ \vdots \\ z_{tn} \end{bmatrix} = \begin{bmatrix} E(y_{t+s-1} | \Omega_t) \\ E(y_{t+s-2} | \Omega_t) \\ \vdots \\ y_t \\ y_{t-1} \\ \vdots \\ y_{t-m} \end{bmatrix}, \ E(\mathbf{z}_{t+1} | \Omega_t) = \begin{bmatrix} E(y_{t+s} | \Omega_t) \\ E(y_{t+s-1} | \Omega_t) \\ \vdots \\ E(y_{t+1} | \Omega_t) \\ y_t \\ \vdots \\ y_{t+1-m} \end{bmatrix},$$

$$\boldsymbol{\omega}_t = \begin{bmatrix} \omega_t \\ 0 \\ \vdots \\ 0 \\ 0 \\ \vdots \\ 0 \end{bmatrix}, \tag{C.13}$$

where $n=m+s$. Then (C.12) will be the first equation in the multivariate equation system

$$B\mathbf{z}_t = AE(\mathbf{z}_{t+1} | \Omega_t) + \boldsymbol{\omega}_t,$$

where

$$\underset{n\times n}{B} = \left[\begin{array}{ccccccc|c} 0 & 0 & \dots 0 & 1 & -\lambda_1 & -\lambda_2 \dots & -\lambda_{m-1} & -\lambda_m \\ \hline & & & I_{n-1} & & & & \underset{(n-1)\times 1}{0} \end{array}\right],$$

$$\underset{n\times n}{A} = \left[\begin{array}{c|cccccccc} \alpha_s & \alpha_{s-1} & \dots & \alpha_1 & 0 & 0 & \dots & 0 & 0 \\ \hline \underset{1\times(n-1)}{0} & & & & I_{n-1} & & & & \end{array}\right],$$

The matrix I_{n-1} stands for the identity matrix of order $n-1$. Given the triangular form of matrices B and A it is easily seen that $|B| = -\lambda_m \neq 0$, and $|A| = \alpha_s \neq 0$. Hence B and A are both non-singular and we have

$$\mathbf{z}_t = DE(\mathbf{z}_{t+1} | \Omega_t) + B^{-1}\boldsymbol{\omega}_t,$$

where $D = B^{-1}A$ is also a non-singular matrix. Using (C.9) the general martingale solution of the multivariate equation will be

$$\mathbf{z}_t = D^{-t}\mathcal{M}_t - \sum_{j=1}^{t-1} D^{-j}B^{-1}\boldsymbol{\omega}_{t-j}, \tag{C.14}$$

where, $\{\mathcal{M}_t\}$ is an n-dimensional martingale vector process. However, in the present case where $\mathbf{z}_t$ includes lagged values of y_t, not all the components of $\mathcal{M}_t$ can be chosen arbitrarily. To see this suppose D has n distinct eigenvalues $\rho_1, \rho_2, \dots, \rho_n$. Then the canonical form $D = P^{-1}RP$ exists, where R is a diagonal matrix with ρ_i as its diagonal elements. Furthermore since D is non-singular we also have

$$D^{-j} = P^{-1}R^{-j}P, \quad \text{for } j = 1, 2, \dots$$

Using this result in (C.14) and post-multiplying the resultant expression by P yields

$$P\mathbf{z}_t = R^{-t}\mathcal{N}_t + \mathbf{q}_t, \tag{C.15}$$

where $\mathcal{N}_t = P\mathcal{M}_t$ is also a multivariate martingale process, and

$$\mathbf{q}_t = -\sum_{j=1}^{t-1} R^{-j}PB^{-1}\boldsymbol{\omega}_{t-j}.$$

Partitioning the $s+m$ equations in (C.15) into s and m equations, in an obvious notation we have

$$P_{11}\mathbf{z}_{t1} + P_{12}\mathbf{z}_{t2} = R_1^{-t}\mathcal{N}_{t1} + \mathbf{q}_{t1}, \tag{C.16}$$

$$P_{21}\mathbf{z}_{t1}+P_{22}\mathbf{z}_{t2}=R_2^{-t}\mathcal{N}_{t2}+\mathbf{q}_{t2}, \tag{C.17}$$

where $\mathbf{z}_{t1}=\{E(y_{t+s-1}|\Omega_t), E(y_{t+s-2}|\Omega_t), \ldots, y_t\}$, and $\mathbf{z}_{t2}=\{y_{t-1}, y_{t-2}, \ldots, y_{t-m}\}$. Notice that $\mathbf{z}_{t2}$ contains only predetermined variables at time t. Therefore it will always be possible to obtain $\mathcal{N}_{t2}$ uniquely in terms of $\mathbf{z}_{t2}$, $\mathbf{q}_{t1}$ and $\mathbf{q}_{t2}$. The general solution of (C.12) depends only on the s arbitrary martingale processes in $\mathcal{N}_{t1}$. Pre-multiplying (C.16) by the inverse of P_{11} we obtain

$$\mathbf{z}_{t1}=-P_{11}^{-1}P_{12}\mathbf{z}_{t2}+P_{11}^{-1}R_1^{-t}\mathcal{N}_{t1}+P_{11}^{-1}\mathbf{q}_{t1}.$$

The general martingale solution of (C.12) is now given by the last equation in the above result. Specifically, this general solution can be written as

$$y_t=\sum_{j=1}^{m}\theta_j y_{t-j}+\sum_{j=1}^{s}\rho_j^{-t}\mathcal{M}_{tj}+\sum_{j=1}^{s}\delta_j\sum_{i=1}^{t-1}\rho_j^{-t}\omega_{t-i}, \tag{C.18}$$

where $\mathcal{M}_{t1}, \mathcal{M}_{t2}, \ldots, \mathcal{M}_{ts}$ are s arbitrary martingales, and the parameters θ_j and δ_j are obtainable from the expressions given above. The parameters $\{\theta_1, \theta_2, \ldots, \theta_m\}$ are given by the last row of matrix $-P_{11}^{-1}P_{12}$, and the eigenvalues $\rho_1, \rho_2, \ldots, \rho_s$ are the roots of the determinantal equation

$$|D-\rho I_n|=0,$$

or

$$|A-\rho B|=0.$$

It is also easily seen that the roots of this equation will be the same as the roots of the nth-order polynomial equation, $(n=s+m)$

$$\sum_{i=1}^{m}\lambda_i\rho^i+\sum_{i=1}^{s}\alpha_i\rho^{-i}=1. \tag{C.19}$$

Notice also that the matrix P is formed from the characteristic vectors of $D=B^{-1}A$.

The unique stationary solution of (C.12) 'if it exists' is given by the autoregressive forward solution

$$y_t=\sum_{j=1}^{m}\theta_j y_{t-j}+\sum_{j=1}^{s}\delta_j\sum_{i=0}^{\infty}\rho_j^iE(\omega_{t+i}|\Omega_t), \tag{C.20}$$

where $\rho_1, \rho_2, \ldots, \rho_s$ are those roots of the polynomial equation (C.19) that fall inside the unit circle.

C.2.2 General Martingale Solution when A *is Non-invertible*[4]

Consider now the more prevalent case where matrix A in (C.8) is singular, and suppose that it has $n_1(\leqslant n)$ non-zero characteristic roots. Then matrix A has

[4] The material in this section draws from Pesaran (1981), and Broze and Szafarz (1985).

the Jordan canonical form $A = T\Lambda T^{-1}$, where T is a non-singular matrix and Λ is an $n \times n$ block-triangular matrix

$$\Lambda = \begin{pmatrix} \Lambda_1 & 0 \\ 0 & \Lambda_2 \end{pmatrix}, \tag{C.21}$$

where Λ_1 which is of order $n_1 \times n_1$ is the block associated with the non-zero characteristic roots of A and Λ_2 which is of order $n_2 \times n_2 (n_1 + n_2 = n)$ is the block associated with the zero characteristic roots of A. Notice that Λ_1 is non-singular and Λ_2 is a nil-potent matrix of order n_2. That is $\Lambda_2^j = 0$ for $j \geqslant n_2$, although for values of $j < n_2$, Λ_2^j may be non-zero.

Using the Jordan form of A, (C.8) becomes

$$\bar{\mathbf{z}}_t = \Lambda E(\bar{\mathbf{z}}_{t+1} \mid \Omega_t) + \bar{\boldsymbol{\omega}}_t,$$

where

$$\bar{\mathbf{z}}_t = T^{-1}\mathbf{z}_t, \text{ and } \bar{\boldsymbol{\omega}}_t = T^{-1}\boldsymbol{\omega}_t. \tag{C.22}$$

But in view of (C.21), the above canonical form can be written in the form of two separate blocks of equations:

$$\bar{\mathbf{z}}_{t1} = \Lambda_1 E(\bar{\mathbf{z}}_{t1} \mid \Omega_t) + \bar{\boldsymbol{\omega}}_{t1}, \tag{C.23a}$$

$$\bar{\mathbf{z}}_{t2} = \Lambda_2 E(\bar{\mathbf{z}}_{t+1,2} \mid \Omega_t) + \bar{\boldsymbol{\omega}}_{t1}, \tag{C.23b}$$

where $\bar{\mathbf{z}}_t' = (\bar{\mathbf{z}}_{t1}', \bar{\mathbf{z}}_{t2}')$, $\bar{\boldsymbol{\omega}}_t' = (\bar{\boldsymbol{\omega}}_{t1}', \bar{\boldsymbol{\omega}}_{t2}')$. Since Λ_1 is non-singular, the general solution of (C.23a) is straightforward and is already obtained in the previous section. Using (C.9) we have

$$\bar{\mathbf{z}}_{t1} = \Lambda_1^{-t}\mathscr{M}_{1t} - \sum_{j=1}^{t-1} \Lambda_1^{-j}\bar{\boldsymbol{\omega}}_{t-j,1}, \tag{C.24a}$$

where $\{\mathscr{M}_{1t}\}$ is a martingale vector process of order n_1. The solution of (C.23b) can be easily obtained by the forward recursive substitution method discussed in some detail in section 5.3. Application of this method to (C.23b) yields

$$\bar{\mathbf{z}}_{t2} = \Lambda_2^j E(\bar{\mathbf{z}}_{t+j,2} \mid \Omega_t) + \sum_{i=0}^{j-1} \Lambda_2^i E(\bar{\boldsymbol{\omega}}_{t+i,2} \mid \Omega_t).$$

But since Λ_2 is a nil-potent matrix of order n_2, then by setting $j = n_2$ we arrive at the following unique solution for the second block of equations (C.23b),

$$\bar{\mathbf{z}}_{t2} = \sum_{i=0}^{n_2-1} \Lambda_2^i E(\bar{\boldsymbol{\omega}}_{t+i,2} \mid \Omega_t). \tag{C.24b}$$

The above results have a number of interesting implications. Consider first the case where all the non-zero characteristic roots of A fall within the unit circle. Then from the results in the previous section it follows that the unique stationary solution associated with the block (C.24a) is given by

$$\bar{\mathbf{z}}_{t1} = \sum_{i=0}^{\infty} \Lambda_1^i E(\bar{\boldsymbol{\omega}}_{t+i,1} \mid \Omega_t).$$

Combining this result with (C.24b) and recalling that $\Lambda_2^i = 0$, for $i \geqslant n_2$ we obtain

$$\bar{\mathbf{z}}_t = \sum_{i=0}^{\infty} \Lambda^i E(\bar{\boldsymbol{\omega}}_{t+i} \mid \Omega_t).$$

Now using the transformations in (C.22) and noting that $A^i = T^{-1}\Lambda^i T$, we again arrive at (C.10) which establishes that the unique stationary solution obtained for the invertible case is also valid for the case where A is not invertible.

In the 'irregular' case where some or all the non-zero roots of A fall outside the unit circle, the general solutions given above can be simplified by rewriting (C.24a) in the martingale difference form. That is

$$\bar{\mathbf{z}}_{t1} = \Lambda_1^{-1}\bar{\mathbf{z}}_{t-1,1} - \Lambda_1^{-1}\bar{\boldsymbol{\omega}}_{t-1,1} + \boldsymbol{\varepsilon}_{1t}^0,$$

where $\boldsymbol{\varepsilon}_{1t}^0 = \Lambda_1^{-t}(\mathscr{M}_{1t} - \mathscr{M}_{1,t-1})$, is a martingale difference vector of order n_1. Combining this result with (C.24b) and using the transformations in (C.22) we have

$$\mathbf{z}_t = Q\mathbf{z}_{t-1} - Q\boldsymbol{\omega}_{t-1} + \sum_{i=0}^{n_2-1} G_i E(\boldsymbol{\omega}_{t+i} \mid \Omega_t) + \boldsymbol{\xi}_t^0, \tag{C.25}$$

where

$$Q = T\begin{pmatrix} \Lambda_1^{-1} & 0 \\ 0 & 0 \end{pmatrix} T^{-1},$$

$$G_i = T\begin{pmatrix} 0 & 0 \\ 0 & \Lambda_2^i \end{pmatrix} T^{-1},$$

and

$$\boldsymbol{\xi}_t^0 = T\begin{pmatrix} \boldsymbol{\varepsilon}_{1t}^0 \\ 0 \end{pmatrix}.$$

In the special case where A is a nil-potent matrix of order n (i.e. $n_1 = 0$, and $n_2 = n$), the RE model (C.8) has a unique (possibly non-stationary) solution given by

$$\mathbf{z}_t = \sum_{i=0}^{n-1} A^i E(\boldsymbol{\omega}_{t+i} \mid \Omega_t). \tag{C.26}$$

This result can be obtained either by the application of the forward recursive substitution method directly to (C.8), or by utilizing (C.24b). In general the dimension of the multiplicity of the solution sets of (C.8) is determined by n_1, the number of non-zero eigenvalues of A. In the extreme case where all eigenvalues of A are equal to zero, the RE model has a unique solution and is given by (C.26).

Appendix D

Derivation of Present Value of Prospective Yields under the Rational Expectations Hypotheses

Infinite sums of the type

$$y_t = \sum_{j=0}^{\infty} \alpha^j E(\omega_{t+j}|\Omega_t), \quad |\alpha|<1, \tag{D.1}$$

are frequently encountered in the rational expectations literature, either as the forward solution of a first-order RE equation with future expectations of the endogenous variable, or as the expected present value of prospective yields on an asset. In this appendix we obtain simple expressions for such infinite sums under three alternative specifications of the process generating ω_t.

1 Consider first the general case where $\{\omega_t\}$ is a known linear covariance-stationary process with the following infinite moving-average representation

$$\omega_t = \sum_{i=0}^{\infty} f_i \varepsilon_{t-i} = F(L)\varepsilon_t, \tag{D.2}$$

where $F(L)=\Sigma_{i=0}^{\infty} f_i L^i$, is analytic inside the unit circle, $\Sigma_{i=0}^{\infty} f_i^2 < \infty$, and $\{\varepsilon_t\}$ is a martingale difference process with respect to the non-decreasing information set $\Omega_t \supset \Omega_{t-1} \supset \Omega_{t-2} \ldots$ Notice that a white-noise process is a special example of a martingale difference process. Specifically, it will be assumed that

$$E(\varepsilon_{t+i}|\Omega_t)=0, \qquad \text{for } i=1,2,\ldots, \tag{D.3}$$

$$E(\varepsilon_{t-i}|\Omega_t)=\varepsilon_{t-i}, \quad \text{for } i=0,1,2,\ldots \tag{D.4}$$

Now write ω_{t+j} as

$$\omega_{t+j} = \sum_{i=0}^{j-1} f_i \varepsilon_{t+j-i} + \sum_{i=j}^{\infty} f_i \varepsilon_{t+j-i},$$

and then take expectations conditional on Ω_t, using (D.3) and (D.4) to obtain

$$E(\omega_{t+j}|\Omega_t)=\sum_{i=j}^{\infty} f_i\varepsilon_{t+j-i},$$
$$=\sum_{i=0}^{\infty} f_{i+j}\varepsilon_{t-i}.$$

Substituting this result in (D.1) now yields

$$y_t=\sum_{j=0}^{\infty}\alpha^j E(\omega_{t+j}|\Omega_t),$$
$$=\sum_{i=0}^{\infty}\sum_{j=0}^{\infty}\alpha^j f_{i+j}\varepsilon_{t-i},$$
$$=F(\alpha)\varepsilon_t+\{F(\alpha)-f_0\}\alpha^{-1}\varepsilon_{t-1}+\{F(\alpha)-f_0-f_1\alpha\}\alpha^{-2}\varepsilon_{t-2}$$
$$+\{F(\alpha)-f_0-f_1\alpha-f_2\alpha^2\}\alpha^{-3}\varepsilon_{t-3}+\dots,$$

and since $|\alpha|<1$, after some algebraic manipulation we obtain

$$y_t=\left(\frac{LF(L)-\alpha F(\alpha)}{L-\alpha}\right)\varepsilon_t. \qquad \text{(D.5)}$$

This is the same result as the unique linear stationary solution given by (5.38a).

The above expression for y_t can also be written in terms of ω_t. Pre-multiplying both sides of (D.2) by $F^{-1}(L)$, the inverse of $F(L)$, we have $\varepsilon_t=F^{-1}(L)\omega_t$, which is the autoregressive representation of the ω_t process. The assumption that $F(L)$ is analytic on the open unit circle ensures that this autoregressive representatioon does in fact exist. Thus

$$y_t=(L-\alpha)^{-1}\{L-\alpha F(\alpha)F^{-1}(L)\}\omega_t. \qquad \text{(D.6)}$$

2 Suppose now the process $\{\omega_t\}$ has the following stationary $AR(r)$ representation

$$\left(\sum_{i=0}^{r}\rho_i L^i\right)\omega_t=\varepsilon_t, \quad (\rho_0\equiv 1),$$

where $\{\varepsilon_t\}$ is a white-noise process. In this case denoting expectations of ω_{t+j} conditioned on the information set Ω_t by ω^*_{t+j} we can write

$$j=0, \qquad \omega^*_t-\omega_t=0,$$
$$j=1, \qquad \omega^*_{t+1}+\rho_1\omega^*_t+\rho_2\omega_{t-1}+\rho_3\omega_{t-2}+\dots+\rho_r\omega_{t-r}=0,$$
$$j=2, \qquad \omega^*_{t+2}+\rho_1\omega^*_{t+1}+\rho_2\omega^*_t+\rho_3\omega_{t-1}+\dots+\rho_r\omega_{t+1-r}=0,$$
$$\vdots \qquad \vdots \qquad \vdots$$
$$j=r-1, \qquad \omega^*_{t+r-1}+\rho_1\omega^*_{t+r-2}+\dots\dots+\rho_{r-1}\omega^*_t+\rho_r\omega_{t-1}=0,$$

and for $j \geqslant r$,

$$\sum_{i=0}^{r} \rho_i \omega^*_{t+j-i} = 0, \quad (\rho_0 \equiv 1).$$

If we number the above relations in ascending order starting from zero and multiplying the jth relation by α^j and then add them all up, after some algebraic manipulation it follows that

$$\left(\sum_{i=0}^{r} \rho_i \alpha^i\right)\left(\sum_{j=0}^{\infty} \alpha^j \omega^*_{t+j}\right) = \omega_t - \sum_{j=1}^{r-1}\left(\sum_{i=j+1}^{2} \alpha^{i-j}\rho_i\right)\omega_{t-j}.$$

Now assuming α is not a characteristic root of the AR(r) process, that is $(1+\phi_0) = \Sigma_{i=0}^{r} \rho_i \alpha^i \neq 0$, we obtain

$$y_t = \sum_{j=0}^{\infty} \alpha^j \omega^*_{t+j} = (1+\phi_0)^{-1}\left(1 - \sum_{j=1}^{r-1} \phi_j L^j\right)\omega_t, \tag{D.7}$$

where

$$\phi_j = \sum_{i=j+1}^{r} \rho_i \alpha^{i-j}, \quad \text{for } j = 0, 1, 2, \ldots, r-1. \tag{D.8}$$

Now noting that when $\{\omega_t\}$ is stationary then,

$$\omega_t = \left(\sum_{i=0}^{r} \rho_i L^i\right)^{-1} \varepsilon_t,$$

which means that result (D.7) can also be written as

$$y_t = \sum_{j=0}^{\infty} \alpha^j \omega^*_{t+j} = \frac{1}{1+\phi_0}\left(\frac{1 - \sum_{j=1}^{r-1} \phi_j L^j}{1 + \sum_{j=1}^{r} \rho_j L^j}\right)\varepsilon_t. \tag{D.9}$$

This establishes that when $\{\omega_t\}$ follows a stationary AR(r) process, the forward solution $\{y_t\}$ will have an ARMA($r, r-1$) specification with $r-1$ parameter restrictions given by relations (D.8).

3 Consider now the more general case where $\{\omega_t\}$ follows the stationary ARMA(r, s) process

$$\sum_{i=0}^{r} \rho_i \omega_{t-i} = \sum_{i=0}^{s} \gamma_i \varepsilon_{t-i}, \quad (\rho_0 \equiv \gamma_0 \equiv 1).$$

Employing a similar procedure to that used above we can write:

$$j=0, \qquad \omega_t^* - \omega_t = 0,$$

$$j=1, \qquad \omega_{t+1}^* + \rho_1 \omega_t^* + \rho_2 \omega_{t-1} + \ldots + \rho_r \omega_{t-r} = \gamma_1 \varepsilon_t + \gamma_2 \varepsilon_{t-1} + \ldots + \gamma_s \varepsilon_{t+1-s},$$

$$j=2, \qquad \omega_{t+2}^* + \rho_1 \omega_{t+1}^* + \rho_2 \omega_t^* + \ldots + \rho_r \omega_{t+1-r} = \gamma_2 \varepsilon_t + \gamma_3 \varepsilon_{t-1} + \ldots + \gamma_s \varepsilon_{t+2-s},$$

$$\ldots \qquad \ldots \qquad \ldots \qquad \ldots$$

$$j=r-1, \quad \omega_{t+r-1}^* + \rho_1 \omega_{t+r-2}^* + \ldots + \rho_r \omega_{t-1} = \gamma_r \varepsilon_t + \gamma_{r+1} \varepsilon_{t-1} + \ldots + \gamma_s \varepsilon_{t+r-s},$$

and for $j \geqslant r$,

$$\sum_{j=0}^{\infty} \rho_i \omega_{t+j-i}^* = \gamma_j \varepsilon_t + \gamma_{j+1} \varepsilon_{t-1} + \ldots + \gamma_s \varepsilon_{t+j-s}.$$

Again multiplying the above relations by α^j and then adding them all up we have

$$y_t = \sum_{j=0}^{\infty} \alpha^j \omega_{t+j}^* = (1+\phi_0)^{-1} \left(\omega_t - \sum_{j=1}^{r-1} \phi_j \omega_{t-j} + \sum_{j=0}^{s-1} \psi_j \varepsilon_{t-j} \right), \tag{D.10}$$

where ϕ_j's are defined in (D.8), and

$$\psi_j = \sum_{i=j+1}^{s} \gamma_i \alpha^{i-j}, \quad \text{for } j=0, 1, \ldots, s-1. \tag{D.11}$$

Now using the lag operator L, the expression in (D.10) can also be written as

$$y_t = \sum_{j=0}^{\infty} \alpha^j \omega_{t+j}^* = (1+\phi_0)^{-1} \left\{ \left(1 - \sum_{j=1}^{r-1} \phi_j L^j \right) \omega_t + \left(\sum_{j=0}^{s-1} \psi_j L^j \right) \varepsilon_t \right\}, \tag{D.12}$$

and since

$$\omega_t = \left(\sum_{i=0}^{r} \rho_i L^i \right)^{-1} \left(\sum_{i=0}^{s} \gamma_i L^i \right) \varepsilon_t,$$

it follows that $\{y_t\}$ given by (D.12) has an ARMA$(r, r+s-1)$ specification. This result also implies that so long as the stochastic process of ω_t in (D.1) has a moving-average part (i.e. $s \geqslant 1$), the forward solution $\{y_t\}$ will also have a moving-average part with an order *at least* as large as the order of the autoregressive part of $\{\omega_t\}$.

4 The above results can be easily generalized to the case of multivariate random variables. For example, suppose $\mathbf{y}_t$ and $\boldsymbol{\omega}_t$ are $k \times 1$ vectors and that $\{\boldsymbol{\omega}_t\}$ can be represented by the following stationary AR(r) multivariate process

$$\sum_{i=0}^{r} R_i \boldsymbol{\omega}_{t-i} = \boldsymbol{\varepsilon}_t, \quad (R_0 = I_k),$$

where R_i are parameter matrices of order $k \times k$ and $\boldsymbol{\varepsilon}_t$ is a $k \times 1$ vector of white-noise processes. Then employing a procedure similar to the one used for the univariate case we have, assuming as before that $|\alpha| < 1$,

$$\mathbf{y}_t = \sum_{j=0}^{\infty} \alpha^j E(\boldsymbol{\omega}_{t+j} | \Omega_t), \tag{D.13}$$

$$= (I_k + \Phi_0)^{-1} \left(I_k - \sum_{j=1}^{r-1} \Phi_j L^j \right) \boldsymbol{\omega}_t, \tag{D.14}$$

where I_k stands for a $k \times k$ identity matrix and

$$\Phi_j = \sum_{i=j+1}^{r} \alpha^{i-j} R_i, \quad \text{for } j = 0, 1, 2, \ldots, r-1. \tag{D.15}$$

In deriving the above expressions for the present value of the prospective yields formula (D.1) or (D.13), we have assumed $|\alpha| < 1$ and that the 'yields' $\{\omega_t\}$ or $\{\boldsymbol{\omega}_t\}$ follow a covariance stationary process. It is, however, worth noting that the results hold even if $\boldsymbol{\omega}_t$ is not a stationary process. Under $|\alpha| < 1$, the condition that $\boldsymbol{\omega}_t$ is stationary is sufficient but not necessary for the existence of the present value formulae given above. For example, when $\boldsymbol{\omega}_t$ follows a multivariate first-order autoregressive process with parameter matrix R, the necessary condition for the existence of (D.14) is the convergence of the infinite sum $\Sigma_{j=0}^{\infty} (\alpha R)^j$, and this is achieved if the eigenvalues of R (in absolute value) are less than $|\alpha|^{-1}$. For a value of $\alpha = 0.9$, this condition, for instance, allows the $\boldsymbol{\omega}_t$ process to possess non-stationary roots so long as they are less than the value of $1/0.9 = 1.11$.

Data Appendix*

This appendix describes the definitions and sources of the data used in chapters 8 and 9, and provides the data themselves so that other researchers can readily check the empirical results obtained if they so wish.

Π_t: The actual rate of change of manufacturing prices, constructed from monthly price indices of the Wholesale Prices of Manufactured Goods published in various issues of the *Monthly Digest of Statistics*. For each month that the CBI Survey was carried out, we calculated Π_t by the percentage change in the price index from its level 4 months previously. The inflation series were not corrected for seasonal variations since no significant pattern of seasonality could be found. The price series were, however, adjusted for the effect of reductions in VAT-exclusive prices of alcoholic liquor, tobacco and cigarettes, matches and mechanical lighters which took place in April 1973.

R_t, F_t: Fractions of firms respectively reporting a price rise and a price fall.

${}_tR^e_{t+1}$, ${}_tF^e_{t+1}$: Fractions of firms respectively expecting a price rise and a price fall. These statistics are computed from the raw data provided in table A.1 by dividing the appropriate figures in the 'up' and 'down' categories to the sum of the percentages in the three categories 'up', 'same' and 'down'.

Π^e_{tU}: Inflation expectations series based on the uniform distribution.

Π^e_{tL}: Inflation expectations series based on the logistic distribution.

Π^e_{tN}: Inflation expectations series based on the normal distribution.

Π^e_{tR}: Inflation expectations series based on the regression method (computed using the conversion formula (8.39), p. 230).

The time series on Π_t, Π^e_{tU}, Π^e_{tL}, Π^e_{tN}, and Π^e_{tR} over the period 1959(1)–1985(2) are given in table A.2.

*This appendix updates the information already published in Pesaran (1984b, 1985). The author is particularly grateful to Katerina Homenidou for compiling the new data sets and for carrying out the computations involved in the conversion of qualitative responses into quantitative measures.

f_t: Rate of change of Price Index of Materials and Fuel purchased by manufacturing industry; *Economic Trends Annual Supplement (ETAS)*, 1983, 1986.

w_t: Rate of change of Basic Weekly Wage Rates of Manual Workers in manufacturing industry; *ETAS*, 1986.

q_t: Rate of change of Index of Manufacturing output; *ETAS*, 1986.

e_t: Rate of change of Effective Exchange Rate. For the post-1971 period the data on effective exchange rates were taken from various issues of the *Financial Statistics*. For the pre-1971 period e_t were calculated on the basis of changes in the sterling-dollar exchange rates.

m_t: Rate of change of M_3 definition of the Money Supply; *ETAS*, 1986.

RU_t: The overall Rate of Unemployment, adjusted for seasonal variations; *ETAS*, 1986. For 1958 and 1959 1st quarter RU_t is based on monthly averages of percentage rates of unemployment published in the *British Labour Statistics, Historical Abstract 1886–1968*, Department of Employment and Productivity.

FHI_t: The Fels–Hopkin Index of the strength of the prices policies. The values of the index for the period 1959(1)–1973(4) are given in table 6.2 in Coutts et al. (1978). The updated values of this index for the post-1973 period are as follows

	Quarters			
Years	(i)	(ii)	(iii)	(iv)
1974	0.50	0.67	0.75	0.75
1975	0.45	0.45	0.45	0.45
1976	0.45	0.45	0.30	0.20
1977	0.20	0.20	0.15	0.10
1978	0.10	0.10	0.10	0.10
1979	0.10	0.10	0.0	0.0

The index for the period 1980–5 was set equal to zero. The author is particularly grateful to Frank Wilkinson for updating the Fels–Hopkin's index used in this study.

Remark:

Because of the three times yearly frequency of the CBI surveys over the 1958–71 period, we averaged the published quarterly data for the last two quarters of each year during this period before proceeding with the computations of the rate of change of the variables used in this study. In principle by utilizing monthly data it is possible to obtain more accurate estimates of the quarterly rates of change on a tri-annual basis. But for our purposes we did not think the extra precision was worth the extra effort.

The time-series observations for f_t, w_t, q_t, e_t, m_t, and RU_t are given in table A.3.

Table A.1 Past and expected trends in average selling prices of British manufacturing

	Trend over past 4 months				Expected trend over next 4 months			
	Up	Same	Down	N/A	Up	Same	Down	N/A
1958: June	3	66	30	1	2	75	20	3
Oct.	3	66	30	1	7	73	16	4
1959: Feb.	9	62	29	0	3	76	17	4
June	9	64	26	1	7	75	15	3
Oct.	12	67	20	1	10	75	12	3
1960: Feb.	12	70	16	2	14	76	7	3
June	22	66	11	1	12	77	6	5
Oct.	16	71	12	1	13	76	8	3
1961: Feb.	25	64	11	0	21	68	7	4
June	24	64	11	1	15	72	7	6
Oct.	22	64	13	1	11	74	10	5
1962: Feb.	12	70	17	1	13	71	12	4
June	13	66	19	2	13	72	11	4
Oct.	16	66	17	1	11	74	12	3
1963: Feb.	12	68	19	1	11	75	11	3
June	13	69	17	1	11	76	10	3
Oct.	12	75	11	2	13	77	6	4
1964: Feb.	27	63	8	2	28	62	6	4
June	32	58	9	1	14	76	6	4
Oct.	24	63	11	2	25	62	7	6
1965: Feb.	26	67	5	2	32	61	5	2
June	33	58	5	4	23	67	5	5
Oct.	19	72	7	2	16	73	8	3
1966: Feb.	21	70	7	2	29	62	7	2
June	32	60	5	3	30	60	4	6
Oct.	18	67	9	6	5	76	12	7
1967: Feb.	4	78	14	4	8	76	10	6
June	7	75	15	3	14	71	9	6
Oct.	13	69	14	4	18	67	9	6
1968: Feb.	31	58	8	3	45	47	4	4
June	40	51	5	4	25	65	4	6
Oct.	23	69	7	1	20	74	4	2
1969: Feb.	32	62	5	1	40	53	3	4
June	37	57	4	2	35	57	3	5
Oct.	41	51	6	2	39	52	4	5
1970: Feb.	47	46	5	2	56	35	4	5
June:	59	35	4	2	58	35	2	5
Oct.	60	35	2	3	64	29	2	5
1971: Feb.[a]	59	34	3	4	58	35	2	5
June	59	33	5	3	52	41	3	4
Sep.	41	50	6	3	26	67	4	3
1972: Jan.	31	58	8	3	39	54	3	4
April	40	50	7	3	49	44	3	4
July	44	49	5	2	53	43	1	3
Oct.	49	45	4	2	55	42	2	1

Table A.1 – *contd.*

	Trend over past 4 months				Expected trend over next 4 months			
	Up	Same	Down	N/A	Up	Same	Down	N/A
1973: Jan.	36	61	2	1	31	67	1	1
April	23	74	2	1	43	53	2	2
July	44	53	1	2	53	44	1	2
Oct.	58	39	1	2	55	41	1	3
1974: Jan.	65	32	2	1	72	25	1	2
April	77	22	1	0	77	20	1	2
July	77	17	2	4	70	25	2	3
Oct.	75	22	1	2	73	22	2	3
1975: Jan.	74	20	4	2	73	22	4	1
April	72	22	5	1	64	31	3	2
July	62	29	5	4	64	28	4	4
Oct.	57	35	5	3	63	32	2	3
1976: Jan.	59	37	3	1	65	29	3	3
April	60	34	4	2	66	30	2	2
July	63	33	2	2	69	27	1	3
Oct.	68	27	3	2	73	23	1	3
1977: Jan.	70	26	1	3	76	22	1	1
April	73	22	3	2	69	28	1	2
July	59	36	3	2	63	32	3	2
Oct.	52	42	6	0	54	42	4	0
1978: Jan.	43	49	7	1	55	41	3	1
April	48	45	6	1	52	45	2	1
July	44	52	3	1	56	41	2	1
Oct.	44	51	4	1	55	43	1	1
1979: Jan.	47	50	1	2	61	37	1	1
April	59	38	2	1	66	31	1	2
July	67	29	3	1	66	31	1	2
Oct.	62	34	2	2	62	33	2	3
1980: Jan.	58	37	3	2	66	30	1	3
April	61	34	4	1	59	37	3	1
July	46	43	11	0	43	47	10	0
Oct.	29	51	19	1	32	55	12	1
1981: Jan.	25	58	17	0	34	58	8	0
April	27	52	21	0	37	53	9	1
July	28	55	16	1	35	57	7	1
Oct.	30	57	12	1	46	50	4	0
1982: Jan.	36	55	7	2	50	46	3	1
April	38	51	10	1	36	59	4	1
July	29	60	11	0	33	60	6	1
Oct.	19	69	11	1	25	68	6	1
1983: Jan.	15	66	17	2	29	60	9	2
April	26	64	9	1	34	63	3	0
July	31	61	8	0	25	70	4	1
Oct.	26	65	7	2	32	62	5	1

Table A.1 — *contd.*

	Trend over past 4 months				Expected trend over next 4 months			
	Up	Same	Down	N/A	Up	Same	Down	N/A
1984: Jan.	29	63	7	1	48	48	3	1
April	39	54	6	1	40	54	4	2
July	30	62	7	1	28	65	5	2
Oct.	30	62	7	1	39	55	5	1
1985: Jan.	32	62	5	1	43	52	4	1
April	40	54	5	1	34	61	4	1
July	29	64	6	1	29	64	6	1
Oct.	20	72	7	1	24	67	7	2
1986: Jan.	22	63	14	1	34	55	9	2
April	29	61	9	1	26	65	7	2

[a] Estimated.
Source: The Confederation of British Industries — Industrial Trends Survey. The figures refer to the percentage of respondents in the surveys reporting (or expecting) a price change.

Table A.2[a] Actual and expected rates of price changes in British manufacturing (percentages)

		Expected			
		Probability method			
Year	Actual Π_t	Uniform Π^e_{tU}	Normal Π^e_{tN}	Logistic Π^e_{tL}	Regression method Π^e_{tR}
1958: June	0.27	—	—	—	—
Oct.	0.18	—	—	—	—
1959: Feb.	0.36	−0.42	−0.80	−0.91	0.36
June	−0.36	−0.62	−1.32	−1.55	0.13
Oct.	0.27	−0.36	−0.71	−0.81	0.06
1960: Feb.	0.27	−0.09	−0.18	−0.20	0.17
June	1.16	0.31	0.63	0.72	0.49
Oct.	0.35	0.26	0.57	0.67	0.51
1961: Feb.	0.88	0.22	0.45	0.51	0.49
June	1.05	0.70	1.20	1.35	0.84
Oct.	1.12	0.38	0.72	0.83	0.60
1962: Feb.	0.85	0.05	0.09	0.10	0.48
June	0.34	0.05	0.09	0.10	0.72
Oct.	0.51	0.09	0.17	0.20	0.60
1963: Feb.	0.50	−0.05	−0.09	−0.10	0.36
June	−0.17	0.00	0.00	0.00	0.43
Oct.	1.34	0.05	0.09	0.10	0.25

Table A.2[a] — *contd.*

Year	Actual Π_t	Expected: Probability method: Uniform Π^e_{tU}	Normal Π^e_{tN}	Logistic Π^e_{tL}	Regression method Π^e_{tR}
1964: Feb.	0.41	0.31	0.65	0.76	0.67
June	1.81	1.20	1.87	2.05	1.43
Oct.	1.29	0.36	0.73	0.85	0.45
1965: Feb.	1.84	0.98	1.56	1.72	1.39
June	1.96	1.50	2.25	2.44	1.96
Oct.	0.46	0.91	1.57	1.76	1.33
1966: Feb.	0.92	0.37	0.69	0.79	0.62
June	1.21	1.20	1.84	2.00	1.38
Oct.	0.37	1.47	2.26	2.46	1.50
1967: Feb.	0.37	−0.31	−0.69	−0.81	−0.04
June	0.00	−0.09	−0.19	−0.22	0.31
Oct.	0.82	0.24	0.45	0.51	0.62
1968: Feb.	2.07	0.46	0.79	0.88	0.89
June	1.58	2.96	3.61	3.74	3.27
Oct.	0.52	1.10	1.85	2.06	1.17
1969: Feb.	1.98	0.73	1.41	1.61	0.59
June	1.01	2.37	3.15	3.33	2.42
Oct.	1.34	1.90	2.74	2.95	1.79
1970: Feb.	2.48	2.28	3.04	3.21	1.78
June	2.58	5.04	5.15	5.11	3.97
Oct.	2.44	5.42	5.22	5.12	4.02
1971: Feb.	2.96	7.25	6.20	5.93	4.57
June	2.92	5.42	5.22	5.12	3.64
Oct.	1.65	4.05	4.43	4.46	2.89
1972: Jan.	0.99	1.11	1.88	2.09	0.79
April	1.62	2.26	3.07	3.24	1.94
July	1.87	3.54	4.07	4.15	2.97
Oct.	2.89	4.10	4.37	4.39	3.37
1973: Jan.	2.23	4.28	4.53	4.54	3.65
April	1.69	1.52	2.58	2.86	1.62
July	3.67	2.62	3.40	3.57	3.02
Oct.	5.20	4.01	4.32	4.35	4.43
1974: Jan.	6.59	4.47	4.58	4.56	4.70
April	11.94	9.63	6.89	6.37	8.13
July	7.78	12.88	8.05	7.26	10.60
Oct.	7.19	9.22	7.15	6.70	7.48
1975: Jan.	8.98	10.94	7.93	7.33	7.28
April	8.80	10.63	8.48	7.96	7.63
July	6.91	6.67	6.06	5.86	6.26
Oct.	4.20	7.26	6.57	6.35	6.76

Table A.2[a] — *contd.*

Year	Actual Π_t	Expected: Probability method: Uniform Π^e_{tU}	Normal Π^e_{tN}	Logistic Π^e_{tL}	Regression method Π^e_{tR}
1976: Jan.	5.04	6.46	5.79	5.59	5.86
April	4.92	7.25	6.39	6.15	6.09
July	5.33	7.23	6.18	5.91	6.23
Oct.	5.94	8.54	6.46	6.04	6.94
1977: Jan.	8.11	10.61	7.26	6.66	7.86
April	7.88	11.56	7.59	6.90	8.73
July	6.63	8.23	6.33	5.94	7.04
Oct.	2.76	6.36	5.88	5.71	6.16
1978: Jan.	2.70	4.04	4.44	4.48	4.02
April	3.14	4.30	4.59	4.61	3.89
July	2.53	3.77	4.21	4.27	3.69
Oct.	2.55	4.47	4.65	4.64	4.14
1979: Jan.	2.76	4.26	4.46	4.46	3.95
April	4.55	5.50	5.11	4.98	4.82
July	7.11	7.11	5.86	5.57	5.96
Oct.	5.50	7.11	5.86	5.57	6.39
1980: Jan.	5.78	6.16	5.63	5.46	5.73
April	7.42	7.35	5.96	5.66	6.78
July	4.32	5.13	5.13	5.07	5.74
Oct.	2.14	2.33	2.95	3.08	3.47
1981: Jan.	1.25	1.23	1.73	1.85	2.24
April	4.93	1.52	2.16	2.32	2.04
July	2.61	1.79	2.42	2.57	3.44
Oct.	2.19	1.67	2.35	2.51	3.37
1982: Jan.	3.24	2.85	3.53	3.66	3.55
April	3.35	3.46	4.01	4.10	4.10
July	1.55	1.84	2.64	2.83	2.70
Oct.	1.79	1.53	2.23	2.41	2.10
1983: Jan.	1.59	0.95	1.58	1.75	1.58
April	2.49	1.13	1.68	1.83	2.14
July	1.88	1.67	2.53	2.75	2.56
Oct.	1.28	1.02	1.77	1.98	1.62
1984: Jan.	1.83	1.48	2.23	2.42	1.78
April	3.46	3.18	3.80	3.91	3.33
July	1.69	2.26	3.02	3.20	2.91
Oct.	1.36	1.20	1.92	2.12	1.76
1985: Jan.	1.95	2.10	2.84	3.01	2.26
April	3.11	2.54	3.27	3.43	2.70

[a] For definition of variables and sources, see data appendix.

Table A.3[a] Data used in chapters 8 and 9 (percentages)

Year	f_t	w_t	q_t	e_t	m_t	RU_t
1958: June	0.97	0.44	−1.48	0.00	—	2.17
Oct.	0.00	1.72	0.15	−0.50	—	2.37
1959: Feb.	0.32	1.06	1.62	0.14	—	2.83
June	−0.32	0.21	2.88	0.00	—	2.19
Oct.	1.27	0.63	4.17	−0.14	—	2.04
1960: Feb.	0.63	0.84	4.52	−0.22	—	1.77
June	−0.32	0.83	0.13	0.36	—	1.68
Oct.	−1.59	1.23	0.65	0.00	—	1.57
1961: Feb.	−0.32	2.61	−0.39	−0.36	—	1.43
June	0.32	0.40	1.29	−0.36	—	1.45
Oct.	−0.97	0.40	−1.42	0.58	—	1.57
1962: Feb.	1.61	0.78	−0.65	0.14	—	1.70
June	−0.96	1.17	1.68	0.00	—	1.91
Oct.	−0.65	1.91	0.13	−0.36	—	2.19
1963: Feb.	1.92	0.76	−2.07	0.00	—	2.56
June	0.32	0.56	3.60	0.00	1.35	2.42
Oct.	1.57	1.12	4.57	0.00	2.08	2.18
1964: Feb.	2.46	2.74	4.37	0.00	2.86	1.85
June	−0.30	0.90	0.00	0.00	1.36	1.74
Oct.	1.81	1.24	2.40	−0.36	2.13	1.59
1965: Feb.	0.60	1.23	1.12	0.00	2.69	1.42
June	0.00	0.69	0.22	0.36	1.95	1.44
Oct.	−0.30	2.22	0.67	−0.14	2.12	1.45
1966: Feb.	2.36	1.84	2.40	0.14	3.75	1.28
June	1.73	0.99	−0.54	−0.36	−0.72	1.34
Oct.	−2.03	1.47	−1.20	0.00	1.74	1.70
1967: Feb.	−1.18	1.13	0.11	0.00	2.17	2.21
June	−0.59	0.16	0.87	0.36	1.82	2.33
Oct.	3.51	3.15	1.19	−0.36	4.42	2.42
1968: Feb.	7.74	4.54	5.03	−14.68	3.40	2.47
June	−1.88	0.59	1.02	−0.84	2.54	2.50
Oct.	0.81	1.46	1.41	0.00	1.45	2.46
1969: Feb.	1.86	3.28	1.58	0.00	2.09	2.43
June	1.31	0.28	1.75	0.00	−1.72	2.41
Oct.	2.06	1.94	−0.39	0.00	1.42	2.48
1970: Feb.	3.02	4.43	−0.68	0.42	1.99	2.54
June	0.49	2.34	0.87	0.00	3.05	2.59
Oct.	0.98	4.51	0.29	−0.42	3.05	2.66
1971: Feb.	2.17	5.72	−1.16	0.84	6.14	2.65
June	1.89	2.29	0.00	0.42	1.25	3.02
Oct.	0.23	2.90	−0.49	2.06	4.38	3.40
1972: Jan.	0.47	4.83	−2.88	5.09	11.23	3.65
April	0.46	2.79	5.01	−0.55	6.62	3.56
July	2.97	6.31	0.86	−6.19	3.15	3.35
Oct.	5.47	2.83	3.82	−3.12	5.15	3.14
1973: Jan.	8.75	0.46	3.86	−1.55	7.67	2.72
April	5.50	3.28	0.09	0.52	4.40	2.51
July	12.31	5.32	0.79	−5.88	6.65	2.28
Oct.	10.67	2.43	0.26	−1.48	5.26	2.03

Table A.3[a] — *contd.*

Year	f_t	w_t	q_t	e_t	m_t	RU_t
1974: Jan.	22.61	1.64	−5.18	0.19	4.84	2.49
April	−0.23	4.23	6.31	1.84	0.28	2.32
July	0.35	8.53	−0.78	−0.55	1.20	2.43
Oct.	5.68	5.38	−4.34	−1.95	4.11	2.58
1975: Jan.	1.75	5.30	−0.82	−1.70	2.30	2.90
April	3.52	10.28	−5.06	−3.19	0.23	3.43
July	6.39	4.88	−1.55	−4.32	3.27	3.95
Oct.	8.20	5.18	1.26	−2.49	−0.14	4.50
1976: Jan.	4.34	5.82	1.25	−1.16	2.50	4.81
April	7.67	3.66	1.51	−8.55	1.88	5.03
July	3.39	1.66	−0.19	−2.58	3.89	5.12
Oct.	7.47	0.28	2.78	−7.40	1.09	5.13
1977: Jan.	4.16	1.21	1.45	3.52	0.10	5.15
April	2.73	1.02	−2.18	−0.37	2.37	5.24
July	−1.56	1.05	−0.74	0.25	2.73	5.55
Oct.	−2.98	0.68	0.37	2.20	3.77	5.59
1978: Jan.	1.12	1.97	−0.19	2.63	5.19	5.45
April	3.28	15.46	2.20	−5.95	2.92	5.66
July	0.14	1.50	0.09	0.87	2.63	5.20
Oct.	3.57	3.52	−1.00	0.00	3.77	5.00
1979: Jan.	4.50	2.49	−1.94	2.21	1.84	5.00
April	2.69	2.36	4.46	5.43	4.04	4.84
July	1.56	1.74	−3.63	4.82	3.14	4.73
Oct.	5.15	7.03	1.56	−3.12	3.36	4.73
1980: Jan.	4.42	5.66	−2.86	4.96	2.82	4.98
April	−1.58	2.58	−4.30	1.60	5.34	5.53
July	−1.49	1.32	−4.90	2.30	4.82	6.43
Oct.	1.38	3.48	−4.40	3.56	4.18	7.59
1981: Jan.	4.25	2.78	−0.65	1.58	2.09	8.58
April	3.31	1.81	0.54	−4.01	4.07	9.38
July	2.17	0.97	1.81	−7.65	4.69	9.94
Oct.	4.20	1.89	0.42	−1.00	1.83	10.38
1982: Jan.	2.73	1.85	−0.53	1.66	2.53	10.66
April	−1.78	0.93	0.11	−0.99	2.11	10.94
July	−0.43	0.79	−0.95	1.32	2.15	11.29
Oct.	3.41	1.91	−0.96	−2.66	2.16	11.65
1983: Jan.	4.27	1.64	2.86	−10.15	4.67	11.93
April	−0.84	0.74	−0.31	4.61	2.31	12.17
July	0.97	0.59	1.97	0.71	1.10	12.24
Oct.	2.86	1.87	1.33	−2.02	2.37	12.25
1984: Jan.	3.90	—	1.01	−1.82	2.02	12.41
April	0.57	—	0.60	−2.35	2.17	12.52
July	−0.12	—	0.99	−2.28	2.75	12.66
Oct.	4.44	—	−0.10	−3.79	2.70	12.72
1985: Jan.	4.25	—	1.47	−4.08	3.90	12.86
April	−5.23	—	0.39	9.01	2.21	12.98

[a] For definition of variables and sources, see *data appendix*.

References

Abel, A. B. and Mishkin, F. S. (1983) An integrated view of tests of rationality, market efficiency and the short-run neutrality of monetary policy, *Journal of Monetary Economics,* **11**, 3–24.

Ahlfors, L. V. (1966) *Complex Analysis – An Introduction to the Theory of Analytic Functions of One Complex Variable,* Second Edition, McGraw-Hill, New York.

Aiginger, K. (1981) Empirical evidence on the rational expectations hypothesis using reported expectations, *Empirica,* **1**, 25–72.

Albert, A. E. and Gardner, L. A. (1967) *Stochastic Approximation and Nonlinear Regression.* MIT Press, Cambridge, Mass.

Anderson, O. (1951) Konjunkturtest und statistik, *Allgemeines Statistical Archives,* **35**, 209–20.

Anderson, O. (1952) The business test of the IFO-Institute for economic research, Munich, and its theoretical model, *Revue de l'Institut International de Statistique,* **20**, 1–17.

Anderson, T. W. (1971) *The Statistical Analysis of Time Series,* Wiley, New York.

Aoki, M. and Canzoneri, M. (1979) Reduced forms of rational expectations models, *Quarterly Journal of Economics,* **93**, 59–71.

Arrow, K. J. (1951) Alternative approaches to the theory of choice in risk-taking situations, *Econometrica,* **19**, 404–37.

Arrow, K. J. and Hahn, F. H. (1971) *General Competitive Analysis.* Holden-Day, San Francisco.

Attfield, C. L. F., Demery D. and Duck, N. W. (1981) A quarterly model of unanticipated monetary growth, output and the price level in the U.K. 1963–1978, *Journal of Monetary Economics,* **8**, 331–50.

Aumann, R. J. (1976) Agreeing to disagree, *Annals of Statistics,* **4**, 1236–39.

Baillie, R. T., Lippens, R. E. and McMahon, P. C. (1983) Testing rational expectations and efficiency in the foreign exchange market, *Econometrica,* **51**, 553–63.

Barro, R. J. (1976) Rational expectations and the role of monetary policy, *Journal of Monetary Economics,* **2**, 1–32.

Barro, R. J. (1977) Unanticipated money growth and unemployment in the United States, *American Economic Review,* **67**, 101–15.

Barro, R. J. (1978) Unanticipated money, output and the price level in United States, *Journal of Political Economy,* **86**, 549–80.

Bartlett, M. S. (1978) *An Introduction to Stochastic Processes–with special reference to methods and applications,* 3rd edn. Cambridge University Press, Cambridge.

Batchelor, R. A. (1981) Aggregate expectations under the stable laws, *Journal of Econometrics,* **16**, 199–210.

Batchelor, R. A. (1982) Expectations, output and inflation: the European experience, *European Economic Review,* **17**, 1–25.

Batchelor, R. A. (1984) The Measurement and Impact of Inflation and Growth Expectations, Report to the Commission of the European Communities.

Batchelor, R. A. (1986a) The psychophysics of inflation, *Journal of Economic Psychology,* **7**, 269–290.

Batchelor, R. A. (1986b). Quantitative v. qualitative measures of inflation expectations, *Oxford Bulletin of Economics and Statistics,* **48**, 99–120.

Batchelor, R. A. and Dua, P. (1987) The accuracy and reliability of UK consumer inflation expectations: some direct evidence, *Applied Economics* (forthcoming).

Bausor, R. (1983) The rational-expectations hypothesis and the epistemics of time, *Cambridge Journal of Economics,* **7**, 1–10.

Bean, C. R. (1984) A little bit more evidence on the natural rate hypothesis from the U.K., *European Economic Review,* **25**, 279–92.

Begg, D. K. H. (1982a) *The Rational Expectations Revolution in Macroeconomics.* Philip Allan, Oxford.

Begg, D. K. H. (1982b) Rational expectations, wage rigidity, and involuntary unemployment, *Oxford Economic Papers,* **34**, 23–47.

Bennett, A. (1984) Output expectations of manufacturing industry, *Applied Economics,* **16**, 869–79.

Billingsley, P. (1979) *Probability and Measure.* Wiley, New York.

Blanchard, O. J. (1979) Backward and forward solutions for economies with rational expectations, *American Economic Review,* **69**, 114–18.

Blanchard, O. J. and Kahn, C. M. (1980) The solution of linear difference models under rational expectations, *Econometrica,* **48**, 1305–1311.

Blanchard, O. J. and Watson, M. W. (1982) Bubbles, rational expectations, and financial markets. In P. Wachtel (ed.), *Crises in the Economic and Financial Structure.* Lexington Books, Lexington, Mass.

Blume, L. E. and Easley, D. (1982) Learning to be rational, *Journal of Economic Theory,* **26**, 340–51.

Boland, L. A. (1979) A critique of Friedman's critics, *Journal of Economic Literature,* **17**, 503–22.

Boland, L. A. (1982) *The Foundations of Economic Method.* George Allen and Unwin, London.

Bowden, R. J. (1973) The theory of parametric identification, *Econometrica,* **41**, 1069–74.

Bowden, R. J. (1984) Convergence to 'rational expectations' when the system parameters are initially unknown by the forecasters. Unpublished manuscript, University of Western Australia, Australia.

Box, G. E. P. and Cox, D. R. (1964) An analysis of transformations, *Journal of the Royal Statistical Society, B,* **26**, 211–43.

Box, G. E. P. and Jenkins, G. M. (1970) *Time Series Analysis, Forecasting and Control,* Holden Day, San Francisco.

Brandenburger, A. (1985) Information and learning in market games. Unpublished manuscript, Churchill College, Cambridge.

Brandenburger, A. and Dekel, E. (1985) Common knowledge with probability 1, Research paper no. 796R, Graduate School of Business, Stanford University.

Bray, M. M. (1983) Convergence to rational expectations equilibrium. In Frydman, R. and Phelps, E. S. (eds), *Individual Forecasting and Aggregate Outcomes.* Cambridge University Press, Cambridge.

Bray, M. M. (1985) Rational expectations, information and asset markets: an introduction, *Oxford Economic Papers,* **37**, 161–195.

Bray, M. M. and Kreps, D. M. (1984) Rational learning and rational expectations. Unpublished manuscript, Faculty of Economics and Politics, University of Cambridge.

Bray, M. M. and Savin, N. E. (1986) Rational expectations equilibria, learning and model specification, *Econometrica,* **54**, 1129–60.

Brown, B. W. and Maital, S. (1981) What do economists know? An empirical study of experts' expectations, *Econometrica,* **49**, 491–504.

Brown, R. L., Durbin, J. and Evans, J. M. (1975) Techniques for testing the constancy of regression relations over time (with discussion), *Journal of the Royal Statistical Society,* B, **37**, 149–92.

Broze, L. and Szafarz, A. (1984) On linear models with rational expectations which admit a unique solution, *European Economic Review,* **24**, 103–11.

Broze, L. and Szafarz, A. (1985) On econometric models with rational expectations. Discussion Paper Number 8509, Centre d'Economie Mathematique et d'Econometrie, Université Libre de Bruxelles.

Broze, L., Gourieroux, C. and Szafarz, A. (1985) Solutions of linear rational expectations models, *Econometric Theory,* **1**, 341–68.

Buiter, W. H. (1983) Real effects of anticipated and unanticipated money–some problems of estimation and hypothesis testing, *Journal of Monetary Economics,* **11**, 207–24.

Buiter, W. H. and Miller, M. (1983) Real exchange rate over-shooting and the output cost of bringing down inflation: some further results. In Frenkel, J. A. (ed.), *Exchange Rates and International Macroeconomics.* University of Chicago Press, Chicago.

Cagan, P. (1956) The monetary dynamics of hyperinflation. In Friedman, M. (ed.), *Studies in the Quantity Theory of Money.* University of Chicago Press, Chicago.

Caldwell, B. J. (1982). *Beyond Positivism: Economic Methodology in the Twentieth Century.* George Allen and Unwin, London.

Cargill, T. F. (1976) Anticipated price changes and nominal interest rates in the 1950's, *Review of Economics and Statistics,* **58**, 364–67.

Carlson, J. A. (1975) Are price expectations normally distributed? *Journal of the American Statistical Association,* **70**, 749–754.

Carlson, J. A. (1977) A study of price forecasts, *Annals of Economic and Social Measurement,* **6**, 27–56.

Carlson, J. A. and Parkin, M. (1975) Inflation expectations, *Economica,* **42**, 123–38.

Chan-Lee, J. H. (1980) A review of recent work in the area of inflationary expectations, *Welwirtschaftliches Archiv,* **1**, 45–85.

Chow, G. C. (1980) Estimation of rational expectations models, *Journal of Economic Dynamics and Control,* **2**, 241–55.

Coddington, A. (1982) Deficient foresight: a troublesome theme in Keynesian economics, *American Economic Review,* **72**, 480–7.

Coutts, K., Godley, W. and Nordhaus, W. (1978) *Industrial Pricing in the United Kingdom.* Cambridge University Press, Cambridge.

Cumby, R. E., Huizinga, J. and Obstfeld, M. (1983) Two-step two-stage least squares estimation in models with rational expectations, *Journal of Econometrics,* **21**, 333–55.

Cyert, R. M. and De Groot, M. H. (1974) Rational expectations and Bayesian analysis, *Journal of Political Economy,* **82**, 521–36.

Dagli, C. A. and Taylor, J. B. (1984) Estimation and solution of linear rational expectations models using a polynomial matrix factorization, *Journal of Economic Dynamics and Control,* **8**, 341–8.

Danes, M. (1975) The measurement and explanation of inflationary expectations in Australia, *Australian Economic Papers,* **19**, 75–87.

Davidson, P. (1982/83) Rational expectations: a fallacious foundation for studying crucial decision-making processes, *Journal of Post-Keynesian Economics,* **5**, 182–98.

De Finetti, B. (1937) La Prévision: Ses Lois Logiques, Ses Sources Subjectives,

Annales de l'Institut Henri Poincaré, 7, 1–68.

De Leeuw, F. and McKelvey, M. J. (1981) Price expectations of business firms, *Brookings Papers on Economic Activity,* No. 1. pp. 299–314.

De Menil, G. (1974) Rationality in popular price expectations. Unpublished manuscript, Princeton University.

De Menil, G. and Bhalla, S. S. (1975) Direct measurement of popular price expectations, *American Economic Review,* **65**, 169–80.

DeCanio, S. J. (1979) Rational expectations and learning from experience, *Quarterly Journal of Economics,* **93**, 47–57.

Defris, L. V. and Williams, R. A. (1981) Quantitative versus qualitative measures of price expectations: the evidence from Australian consumer surveys, *Economics Letters,* **2**, 169–73.

Demetriades, P. (1987) The relationship between the level of inflation and inflation uncertainty: evidence from the UK. Unpublished manuscript. Central Bank of Cyprus, Cyprus.

Doob, J. L. (1953) *Stochastic Processes.* Wiley, New York.

Dornbusch, R. (1976) Expectations and exchange rate dynamics, *Journal of Political Economy,* **84**, 1161–76.

Dow, A. and Dow, S. (1985) Animal spirits and rationality. In Lawson, T. and Pesaran, H. (eds), *Keynes' Economics: Methodological Issues.* Croom Helm, London.

Dubey, P. and Shubik, M. (1977) A closed economy with exogenous uncertainty, different levels of information, money, futures and spot markets, *International Journal of Game Theory,* **6**, 231–48.

Eichenbaum, M. S., Hansen, L. P. and Singleton, K. J. (1984) A time series analysis of representative agent models of consumption leisure choice under uncertainty. Unpublished manuscript, Carnegie-Mellon University.

Evans, G. W. (1985) Expectational stability and the multiple equilibria problem in linear rational expectations models, *Quarterly Journal of Economics,* **100**, 1217–33.

Evans, G. W. (1986) Selection criteria for models with non-uniqueness, *Journal of Monetary Economics,* **18**, 147–57.

Evans, G. W. and Gulamani, R. (1984) Tests of rationality in the Carlson–Parkin inflation expectations data, *Oxford Bulletin of Economics and Statistics*, **46**, 1–9.

Fair, R. C. (1970) The estimation of simultaneous equation models with lagged endogenous variables and the first order serially correlated errors, *Econometrica,* **38**, 507–16.

Fama, E. F. (1970) Efficient capital markets: a review of theory and empirical work, *Journal of Finance*, **25**, 383–423.

Fama, E. F. (1975) Short term interest rates as predictors of inflation, *American Economic Review,* **65**, 269–82.

Fama, E. F. (1976) *Foundations of Finance.* Basic Books, New York.

Feige, E. L. and Pearce, D. K. (1976) Economically rational expectations: are innovations in the rate of inflation independent of innovations in measures of monetary and fiscal policy? *Journal of Political Economy,* **84**, 499–522.

Figlewski, S. and Wachtel, P. (1981) The formation of inflationary expectations, *Review of Economics and Statistics,* **63**, 1–10.

Fischer, S. (1977) Wage indexation, and macroeconomic stability. In Brunner, R. and Meltzer, A. H. (eds), *Stabilization of the Domestic and International Economy.* North-Holland, Amsterdam.

Fischer, S. (1981) Relative shocks, relative price variability, and inflation, *Brookings Papers in Economic Activity,* **2**, 381–431.

Fishe, R. P. H. and Lahiri, K. (1981) On the estimation of inflationary expectations from qualitative responses, *Journal of Econometrics,* **16**, 89–102.

Fisher, F. M. (1966) *The Identification Problem in Econometrics.* McGraw-Hill, New York.

Flood, R. P. and Garber, P. M. (1980) Market fundamentals versus price-level bubbles: the first tests, *Journal of Political Economy,* **88**, 745–70.

Foster, E. (1978) The variability of inflation, *Review of Economics and Statistics,* **60**, 346–50.

Fourgeaud, C., Gourieroux, C. and Pradel, J. (1986) Learning procedures and convergence to rationality, *Econometrica,* **54**, 845–68.

Frenkel, J. A. (1975) Inflation and the formation of expectations, *Journal of Monetary Economics,* **1**, 403–21.

Frenkel, J. A. (1977) The forward exchange rate, expectations and the demand for money: the German hyperinflation, *American Economic Review,* **67**, 653–70.

Frenkel, J. A. (1982) A technique for extracting a measure of expected inflation from the interest rate term structure, *Review of Economics and Statistics,* **64**, 135–42.

Friedman, B. M. (1979) Optimal expectations and the extreme information assumption in 'rational expectations' macromodels, *Journal of Monetary Economics,* **5**, 23–41.

Friedman, B. M. (1980) Survey evidence on the 'rationality' of interest rate expectations, *Journal of Monetary Economics,* **6**, 453–65.

Friedman, M. (1953) *Essays in Positive Economics,* University of Chicago Press, Chicago.

Friedman, M. (1968) The role of monetary policy, *American Economic Review,* **58**, 1–17.

Frisch, R. (1934) *Statistical Confluence Analysis by Means of Complete Regression Systems,* Universitetets Økonomiske Institutt, Oslo.

Frydman, R. (1982) Towards an understanding of market processes, individual expectations: learning and convergence to rational expectations equilibrium, *American Economic Review,* **72**, 652–68.

Frydman, R. and Phelps, E. S. (eds) (1983) *Individual Forecasting and Aggregate Outcomes: 'Rational Expectations' Examined.* Cambridge University Press, Cambridge.

Frydman, R. and Rappoport, P. (1984) An examination of econometric tests of the proposition central to the new classical macroeconomics. Unpublished manuscript, Department of Economics, New York University, New York.

Gibson, W. E. (1972) Interest rates and inflationary expectations: new evidence, *American Economic Review,* **62**, 854–65.

Glynn, D. R. (1969) The CBI industrial trends survey, *Applied Economics,* **1**, 183–96.

Gourieroux, C., Laffont, J. J. and Monfort, A. (1982) Rational expectations in dynamic linear models: analysis of the solutions, *Econometrica,* **50**, 409–25.

Granger, C. W. J. (1969) Investigating causal relations by econometric models and cross-spectral methods, *Econometrica,* **37**, 424–38.

Granger, C. W. J. and Newbold, P. (1973) Some comments on the evaluation of economic forecasts, *Applied Economics,* **5**, 35–47.

Gregory, A. W. (1986) Estimating equations with combined moving average error processes under rational expectations. Unpublished manuscript, Queen's University, Canada.

Grossman, S. J. (1976) On the efficiency of competitive stock markets where traders have diverse information, *Journal of Finance,* **31**, 573–85.

Grossman, S. J. (1977) The existence of futures markets, noisy rational expectations and informational externalities, *Review of Economic Studies,* **44**, 431–49.

Grossman, S. J. (1978) Further results on the information efficiency of competitive stock markets, *Journal of Economic Theory,* **18**, 81–101.

Grossman, S. J. (1981) An introduction to the theory of rational expectations under asymmetric information, *Review of Economic Studies,* **48**, 541–59.

Grossman, S. J. and Stiglitz, J. E. (1976) Information and competitive price systems, *American Economic Review,* **66**, 246–53.

Grossman, S. J. and Stiglitz, J. E. (1980) On the impossibility of informationally efficient markets, *American Economic Review,* **70**, 393–408.

Haavelmo, T. (1958) The role of the econometrician in the advancement of economic theory, *Econometrica,* **26**, 351–7.

Hahn, F. (1952) Expectations and equilibrium, *Economic Journal,* **62**, 802–19.

Hamilton, J. D. and Whiteman, C. H. (1985) The observable implications of self-fulfilling expectations, *Journal of Monetary Economics,* **16**, 353–73.

Hansen, L. P. (1982) Large sample properties of generalized method of moments estimators, *Econometrica,* **50**, 1029–54.

Hansen, L. P. and Hodrick, R. J. (1980) Forward exchange rates as optimal predictors of future spot rates: an econometric analysis, *Journal of Political Economy,* **88**, 829–53.

Hansen, L. P. and Sargent, T. J. (1980) Formulating and estimating dynamic linear rational expectations, *Journal of Economic Dynamics and Control,* **2**, 7–46.

Hansen, L. P. and Sargent, T. J. (1982) Instrumental variable procedures for estimating linear rational expectations models, *Journal of Monetary Economics,* **9**, 263–96.

Harvey, A. C. (1981) *Time Series Models,* Philip Allan, London.

Hayashi, F. and Sims, C. (1983) Nearly efficient estimation of time series models with predetermined, but not exogenous instruments, *Econometrica,* **51**, 783–98.

Hayek, F. A. (1937) Economics and knowledge, *Economica* (new series), **4**, 33–54.

Hayek, F. A. (1945) The use of knowledge in society, *American Economic Review,* **35**, 519–30.

Hey, J. D. (1984) Decision under uncertainty. In van der Ploeg, F. (ed.), *Mathematical Methods in Economics.* Wiley, New York.

Hicks, J. R. (1939) *Value and Capital,* Clarendon Press, Oxford.

Hirshleifer, J. and Riley, J. G. (1979) The analytics of uncertainty and information: an expository survey, *Journal of Economic Literature,* **17**, 1375–1421.

Hodgson, G. (1985) Persuasion, expectations and the limits to Keynes. In Lawson, T. and Pesaran, H. (eds), *Keynes' Economics: Methodological Issues.* Croom Helm, London.

Holden, K. and Peel, D. A. (1977) An empirical investigation of inflationary expectations, *Oxford Bulletin of Economics and Statistics,* **39**, 291–9.

Holden, K., Peel, D. A. and Thompson, J. L. (1985) *Expectations: Theory and Evidence.* Macmillan, London.

Hume, D. (1975) Enquiries concerning human understanding and concerning the principles of morals. L. A. Selby-Bigge (ed.), 3rd edn revised by P. H. Nidditch. Oxford University Press, Oxford.

Jacobs, R. L. and Jones, R. A. (1980) Price expectations in the United States: 1947–75, *American Economic Review,* **70**, 269–77.

Jordan, J. S. and Radner, R. (1982) Rational expectations in microeconomic models: an overview, *Journal of Economic Theory,* **26**, 201–23.

Juster, F. T. (1974) Savings behavior, uncertainty and price expectations, The Economic Outlook for 1974. University of Michigan, Ann Arbor.

Katona, G. (1951) *Psychological Analysis of Economic Behaviour.* McGraw-Hill, New York.

Katona, G. (1958) Business expectations in the framework of psychological economics (towards a theory of expectations). In Bowman, M. J. (ed.), *Expectations, Uncertainty, and Business Behaviour.* Social Science Research Council, New York.

Kawasaki, S., McMillan, J. and Zimmermann, K. F. (1982) Disequilibrium dynamics: an empirical study, *American Economic Review,* **72**, 992–1004.

Kawasaki, S., McMillan, J. and Zimmermann, K. F. (1983) Inventories and price inflexibility, *Econometrica,* **51**, 599–610.

Kennan, J. (1979) The estimation of partial adjustment models with rational expectations, *Econometrica,* **47**, 1441–55.

Keynes, J. M. (1921) *A Treatise on Probability,* Macmillan, London.

Keynes, J. M. (1936) *The General Theory of Employment, Interest and Money.* Macmillan, London.

Keynes, J. M. (1937) The general theory of employment, *Quarterly Journal of Economics,* **51**, 209–23.

Klein, L. R. (1954) Applications of survey methods and data to the analysis of economic fluctuations. In Klein, L. R. (ed.), *Contributions of Survey Methods to Economic Fluctuations,* Columbia University Press, New York.

Klein, P. A. and Moore, G. H. (1981) Industrial surveys in the UK: part I new orders, *Applied Economics,* **13**, 167–79.

Klepper, S. and Leamer, E. E. (1984) Consistent sets of estimates for regressions with errors in all variables, *Econometrica,* **52**, 163–83.

Knight, F. K. (1921) *Risk, Uncertainty and Profit.* Frank Cass, London.

Knöbl, A. (1974) Price expectations and actual price behaviour in Germany, *International Monetary Fund Staff Papers,* **21**, 83–100.

Koenig, H., Nerlove, M. and Oudiz, G. (1981) On the formation of price expectations: an analysis of business test data by log-linear probability models, *European Economic Review,* **16**, 103–38.

Koopmans, T. C., Rubin, H. and Leipnik, R. B. (1950) Measuring the equation systems of dynamic economics. In Koopmans, T. C. (ed.), *Statistical Inference in Dynamic Economic Models,* Cowles Commission Monograph 10, John Wiley, New York.

Koyck, L. M. (1954) *Distributed Lags and Investment Analysis.* North-Holland, Amsterdam.

Lahiri, K. (1976) Inflationary expectations: their formation and interest rate effects, *American Economic Review,* **66**, 124–31.

Lahiri, K. (1981) *The Econometrics of Inflationary Expectations.* North-Holland, Amsterdam.

Lancaster, K. (1968) *Mathematical Economics.* Macmillan, London.

Lawson, T. (1981) Keynesian model building and the rational expectations critique, *Cambridge Journal of Economics,* **5**, 311–26.

Lawson, T. and Pesaran, M. H. (eds) (1985) *Keynes' Economics: Methodological Issues.* Croom Helm, London.

LeRoy, F. S. and Porter, R. D. (1981) The present-value relations: test based on implied variance bounds, *Econometrica,* **49**, 555–74.

Leiderman, L. (1980) Macroeconomic testing of the rational expections and structural neutrality hypotheses for the United States, *Journal of Monetary Economics,* **6**, 69–82.

Leonard, J. S. (1982) Wage expections in the labour markets: survey evidence on rationality, *Review of Economics and Statistics,* **64**, 157–61.

Lippman, S. A. and McCall, J. J. (1981) The economics of uncertainty: selected topics and probabilistic methods. In Arrow, K. J. and Intriligator, M. (eds), *Handbook of Mathematical Economics,* vol. 1. North-Holland, Amsterdam.

Logue, D. E. and Willet, T. D. (1976) A note on the relation between the rate and the variability of inflation, *Economica,* **43**, 151–8.

Lovell, M. C. (1986) Tests of the rational expectations hypothesis, *American Economic Review,* **76**, 110–24.

Lucas, R. E. (1972a) Econometric testing of the natural rate hypothesis. In Eckstein, O.

(ed.), *The Econometrics of Price Determination,* Conference, Washington, DC.
Lucas, R. E. (1972b) Expectations and the neutrality of money, *Journal of Economic Theory,* **4**, 103–24.
Lucas, R. E. (1973) Some international evidence on output–inflation trade-offs, *American Economic Review,* **63**, 326–44.
Lucas, R. E. (1975) An equilibrium model of the business cycle, *Journal of Political Economy,* **83**, 1113–44.
Lucas, R. E. (1976) Econometric policy evaluation: a critique, in Brunner, K. and Meltzer, A. H. (eds), *The Phillips Curve and Labor Markets.* Carnegie-Rochester Conference Series on Public Policy, vol. 1. North-Holland, Amsterdam.
Lucas, R. E. and Sargent, T. J. (1981) *Rational Expectations and Economic Practice,* George Allen and Unwin, London.
Marschak, J. and Radner, R. (1972) *Economic Theory of Teams.* Cowles Foundation Monograph 22, Yale University Press, New Haven.
Marshall, A. (1964) *Principles of Economics,* 8th edn. Macmillan, London.
McCallum, B. T. (1976) Rational expectations and the estimation of econometric models: an alternative procedure, *International Economic Review,* **17**, 484–90.
McCallum, B. T. (1979) On the observational inequivalence of classical and Keynesian models, *Journal of Political Economy,* **87**, 395–402.
McCallum, B. T. (1983) On non-uniqueness in rational expectations models, *Journal of Monetary Economics,* **11**, 139–68.
McDonald, J. (1983) A solution to an estimation problem involving models with rational expectations, *Journal of Monetary Economics,* **11**, 381–6.
McGuire, C. B. (1972) Comparison of information structures. In McGuire, C. B. and Radner, R. (eds), *Decision and Organization, A Volume in Honour of Jacob Marschak,* North-Holland, Amsterdam.
McGuire, T. W. (1976) Price change expectations and the Philips curve. In Brunner, K. and Meltzer, A. (eds), *The Economics of Price and Wage Control.* Carnegie-Rochester Series on Public Policy, No. 2, North-Holland, Amsterdam.
McIntosh, J., Schiantarelli, F. and Low, W. (1986a) Firm's expectations and the adjustment of prices and output: econometric evidence from categorical survey data. Discussion Paper Series, No. 291, Department of Economics, University of Essex.
McIntosh, J., Schiantarelli, F. and Low, W. (1986b) A qualitative response analysis of U.K. firms' employment and output decisions. Discussion Paper Series, No. 298. Department of Economics, University of Essex.
Meiselman, D. (1962) *The Term Structure of Interest Rates,* Prentice-Hall, Englewood Cliffs, NJ.
Mills, T. C. (1981) Modelling the formation of Australian inflation expectations, *Australian Economic Papers,* **20**, 150–60.
Mincer, J. (1969) Models of adaptive forecasting. In Mincer, J. (ed.), *Economic Forecasts and Expectations: Analysis of Forecasting Behaviour and performance,* NBER, Columbia University Press, New York.
Mishkin, F. S. (1982) Does anticipated monetary policy matter? An econometric investigation, *Journal of Political Economy,* **90**, 22–51.
Mishkin, F. S. (1983) *A Rational Expectations Approach to Macroeconomics – Testing Policy Ineffectiveness and Efficient-Markets Models.* NBER Monograph. University of Chicago Press, Chicago.
Modigliani, F. and Sauerlender, O. W. (1955) Economic expectations and plans of firms in relation to short-term forecasting, in *Short-term Economic Forecasting,* NBER Studies in Income and Wealth, no. 17. Princeton University Press, Princeton.
Mullineaux, D. J. (1978) On testing for rationality: another look at the Livingston price expectations data, *Journal of Political Economy,* **86**, 329–36.

Mullineaux, D. J. (1980) Inflation expectations and money growth in the United States, *American Economic Review,* **70**, 149–61.

Murphy, K. M. and Topel, R. H. (1985) Estimation and inference in two-step econometric models, *Journal of Business and Economic Statistics,* **3**, 370–9.

Muth, J. F. (1960) Optimal properties of exponentially weighted forecasts, *Journal of the American Statistical Association,* **55**, 299–306.

Muth, J. F. (1961) Rational expectations and the theory of price movements, *Econometrica,* **29**, 315–35.

Nagel, E. (1963) Assumption in economic theory, *American Economic Review* (Papers and Proceedings), **53**, 211–19.

Neftci, S. N. and Sargent, T. J. (1978) A little bit of evidence on the natural rate hypothesis from the U.S.; *Journal of Monetary Economics,* **4**, 315–19.

Nelson, C. R. (1972) The prediction performance of the FRB–MIT–PENN model of the US economy, *American Economic Review,* **62**, 902–17.

Nelson, C. R. (1979) Granger causality and the natural rate hypothesis, *Journal of Political Economy,* **87**, 390–4.

Nerlove, M. (1958) Adaptive expectations and cobweb phenomena, *Quarterly Journal of Economics,* **72**, 227–40.

Nerlove, M. (1983) Expectations, plans, and realizations in theory and practice, *Econometrica,* **51**, 1251–79.

Nerlove, M., Grether, D. M. and Carvalho, J. (1979) *Analysis of Economic Time Series: A Synthesis.* Academic Press, New York.

Newey, W. K. (1984) A method of moments interpretation of sequential estimators, *Economics Letters,* **14**, 201–6.

Newey, W. K. and West, K. D. (1985) A simple, positive definite, heteroskedasticity and autocorrelation consistent covariance matrix. Discussion Paper No. 92, Woodrow Wilson School, Princeton.

Pagan, A. R. (1984) Econometric issues in the analysis of regressions with generated regressors, *International Economic Review,* **25**, 221–47.

Pagan, A. R. (1986) Two stage and related estimators and their applications, *Review of Economic Studies,* **53**, 517–38.

Pagan, A. R. and Ullah, A. (1986) The econometric analysis of models with risk terms. Centre for Economic Policy Research Discussion Paper, London.

Pagan, A. R., Hall, A. D. and Trivedi, P. K. (1983) Assessing the variability of inflation, *Review of Economic Studies,* **50**, 585–96.

Papandreou, A. G. (1963) Theory construction and empirical meaning in economics, *American Economic Review* (Papers and Proceedings), **53**, 205–10.

Patinkin, D. (1984) Keynes and economics today, *American Economic Review* (Papers and Proceedings), **74**, 97–102.

Pesando, J. E. (1975) A note on the rationality of the Livingston price expectations, *Journal of Political Economy,* **83**, 849–58.

Pesaran, M. H. (1981) Identification of rational expectations models, *Journal of Econometrics,* **16**, 375–98.

Pesaran, M. H. (1982) A critique of the proposed tests of the natural rate-rational expectations hypothesis, *Economic Journal,* **92**, 529–54.

Pesaran, M. H. (1984a) The new classical macroeconomics: a critical exposition, in van der Ploeg, F. (ed.), *Mathematical Methods in Economics.* John Wiley, New York.

Pesaran, M. H. (1984b) Expectations formations and macro-econometric modelling, in Malgrange P. and Muet, P.-A. (eds), *Contemporary Macroeconomic Modelling.* Basil Blackwell, Oxford.

Pesaran, M. H. (1985) Formation of inflation expectations in British manufacturing industries, *Economic Journal,* **95**, 948–75.

Pesaran, M. H. (1986) Two-step, instrumental variable and maximum likelihood estimation of multivariate rational expectations models. Unpublished manuscript, Trinity College, Cambridge.

Pesaran, M. H. (1987) Global and partial non-nested hypotheses and asymptotic local power, *Econometric Theory*, **3**, 69–97.

Pesaran, M. H. and Pesaran, B. (1987) *Data-FIT: an interactive econometric software package*. Oxford University Press, Oxford (forthcoming.)

Pesaran, M. H. and Slater, L. J. (1980) *Dynamic Regression: Theory and Algorithms*, Ellis Horwood, Chichester.

Phelps, E. S. (1970) Introduction: the new microeconomics in employment and inflation theory, in Phelps, E. S. et al. (eds), *Microeconomic Foundations of Employment and Inflation Theory*. Macmillan, London.

Popper, K. R. (1972) *Objective Knowledge: An Evolutionary Approach*. Oxford University Press, Oxford.

Pudney, S. E. (1982) The identification of rational expectations models under structural neutrality, *Journal of Economic Dynamics and Control*, **4**, 117–21.

Pyle, D. M. (1972) Observed price expectations and interest rates, *Review of Economics and Statistics*, **54**, 275–80.

Radner, R. (1982) Equilibrium under uncertainty, in Arrow, K. J. and Intriligator, M. D. (eds), *Handbook of Mathematical Economics*, vol. 2. North-Holland, Amsterdam.

Radner, R. (1983) Comment on convergence to rational expectations equilibrium, in Frydman and Phelps (1983).

Ramsey, F. P. (1931) Truth and probability, in Braithwaite, R. B. (ed.), *The Foundations of Mathematics and Other Logical Essays*. Kegan Paul, Trench, Trubner and Co., London.

Ravankar, N. S. (1980) Testing of the rational expectation hypothesis, *Econometrica*, **48**, 1347–63.

Robinson, J. (1971) *Economic Heresies*. Macmillan, London.

Rose, D. E. (1972) A general error-learning model of expectations formation, paper presented at the European Meeting of the Econometrics Society. Unpublished manuscript.

Rose, D. E. (1976) Expectations formation as optimal forecasting and error learning. Unpublished Ph.D. dissertation, Department of Economics, University of Manchester.

Rothenberg, T. J. (1971) Identification in parametric models, *Econometrica*, **39**, 577–91.

Rotter, J. B. (1954) *Social Learning and Clinical Psychology*. Prentice-Hall, Englewood Cliffs, NJ.

Samuelson, P. (1963) Problems of methodology: discussion, *American Economic Review* (papers and proceedings), **53**, 231–6.

Sargan, J. D. (1958) The estimation of economic relationships using instrumental variables, *Econometrica*, **26**, 393–415.

Sargan, J. D. (1983) A reformulation and comparison of alternative methods of estimating models containing rational expectations. Unpublished manuscript, London School of Economics.

Sargan, J. D. (1984) Alternative models for rational expectations in some simple irregular cases. Unpublished manuscript, London School of Economics.

Sargent, T. J. (1973) Rational expectations, the real rate of interest and the natural rate of unemployment, *Brookings Papers on Economic Activity*, no. 2, 429–72.

Sargent, T. J. (1976a) A classical macroeconomic model for the United States, *Journal of Political Economy*, **84**, 207–37.

Sargent, T. J. (1976b) The observational equivalence of natural and unnatural rate theories of macroeconomics, *Journal of Political Economy*, **84**, 631–40.

Sargent, T. J. (1978) Estimation of dynamic labour demand schedules under rational expectations, *Journal of Political Economy,* **86**, 1009–44.
Sargent, T. J. (1979a) *Macroeconomic Theory.* Academic Press, New York.
Sargent, T. J. (1979b) Causality, exogeneity, and natural rate models: reply to C. R. Nelson and B. T. McCallum, *Journal of Political Economy,* **87**, 403–9.
Sargent, T. J. and Wallace, N. (1973) Rational expectations and the dynamics of hyperinflation, *International Economic Review,* **14**, 328–50.
Savage, L. J. (1954) *The Foundations of Statistics,* Dover Publications, Inc., New York.
Schotter, A. (1981) *The Economic Theory of Social Institutions.* Cambridge University Press, Cambridge.
Schotter, A. and Schwödiauer, G. (1980) Economics and the theory of games: a survey, *Journal of Economic Literature,* **18**, 479–527.
Severn, A. K. (1983) Formation of inflation expectations in the UK: pitfalls in the use of the error-learning model, *European Economic Review,* **20**, 349–63.
Shackle, G. L. S. (1949) *Expectations in Economics.* Cambridge University Press, Cambridge.
Shackle, G. L. S. (1955) *Uncertainty in Economics.* Cambridge University Press, Cambridge.
Shaw, G. K. (1984) *Rational Expectations: An Elementary Exposition.* Wheatsheaf Books, Brighton.
Shiller, R. J. (1978) Rational expectations and the dynamic structure of macroeconomic models: a critical review, *Journal of Monetary Economics,* **4**, 1–44.
Shiller, R. J. (1981) Do stock prices move too much to be justified by subsequent changes in dividends?, *American Economic Review,* **71**, 421–36.
Shuford, H. (1970) Subjective variables in economic analysis: a study of consumer's expectations. Unpublished manuscript, Yale University.
Simon, H. A. (1958) The role of expectations in an adaptive or behavioristic model, in Bowman, M. J. (ed.), *Expectations, Uncertainty, and Business Behavior.* Social Science Research Council, New York.
Sims, C. A. (1980) Macroeconomics and reality, *Econometrica,* **48**, 1–48.
Smith, G. W. (1978) Producers' price and cost expectations, in Parkin, M. and Summer, M. T. (eds), *Inflation in the United Kingdom.* Manchester University Press, Manchester.
Smith, G. W. (1982) Inflation expectations: direct observations and their determinants, in Artis, M. J. (ed.), *Demand Management, Supply Constraints, and Inflation.* Wiley, New York.
Stigler, G. J. (1961) The economics of information, *Journal of Political Economy,* **69**, 213–25.
Taylor, J. B. (1975) Monetary policy during a transition to rational expectations, *Journal of Political Economy,* **83**, 1009–21.
Taylor, J. B. (1977) Conditions for unique solutions in stochastic macroeconomic models with rational expectations, *Econometrica,* **45**, 1377–85.
Taylor, J. B. (1979) Estimation and control of a macroeconomic model with rational expectations, *Econometrica,* **47**, 1267–86.
Taylor, J. B. (1980) Aggregate dynamics and staggered contracts, *Journal of Political Economy,* **88**, 1–23.
Theil, H. (1952) On the time shape of economic microvariables and the Munich business test, *Revue de l'Institut International de Statistique,* **20**, 105–120.
Theil, H. (1955) Recent experiences with the Munich business test: an expository article, *Econometrica,* **23**, 184–92.
Theil, H. (1966) *Applied Economic Forecasting.* North-Holland, Amsterdam.
Townsend, R. M. (1978) Market anticipations, rational expectations and Bayesian analysis, *International Economic Review,* **19**, 481–94.

Townsend, R. M. (1983) Forecasting the forecasts of others, *Journal of Political Economy,* **91**, 546–88.

Trivedi, P. K. (1973) Retail inventory investment behaviour, *Journal of Econometrics,* **1**, 61–80.

Turkington, D. A. (1985) A note on two-stage least squares, three-stage least squares and maximum likelihood estimation in an expectations model, *International Economic Review,* **26**, 507–10.

Turnovsky, S. J. (1969) A Bayesian approach to the theory of expectations, *Journal of Economic Theory,* **1**, 220–27.

Turnovsky, S. J. (1970) Empirical evidence on the formation of price expectations, *Journal of the American Statistical Association,* **65**, 1441–54.

Turnovsky, S. J. and Wachter, M. W. (1972) A test of the 'expectations hypothesis' using directly observed wage and price expectations, *Review of Economics and Statistics,* **54**, 47–54.

Visco, I. (1981) On the derivation of the reduced forms of rational expectations models, *European Economic Review,* **16**, 355–65.

Visco, I. (1984a) On linear models with rational expectations – an addendum, *European Economic Review,* **24**, 113–15.

Visco, I. (1984b) *Price Expectations in Rising Inflation,* North-Holland, Amsterdam.

Visco, I. (1986) The use of Italian data in the analysis of the formation of inflation expectations. Unpublished manuscript, Banca d'Italia.

Wallis, K. F. (1980) Econometric implications of the rational expectations hypothesis, *Econometrica,* **48**, 49–73.

Watson, M. W. (1986) Recursive solution methods for dynamic linear rational expectations models. Unpublished manuscript, Northwestern University.

Wegge, L. L. (1965) Identifiability criteria for a system of equations as a whole. *Australian Journal of Statistics,* **7**, 67–77.

Wegge, L. L. and Feldman, M. (1983a) Identifiability criteria for Muth-rational expectations models, *Journal of Econometrics,* **21**, 245–254.

Wegge, L. L. and Feldman, M. (1983b) Comment to the editor, *Journal of Econometrics,* **21**, 255–6.

White, H. (1980) A heteroskedasticity-consistent covariance matrix estimator and direct test for heteroskedasticity, *Econometrica,* **48**, 817–38.

Whiteman, C. H. (1983) *Linear Rational Expectations Models: A User's Guide.* University of Minnesota Press, Minneapolis.

Wickens, M. R. (1982) The efficient estimation of econometric models with rational expectations. *Review of Economic Studies,* **49**, 55–67.

Wickens, M. R. (1986) The estimation of linear models with future rational expectations by efficient and instrumental variable methods. Centre for Economic Policy Research Discussion Paper No. 111.

Wong, S. (1973) The 'F-Twist' and the methodology of Paul Samuelson, *American Economic Review,* **63**, 312–25.

Wren-Lewis, S. (1986) An econometric model of UK manufacturing employment using survey data on expected output, *Journal of Applied Econometrics,* **1**, 297–316.

Zellner, A. (1962) An efficient method of estimating seemingly unrelated regressions and tests for aggregation bias, *Journal of the American Statistical Association,* **57**, 348–68.

Index of Subjects

Index of Authors